Seduction and Repetition
in Ovid's *Ars Amatoria* 2

Seduction and Repetition in Ovid's *Ars Amatoria* 2

Alison Sharrock

CLARENDON PRESS · OXFORD

1994

Oxford University Press, Walton Street, Oxford OX2 6DP
Oxford New York Toronto
Delhi Bombay Calcutta Madras Karachi
Kuala Lumpur Singapore Hong Kong Tokyo
Nairobi Dar es Salaam Cape Town
Melbourne Auckland Madrid
and associated companies in
Berlin Ibadan

Oxford is a trade mark of Oxford University Press

Published in the United States
by Oxford University Press Inc., New York

British Library Cataloguing in Publication Data
Data available

Library of Congress Cataloging in Publication Data
Seduction and repetition in Ovid's Ars amatoria II
Alison Sharrock.
Based on the author's thesis (Ph. D.—University of
Cambridge), 1988. Includes bibliographical references and indexes. 1. Ovid,
43 B.C.–17 or 18 A.D. Ars amatoria. 2. Erotic poetry, Latin—History and
criticism. 3. Seduction in literature. 4. Repetition (Rhetoric) 5. Rome in
literature. 6. Rhetoric, Ancient. 7. Sex in literature. I. Title.
PA6519.A84S53 1994 871'.01—dc20 94-10
ISBN 0-19-814959-X

1 3 5 7 9 10 8 6 4 2

Typeset by Datix International Limited, Bungay, Suffolk
Printed in Great Britain on acid-free paper by
Bookcraft (Bath) Ltd. Midsomer Norton

To Tim

PREFACE

The *Ars Amatoria* is a poem about poetry, and sex, and poetry as sex. Despite the Ovidian renaissance of recent years, there has been little close reading of the *Ars Amatoria*, particularly outside the first book. Book 1 has an excellent standard commentary by Hollis (1977), and general readings have also tended to concentrate on the first book.[1] Advances in the classical application of the techniques of modern literary criticism and theory are now reaching Ovid, the most notable example being Duncan Kennedy's new book on elegy (1993). It is in this context that the present work aims to offer a reading of the poem based on a paradigmatic close reading of three significant passages. The tradition of 'selections from the *Ars Amatoria*' is perhaps not entirely a happy one, since it would seem that the three editions we have of selections for school and undergraduate readers are seeking, among other things, to trim Ovid of his supposed excess.[2] These selections constitute examples of what, one feels, some scholars writing for more senior audiences might like to do in order to tidy Ovid up. Griggs, for example, in his self-confessed concentration on the overtly didactic parts of the *Ars*, excises the 'embroidery' such as the Daedalus story, with its 'tenuous' connection with the main text. Of the three editors of selections, only Thompson includes the Daedalus episode. His criterion for selection is apparent from one example: he prints (vv. 459–60) *oscula da flenti . . . | Pax erit ! hoc uno soluitur ira modo* ('give her kisses as she is crying . . . there will be peace; anger is dissolved in this way only').

---

[1] On the whole work still the best and essentially the only commentary is that of Brandt (1902), while we are still indebted to that of Burman (1727) for many valuable comments. The best bibliographical sources for the *Ars* are: Lenz (1939) covering 1928–37, Pridik (1970) covering 1936–68, Gariépy (1970) covering 1958–68, Coletti (1981) covering 1958–78. See also Myerowitz (1985: 223–36).

[2] Thompson (1958), Griggs (1971), Murgatroyd (1982). I have found Murgatroyd of most use.

Say no more! The missing words are, of course, *Veneris da gaudia flenti* ('make love to her as she is crying').

It is not my intention to produce an abridged version of the poem, but to use exemplars to suggest ways of reading: reading, that is, of the passages, of Book 2, of the *Ars Amatoria*, and of didactic poetry generally. My treatment of the poem has disrupted the 'natural' order of reading, for the material of Chapter 2 comes after that of Chapter 3 in the poem: this has been done partly because the subject matter of the first two chapters (the seduction of the reader) and of the last two (Callimachean poetics) are particularly closely related, and partly to emphasize the questions of re-reading which are considered throughout the book.

One factor in the selection of passages for close reading has been that they display a feature of Ovidian poetry which is much censured, but also often most fruitful: in a word—excess. There have been studies of the role of exempla and other set-pieces, among which Watson, Myerowitz, Leach, Blodgett, and Weber have been most favourable, while Otis, Wilkinson, Tolkiehn, Frécaut, and Krokowski represent a cross-section of the others, but the orthodoxy remains that the facile nature of Ovidian poetry can be seen with particular clarity in his supposed digressions. Much of the scholarly attention afforded the poem has, however, been concerned with the sense in which it might be called 'didactic' (is it really teaching?) and hence its political status *vis-à-vis* the Augustan moral reforms. While earlier scholars were concerned with the poet's intention and sincerity, more recent critics, perhaps reacting against the previous methodology, have tended to concentrate on formal didactic elements. The effect of this change of emphasis is that these critics have been asking a different question from the earlier scholars, or formulating both question and answer in poetic rather than in intentionalist terms, so that the question 'does the poem actually seek to teach' becomes 'does the poem display the characteristic features of the didactic genre?'. The antithesis of intentionalism might perhaps be called 'the literary fallacy': that is, the belief or practice, fallacious in my view, that the literary text is a sealed unit divorced from any social setting, be it of original production or in the history of its reception by readers through the ages.[3] The most significant recent study of the *Ars*, in English, is that of Myerowitz (1985), a work written in what might be called the 'serious tradition' of scholarship on the *Ars*, coming particularly from America.[4] As the first major study of the work in English, Myerowitz's book follows the pioneering work of Wilkinson, Kenney, Hollis, and others, and brings Ovidian erotodidactic studies to the point at which a close reading seems timely. My book is concerned with the relationship between the various levels of author, text, and reader, and particularly the role in the seduction of the reader played by Callimachean poetics.

In an effort to make this book more accessible to non-classicists, and to students of Classics who have come late to the study of Latin and Greek, I have included translations, my own except where otherwise stated. The translations are intended as an aid to the reader: they make no claim to be elegant. Since the provision of translations for all Latin and Greek used would add very considerably to the weight of the book, I have translated all non-English in the main text (except where to do so would be too awkward) but not always in the notes. I appreciate that this compromise is not without its ironies. The text of the *Ars Amatoria* I have used is Kenney's *Oxford Classical Text*.

This book is based on my Ph.D. dissertation, which was written under the supervision of John Henderson, to whom I owe the greatest debt of gratitude. Duncan Kennedy and

---

[3] On the subject of the political status of the poem, not significantly addressed here, see my forthcoming article. Holzberg (1981) rightly exposes the differences in approach between earlier and more modern critics. In the first group (the distinction is necessarily rough, for members of what I have designated the first group also discuss formal didactic elements) come Zingerle (1867–71), Kroll (1924), Wilkinson (1955), Krokowski (1963), Kenney (1958), a work of great value for the discussion of formal didacticism in the *Ars*, Effe (1977). Loosely in the second group come Leach (1964), Binnicker (1967), Hollis's commentary on *Ars* 1 (1977), Durling (1958), Solodow (1977), Myerowitz (1985), Pöhlmann (1973), Kettemann (1979), Küppers (1981), Holzberg (1981), Weber (1983), Kling (1970) (the Germanic writers often give highly structural analyses of the *Ars*), Dilke (1982), Kleve (1983).

[4] Representatives of what I am calling the serious tradition are Fyler (1971), Romano (1972), Shulman (1981), Solodow (1977). The most important works relating to the *Ars* not in English are probably those of Labate (1984), which is concerned with Ovid's erotic poetry generally, and Scivoletto (1976).

Stephen Hinds gave generously of their time and wisdom. The dissertation was examined by Michael Reeve and Anna Wilson, to whom appreciation is also due. Many other friends have advised and supported me, both in Cambridge and here at Keele, where I would particularly like to mention Gerry Nussbaum. More recently, Charles Martindale read and very helpfully criticized a late draft of the book. I am indebted also to the expertise of Hilary O'Shea and other members of the staff of Oxford University Press, and to the helpful suggestions of the Press's readers. My thanks finally to Tim Sharrock, whose support, encouragement, and knowledge of computers have made the writing of this book possible.

CONTENTS

Abbreviations   xiii

1. The Art of (re-)Reading   1

2. First Catch Your Reader   21

3. *Amor Artis*: The Daedalus Episode   87

4. Callimachean Apollo and the Long and Short of   197
   Art

5. Thus We See? Re-reading 'Reading the *Ars*   291
   Amatoria'

References   297

Index Locorum   311

General Index   316

ABBREVIATIONS

Titles of Latin works are generally abbreviated as in *Oxford Latin Dictionary*, except that Horace *Satires* betcomes *Sat.*, Virgil's *Georgics* and *Aeneid* become *Georg.* and *Aen.*, and Ovid *Heroides* becomes *Her.*

AJA	*American Journal of Archaeology*
A.J.Ph.	*American Journal of Philology*
ANRW	*Aufstieg und Niedergang der römischen Welt*
AUMLA	*Journal of the Australasian Universities Language and Literature Association*
BICS	*Bulletin of the Institute of Classical Studies of the University of London*
CAH	*Cambridge Ancient History*, ed. I. E. S. Edwards, C. J. Godd, N. G. L. Hammond, and E. Sollberger, 3rd edn. (1970–)
CJ	*The Classical Journal*
Cl.Ant.	*Classical Antiquity*
C.Ph.	*Classical Philology*
CQ	*Classical Quarterly*
CR	*Classical Review*
CSCA	*California Studies in Classical Antiquity*
CW	*Classical World*
G&R	*Greece and Rome*
GRBS	*Greek, Roman, and Byzantine Studies*
H.S.Ph.	*Harvard Studies in Classical Philology*
JRS	*Journal of Roman Studies*
JWI	*Journal of the Warburg and Courtauld Institutes*
LCM	*Liverpool Classical Monthly*
LEC	*Les Études classiques*
MD	*Materiali e Discussioni per l'analisi dei testi classici*
MDAI(R)	*Mitteilungen des Deutschen Archäologischen Instituts (Röm. Abt.)*

MH	*Museum Helveticum*
OCD	*Oxford Classical Dictionary*
OLD	*Oxford Latin Dictionary*
P.C.Ph.S.	*Proceedings of the Cambridge Philological Society*
Ph.Q.	*Philological Quarterly*
PLLS	*Papers of the Liverpool Latin Seminar*
QIFL	*Quaderni dell'Istituto di Filologia latina dell' Università di Padova*
RE	*Real-Encyclopädie der classischen Altertumswissenschaft*, ed. A. Pauly, G. Wissowa, and W. Kroll (Stuttgart, 1894–1980)
REG	*Revue des Études Grècques*
REL	*Revue des Études Latines*
RFIC	*Rivista di Filolgia e di Istruzione Classica*
SO	*Symbolae Osloenses*
T.A.Ph.A.	*Transactions and Proceedings of the American Philological Society*
TLL	*Thesaurus Linguae Latinae*
WS	*Wiener Studien*
ZPE	*Zeitschrift für Papyrologie und Epigraphik*

I

The Art of (re-)Reading

Ovid's *Ars Amatoria* is a pivotal work within the poet's œuvre. Roman writers and readers might see in the corpus of a poet a developmental process like the *cursus honorum* of civic life. Virgil, a textbook case, begins with the light *Eclogues* (written *gracili . . . hibisco*, 'with a delicate mallow-reed': 10. 71) and advances through didactic epos (the *Georgics*) to graduate in the *Aeneid*, the height of honour, the consulship of poetry. A similar progression can be discerned in the Horatian œuvre, from the *Epodes* and *Satires* appropriate to youth, developing through *Odes* 1–3 and the first book of *Epistles*, to the *Carmen Saeculare*, *Odes* 4, and *Epistles* 2, especially the *Ars Poetica*, where we see the philosophical reflection considered appropriate to old age, a stage which Virgil could be perceived as never reaching because of his untimely death. We are dealing here with people's perceptions and expectations of literary career-progress rather than facts of exact age. Whether the story in the *Vitae* (35), that Virgil planned to devote himself entirely to philosophy after completing the revision of the *Aeneid*, arises from reality, in any sense, or from Donatus' view of what would be appropriate, it must indicate awareness of this developmental process.[1] Such awareness may be found in one modern critic, who comments of the *Metamorphoses*: 'Furthermore, Ovid had ample precedent for writing a more serious kind of narrative. Virgil had, before him, graduated from bucolic and didactic to epic; Horace from

---

[1] Most (1987) argues that the writer of the *Culex* constructs his poem around the triadic literary career of Virgil. Such biographical statements should be read at least in part as literary-critical statements. On this subject see Lipking (1981), esp. p. xi: 'to consider the question of how a poet molds a career . . . is almost necessarily to consider Virgil, who supplied the pattern of a career to so many later poets'. See also p. 77, where he too describes the three works of Virgil as the poet's *cursus honorum*.

satires and iambics to the classical lyric.' (Otis 1966: 43.)
The didactic *Ars* bears the same relationship to the *Amores*
(and *Heroides*) and to the *Metamorphoses* (and *Fasti*) as
Virgil's didactic *Georgics* does to the *Eclogues* and to the
Aeneid. Even if the triadic career in Virgil's case can only
be seen with hindsight, a possibility which would itself not
stop such a perception forming part of poet's reception, in
Ovid's case the comparison with his great predecessor
allows the development greater visibility. It is a not uncommon evaluation of the mythological episodes in the *Ars* that
one of their most important functions is as a practice run
for the *Metamorphoses* (Krokowski 1963: 147). This judgement reflects the extent to which many classical scholars
judge poetry by the canons laid down by classical authority.
Epic is the best, the only important subject for a mature
poet, and the value of earlier poetry consists in the extent to
which it furthers the epic goal.

Book 2, in particular, provides a challenge highlighted by
its pivotal nature. It is, as we have it and must, albeit
carefully, read it, the middle poem in a three-book collection, in which the attractions of reading ahead and re-reading retrospectively are maximized. The book presents the
problems of continuation, which in this case is a matter of
repeating with a difference, since much of the material is
notionally the same, the conventions of elegy. Ovid's comment on Ulysses' rhetorical skills could almost be a programmatic statement of his own (*Ars* 2. 128):

> *ille referre aliter saepe solebat idem*
>
> He used often to relate the same thing in different ways.

The Daedalus episode, in particular, can be paradigmatic of
this problematic opportunity, being a story well known
from the great authors, and one which Ovid will treat
again. Middle books in Latin texts often lend themselves to
reflection—in the manner of *Aeneid* 6—and this is certainly
the case with *Ars* 2.

1a Postscript: Writing after a Tradition

Critics from Seneca to the present day have found fault with Ovid for repetitive use both of the traditions of elegy and of his own material. The judgements of two influential critics may be taken as representative of the long and dominant tradition in Ovidian scholarship, which, although it has been challenged in recent years, remains the orthodoxy. Wilkinson says of Ovid's didactic poetry: 'Quite apart from the sameness of tone, there is too much *crambe repetita*. Surely we have heard before, and more than once, of lovers communicating by writing on the table in wine, exchanging glances and signs, drinking from the side of the cup where the other has drunk, and touching hands' (Wilkinson 1955: 143). This view is echoed by Otis (1966: 18): 'so many of the same themes [as in the *Amores*] are repeated and so often repeated in a much less striking way.' According to this view, the *Ars* is rather a heavy reworking of the well-known topoi of Latin love elegy, strung together and padded out by 'embroidery' in the form of mythological and other exempla, which have a tenuous connection with the main text, and by scene-painting such as the Epiphany of Apollo. I wish to address the common and ancient charge against Ovid of narcissistic and empty display of a trivial skill. I shall suggest that the text itself by this very excess challenges our response to its exhibitionist display of art, which is at the same time pure self-indulgence and a tight artistic structure. Recent critical interest in paralleling themes has led readers of the *Ars* to condemn it for excessive repetition of commonplaces, but often the very conventionality is the point, and this is the basis for Ovid's readers to concentrate on the manipulation *as* the point.[2] Part of the problem, I suggest, derives from insufficient attention to two points: the workings of writing in a tradition, and the nature of didactic poetry.

Already in the *Amores* Ovid is writing not only in but

[2] Myerowitz (1985: 35) makes this point briefly: 'the more traditional sources the poem is demonstrated to draw upon, the more original it becomes.' Weber (1983: 113) notes this repetition of material, but ascribes its explanation to his structural analysis of the two books.

that depends on your definition of elegy

moreover at the end of a tradition, the tradition of Roman elegy. In the *Ars* this situation is reduplicated twice: firstly, in that the *Ars* responds to the *Amores* in a way not dissimilar to the relationship between the *Amores* and earlier elegy; and secondly in that Ovid is now working in another tradition alongside the first, that of didactic poetry. This reduplication is further redoubled in the second book, for at one level keeping a mistress is not so very different from catching her, since both activities depend on the conventions of elegiac erotic discourse. The central artistic problem of Book 2 is that of repetition. How is the interest of both pupil and reader to be sustained in what is in many ways the same material over again? Of course Ovid uses the commonplaces of elegy: that is what writing in a tradition is all about. How else would we recognize it? As is becoming increasingly recognized, Roman poets are deeply self-conscious about the workings of literary traditions and about their own place in them. Here, perhaps, is the difference between traditional source-criticism and the approach sometimes called intertextuality. (See Worton and Still 1990.) If the aim is simply to identify and categorize the conventions employed by Ovid, a certain boredom at his apparent lack of originality is the almost inevitable result. If, however, one accepts the ancient and particularly Ovidian premiss of the positive, even necessary literary value of working with and within a tradition, then one can analyse the *manipulation* of topoi, which depends for its effectiveness on them being pointedly traditional and easily identifiable as such. (See G. Williams 1968 and Woodman and West 1979.) It is that manipulation of a tradition which makes the *Ars* such a self-consciously intertextual poem. Secondly, and the points are related, it is part of the didactic stance to be ostentatiously traditional. Up to a point, it is in the generic nature of a didactic poem to be 'boring', for that is a traditional aspect of pedagogy. That boringness must, of course, be of a stylized and carefully judged variety, and so on another level of reading it will itself be a source of interest. To put it another way, the *Ars* is and is not boring.[3]

[3] It is one of those pleasing paradoxes of literary study that the representation of boringness is itself precisely not boring. One might think of 'the bore' in Hor.

1b The Reader of the *Ars*

How to keep a girl, a lover, a reader? ⌐

In the process of signification which we call a text, readers play all sorts of crucial roles. Whether the locus of the production of meaning exists in the author's intention, or the reader's interpretation, or some mixture of the two, has been one of the most important debates in literary studies this century. The group of writings which can be, and indeed are, labelled 'reader-response criticism' do not form a critical school like 'new criticism', 'phenomenology', or 'deconstruction', but rather consider the philosophy of reading from a wide variety of critical viewpoints. Classicists in general have been slow to join the debate, with notable exceptions.[4] This is not the place for extended theoretical debate: interested readers (mine!) may find illuminating surveys of reader-response criticism in Tompkins (1980) and Freund (1987). An excellent, although idiosyncratic, discussion can be found in Fish's analysis of Iser (Fish 1989: 68–86). Fish's main point seems to be that *all* reading is interpretation (a view to which I would subscribe), as indeed is real-life perception, but that there is no worry about wild subjectivity because *all* interpretation is constrained by assumptions. He claims, as I understand him, that what he calls the interpretative community (see Fish 1980) controls the proliferation of readings. Some readers may feel that this notion reintroduces issues surrounding authority, in that it perhaps does not fully confront the question of who constitutes the 'interpretative community'.

Sat. 1. 9, or, as Charles Martindale suggested to me, Miss Bates in Jane Austen's *Emma*.

[4] The best work of classical scholarship on reader response is Martindale (1993). There is also an issue of *Arethusa* (1986) devoted to the subject. In Ovidian studies the other main critiques which could be labelled 'reader response' are Kettemann's use of the Germanic tradition of Rezeptionsästhetik (1979), of which Iser (1978) and Jauss (1982) are representative, and von Albrecht's discussion of Ovid's relationship with his audience with regard to the *Metamorphoses* (1982). More recently, there has been an excellent study of the erotic and narrative triangle in which Ovid, his characters and his readers are involved in the *Metamorphoses*, by Nagle (1988). E. F. Wright's article (1984), although mainly concerned with the narrators of the *Ars*, also makes some use of 'the reader'.

Culler's books on structuralism, deconstruction, and semiotics (1975; 1981; 1983; 1988) set the role of the reader within the wider critical debate. The common factor in reader-response criticism is an emphasis on the activity of the reader, both within the text (in the case, for example, of the 'narratee' of Prince, or the 'implied reader' of Iser) and outside it (of which there is a whole array of mock readers, super-readers, contemporary readers, etc.). Recent feminist criticism has shown what difference it makes to read as a woman, by postulating a 'woman' reader (who need not be biologically female) to expose the genderedness of the history of reading. (See for example Fetterly 1978 and Jacobus 1986.) The concept of the reader has to be understood in all sorts of ways: most reader-response critics would posit a variety of readers, both real and imaginary, while those influenced by deconstruction would want to stress the potential dissolution of the distinction between the reader in and out of the text. These comments bear upon reading generally: what is specific in didactic texts is the foregrounding of the act of reading by the presence of an *involved* Reader who receives the text's instruction. Didactic poetry makes explicit the activity of readers by purporting to teach—someone.

Didactic poetry traditionally, indeed generically, has an addressee. From the very beginnings of the tradition, wisdom literature has stressed a notional addressee, often the son of the speaker, or a ruler.[5] For Ovid's great predecessors in didactic, Hesiod, Lucretius, and Virgil, it is Perses, Memmius, and Maecenas respectively. For Ovid (*Ars* 1. 1) it is whoever

> *in hoc artem populo non novit amandi.*

> in this population does not know the art of loving.

Anyone, the Roman world, perhaps the whole world. At significant moments throughout the poem, Ovid pointedly

---

[5] See West (1978: 3–25, and 1969: 122). Welcker, in the preface to his 1826 edition of Theognis (p. lxxvii), argued that 'it was a conventional device of ancient poets to address their reflections to an individual, so as to give the impression of genuine concern for a friend rather than severe determination to improve strangers' (I quote here from West 1978: 33–4).

directs his advice towards an addressee, with the didactic phrase, *si quis*. The phrase implies the 'anyone' who might understand, and has similarities with Lucretian usage, while Virgil also uses the formula, though in a less formally didactic manner.[6] In each case, *quis* stands for the didactic 'you'. The generality of the address, which encompasses the whole world in its ambit, informs us of our involvement in the text, for it does not allow us neatly to partition the addressee off from ourselves as readers. At the same time, however, it is possible for us to identify an addressee of a more specific and distinct nature, as we shall see.

The convention of the didactic addressee allows the teacher to criticize within the bounds of literary tact, and allows the reader both to identify with the disciple and to distance himself. Ovid stands at the end of a sophisticated didactic tradition of reader/addressee interrelations, and his addressee is an unusually subtle creation. I shall frequently refer to the Reader, by which I mean the notional addressee. I use the term 'Reader' in preference to 'addressee' in order to encourage the potential slippage between Reader and reader which I am suggesting, while at the same time retaining a sense of difference by the use of the upper case R. The relationship between this Reader and other readers is central to my discussion. Whether we choose to be Ovid's *ideal* reader or not, simply by following the text we are involved because the subject is so universal. Ovid himself self-deprecatingly ironizes this universality when in exile he describes the *Ars* as teaching *quod nemo nescit, amare* ('what no one is ignorant of—love', *Tr.* 1. 1. 112). So

---

[6] See e.g. Lucr. 2. 225–9 *quod si forte aliquis credit grauiora potesse | corpora . . . auius a uera longe ratione recedit*, 931 *quod si forte aliquis dicet*. Cf. Virg. *Georg.* 2. 49–51 *tamen haec quoque, si quis | inserat . . . | exuerint siluestrem animum*, 3. 49 (the most like Lucretian and Ovidian usage) *seu quis Olympiacae miratus praemia palmae | pascit equos, seu quis fortis ad aratra iuuencos, | corpora praecipue matrum legat*, 3. 474 *aerias Alpis et Norica si quis | castella in tumulis et Iapydis arua Timaui | nunc quoque post tanto uideat*. It occurs at the opening of the *Ars* (thus gaining a certain titular force), and at 1. 267 *quisquis ubique uiri, dociles aduertite mentes*, 440 *nec exiguas, quisquis es, adde preces*, 2. 99 *fallitur, Haemonias si quis decurrit ad artes*, 144 *quisquis es*, 241–2 *exue fastus, | curam mansuri quisquis amoris habes* (very much a round-up formula), 511 *quisquis sapienter amabit*; *Rem.* 15 *at si quis male fert indignae regna puellae, | ne pereat, nostrae sentiat artis opem*, 249 *uiderit, Haemoniae si quis mala pabula terrae | et magicas artes posse iuuare putat*.

while on the one hand the Reader is separate from us, at the same time also we are the reader.

In contrast with his most important predecessors, Ovid's didactic poem has no named addressee. This highlights the question: to whom is this advice addressed? The lack of a specific person behind the addressee allows for easier accommodation of addressee to context, and facilitates slippage between the Reader and the reader. At the same time, however, the very unconventionality of the addressee forces us to focus on the distinctions between Reader and reader. *We* are that Reader—anyone—and yet also we are not, but are persuaded to view ourselves as a sophisticated external audience watching, at a stage removed, the lover's progress in his studies. It is impossible to ignore or to depersonalize the second-person addresses in didactic writing: to do so is to ignore a central feature of didactic poetry, that it is intended to teach someone, and to show that teaching taking place. The complicated but necessary result is that of readers watching Readers: it is this duplicity of readership that is essential to our understanding of the *Ars*. The logical conclusion, so to speak, of this is an infinite series of levels of reader each viewing the one ahead, for it is on the difference of the repetition in re-reading that our stake and interest in the text depends. The implied ideal reader of our text must be able both to identify with the Reader and to dissociate himself.

More than ever before, the addressee becomes a character in the drama, whose manipulation by Ovid adds considerably to the reader's appreciation. That character, the Reader, is in fact two: man and woman. This raises the problematical question of the gender of the reader also, implied and real. Although row upon row of the infinite series of readers which I postulated above are constructed as masculine, yet it must be possible for there to be a female reader of this text, because real women have read it. Women reading are not necessarily woman readers of course. I do not propose to go into this question in detail here, but simply to note the problems raised by my use of the inclusive 's/he' to designate the reader, and equally by my use of the exclusive 'he'. I have often used the exclusive pronoun when referring to the reader (as above), because what we might call the 'initial implied reader' of Book 2 is male; but it should be stressed also that reading involves playing out many roles, including those of the opposite gender. The instability of the reader's gender is an indication of the complex of identification with and distancing from the Reader which the response to this text demands.

A pedagogic relationship develops between poet and addressee, which treads a precarious line between submission and dominance. On one model of the pedagogic relationship, and perhaps that most familiar to the Roman audience, the interaction of *magister* ('master/teacher') and *iuuenis* ('young man') is financially and socially structured so that the hired (inferior) is in a position of ambiguous authority over the hiring (superior = son of the father). (See Bonner 1977: 146.) Ovid usurps and subverts the correct pedagogic role, by calling for *komoi* not lessons, girls not books, in direct opposition to the pedagogue's normal social function. The equivocation of teacher/pupil relationship is highlighted by the problematical status of Maecenas *vis-à-vis* Virgil in the *Georgics*. Here is a didactic poem about farming the land addressed to a man who, in the context of the post-Actian resettlement, has a very special stake in the land of Italy; a poem about the social order addressed to a man who is the penultimate authority in the social restructuring of Italian life; a poem which connects poet and addressee as 'singer and patron, teacher and the everyman "you" who might understand'.[7] Teachers are figures of authority—they might, for example, be fathers rather than father-substitutes—but are also dependent on their pupils: Ovid's didactic game is one of the struggle for power.

When we watch Ovid's games with his would-be lover, the Reader, as if from high up on a Lucretian mountain, we are continually forced to remember that we too are the victim and are involved in the text.[8]

---

[7] I quote from Putnam (1979: 18), who does not make explicit the tension in his statement.

[8] On the subject of the reader being 'forced' into a certain reading, see the writings of Riffaterre, for example his essay on 'compulsory reader response' (1990). Fish's criticism of this kind of approach is a necessary balance.

1c Didactic Readers

This heading is intended to refer here not only to the
specific addressees (Readers) and wider audiences (readers)
of the didactic tradition, but also to some very specific
members of wider audiences (readers)—the critics; and furthermore to link self-referentially with the *Ars* by hinting at
the tradition of handbooks on a subject, in the manner of an
'Anglo-Saxon Reader'. The *Ars Amatoria* itself is such a
handbook. Have I just killed the joke by explaining it?

Since the text is pointedly didactic, it will be helpful to
consider how a contemporary audience might have viewed
itself as didactic audience. This brings with it a host of
problems. Which 'contemporary audience'? A group of
Ovid's literary friends? A 17-year-old Roman boy alone
with the text? Augustus? How do we know? I pose these
unanswerable questions to be borne in mind along with my
use of idealized terms such as 'readers' and 'audiences'.
Since the text is a sign of social discourse, some knowledge
of the kinds of reading performances for which it is designed
may help to define an original audience, although this
cannot take us far along the road to an understanding of its
reception. It should perhaps be stated that the terminology
of 'reading' should be taken in general terms, since many
ancient readers probably did not actually read their literature themselves, but had it read to them. The mode of
didactic discourse which might be termed moral-social constitutes, questions, and so reconstitutes a society—of readers.[9] For what it is worth, which is probably not a lot, I
would suggest that we take as the implied readership of this
work (that is, a stage between the Reader and the reader,
any reader) to be, very broadly, educated Roman men of a
detached and mildly subversive frame of mind, contemporary with Ovid.

---

[9] The constitution of this 'society of readers' allows the poem to address and
simultaneously to avoid the problem of its relationship with the contemporary
political ambience, a subject which I have avoided here. It is addressed in my
forthcoming article on 'Ovid and the Politics of Reading', as is the nature of the
original situation of reception.

tute tibi: *Who is the Didactic 'You'?*

Didactic poetry has an internal addressee (Reader), a wider intended audience (reader), and abundant use of the second person singular (and sometimes plural). Who is the referent of the second person singular? A certain ambiguity arises between addressee (Reader) and audience (reader). Since the *Ars* is written consciously, indeed self-consciously, within the tradition of didactic literature, it will be instructive to consider for a moment the Readers and readers of his great predecessors, Hesiod, Lucretius, and Virgil. In each case, scholars have been concerned to distinguish between the named addressee and the generalized 'you', often imposing distinctions for the sake of certain interpretative strategies—as we all do, it being in the nature of reading.

The employment of the biographical imperative leads to misconception of the nature of second-person addresses in didactic. West (1978: 39) claims that the tone of second-person address after *Erg.* 316 is such that we do not think particularly of Perses but apply it to anyone. But surely the point about such second-person addresses in didactic is that they designedly *blur* such distinctions. Simply by our involvement in the text we are—in some sense—all Perses. In this poem about how to behave in society (the family being the base unit of society), the poet addresses the object of his concern, but one very near to him, his second self, his brother—this, whether or not a real brother exists. Any reader is Hesiod's metaphorical brother. The replacement of the father–son relationship, more usual in wisdom literature, by that between brothers (perhaps with an implied age difference), although it raises the question of authority, allows the poet to assume a less threateningly authoritarian stance with regard to his audience.

The same sort of problems arise in Heath's important and illuminating study of didacticism (1985), where he seeks to distinguish between 'formal' didacticism, which is 'purporting to be intended to instruct', and 'final' didacticism, which is actually 'intended to instruct' (the terms are his). Distinctions such as formal and final, real and literary device, also made by Heath, are imposed by particular readers for particular purposes, and are precisely those blurred in the didactic work. Heath's vagueness as to who it is who is being instructed—addressee or audience—in each of these works is indicative of the same trap as that caused by dogmatic distinction between the ostensible addressee and the generalized second-person address. Hesiod's advice to his brother, much of it not specifically personal, must be at least *purporting to be* general advice on how to live well, and therefore be formally didactic, in an already established tradition of wisdom literature—else why *write* at all? The nature of reading, and particularly of reading didactic poetry with a specific addressee, precludes so rigorous a distinction between named addressee and assumed reader.

The function of the addressee Memmius in Lucretius has caused considerable scholarly concern, over whether the work is primarily intended to persuade the real man to embrace Epicureanism, or is more concerned with the general reader. Some discussions seem in danger of the belief that the work might really have been written purely to persuade Memmius and not be concerned with the general reader at all.[10] The question is surely whether or to what extent the poem *presents itself*—to any reader—as being designed for the conversion of Memmius. Since it is an established convention that books can be dedicated simply by addressing the dedicatee, a third participant (a general reader) plays a necessary role as audience before whom the dedication is being played out. The question, rather, is surely what role the character of the addressee, Memmius, might play in the design of the book as literature.[11] The problem relates partly to why Memmius only appears in clusters in the first two and the fifth books,[12] partly to the conflict between what we know of the historical Memmius's

[10] Compare Farrington's case (1965): the whole poem is very heavily directed towards Memmius and is not so much to provide information as to turn Memmius to the moral life.

[11] Classen (1968) appreciates this universality of the 'listener', as he argues that the poem follows the canons of rhetorical theory in order to persuade its Roman audience, epitomized by Memmius. See esp. pp. 92–3, 95–6.

[12] For example, Townend (1978), whose thesis is that the highlighting of Memmius in the first two and the fifth books indicates that they were written earlier with a more specifically evangelistic intent.

lifestyle and attacks by the poet on similar behaviour, as in the discussion of political ambition in 3. 59–84.[13] Clay (1983) seeks to solve this problem by seeing two distinct characters in Memmius, the Roman aristocrat and the constructed reader (Reader, in my terminology) of the poem, and claiming that we learn little or nothing about each from the other (212). This avoids the problem, by making the affair purely literary. The problem for addressee-function in didactic discourse lies partly in asking too narrowly biographical questions, and partly in the use of preconceived assumptions about what can and cannot be said to a patron, within the bounds of literary licence and of tact.[14]

Clay's study is perhaps the best discussion of Lucretius' Memmius and addressee-function in classical texts. The Reader is to be seen as a character in the poem by himself being actively involved, *tute tibi* ('you yourself for yourself'), when Lucretius says that he has provided him with enough evidence to penetrate the truth himself (1. 403, 407, 5. 1281, 6. 527–34). He is brought to face the prospect of death (3. 1025–52), the power of his own passions and their bondage (4. 1150), and finally the plague, and asked to view them with a tranquil mind. Without the Reader, a person undergoing instruction and through whom the poet can suggest an appropriate response, the reading of readers would be greatly diminished. The failure of Clay's reading, for me, is the complete disjunction he wants to make between the historical reality of C. Memmius and the 'Memmius' in the poem. The identification is not total or simple, certainly, but nor is it irrelevant.

Virgil's *Georgics* are clearly a central work to consider for any formal discussion of the *Ars*. In the case under consideration, that is the interrelations of readers and addressees, no single model emerges for the reader's self-image, since we are faced with a multiplicity of addressees.[15] First

[13] M. F. Smith, in the Loeb edition of Lucretius (1975), proposes that the address to Memmius is not flattering but provocative in its clear discrepancies with his known lifestyle.

[14] This is too large a subject to tackle here. See Zetzel (1982).

[15] Of addressees, that is, who could reasonably act as that model. I do not imagine that we should identify with every apostrophe: in the *Ars*, that would involve reception of Ovid's address *in liquida, pisces, delituistis aqua* ('ye fishes,

comes the poem's dedicatee, Maecenas, under whom we might see and identify with the whole society of the cultured Roman upper classes, who constituted the original intended audience. In order to read the poem, one of the roles any reader must play is to become an educated Roman citizen (perhaps aristocrat), but even as such one has to face the problem of the extent to which the actual advice of the poem is addressed to Maecenas. The *coloni* ('farmers') seem to be a separate group.[16] The *tu* to whom the advice is addressed can hardly be Maecenas.

Or can it? If, as is presumably the case, the text follows the didactic tradition of presenting itself for the instruction—in some form—of its Reader and readers, to separate the *coloni* entirely from the intended audience (Reader = Maecenas and readers = Roman aristocrats) is to violate generic constraints and lose the didactic force of the poem. Moreover, as Miles (1980) has proposed, the poem must be seen against the background of the hero-worship of farmers and the myth that agriculture embodied the origins of civilization, and therefore as addressed to the broader responsibilities of the statesman as well as the farmer. The prayer to Augustus to pity ignorant farmers would then take on an even more political aspect, since those farmers would also be statesmen.[17] The text contributes to the social discourse of farming as the restructuring of society, collectively assigned to Augustus as a focus for the new reality. The *Georgics* tell you 'how to run a farm': 'how', that is, cosmically, socially, morally, rather than at a purely mechanical level. Maecenas, then, is metaphorically a 'farmer'. We, with Maecenas, *must* identify with the *coloni*.[18]

---

you hid in the clear water', 2. 472). On the subject of multiple addressees in didactic, note Osborne's argument (1987: 31–2) that the *Physics* and *Katharmoi* of Empedocles are in fact one and the same poem, and that scholars have been misled into separating them by the appearance of two addressees.

[16] Putnam (1979: 88) points to two separate addressees: 'Virgil voices two more apostrophes, first to the farmers who carry out his didactic precepts, second to Maecenas who is asked to join in finishing the creative voyage already begun.'

[17] If Miles's thesis is correct, the subject matter of the imitative *Ars* is rendered even more outrageous.

[18] Kromer's comments (1979: 9) are instructive. 'On one level, then, the portrait of the conscientious farmer or astronomer or student of Epicureanism is a

The Naïve and the Sophisticated

At the same time, since the moral status of civilization is problematical, we both remain aloof in our Roman sophistication from the boorish simplicity of the rustics, and also use them as a measure for our own civilization. In this regard, the *coloni* fulfil a function often accorded to the Reader in didactic texts. The Reader, as the direct recipient of the teacher's wisdom, is constructed as necessarily naïve and unsophisticated, necessarily, since as such he stands in need of the poet's advice. He is putty in the teacher's hands. The readers, by contrast, are encouraged, enticed, and seduced into perceiving themselves (ourselves) as sophisticated onlookers who take pleasure in the informing of the Reader's naïvety.[19] As we watch the instruction of Memmius (for example) taking place, and working, the poet's flattery attracts *us* into his philosophy and his poem. Keeping our sight on the Reader allows us to see how Lucretius entices and manipulates him through his distancing and associating with him: then we must see the enticing manipulation happening also to ourselves.[20]

Clay uses the theme of religion to examine Lucretius' text's relationship with its Reader. He begins as a real Roman religious, even superstitious Reader, terrified of the heavens, in contrast with and in need of the understanding and true piety of Epicurus. Clay shows how he can actually be seen as making progress through the poem (as does Ovid's young lover). In 6. 86 the Reader reacts in a terrified Etruscan manner to the thunderstorm, but by 6. 380, once

---

metaphor for the good reader of a given text.' The incomplete identification of the actual audience with the ostensible one has the result that 'the actual readers are not directly criticized but are permitted to feel that the learning process is taking place at one remove from themselves' (p. 10).

[19] A similar point is made by Griffith (1983: 55) on Theognis.

[20] Compare Clay (1983: 219): 'Lucretius can associate himself with his reader in the self-sufficient relation of "you" and "I"; he can indicate the gap that separates him from his reader by speaking of "us" (Epicureans); he can join Memmius and contemplate the rest of mankind from a distance; and he and his reader can join the large company of the fearful and unenlightened (1. 114 and 134).' Such sympathetic association is itself a form of enticement, as for example in 5. 1218–21, where Lucretius professes to join his Reader in fear of thunder and lightning so that he can draw him to *ratio* (cf. Clay: 223), and of flattery, as the poet draws the Reader up to his own vantage point.

he has understood the nature of thunder and lightning, he is no longer possessed by these fears. 'Lucretius has given his religious reader an alternative view of the world gradually to replace his Roman, native and naïve conception of the nature of things' (Clay 1983: 224.) Now—and this Clay does not mention—*this* points to a really naïve Reader. No reader of Lucretius was simply 'Roman, native, and naïve', but he must bring to his reading an experience of culture as a Roman difference from Greek culture. Lucretius' readers watch with a pleasant sense of superiority the simplicity of Lucretius' Reader.

But inevitably the distinction between the naïve Reader in the text and the sophisticated reader keeping her/his distance from the text, as an amused and detached onlooker, breaks down in the very act of reading. The opening prayer to Venus is an enticement to the very Roman Reader to come to the poem, by flattering mention of his deeds and family, and by a veneer of Roman patriotism shared between poet and Reader.[21] But Venus is gradually eclipsed by Natura, *uenus*, and a philosophical understanding of the gods and the nature of things, as the Reader matures philosophically (Clay 1983: particularly 226). According to Clay (1983: 231), Lucretius *intends* his Reader to recognize the contradiction between his invocation and his theology, and by a retrograde reading to 'realize that the Roman goddess who first attracted him to the poem cannot herself be attracted by any human appeal'. For the reader, the invocation, as a beautiful piece of poetry, and the portrayal of the Reader's development are the honey (which, oddly, Clay does not mention) which attracts him into the poem. We, as readers of the *Ars*, see the addressee (the young man in the first two books) as this inexperienced audience and ourselves as enlightened readers on a level with Ovid, until we are forced to give up, to some extent, this self-image of superiority when we remember that the poem is addressed to *si quis in hoc ... populo*, and that Ovid has himself

---

[21] Memmius here epitomizes the Roman aristocratic readers who are Lucretius' intended audience, for which some version, perhaps an ideal one, of his historical character is essential. This is where I find Clay's distinction between C. Memmius and 'Memmius' unhelpful.

contrived our lofty viewpoint, so that we are his victims no less than the *iuuenis* ('young man').

One difficulty scholars have found in reading the didactic addressee as a character in the drama is the perceived inconsistency of that character. This concern is prompted in part by the imperative to ask unanswerable biographical questions. West (1978: 33), seeking to overturn the previous orthodoxy that Hesiod wrote as he did to suit the real character of Perses, argues that his character changes, sometimes inconsistently, as suits the purpose of the instruction: Perses' character is inconsistent, *therefore* the demands of the context have determined his 'character' at any one point.[22] But to adopt this position is to rely on preconceived assumptions about what constitutes consistency and inconsistency in character. Real people and didactic addressees are equally capable of being inconsistent, so a distinction between them which uses such a criterion cannot be valid. It is true also of Memmius that he is inconsistent. Like Hesiod's Perses, the addressee of the *De Rerum Natura* undergoes changes in identity, and for this reason, according to Townend, cannot connect with Memmius throughout. He says on 3. 968 'the addressee is not the philosopher's disciple of book 1, but the satirist's butt' (Townend 1978: 276). True, but is it impossible for the same person in different situations to take on both these images, particularly when they are self-images? Again preconceptions about what is contradictory in character confuse the function of the didactic addressee. In the *Ars* also, the lover changes his status and situation to suit the precept: so it might seem from, for example, the contrast between his powerful position in 2. 287–94 (master of slaves, allowing his 'mistress' to *feel* in control), and his 'poverty' in the couplets immediately preceding (vv. 261–84) and his slave-like behaviour for much of the section vv. 145–336. But this is a poem about behaviour and self-image. There is no simple consistent picture of a Roman man-in-the-street.

---

[22] He assumes support for this from the *Scholia Vetera in Hesiodi Opera et Dies* 3. 13P, quoted by West (1978: 33 n. 1) and Clay (1983: 333 n. 112): 'Hesiod fashioned this persona and borrowed it from his brother Perses, either in truth or in accordance with its plausibility and suitability to his argument.'

1d How Many Books Make Three?

The prevailing view of the chronology of the *Ars* is that Book 3 is a later addition, an afterthought tagged on to the important part, with little concern for integration. Hollis subscribes to the opinion, arguing particularly from the didactic table of contents in *Ars* 1. 35–40.[23] The orthodoxy has it that *Ars* 1 and 2 were published together, probably around 2 BC, with *Ars* 3 coming sometime later, probably around AD 2, possibly as part of a second edition of the whole poem, although this last point is not accepted by Hollis.[24] I shall argue that the appearance of a two-book poem is deceitful, whether or not there were two editions.[25] The question is, rather, one of the extent of integration.

We have a three-book work: when reading the second book, how far should we be aware of the existence of the third? Are we reading the last of two or the middle of three? The answer is 'both', inevitably, but on different levels. In so far as we identify with the Reader, who is a character in the drama, we should impose blinkers on ourselves in order to be unaware of the betrayal which is to happen at the end of Book 2. But if we, as *readers*, are aware of the existence of the different perspective of Book 3, then our pleasure is enhanced by the joke played on the lover/Reader. This simultaneous suspension of critical faculties, together with an awareness that we are deliberately 'not-knowing' what we know, is an essential part of reading, particularly of re-

[23] See Hollis (1977: pp. xii–xiii and ad loc.). For the argument see Sabbadini (1909). This view is echoed e.g. by Marchesi (1918: 42, 61), Wilkinson (1955: 122), Fränkel (1945: 65), Dilke (1982: 12). For a contrary view see Romano (1972: 817), Weber (1983). Murgia (1986) argues for a second edition, and places it as late as close to AD 8. This strikes me as too convenient (as an explanation for the poet's exile). See Syme (1978: 9–20), particularly 15, for arguments for an earlier date, also probably in two editions.

[24] The argument for the dates is generally taken, as is explained by Hollis (1977: p. xiii), to stem from the reference to the mock sea-battle of 2 BC (*Ars* 1. 171), and that to Gaius being in the East but apparently not having met the Parthian king Phraataces (a meeting which took place in AD 2) at *Rem.* 155–6, the *Remedia Amoris* being taken to be close in time to *Ars* 3.

[25] Indeed, I wonder how far we are justified in seeing publication as the fixed and final event which it is for us today. At some point presumably the text must have been standardized in time to be corrupted by the manuscript tradition, but it seems to me likely that ancient authors and readers would have had a more fluid conception of composition than is generally acknowledged.

reading. Take the simple example of reading a novel where the resolution is already known. In order to enjoy the experience of surprise, we must posit a reader who does not know the ending, and identify with him/her. At the same time, however, we take pleasure in perceiving the clues in the text towards the resolution, which we missed on our first reading, and which our implied unknowing reader is missing. If I may be allowed a self-quotation: '[w]henever we identify a reading (and hence a reader) of (or in) a text, we have just been transformed into yet another reader in the act of reading the previous level: and so readers watch readers going all the way down in a constant metamorphosis on the shifting sands of meaning' (Sharrock 1991).

Let us return to the table of contents. Admittedly, *Ars* 1. 35–40 looks like an original plan for the work, addressed only to men, which Ovid did not bother to revise when he added the third book.

> *Principio quod amare uelis, reperire labora,*
> *qui noua nunc primum miles in arma uenis;*
> *proximus huic labor est placitam exorare puellam;*
> *tertius ut longo tempore duret amor.*
> *hic modus; haec nostro signabitur area curru;*
> *haec erit admissa meta premenda rota.*

First of all, you who now for the first time come
as a soldier into these new arms, make an effort
to find an object you want to love;
the next task is to prevail upon the girl who has pleased you;
the third that love should remain for a long time.
This will be the end [due measure]; this arena will be marked out
by my chariot;
this *meta* [goal and turning-post] will be scraped by my flying
wheel.

It would really be rather surprising if Ovid *did* make reference here to his volte-face of the third book. The young man must be given the impression that the teacher is wholly on his side; he should not be told that his master will help him first, and then give subversive assistance to the opposition. The reader, however, can see the subtle jokes being played on the would-be lover, and a couple of hints are given that the catalogue is not so straightforward.

Firstly, the catalogue suggests a tripartite structure to the

work: *principio . . . proximus . . . tertius* ('first . . . next . . .
thirdly'). Now, while it is possible to refer 'first find your
girl, then catch her' to two halves of the first book, and
apply 'thirdly' to the second book, there is something funny
about using the term *tertius* to apply to the *second* book of a
three-book work which is pretending at the moment that
the actual third book does not exist. The joke hinges on the
meta in 1. 40. This is both the goal and the turning post, the
end and the change of direction. In the middle of *Ars* 2 and
therefore at the centre of the three-book work, the chariot
of the *Ars* skids around a *meta* which has to be a turning-
post, as Ovid changes from advising the lover to hide his
infidelities to pointing out the advantages of displaying
them (2. 426). Then, at the end of Book 2, the lovers are
hurrying together towards the *meta*—the goal of love-
making. But while the erotic *meta* is very clearly a goal and
so an end, the poetic *meta* turns out also to be a turning-
post, and the work goes on. *Finis adest operi* ('The end of
the work is here'), Ovid claims (2. 733), referring both to
the poem and to the erotic *opus* of v. 730, but the ambiguity
of the 'work' (sex or poetry) and of the carefully chosen
meta (in 1. 40 and 2. 727) allows the poem both to end and to
change direction. The *meta* of 2. 727 is a goal pure and
simple for the Reader, but for the reader it is both a goal
and a turning-post towards *Ars* 3.

While the first two books pretend that the third does not
exist, the third is equally coy about the presence of 1 and 2.
In the catalogue of works which a *docta puella* ('learned
girl') should read (*Ars* 3. 329–45), including the *Amores* and
Heroides, conspicuous by their absence are *Ars* 1 and 2. We
would perhaps be surprised if they were mentioned, but we
should be no more surprised that Book 3 is not mentioned
in the first two books.[26] As we have it there are two books
for the male Reader and one for the female, and three for
the reader.

[26] I would have to admit that *Ars* 3 opens with a reference to the aid Ovid has
given to men (the opening word *Arma* links it as much to *Am.* 1. 1—and through
that to the opening of the *Aeneid*—as it does to *Ars* 1. 1). But after that very
general reference, itself perhaps part of the 'extra-dramatic' link between the
books, the advice to men disappears at the primary level.

2

First Catch Your Reader

2a How to Catch a Reader

The reader is and is not the Reader. The act of reading this text necessarily involves both identification with and separation from the aspiring lover to whom it is notionally addressed. So it is that we are able 'voyeuristically' to watch the lover's progress through his apprenticeship, identifying with him, but with a detached amusement. We see him as seducer and also as victim of seduction, and that in two ways. First, there are times when we may suspect that he is as much seduced by the girl and/or love as seducing it/her. Someone, a *praeda petita* ('a desired prey'), *decidit* ('fell') into Ovid's *casses* ('trap') in the first pentameter of our book. Who was it? The girl certainly: but if we are alert to the games which, I shall suggest, Ovid plays with his reader, we may re-read the line with the lover also subliminally signified or at least hinted at by *praeda*. The *lover* has fallen into Ovid's trap, in that he is involved in the poem and enthusiastically following its advice. He is a victim of seduction by the poet/teacher. If the lover is signified, then so is the reader, for when we see the lover caught in the trap and held in the text's embrace we must realize that we too are the victims of the text's seduction. At times we too are deceived for the moment, and then are made to laugh at our own gullibility. Moreover, when the reader takes the hint and realizes Ovid's deception of the lover, he gains satisfaction from his vantage-point with Ovid, looking down on the student/lover. By letting us in to his superior dwelling-place, Ovid has done to us what he has done to the girl and the lover. We have bitten and are caught—we are reading the book. The pleasure of the lover, the pleasure of reading, the erotics of the text, its figuration as seduction:[1] that is what is especially explicit in Ovid. Any pleasure we derive from reading the poem is *amor* ('love') for its *ars* ('art').

Ovid, in the *Remedia Amoris*, answers his own earlier line, perhaps confirming our suspicions that lovers may also fall into traps, when he says (*Rem.* 501–2):

> *deceptum risi, qui se simulabat amare*
> *in laqueos auceps decideratque suos*

I have laughed at a man who pretended to be in love
to see him deceived and, a bird-catcher, falling headlong into his
  own trap.

Ovid created a trap for women and taught it to his pupil, in such a way that it became a trap also for the man himself. He was told in the *Ars Amatoria* to pretend to be in love in order to catch his girl, but it turns out in the *Remedia Amoris* that this very pretence of love may have trapped him. The love which began in the *Ars* as a manipulative pretence on the young lover's part must become for him a real love, a love which catches him also, putting him in need of the advice of the *Remedia Amoris*. Ovid hints at a warning of the reciprocal nature of erotic trapping in the first book of the *Ars*, in a couplet of cleverly ambiguous gender (*Ars* 1. 645–6):

> *fallite fallentes; ex magna parte profanum*
> *sunt genus: in laqueos, quos posuere, cadant*

Deceive the deceptive; they are a wicked race, most of them:
let them fall into the traps which they have laid.

At the moment of transition between Books 1 and 2, the trap snaps shut. The prey—whoever it may be—is caught. The task now is to hold on to it—*hoc erit artis opus* ('this will be a work of art', v. 14). Winning the girl, writing Book 1: these are not enough, Ovid claims in his self-advertising prologue (vv. 11–12).

> *non satis est uenisse tibi me uate puellam:*
> *arte mea capta est, arte tenenda mea est*

---

[1] See Chambers's (1984) exposition of the seductive power of narrative, esp. his final ch., 'Authority and Seduction: The Power of Fiction' (205–23).

It is not enough that the girl has come to you through my poem:
by my art she has been caught, by my art she must be kept.

Capta ('caught') and *tenenda* ('kept') in the pentameter
refer back to *puellam* ('girl') in the hexameter, of course,
but an astute reader may read Ovid's proclamation about
the girl, and then reflect that something very similar is
happening to the lover; and if he is attuned to the suggestive
rapacity of Ovidian art he may suspect that he too is being
held captive by the art/Art, and will be held, along with the
girl, through the second book. It is not just the *puella*
which is the antecedent of *tenenda*, but, secondarily and
subliminally, the ambiguously feminine *praeda*, in the
second line, which may be, alternately or simultaneously,
girl, lover, or reader.[2]

In this book about 'holding', *teneo* gains programmatic
significance, as it recurs (with compounds) as a leitmotif
throughout the book, drawing on the wealth of meaning the
word has acquired in love elegy. (See Pichon 1902, and
Pease 1935 on Virg. *Aen.* 4. 308.) It can mean 'hold'; sexually
'embrace';[3] 'stop' the lover leaving;[4] inflame passion by
'delay';[5] 'hold back' in love-making;[6] mesmerize, 'keep'

[2] The problem of the gender-specification of 'reader' which I mentioned in Ch.
1 arises forcibly here. The practice of signifying the reader with 's/he' seems
oddly inappropriate here, where the Reader is so clearly and necessarily male, and
so is the implied reader. Is it the moral of this story that this text only allows a
male reading? Or at least that my reading of it does? A female reader inscribed in
my reading would inevitably carry different and further connotations in the
schema of seduction which I am offering as a sophisticated metaphor. We are all
trapped.

[3] Cf. e.g. Catul. 11. 18; Tib. 1. 5. 39, 1. 6. 35, 2. 6. 52 *quisue meam teneat, quot
teneatue modis* ('who holds my beloved, and in what ways he holds her'); Ov. *Am.*
3. 7. 3.

[4] Cf. e.g. Catul. 55. 17; Tib. 1. 1. 55 *me retinent uinctum formosae uincla puellae*
('the chains of a lovely girl hold me back'), so that he cannot go on campaign; Ov.
Her. 16. 213; *Rem.* 213, 529.

[5] Cf. e.g. Tib. 1. 8. 73–4 *et cupidum ficta detinuisse mora* ('and to have held me
back me in my desire with imagined delay').

[6] Cf. Ov. *Rem.* 405, come to your beloved already worn out from sex with
another, because *sustentata Venus gratissima* ('delayed sex is most welcome');
Mart. 1. 46 *Cum dicis 'propero, fac si facis,' Hedyle, languet | protinus et cessat
debilitata Venus. | expectare iube. uelocius ibo retentus. | Hedyle, si properas, dic mihi,
ne properem* ('When you say, "I'm close, come if you are going to," Hedyle,
straight away my weakened desire languishes and fails. Order me to wait. I'll go
faster when held back. Hedyle, if you are close, tell me not to come.'); and see also
Adams (1982: 144).

spellbound.[7] This is what the *Ars* does to us: it holds on to us, controls us, keeps us spellbound, embraces us with the erotics of its text. The poem inflames our poetic and erotic interest by its delay: it holds us back to hold on to us. In this highly programmatic line (12), the *ars/Ars* game (the play between *ars* = skill/art, and *Ars* = the poem) works four ways: *ars ... Ars, Ars ... ars, ars ... ars, Ars ... Ars.* The fifth, and most tenacious (*'teneo*-ing') reading is the act of working out the play.

Almost one hundred lines into Book 2, after the prologue and the extended discursus on Daedalus and Icarus (which will be discussed in the next chapter), the teacher impresses on his pupil the need to be lovable in order to be loved; and the poet exemplifies the complexities of 'holding', here particularly intensified. The lover is told not to rely on magic, or on looks, but on *ars* (and therefore the *Ars*), and is presented with an example of artistic loving in the story of Ulysses and Calypso. It is this passage, vv. 99–144, which is the main focus of this chapter. For the reader's convenience, I shall quote vv. 99–122 here, and again in discussion of them, and vv. 123–44 (*Ulysses and Calypso*) later.

> *fallitur, Haemonias si quis decurrit ad artes*
> *datque quod a teneri fronte reuellit equi.* 100
> *non facient, ut uiuat amor, Medeides herbae*
> *mixtaque cum magicis nenia Marsa sonis:*
> *Phasias Aesoniden, Circe tenuisset Ulixem,*
> *si modo seruari carmine posset amor.*
> *nec data profuerint pallentia philtra puellis;* 105
> *philtra nocent animis uimque furoris habent.*
> *sit procul omne nefas! ut ameris, amabilis esto;*
> *quod tibi non facies solaue forma dabit.*
> *sis licet antiquo Nireus adamatus Homero*
> *Naiadumque tener crimine raptus Hylas,* 110
> *ut dominam teneas nec te mirere relictum,*
> *ingenii dotes corporis adde bonis.*
> *forma bonum fragile est, quantumque accedit ad annos,*
> *fit minor et spatio carpitur ipsa suo.*
> *nec uiolae semper nec hiantia lilia florent,* 115
> *et riget amissa spina relicta rosa;*

---

[7] Cf. Tib. 1. 2. 27; Ov. *Her.* 9. 12, 13. 20, 20. 125.

et tibi iam uenient cani, formose, capilli,
  iam uenient rugae, quae tibi corpus arent.
iam molire animum, qui duret, et adstrue formae:
  solus ad extremos permanet ille rogos.   120
nec leuis ingenuas pectus coluisse per artes
  cura sit et linguas edidicisse duas.   (*Ars* 2. 99–122)

Anyone who has recourse to Haemonian arts, and gives
that which is torn from the brow of a young horse,
is deceived. The grasses of Medea will not make
love live, nor the Marsian chant mixed with magic noises.
The Phasian [Medea] would have held the son of Aeson,
and Circe Ulysses, if love could really be kept by a song-spell.
Nor do pallid potions applied to girls bring profit;
potions are harmful to minds and contain the violence of
  madness.
Begone, all evil! In order to be loved, be lovable—
something which beauty will not give you, nor form alone.
Even if you are like Nireus loved by ancient Homer
and tender Hylas stolen by the crime of the Naiads,
in order that you should 'hold' your mistress, and not
marvel at being left [left behind], add gifts of the mind
to the delights of your body.
Beauty is a fragile blessing, and as much as it increases in years,
it diminishes and is plucked by its own extent.
Neither violets nor gaping lilies flower for ever,
and the thorn left alone grows hard when the rose is lost.
Even to you, handsome boy, white hairs will come soon,
soon wrinkles will come, which will furrow your body.
Now build up your mind to endure, and build on your beauty/
  form.
Mind alone remains to the final pyre.
Let it be no light concern to cultivate your spirit
through the freeborn arts and to learn the two languages.

But first let us look back a line to *detinuisse* ('to have held
back/down/on to', v. 98).[8] The word occurs at the end of
the protracted exemplum of Daedalus, and acts as a pointer
to one of its functions. The poet is holding back, restraining,
the love-god in and with his poem. It should be noted that
the word occurred in exactly this form in Tib. 1. 8. 74, where
it signified 'inflame passion by delay'. Likewise Ovid has

---

[8] Yes, I am delaying you just as Ovid does his reader (and Reader).

held back his instruction by his 'irrelevant' tale, using the well-known erotic technique of keeping us and the lover on tenterhooks, but at the same time seductively tempting us with his tale into reading on. At the end, we and the lover are all the more desperate to get on with the matter in hand, and that desperation is seen through a sexual metaphor.

A question at issue in the whole of the second book, and intensified in the passage vv. 99–144, is 'who is holding whom?' Is the lover holding the girl, or the other way round? The uncertainty is signified by the paradoxical juxtaposition *ut dominam teneas* ('so that you may hold your mistress', v. 111). How to *tenere* a girl—this is the point of this book. But by using the term *domina*, Ovid implies that state of elegiac power relations in which the lover is a slave to his mistress, and so introduces an incongruity: the slave is holding on to his mistress, who by implication is trying to get away. We would expect the slave to be the one doing the fleeing. Using the term *domina*, Ovid is manipulating his pupil's self-image into that of the elegiac willing slave, but one who is—or thinks he is—really in control. The sentence continues *nec te mirere relictum* ('and not marvel at being left behind'). The art of love is never to be left (and left behind) by someone you are trying to hold (back/on to). It is essential to get the timing right, and to be fully aware of the stage the relationship has reached (see vv. 337–52, 349–50). This instruction comes to a head in the description of artistic love-making (vv. 725–6):

> *sed neque tu dominam uelis maioribus usus*
> *defice, nec cursus anteeat illa tuos.*

> But don't fail your mistress, using greater sails,
> and don't let her get ahead of you in the race.

So, at v. 111, we may be intended to understand a sexual hint in *dominam teneas*: if the lover sharpens his intellect—by reading the book—he will finally learn how to avoid being—sexually—*relictum* ('left').

The sexual relationship of the lover and the girl becomes a metaphor in the relationship of the lover and Ovid. Ovid, I suggest, is 'holding' the lover (in all the word's complexity), and when we take the point of that he is 'holding' us too . . . and we should smile again to see ourselves as victims of his rapacious art. I submit that in this passage a sub-text develops exploiting the language of the 'persuasion to love' to a *puer delicatus* ('beloved boy'), which realizes Ovid's poetic seduction of Reader and reader in erotic terms. While the pupil learns the art of seduction, he is himself being seduced, both by the girl and by Ovid. And so are you, dear reader, both in that 'you' are the addressee, and through the fun of your seeing the point.

Now of course this is only a metaphor.[9] It would be simplistic to find an impossible contradiction between this pederastic imagery and the avowed claim of Ovid (*Ars* 2. 683–4) that

> *odi concubitus, qui non utrumque resoluunt:*
> *hoc est, cur pueri tangar amore minus*

> I hate sex which does not release both.
> That is why I am affected by the love of boys—less.

Before we agonize over the poet's sincerity, we must investigate the poetic point of the statement. We might perhaps paraphrase the point in its context: 'I am teaching the ultimate skill of two-sided love(-making), far more artistic than any art of pederasty, as, for instance, Tibullus 1. 4.' Moreover, with typical Ovidian undercutting, the last word forces us to reinterpret the sense of the whole couplet: 'I am touched by the love of boys—less.'[10]

2b Lovers and Beloveds

My reading suggests that the aspiring young lover is subliminally forced to play *puer delicatus* to Ovid's sexual and poetic seductive power. For this reading, it is important to remember that ancient erotic relations are more frequently formulated as 'lover and beloved' than as 'two lovers', and

---

[9] I appreciate the problems raised by the phrase just used. See Kennedy (1993: 46–63).

[10] *Minus* can actually make a full, albeit mild negative. Cf. *OLD minus* 4 and Nisbet and Hubbard (1970) on Hor. *Carm.* 1. 2. 27: 'an idiomatic understatement for *non*'. Ovid's statement, then, teasingly opens itself to ambiguity: does he—or does he not—care for boys?

that this affects the balance of power. Cynthia is not Propertius' lover, but his beloved. This is not to say that 'two
lovers' is never an accurate description of ancient erotic
relations but that it is frequently and normally not so. This
is not simply to say, either, that there are not female lovers
in antiquity: Dido and Medea are obvious examples of
'lovers', but they, tellingly, belong more to tragic discourse
than to subjective erotic. In elegy particularly, there is a
loving subject and a loved object, divided by gender and
invested with an automatic rule of relative power-status. In
literary homosexuality there is again a loving subject and a
loved object, this time divided by age, with the same rule of
power. As is well known, the penetrator has power over the
penetrated. Interestingly, when goddesses court mortal men
they behave like older, active-homosexual *men* (Dover 1978:
172). Erotic discourse can only accommodate the anomalous
position of a goddess, both female and powerful, in male
terms.[11]

As he grows up, a young, passive *erōmenos* ('beloved
boy') goes through rites of passage into an adult active
lover, of boys or women. On the threshold, in his ambivalent, one might say ephebic, stage between the two states, a
young man can be simultaneously lover and beloved, in
different relationships. The story of Narcissus in the *Metamorphoses* (3. 339–510) is a *reductio* of this type of situation.
Narcissus' liminal status is signified early in the story by
the comment (*Met.* 3. 352–5) that

> poteratque puer iuuenisque uideri:
> multi illum iuuenes, multae cupiere puellae;
> sed—fuit in tenera tam dura superbia forma—
> nulli illum iuuenes, nullae tetigere puellae.

> He was able to seem both a boy and a young man:
> many young men desired him and many girls;
> but—so hard was the arrogance in the tender form—
> no young men touched him, and no girls.

Echo, fudging/fusing the roles of elegiac *puella* unable to

[11] It is telling in this regard that some scholars have reacted to the imagery of
seruitium amoris ('slavery of love') in Propertius by assuming that Cynthia must be
older than the poet, for how else could she have such power over him?

speak first and goddess-lover pursuing a mortal man, is placed in an impossible situation. One of Narcissus' male lovers calls down nemesis (3. 404–6). Narcissus, of course, can only love himself, and as he stares at the beloved reflection in the pond, he encapsulates the moment of sexual double identity (*Met.* 3. 465):

> *roger, anne rogem*
> Should I be asked, or ask?

Active and passive, lover and beloved in one person.

Of particular interest to us, of course, is the case of a beloved boy having active heterosexual interests. Acontius, for example, begins his love for Cydippe while still himself loved by older men (Call. *Aet.* frr. 68–70).[12] Frequently a *paiderastēs* ('lover of boys') will reproach an unyielding boy with the threat that he too will one day be rejected by a beloved, boy or woman. In Horace *Odes* 3. 20, a man and a woman fight over a boy, in that ambivalent stage where he is attractive to both sexes. Oblivious of either, the boy is (*Carm.* 3. 20. 15–16)

> *qualis aut Nireus fuit aut aquosa*
> *raptus ab Ida.*
>
> such as Nireus was or the boy stolen
> from watery Ida.

The comparison with Nireus, coupled with Ganymede, in this *Ode* about a sexually liminal young man is a strong indicator of the sub-text of our passage. The point will be discussed further below.

Perhaps the *locus classicus* of the liminal beloved–lover is the situation envisaged in Tibullus 1. 8 and 9. In the first poem of this diptych, Tibullus sympathizes with his boy Marathus' amatory state—he is in love with a girl. There is no more than a gentle reproach tempering the older lover's support for his beloved's active case. That reproach is the hint in the closing lines at traditional nemesis, which the poet altruistically prays will not be brought to fulfilment in

---

[12] References to the fragments of Callimachus use the numbering system of Pfeiffer (1949 and 1953). Cf. Theocr. 7. 118, 13. 47; *AP* 12. 109 (Meleager).

Marathus' case, but rather that of the boy's own beloved (*Tib.* 1. 8. 71–8):

> hic Marathus quondam miseros ludebat amantes,
>   nescius ultorem post caput esse deum;
> saepe etiam lacrimas fertur risisse dolentis
>   et cupidum ficta detinuisse mora:
> nunc omnes odit fastus, nunc displicet illi
>   quaecumque opposita est ianua dura sera.
> at te poena manet, ni desinis esse superba.
>   quam cupies uotis hunc reuocare diem!

This Marathus once deceived unhappy lovers,
unaware that a vengeful god stood behind his head;
often he is said to have laughed at grieving tears
and to have held his lover back with pretended delay:
now he hates all pride, now he is displeased, whenever
the hard door is locked with a bolt.
But punishment is waiting for you (girl), if you do not stop being
    arrogant.
How you will want to call back this day with prayers!

The second poem, by contrast, is violent in its condemnation of Marathus' sexual relations with a third party, an older man. In both poems, Tibullus aids his beloved's affair with the girl, as an act of loving service for which he expects a sexual reward. The tripartite affair Tibullus–Marathus–Pholoe is mirrored in the *Ars* by a triptych Ovid–Reader–*puella*. Like Tibullus, Ovid has arranged for the girl to come to the boy. Unlike Tibullus, Ovid has nevertheless maintained his own position of sexual authority.

2c The Teacher as Pederastic Pedagogue

There are precedents for the didactic use of pederasty. We have already looked at a number of models for the teacher–pupil relationship. Another such model—and we must perforce think in erotic terms—is the pederastic connection between older (active) *erastēs* and younger (passive) *erōmenos*. (See Dover 1978: 84–7.) The great inducement for the *erōmenos* in *paiderastia* ('love of boys') is the promise of intellectual and moral advancement; submission effected with this goal in mind is honourable, while dishonour consists in submission to a bad *erastēs*. Such are the relationships envisaged in Plato's *Symposium*.[13] The greatest honour consists in desire for submission to the best *erastēs*—Socrates himself. The reward for such submission is nothing less than access to Socratic philosophy.

In early Greek society, pederasty played an important social role in the formation of *philos* ('friend')-relationships among the aristocracy and in the education, particularly the moral and social education, of the young. In his discussion of Eros and the *polis* (city) in Theognis, Lewis says this of the social role of Eros: '[t]aming the φρένες of men, he [Eros] incites them to form φίλος relationships with one another, making possible through παιδεία/παιδεραστία the transmission of values from one generation to the next' (Lewis 1985: 221). Theognis uses his pederastic poetry to impart to his beloved Cyrnus precepts on right social behaviour.[14] In this case, then, the didactic poet and his addressee are involved in a pederastic relationship which is integral to the didactic process, that is, the transfer of wisdom from teacher to pupil. The Socratic writings of Plato, although not generically didactic poetry, should also be seen in this pedagogic-pederastic tradition, especially when the subject is Eros, as for example in the *Symposium* and the *Phaedrus*. The model extends also into the realm of the transmission of more objective scientific knowledge. Diogenes Laertius reports (8. 61) the statement of Aristippus and Satyrus, that Empedocles' addressee, Pausanias, was the poet's *erōmenos*.

In view of the authoritative role of the father-figure in didactic, particularly wisdom literature (see West 1969), it should be noted that the affection felt by the *erastēs* for the

---

[13] Pausanias in particular hymns a noble love in which the greatest joy to the *erastēs* is that of watching his *erōmenos* maturing under his guidance and growing in spiritual stature. See Penwill (1978). His contention (p. 146) that the *Symposium* shows that, even in the case of Socrates, this supposedly noble love does not work, does not undermine Ovid's employment of the relationship.

[14] See also Cartledge (1981). Shapiro (1981) shows how the occurrence of certain types of pederastic vases correlates with the Peisistratid period just before the rise of the democracy in Athens, and therefore is to be associated with aristocratic values.

erōmenos, concerned as it is with the maintenance and smooth running of the *polis*, is sometimes expressed in terms of the father-son relationship. Now, of course, *paiderastia* ('love of boys') is notoriously Greek. It almost goes without saying that Ovid's literary ancestry is inextricably Graeco-Roman, so his use of a Greek motif is not of itself remarkable. But there is an amusing contrast between the model, however hypothetical or mythical, of pederasty handing down the values of the *polis* and Ovid's pretence at imitating it. According to the official values of his society, his text is decadent and subversive. Romans do not use *paiderastia* as a means of transferring social values between the generations of the aristocracy; nor do they, in their 'official' discourse, consider artistic seduction a valuable socio-moral asset.

The *erōmenos* learns from his *erastēs* the wisdom, values, and skills of his society. Our aspiring lover, if he is to become an adult, active member of his society, must add *ingenii dotes* ('a dowry of intellect') to the attractions of his body (v. 112). As in the case of Socratic *erōmenoi*, this intellectual and moral advancement is what he will gain from submission to his *erastēs*. The question arises: to whom are these mental and physical attributes attractive? On the surface, the answer must be the woman on whom the Reader has designs, but it is also, subliminally, subversively, Ovid himself. This is inherent in the pederastic promise of moral advancement, that the intellectual attractions of the *erōmenos* are as much for the sake of the lover as the beloved. Ovid is training the perfect reader for his text.[15]

2d *ut ameris, amabilis esto*

The central precept of the passage under consideration in this chapter is that in order to keep your girl you have to be

[15] *Dotes*, responding with *dabit* in v. 108, can mean a gift or attribute which will attract. Cf. Ov. *Am.* 2. 4. 17 *siue es docta, places raras dotata per artes*, 38 *ornata est: dotes exhibit ipsa suas*; *Ars* 1. 596 *et, quacumque potes dote placere, place*, 3. 257–8; *Rem.* 325, 331. In exile the word is used of the poetic skill in the *Ars* which made Ovid pleasing ('pleasing' being another concept which has erotic as well as poetic overtones): *perii dotibus ipse meis* (*Pont.* 2. 7. 48).

loved, and in order to effect that situation you have to be lovable, something which you can only achieve by reading the *Ars* (vv. 107–8):

> *ut ameris, amabilis esto;*
> *quod tibi non facies solaue forma dabit.*

In order to be loved, be lovable—
something which beauty will not give you, nor form alone.

It is a commonplace that love is produced not by looks alone but by character, a commonplace which is used by Ovid's most obvious predecessor in erotodidaxis, Tibullus, in addressing Priapus (1. 4. 3–4):

> *quae tua formosos cepit sollertia? certe*
> *non tibi barba nitet, non tibi culta coma est*

What cleverness of yours has caught beautiful boys? Certainly your beard does not shine, nor is your hair well groomed.

It is worth noting the difference between our passage and Tibullus'. Priapus is most emphatically *not* beautiful; rather it is his beloveds who are *formosi* ('beautiful'). In our case, by contrast, it is the supposedly active lover who has *forma* ('beauty'). Ovid indirectly praises the boy's physical attractions in the very act of denying their sufficiency in active, artistic loving.[16]

Just as Lucretius in his proem drew Memmius, and through him the reader, into the web of his poem through flattery, so Ovid attracts his young lover by this backhanded praise of his physical assets. It is only when we are alerted to his game by the next few couplets, however, that we begin to question whether this might be a rather barbed compliment. *Forma* might be an acceptable subject for praise in a man, but to mention the pretty face of an aspiring active, virile lover is somewhat precarious. The precise tone of many passages using terms like *forma* and *facies* is hard to assess (*facies* can of course mean 'appearance' as well as simply 'face'), but a number of examples suggest that this praise is more appropriate to a woman

---

[16] Note that v. 108 originally seems to make a stronger claim than it eventually realizes. After the central pause, the *facies* which appeared to stand alone has to be modified and re-read as *non sola facies*, by the *apo koinou* construction.

(or—more importantly—a beautiful boy) than a man.[17]
Ovid does not yet overtly use the terminology of beautiful
boys, and it is essential that he should not if his tease is
to work. He treads a fine line, keeping the lover in ignorance, but giving a hint to his ideal, astute reader, whom
we, as readers, are trying to be. For Ovid, to write v. 108,
to draw flattering attention to 'your' (that is, the Reader's)
facies and *forma* is a way to *adamare* (v. 109) 'you', as
Reader. Constructing a beautiful boy in the text, giving
him *facies* and *forma* in writing, is a way of loving
him.

The same sort of backhanded compliment occurs in
v. 112, where the lover is told to add something *corporis . . .
bonis* (to 'the blessings of the body'). In the very act of
demanding an artificial addition to 'nature's own red and
white', Ovid subtly hymns his beloved's beautiful body,
just as Propertius does in his second poem, where celebration of her body is couched as vociferous objection to his
puella's use of cosmetics. With our v. 112, we might compare
particularly Propertius 1. 2. 6:

> *nec sinere in propriis membra nitere bonis.*

> and not to allow your limbs to shine in their own right [with
> their own blessings].

Continuing his flattery, Ovid compares the boy to two
epitomes of male beauty, Nireus and Hylas. A cursory
glance might dismiss these comparisons as obvious: a closer
look, however, will expose their telling incongruities
(vv. 109–10).

> *sis licet antiquo Nireus adamatus Homero*
> *Naiadumque tener crimine raptus Hylas*

> Even if you are like Nireus loved by ancient Homer
> and tender Hylas stolen by the crime of the Naiads . . .

---

[17] All of the following examples occur in erotic contexts, where the *facies*
belongs to the passive beloved. Naev. *Trag.* 3 *contempla . . . formam et faciem
uirginis*; Ov. *Am.* 1. 10. 41–2 *turpe . . . faciem lucro prostituisse suam*, 2. 8. 11
Thessalus ancillae facie Briseidos arsit; *Ars* 1. 621 *nec faciem nec te pigeat laudare
capillos*, 3. 137; *Rem.* 584; *Fast.* 4. 223 *Phryx puer in siluis, facie spectabilis, Attis |
. . . uinxit amore deam*; *Met.* 3. 474 *Narcissus ad faciem rediit male sanus eandem*.

The proverbially good-looking Nireus[18] makes at first sight a highly appropriate paradigm: but the totality of this character includes frequent overtones of effeminacy. He is more καλός ('lovely') than ἥρως ('hero'). In Homer (*Il.* 2. 672–5):

Νιρεὺς Ἀγλαΐης υἱὸς Χαροποιό τ᾽ ἄνακτος
Νιρεύς, ὃς κάλλιστος ἀνὴρ ὑπὸ Ἴλιον ἦλθε
τῶν ἄλλων Δαναῶν μετ᾽ ἀμύμονα Πηλεΐωνα.
ἀλλ᾽ ἀλαπαδνὸς ἔην, παῦρος δέ οἱ εἵπετο λαός.

Nireus, the son of Aglaia and the lord Charopus,
Nireus, who was the most beautiful of all the Danaans
who came to Troy, after the excellent son of Peleus.
But he was weak, and only a few people followed him.

Aristotle says (*Rh.* 3. 12. 4) that Homer repeats the name of Nireus to increase his reputation, although he is not mentioned again. Ovid has perhaps eroticized comments of this nature in the tradition of Homeric criticism, when he describes Nireus as loved by Homer. Indeed, there may be a joke intended in *antiquo . . . Homero* ('by ancient Homer') that not only does this example come from the oldest and therefore most authoritative source, but also that Homer was 'older than Nireus', and therefore his lover. Active homosexual lovers are of course generally older than their beloveds. The Homer–Nireus parallel suggests that the relationship between Ovid and the Reader is analogous. We are forced to remember that the young man values Ovid above his illustrious predecessor. In the opening triumph of this book (vv. 3–4)

laetus amans donat uiridi mea carmina palma
praelata Ascraeo Maeonioque seni.

The happy lover presents my songs with the green palm
(triumphal crown),
songs preferred to the Ascraean and Maeonian old men.

[18] Cf. Eur. *IA* 204–5; Diod. 5. 53; Hyg. *Fab.* 270; Hor. *Epod.* 15. 22, *Carm.* 3. 20. 15; Prop. 3. 18. 27; Ov. *Pont.* 4. 13. 6; Lucian *Tim.* 23; Apoll. *Ep.* 3. 13; Otto (1962) 243–4.

Antiquo . . . Homero in our passage must echo *Maeonio . . . seni* in the earlier line. The Homer and Hesiod are presented as rivals for the Reader's erotic favour, and, in a very real sense, the reader's, with erotic favour as a metaphor for reading.

The post-Homeric literary history of Nireus develops the hint of pederasty. Philostratus (*Epist.* 57) attempts to seduce a boy by comparing him with Nireus and Achilles. The *exempla* compliment his looks, but also suggest effeminacy, for here we may think of Achilles on Skyros as much as Achilles before the walls of Troy—although perhaps the boy is to think of the latter! As in our work, the letter has a notional addressee, who would be delighted by the comparisons, and a more sophisticated audience, who would be amused. In Philostratus, as in our work, there is a risk in making too clear a distinction between the naïve Reader and sophisticated reader. Horace uses Nireus twice. At *Epod.* 15. 22 (*formaque uincas Nirea*, 'and you may conquer Nireus in looks'), he may intend the same barbed compliment, hinting at effeminacy, to the man who has stolen his girl. Secondly, *Carm.* 3. 20. 15 unambiguously links Nireus with Ganymede, as *pueri delicati*.

> *qualis aut Nireus fuit aut aquosa*
> *raptus ab Ida.*

> such as Nireus was or the boy stolen from watery Ida.

As mentioned above, this poem describes the indifference of a liminal beloved boy to the battle raging over him between a man and a woman. Ganymede is a classic *erōmenos*; Nireus is more ambiguous, signifying the potentiality of active eros in a boy on the boundaries. A final element in the pederastic history of Nireus is a variant, non-Homeric myth, reported in *RE* 17. 708, in which Nireus was the beloved of Hercules. Despite the lack of a direct reference, Hercules clearly features in the pentameter, so there could be a covert allusion to the affair here.

After the (possibly) worryingly misfitting comparison with Nireus, the young man's potential qualms are now allayed by a straightforward heterosexual one, as he is likened to Hylas stolen by the nymphs. A promise that this great male fantasy will be fulfilled? We might paraphrase: 'if you are good looking, you will be loved by nymphs.' But

Hylas was seized by the nymphs, and he was (in some sense) the *passive* partner in that liaison. As goddesses pursuing a mortal man, the nymphs inevitably force Hylas into the position of *erōmenos*. Moreover, Hylas is *raptus* ('stolen'), as Nireus is *adamatus* ('loved'), the passive syntax reflecting their passive sexuality. Hylas was not only stolen but raped. Pichon (1902: 250) cites two examples of *rapere* meaning rape (*Her.* 15. 162, 17. 43), but says that it most commonly means 'ui abducere puellam' ('to abduct a girl by force'). To distinguish between the two is surely difficult. Amusingly, the *puer delicatus* can be 'raped' (so to speak) into playing an active sexual role. The lover's— Hylas' and our pupil's—introduction into active (heterosexual) love is seen through the image of passive (homosexual) seduction. Alerted by the significance of the passive syntax here, the reader may return to note the similar passivity in the instruction *ut ameris, amabilis esto*. We had assumed that Ovid meant 'in order that you should be loved by girls', but we now realize that he subliminally signalled 'in order that you should be loved by me'. Perhaps Hylas is not such a fitting exemplum after all. Indeed, the implication of homosexuality is still lurking in the background. Hylas' main love-affair, *tener* ('soft') and passive as he is, is with Hercules. He is *raptus* ('stolen') by the nymphs *from* Hercules. If the 'Nireus' paradigm is suspect, 'Hylas' offsets it, but even as it does, it places itself under suspicion. Each deceives with an ambiguous appearance of flattery.

Apollonius, according to Gow (1952), does not give the relationship of Hylas and Heracles an erotic side (1. 1207–72), unless we are to infer it from Heracles' distress at the loss of Hylas.[19] It is most explicit in Theocritus, however (13. 5–7):

> ἀλλὰ καὶ ᾿Αμφιτρύωνος ὁ χαλκεοκάρδιος υἱός
> . . . ἤρατο παιδός,
> τοῦ χαρίεντος ῞Υλα, τοῦ τὰν πλοκαμῖδα φορεῦντος.

But the bronze-hearted son of Amphitryon
loved the child, the lovely Hylas
of the curling locks.

---

[19] Gow (1952: 232) on Theocr. 13, condemns as a 'clumsiness' of Apollonius 'the omission of any tender relation between Heracles and Hylas to account for the former's dismay'.

It was a popular Hellenistic subject, being treated by Callimachus (fr. 596), and at length by Nicander (ap.
Ant. Lib. 26).[20] The story is again paradigmatic in Propertius 1. 20 (see Bramble 1974), which advises its addressee to
keep a guard over his beloved boy, lest he be snatched away
as Hylas was. Virgil includes the story of Hylas in the Song
of Silenus (*Ecl.* 6. 43–4):[21]

> *his adiungit, Hylan nautae quo fonte relictum*
> *clamassent, ut litus 'Hyla, Hyla' omne sonaret*

> To these he added the spring at which the sailors shouted
> for lost [left] Hylas, so that the whole shore resounded
> 'Hylas, Hylas'.

The dying echo of *-rē -re -re* which occupies the fifth foot
in our line 112 (*mirere relictum*), makes us hear a variant on
Hylā Hyla (*Ecl.* 6. 44).[22] This couplet continues the sentence
from the previous one, and acts as a covert hint at the
inappropriateness of the Hylas paradigm. The young man
is meant to identify with Hylas; but it was not *Hylas* who
was left, but Hercules. And he was doubly left, both by
Hylas and by the Argonauts. *Relictum* was, it is true, applied
to Hylas by Virgil, but the leaving of Hylas belongs primarily to his erotic relationship with Hercules. Ovid's consecutive lines ending *Hylas* and *relictum* must surely be an
echo of Silenus.

Hylas is *tener*, young and soft like the foal (v. 100), but in
contrast with the asexuality of the foal, he is also erotically
soft and tender. Sexual connotations are highlighted in the
word's appearance in love poetry. Virgil's Gallan reference
to *teneras . . . plantas* ('tender soles', *Ecl.* 10. 49) may suggest
that it was commonly used by the father of love elegy.
Catullus' description of the poet Licinius as *poeta tener* ('a
tender poet', in poem 50) gives the term programmatic
significance for love poetry, as well as itself being involved

[20] See the scholia on Ap. Rhod. 1. 1236 and Theocr. 13. 6.

[21] Although an appropriate subject for a neoteric/Roman-Callimachean poet,
by *Georg.* 3. 6 the story is paradigmatic of the well-worn themes rejected by the
poet. The tension perhaps lies in the polemic of the *Georgics* as original *didactic*
poetry.

[22] See Bömer (1969) on *Met.* 2. 97 for parallels of Silbenwiederholung, which
he says can be artistic play in high poetry, or cacophony for effect.

in the language of *pueri delicati*.[23] The word can also have overtones of effeminacy.[24] So the exemplum, and therefore also the *illustrandum*, is erotic, with a delicate hint of passivity. Hylas is stolen by the *crimen* of the nymphs. Although this word can be used in love elegy of rape,[25] the usage is uncommon. From whose point of view is it a crime? The absent Hercules? Hylas himself? We need only look back to the last couplet for another crime, the *nefas* of magic. The enchanting allurement of the nymphs is very like a spell over which Hylas has no control.

As the poet spins his seductive web more tightly, he gradually begins to show his hand to the astute reader, with a mixture of flattery and erotic threat towards the Reader (vv. 113–18).

> *forma bonum fragile est, quantumque accedit ad annos,*
> *fit minor et spatio carpitur ipsa suo.*
> *nec uiolae semper nec hiantia lilia florent,*
> *et riget amissa spina relicta rosa.*
> *et tibi iam uenient cani, formose, capilli,*
> *iam uenient rugae, quae tibi corpus arent.*

Beauty is a fragile blessing, and as much as it increases in years, it diminishes, and is plucked by its own extent.
Neither violets nor gaping lilies flower for ever, and the thorn left alone grows hard when the rose is lost.
Even to you, handsome boy, white hairs will come soon, now wrinkles will come, which will plough your body.

The threat that youth and beauty will not last for ever is an extremely common topos of *komoi* and other persuasions to love, urging the beloved to make use of the time available. The threat is especially pertinent to boys, since their passive

---

[23] Examples of the sexual connotations of *tener* abound. Cf. Catul. 17. 15 *et puella tenellulo delicatior haedo*, 61. 100–1 *(nec) a tuis teneris uolet | secubare papillis*, 69. 1–2 *quare tibi femina nulla, | Rufe, uelit tenerum supposuisse femur*; Tib. 1. 3. 63, 1. 4. 9 *o fuge te tenerae puerorum credere turbae*; Ov. *Am.* 3. 3. 25, 3. 7. 53 *a tenera quisquam sic surgit mane puella*; *CIL* 4. 1824. 3 *SI POTEST ILLA* (i.e. *Venus*) *MIHI TENERVM PERTVNDERE PECTVS*. Perhaps particularly worth quoting is Afran. *Com.* 380 *aetas et corpus tenerum . . . haec sunt uenena formosarum mulierum*. It is a standard epithet of Cupid. See e.g. Tib. 2. 6. 1; Ov. *Am.* 2. 18. 4, 3. 15. 1; *Ars* 1. 7, *Tr.* 3. 3. 73.

[24] Cf. Cic. *Pis.* 89 *cum tuis teneris saltatoribus*.

[25] Cf. Ov. *Her.* 15. 326, 19. 37–8 *per gladios alii placitas rapuere puellas, | scripta mihi caute littera crimen erit?*

erotic career has a more definitive end. It is used by Theognis, a writer who has been argued to be a model, directly or indirectly, for Ovid in eroticized didactic (1305–7).

θυμῷ γνοὺς ὅτι παιδείας πολυηράτου ἄνθος
  ὠκύτερον σταδίου, τοῦτο συνεὶς χάλασον
δεσμοῦ

Knowing in your heart that the bloom of much-loved boyhood
is swifter than a race, bring a loosening of my chain.

The following list is no more than a taste of the spread of the topos. Theocr. 29. 26, a persuasion to a boy to love, because he is not getting any younger and youth cannot be recalled; [Theocr]. 27. 8 in a persuasion to love (to a woman), τάχα γάρ σε παρέρχεται ὡς ὄναρ ἥβη ('for youth passes you swiftly like a dream'); *AP* 5. 12 (Rufinus) βαιὸς ὁ χαιρόντων ἔστιν βίος. εἶτα τὰ λοιπὰ | γῆρας κωλύσει ('The life of pleasure is short. Soon old age will prevent the rest'); 28 (idem) addressed to a boy whom the speaker refuses now that he is no longer young—the working out of the punishment-threat; *AP* 5. 79 (Plato) σκέψαι τὴν ὥρην ὡς ὀλιγοχρόνιος ('reflect how short-lived is the bloom of youth'); *AP* 12. 29 (Alcaeus) threat of loss of youth and warning that the boy will wish for the speaker when he is no longer young; *AP* 12. 32 (Thymocles) to a boy, a fulfilment; Hor. *Carm.* 1. 25 (see Nisbet and Hubbard 1970 for parallels) no more *komoi* for the aged Lydia; 4. 13. 2, fulfilment of the threat (to a woman); Tib. 1. 6. 77–84, where nemesis for the faithless beloved is to be a poor, ugly old woman scorned by young men like the one she now rejects; 1. 8. 41 (warning to a girl to treat her lover well) *heu sero reuocatur amor seroque iuuentus | cum uetus infecit cana senecta caput* ('Alas, love and youth are recalled when it is too late, when white age has infected the old head': note this also for our v. 117); Tib. 1. 9. 13 to a boy again (see Murgatroyd's note: 1980); Ov. *Am.* 1. 8. 49, spoken by the *lena* Dipsas, *labitur occulte fallitque uolatilis aetas | et celer admissis labitur annus equis* ('fleeting age slips by in stealth and thus deceives, and the swift year slips by on unchecked horses').

One Propertian example has a proverbial tone which is also present in our passage (Prop. 2. 28. 57):

nec forma aeternum aut cuiquam est fortuna perennis
No one has beauty eternally, nor perennial fortune.

The topos is a formulaic maxim in non-erotic contexts.[26] The effect is to evoke a philosophical, slightly melancholic atmosphere reminiscent, perhaps, of Horatian musing on life and death. But the proverb combines with a quasi-paradox—beauty becomes less as that which has beauty increases. What *is* the *spatium* of beauty? The age of the beautiful one? The rhetoric is specious, seeming to make more of a point than it actually does.[27] It is part of the game of the *Ars Amatoria* to play with such apparent contradictions between form (proverbial maxim) and content (paradoxical inanity—or is it?).

Reflections on the brevity of life and love are frequently formulated by the use of flower imagery. Ovid is using a conventional idea 'youth is short', expressed in conventional terms 'the bloom will fade'. What is unconventional is the use to which these challengingly obvious motifs are put—the seduction of a Reader and a reader. Flower imagery is a common metaphor, in English as well as Latin, for the bloom of youth. Instances are legion:[28] there is one particular example which illuminates our passage, be it by direct echo or a more general community of symbolism. That is [Theocritus] *Idyll* 23. 29–33, a *komos* to a boy.

καὶ τὸ ῥόδον καλόν ἐστι, καὶ ὁ χρόνος αὐτὸ μαραίνει
καὶ τὸ ἴον καλόν ἐστιν ἐν εἴαρι, καὶ ταχὺ γηρᾳ.
λευκὸν τὸ κρίνον ἐστί, μαραίνεται ἀνίκα πίπτει
. . . καὶ κάλλος καλόν ἐστι τὸ παιδικόν, ἀλλ’ ὀλίγον ζῇ.

The rose also is lovely, and time withers it;
and the violet is lovely in the spring, and quickly grows old.
the lily is white, but it withers when it falls . . .
and childish beauty is lovely, but it lives a short time.

---

[26] Cf. Theogn. 985; Sal. *Cat.* 1. 4 *nam diuitiarum et formae gloria fluxa atque fragilis est*; Sen. *Phaedr.* 773 *res est forma fugax*; Nemes. *Ecl.* 4. 24. See Nisbet and Hubbard (1978) on Hor. *Carm.* 2. 14; Otto (1962) 141.

[27] 'Actually' should perhaps be in inverted commas, as should many words.

[28] See e.g. *AP* 5. 124 (Philodemus) οὔπω σοι καλύκων γυμνὸν θέρος; 5. 118 (Marcus Argentarius), a blooming garland which will soon fade is a symbol of the beloved's youth; 12. 91 (Polystratus) λιπαρῶν ἄνθεμον ἠϊθέων (v. 4), Παφίης ἔρνος ἰοστεφάνου (v. 6); 12. 107 (anon.), Tib. 1. 8. 47 *at tibi dum primi floret tibi temporis aetas | utere*.

The three flowers mentioned by Ovid, violets, lilies, and roses, are exactly the three mentioned by the poet of *Idyll* 23. In this persuasion to a boy, the *erōmenos'* career in passive homosexuality is the referent of the flower's brief bloom, and is the basis for his seduction. Secretly, Ovid shows his hand to the artistic reader, and flatters us into placing ourselves in that position.

As 'old age' advances, the rose is replaced by prickly thorns. Rufinus (*AP* 5. 28) rejects a boy because he has reached the nemesis of haughty boys and is no longer young and beautiful. His cheeks are no longer smooth, but he is growing hair, the sign of the end for an *erōmenos*. The metaphor of the rejection is familiar, the rose and the thorns.

> ἀντὶ ῥόδου γὰρ ἐγὼ τὴν βάτον οὐ δέχομαι.

> I do not accept a thorn in place of a rose.

A rose is a beautiful boy; thorns are the hair which will come all too soon. The topos of the growth of hair (and not only on the face) commonly signals the end of amatory boyhood.[29] The same imagery informs a Horatian threat-prophecy (*Carm.* 4. 10. 3–5):

> *et, quae nunc umeris inuolitant, deciderint comae,*
> *nunc et qui color est puniceae flore prior rosae,*
> *mutatus Ligurinum in faciem uerterit hispidam*

> and the hairs which now flow around your shoulders
> will have fallen, and the colour which outshines the flower
> of a red rose
> will be changed and will have turned Ligurinus into a
> hairy face.

Our young man may not have noticed it, but he is described as a hairless boy, who is ripe for seduction.

Just as the whole passage suggests and fudges the question of who is seducing whom, so too this line can be taken simultaneously in two opposite ways. Following my argu-

---

[29] See Murgatroyd (1980) on Tib. 1. 9. 14, to which add *AP* 12. 31 (Phanias), 12. 36 (Asclepiades of Adramyttium), 12. 215 (Strato), 12. 220 (idem). Note also 12. 40. 3–4 (anon.), amongst poems about boys growing hair, γυμνὴν Ἀντιφίλου ζητῶν χάριν, ὡς ἐπ᾽ ἀκάνθαις | εὑρήσεις ῥοδέαν φυομένην κάλυκα.

ment, the bloom of the boy's youth will soon give way to prickly old age (manhood being the 'old age' of a beautiful boy), so he should submit to Ovid while he can, to benefit from his wisdom. But the wisdom he seeks is how to keep a girl, and the image works equally well actively. *Rosa* is a term of endearment,[30] and at *Peruigilium Veneris* 32 stands metaphorically for girls about to marry. If the lover does not submit to Ovid (a play is hinted at between sexual and intellectual submission), he will lose his rose and be left all alone, as was threatened in v. 111: *nec te mirere relictum.* 'Rose' can be used of the female *pudenda*, as of the boyish male.[31] These two mutually exclusive readings of the situation combine to constitute a reading of the passage in which Ovid winks at the reader while hoodwinking the Reader.

Having again allayed the Reader's potential qualms by the mention of the *rosa* (on the active reading), Ovid becomes at once more explicit in his seduction and more deceptive. He addresses the addressee as *formose* ('beautiful boy'). This is another signification of the *puer delicatus*, since *formosus* is almost a *uox propria* of beloveds. For beloved *formosi* we might compare particularly Virg. *Ecl.* 2. 1 *formosum pastor Corydon Alexin* ('the shepherd Corydon [loved] the beautiful Alexis'), 17, 45; Tib. 1. 4. 3 *quae tua formosos cepit sollertia?* ('what cleverness of yours has caught beautiful boys': addressed to the pederastic Priapus); 1. 9. 5–6 *aequum est impune licere | numina formosis laedere uestra semel* ('it is fair to allow beautiful boys to get away with taking your godheads in vain once'); Prop. 1. 20. 51–2 *his, o Galle, tuos monitus seruabis amores, | formosum Nymphis credere uisus Hylan* ('warned by these stories, Gallus, you will guard your beloved; since you have seemed to trust your beautiful Hylas to the nymphs').[32] It will be worth noting here that the word *pais* ('boy') is always applied to

---

[30] Cf. e.g. Pl. *As.* 664, *Bac.* 83, *Men.* 191.

[31] *AP* 5. 35 (Rufinus), 36 (idem), 54 (Dioscorides), 55 (idem), 81 (Dionysius the Sophist), by suggestion. It is most explicit in 62 (Rufinus), where apples and roses stand for breasts and *pudenda*.

[32] For *formosae* e.g. Tib. 1. 1. 5 *me retinent uinctum formosae uincla puellae*, 2. 3. 65; Prop. 1. 4. 7, 1. 15. 8, 2. 18. 30 *mi formosa satis, si modo saepe uenis*, 2. 34. 91.

passive homosexuals.[33] A *formosus* is a *pais/puer* is a beloved boy.

The threat is the approach of grey hair and wrinkles. Again the language is highly conventional, for grey hair as a sign of ageing is a topos of the persuasion to love.[34] Now, on the one hand, these features belong to the persuasion to a woman, not a boy, and—superficially—grey hair in this context reflects the topos of the inappropriateness of elderly love,[35] for the end comes much earlier than grey hair for a *puer delicatus*. That is all the Reader is meant to see. On the other hand, given the seductive context, the reader should note that the expression belongs much more closely to the discourse of persuasion than to the topos of elderly love. Moreover, the overt and safe allusion to hair here acts as an indicator towards the covert and subversive allusion to hair in the previous line.

In the third book of the *Ars*, there is a passage which is closely parallel with ours, and which, being more explicit in its function, can direct our reading of the *Ars* 2 passage. This passage occupies an analogous structural position to ours, coming after the programmatic reflection on art and the status of the book, and performing the same function of persuading the addressee, a girl now, to read the book and follow the instruction (*Ars* 3. 59–82):

> *uenturae memores iam nunc estote senectae,*
> *   sic nullum uobis tempus abibit iners.*   60
> *dum licet et ueros etiam nunc editis annos,*
> *   ludite: eunt anni more fluentis aquae.*
> *nec, quae praeteriit, iterum reuocabitur unda*
> *   nec, quae praeteriit, hora redire potest.*

---

[33] So Dover (1978: 86). The word is also of course used of a slave—any male who is 'not a man'.

[34] Cf. (among many) *AP* 5. 23 (Call.) ἡ πολιὴ δὲ | αὐτίκ' ἀναμνήσει ταυτά σε πάντα κόμη. For grey hair and wrinkles in the fulfilment of the threat cf. *AP* 5. 21 (Rufinus) νῦν ῥυτίδες καὶ θρὶξ πολιὴ καὶ σῶμα ῥακῶδες; for the two again in a fulfilment Hor. *Carm.* 4. 13. 11–12 *quia rugae | turpant et capitis niues*; for the hair alone in a threat Prop. 3. 25. 13 *uellere tum cupias albos a stirpe capillos.* For wrinkles in amatory contexts see Hor. *Carm.* 4. 13. 1; Tib. 2. 2. 20; Prop. 2. 18. 6, 3. 25. 12, 4. 5. 59–60; Ov. *Med.* 46, *Ars* 3. 73.

[35] For which see e.g. Pl. *Mer.* 305 (it is very common in comedy); Hor. *Carm.* 3. 14. 25; Tib. 1. 1. 71–2 *iam subrepet iners aetas, nec amare decebit, | dicere nec cano blanditias capite* (with Murgatroyd 1980), 1. 2. 92 as punishment for a scoffer.

utendum est aetate: cito pede labitur aetas 65
    nec bona tam sequitur quam bona prima fuit.
hos ego, qui canent, frutices uiolaria uidi;
    hac mihi de spina grata corona data est.
tempus erit, quo tu, quae nunc excludis amantes
    frigida deserta nocte iacebis anus, 70
nec tua frangetur nocturna ianua rixa,
    sparsa nec inuenies limina mane rosa.
quam cito, me miserum, laxantur corpora rugis
    et perit, in nitido qui fuit ore, color,
quasque fuisse tibi canas a uirgine iures 75
    sparguntur subito per caput omne comae!
anguibus exuitur tenui cum pelle uetustas,
    nec faciunt ceruos cornua iacta senes;
nostra sine auxilio fugiunt bona: carpite florem,
    qui, nisi carptus erit, turpiter ipse cadet. 80
adde quod et partus faciunt breuiora iuuentae
    tempora: continua messe senescit ager.

Be ye mindful now of fast-approaching eld,
and thus no time will desert ye, inactive.
While it is allowed and you still give your true age, play:
the years pass like flowing water.
The wave which once has passed will never be recalled again,
nor can the hour return which once has passed.
Youth is to be used: age slips on swift foot, and the age which
    follows
is not so good as the first.
I saw those shoots, which now are white, when they were violets;
from this thorn a welcome garland was given to me.
The time will come when you, who now lock out your lovers,
will lie, a chill old woman, through the lonely night,
nor will your door be broken by night-time brawls, nor will you
    find
your threshold scattered with roses in the morning.
Alas, how swiftly bodies are undone by wrinkles
and the complexion which once had been in the shining face
    perishes.
And the hairs which you swear have been white since you were a
    little girl
are suddenly scattered all over your head.
Old age is shrugged off by snakes along with a thin skin,
and the loss of horns does not make stags old;
our blessings flee without replacement: pluck the flower, which
unless it be plucked, will fall foully of its own accord.

Add also that childbirth shortens the days of youth:
the field grows old with continual harvesting.

He goes on to prove that women have nothing to lose—or
at least to pretend to prove this. This is a fairly straightforward persuasion to love, concerned mostly with the topos
that 'time for love is short', a threat which by its extreme
conventionality might perhaps be described as a programmatic signifier for literary seduction. The language of seduction is more overt, since what the poet *says* bears a closer
and easier relationship to what he *does* than in our passage.
Both are invitations to love, that to the girl overtly a
seduction, that to the boy covertly using the terminology of
seduction to *persuade* him to love. The major difference in
content between the two versions seems to be that the boy
is promised advancement in wisdom through his submission, while the girl is only promised that she has nothing to
lose.

Particularly close parallels occur in the use of flower
imagery. At a number of points, the passage from Book 3
exposes the workings of the earlier seduction. Addressing
the boy-Reader, Ovid threatens that his *forma* will be
plucked (*carpitur*). That there is a hint at a flower–sexual
metaphor here is, I think, fortified by the more explicit
association of flowers, age, the transience of erotic beauty,
and '*carpe diem*' ('pluck the day') in the later passage (3. 79–
80):

> *nostra sine auxilio fugiunt bona: carpite florem,*
> *qui nisi carptus erit, turpiter ipse cadet.*

Our blessings flee without replacement: pluck the flower, which
unless it be plucked, will fall foully of its own accord.

Likewise, the comment in *Ars* 2 about flowers, which, I
suggested, involves an oblique reference to hair, has a
parallel in Book 3 with a more explicit connection with hair
and a more explicit sexual hint.

> *hos ego, qui canent, frutices uiolaria uidi;*
> *hac mihi de spina grata corona data est.*   (3. 67–8)

I saw those shoots, which now are white, when they were violets;
from this thorn a welcome garland was given to me.

quasque fuisse tibi canas a uirgine iures
    sparguntur subito per caput omne comae! (3. 75–6)

And the hairs which you swear have been white since you
    were a little girl
are suddenly scattered all over your head.

The parallel imagery helps to tie the passages. The later
passage's clearest threat of grey hair quite closely echoes
the earlier. The two passages are tied not only by subject
but also by verbal echoes: *uiolae/uiolaria, cani ... capilli/
canas ... comae.*

Once the beloved Reader is well and truly caught, he is
encouraged to build up his mind and take advantage of the
wisdom Ovid can supply (vv. 119–22):

iam molire animum, qui duret, et adstrue formae:
    solus ad extremos permanet ille rogos.
nec leuis ingenuas pectus coluisse per artes
    cura sit et linguas edidicisse duas.

Now build up your mind, which will endure, and build
    on your beauty/form.
Mind alone remains to the final pyre.
Let it be no light concern to cultivate your spirit
    through the freeborn arts and to learn the two languages.

Pedagogy again is foregrounded, as the instruction is given
in the language of athletic training. The words *molire ...
duret ... adstrue* all convey notions of building up, strength-
ening, making firm, amusingly applying *material* terms to
the mind, when it is contrasted with the physical, material
body. If we are thinking about Greek pedagogy, then the
association of pederasty and the gymnasium is hard to
resist. The pupil is to perform mental gymnastics under the
pederastic pedagogue's tuition.[36]

Beauty may be transient, but a beautiful mind lasts a
lifetime.[37] The rhetoric is highly conventional, and deliberately overdone, for the mind is not strictly the only thing to

---

[36] Cf. e.g. *AP* 12. 34 (Automedon), 206 (Strato), 222 (Strato). The gymnasium
is the goal of the beloved boy in Hor. *Carm.* 3. 20. *AP* 12. 219 (Strato) depicts
schoolmasters as pederasts.

[37] An allusion, perhaps, to Lucr. 3. 338 *neque post mortem durare uidetur
[corpus]*, or at least designed to create a generally philosophical atmosphere.

remain till the end of life. The prefix *per*(*manet*) is emphatic, while to use the two words *extremos . . . rogos* ('last pyres') is almost redundant to the simple sense.[38] Such romantic rhetoric is common in elegy. Compare for example Prop. 1. 19. 2 *nec moror extremo debita fata rogo* ('nor do I care about the fates owed to the final pyre'), 2. 11. 4 *auferet extremi funeris atra dies* ('the black day of the final funeral will take away'), 2. 20. 17 *me tibi ad extremas mansurum, uita, tenebras* ('that I will stay with you, my darling, until the final shadows').

It is his mind or character that the would-be lover is to cultivate: art adds to nature a supplement to physical attractions.[39] The mind–body opposition reflects the two books of the *Ars*, as the Reader knows it. The first was about catching a girl (body); the second about keeping her, and the way to keep her is to captivate her (mind). In this way he will keep her to the end of his life, the romantic wish of elegy espoused by Tibullus and Propertius.[40] The wish is unrealizable, for the elegiac mistress is *leuis*, flighty, fickle—and love elegy is poetry of longing, for which a happy and uneventful relationship would spell disaster. Ovid's trainee, on the other hand, will have such a character that he will keep *girls* to the end of his life. Ovid never says anything about *one* girl, except specifically to allow for diversity.[41] Attempts have been made to make Ovid more morally and emotionally acceptable by claiming that he was imagining long relationships,[42] but the concept of temporal normality is problematized in a poem where the absence of Ulysses from Penelope was an artistic *mora . . . breuis* ('short

---

[38] *Rogus* is synonymous with death (e.g. Prop. 3. 5. 46 *timor haud ultra quam rogus esse potest*) but with all the pathos of funerals, while *extremus* also can mean something pertaining to death; see *TLL* 5. 2. 2002. 65, and e.g. Manil. 5. 623 *patres cupiant extrema suorum oscula.*

[39] Cf. *AP* 5. 67 (Capito), beauty without charm is a bait without a hook; Ov. *Med.* 45–50 *certus amor morum est; formam populabitur aetas* | *. . . sufficit et longam probitas perdurat in aeuum,* | *perque suos annos hinc bene pendet amor.*

[40] Cf. e.g. Prop. 2. 6. 42 *semper amica mihi, semper et uxor eris*; Tib. 1. 6. 85–6 *nos, Delia, amoris* | *exemplum cana simus uterque coma,* 2. 2. 19–20 (for Cornutus).

[41] *Ars* 2. 387–8 *nec mea uos uni donat censura puellae;* | *di melius! uix hoc nupta tenere potest* ('my judgement does not hand you over to one girl only; good heavens! a bride can hardly manage that').

[42] Wilkinson (1955: 122) claims that Ovid envisages 'fairly permanent liaisons'. See also Fränkel (1945: 55, 59).

delay', 2. 357), but that of Menelaus from Helen was dangerously long (2. 359–72). How long does a relationship have to
be to rate as 'long'? You can only judge the answer by Art.

In order to improve his mind, the lover must take care to
cultivate the *ingenuae artes* ('freeborn arts'), the arts suitable
for a young man of good family.[43] The freeborn arts that
the disciple learns in order to make himself lovable are his
reward for submitting to the pedagogue. In this case, the
primary *ingenua ars* to be cultivated is the *Ars Amatoria*. If
we had not already guessed that *artes* refers to *Artes Amatoriae*, Ovid assists our interpretation at *Pont.* 2. 7. 47–8:

> *artibus ingenuis quaesita est gloria multis:*
> *infelix perii dotibus ipse meis.*

Glory has been achieved by many through their freeborn arts:
I—wretched—have perished by my own resources.

The *dotes* (dowry, gifts, resources) which destroyed him, as
he repeatedly tells us, were the poetic ability to write the
Ars. Artes ingenuae are, for Ovid, the *Ars.* The *ingenuae
artes* at this point link the exilic line with the programme of
our v. 17, where the poet promised to teach *quas . . . per
artes* ('through which arts') love can be kept, and its first
attempt at an answer in v. 99—not Haemonian (that is,
magical). It is through these *ingenuae artes*—the *Ars Amatoria* itself—that love can be kept. They are not of course
really ingenuae. The joke of transplanting *paiderastia* to
Rome and to a purely erotic (and heterosexual) context is
that this is precisely the sort of promise made in Socratic
discussions of homosexual love.

It is through reading the *Ars Amatoria*, it is claimed, that
the lover will learn knowledge and wisdom. Again the
erotic and poetic responses to the poem are intertwined, for
just as the lover cultivates his mind on noble arts, so the
poet or reader cultivates poetry.[44] To help him (us) in his
amatory exploits, a lover must appear bilingually learned to
impress the *docta puella* ('learned girl'); to read the poem

---

[43] Cf. Cic. *de Orat.* 1. 73 *omnibus ingenuis artibus instructus.*

[44] Cf. Tib. 2. 4. 15 *ite procul, Musae, si non prodestis amanti:* | *non ego uos, ut
sint bella canenda, colo*; Prop. 2. 26. 26 *carmina tam sancte nulla puella colit*, 3. 5.
19 *me iuuat in prima coluisse Helicona iuuenta.*

we (he) must pick up the allusions to Greek poetry which show us not only the seduction of this passage, but also that of the next. Not only must the Reader read the poem to get at the information, but also the reader must have a working knowledge of Latin and Greek to follow the subliminal twists through which the poem leads us.[45] Moreover, in the section vv. 99–122, Ovid's 'two languages' have been a straightforward one and a subliminal, seductive one; in the next passage (the tale of Ulysses and Calypso), they are not only the Greek and Latin versions of the story, but also the two opposing seductions (of Ulysses by Calypso and Calypso by Ulysses), and the two purposes of the paradigm, which are an example of the amatory effectiveness of eloquence for the Reader, and a joke about seduction for the reader. Finally, the *duae linguae* ('two tongues') are a covert signifier of the seductive deception of this passage and poem, for 'double-tongued' can, in Latin as in English, mean 'deceitful', as is shown by Virg. *Aen.* 1. 661 *Tyriosque bilinguis* ('and the double-tongued (= deceitful) Tyrians').

2e Doctor Love

The contagiousness of deceit, its pharmacological duplicity, is an essential part of the ancient understanding of poetry, and is recognized by Walsh (1984) as its basic property. For the remainder of this chapter, I shall be concerned with the magical associations of erotic and poetic seduction, in order to elucidate the complex of seductions of Reader and reader which is under discussion.

The *Ars Amatoria* is concerned with its own seductive power; and the two ideas, seduction and poetry, are explored through the ambivalent language of magic (vv. 99–108).

> *fallitur, Haemonias si quis decurrit ad artes*
> *datque quod a teneri fronte reuellit equi.*
> *non facient, ut uiuat amor, Medeides herbae*
> *mixtaque cum magicis nenia Marsa sonis:*
> *Phasias Aesoniden, Circe tenuisset Ulixem,*
> *si modo seruari carmine possit amor.*

[45] For 'two languages' meaning Latin and Greek see *TLL* 7. 1451. 51.

nec data profuerint pallentia philtra puellis;
philtra nocent animis uimque furoris habent.
sit procul omne nefas! ut ameris, amabilis esto;
quod tibi non facies solaue forma dabit.

Anyone who has recourse to Haemonian arts, and gives
that which is torn from the brow of a young horse
is deceived. The grasses of Medea will not make
love live, nor the Marsian chant mixed with magic noises.
The Phasian [Medea] would have held the son of Aeson,
and Circe Ulysses, if love could really be kept by a song-spell.
Nor do pallid potions applied to girls bring profit; potions
are harmful to minds and contain the violence of madness.
Begone, all evil! In order to be loved, be lovable—
something which beauty will not give you, nor form alone.

The ostensible didactic point of this passage is the injunction against the use of magic or drugs. Fränkel (1945: 62)
gets mileage from this passage for his attempt to make an
honest man of Ovid, when he says that it reflects a genuine
dislike for magic and drugs on the poet's part. Perhaps, but
we cannot know. Apart from the fact that a poem (still less
a passage) is a dangerous hunting-ground for the real
author's genuine likes and dislikes, this contention fails to
recognize the didactic function of the disclaimer, and the
complexities of magic as reality and as symbol.[46] At one
level of reading, this is a straightforward claim for didactic
authority. The teacher's condemnation of mere conjurers
stands in direct opposition to the elegiac norm, which
generally purports to respect the illusion of magic.[47] Elegiac
romantic self-deception resorts to magic, even perhaps in
knowledge of its uselessness. Ovid, by contrast, stands as
the voice of true reason. Emulating Lucretius in his tirade
against *religio* (1. 62–79), he poses as the sophisticated scientist of the art of love enlightening the ignorance of the

---

[46] Luck's comments (1985) 3–53 about ancient attitudes to magic are helpful
here. See also Tupet (1976: 379, 384).

[47] See Tib. 1. 2. 41–56. Murgatroyd (1980) is convinced that Tibullus had no
doubts about the efficacy of magic; see particularly the note on 59–60, that the
suggestion that Tibullus has any doubts 'ruins the whole point of the section on
magic'. See also Tib. 1. 5. 11–16, 41, 49–58, 1. 8. 17–22; Prop. 1. 1. 19, 2. 1. 51–2,
4. 5 *passim*; Ov. *Am.* 1. 8 *passim*, 2. 1. 23–8, 3. 7. 31–6, all of which use the
terminology of magic positively.

superstitious. The opening claim for ignorance on the part
of the opposition is Lucretian.[48] Just as anyone who does
not follow Lucretian Epicureanism is going to fail, con-
fronted by reason, so anyone who tries magic to keep a girl
is going about it in the wrong way.

The terms of the claim that only erotic and not magical
means of keeping a girl are effective are, however, deeply
problematical. The essence of the problem lies in the ambiguity of the *pharmakon*. I base the following discussion
around the word *pharmakon* and its relatives, because the
term has become a motif in the discourse on magic and its
relations. I should here contextualize my reading of magic
in the *Ars Amatoria* by ackowledging a debt to Derrida's
(1981) essay, 'Plato's Pharmacy'. In that work, Derrida is
concerned with the relationship between present speech
and (so to speak) absent writing in Platonic and Western
metaphysical thought. Writing is a *pharmakon* for memory:
a cure, but also a poison. What is particularly useful to me
is his exposure of the manifold ambiguities of the *pharmakon*
and its relatives, which act as a leitmotif throughout his
essay.[49] 'This *pharmakon*, this "medicine", this philter,
which acts as both remedy and poison . . . This charm, this
spellbinding virtue, this power of fascination, can be—alternately or simultaneously—beneficent or maleficent . . . Oper-
ating through seduction, the *pharmakon* makes one stray
from one's general, natural, habitual paths and laws' (Derrida 1981: 70). This was an ambiguity already discussed in
antiquity, for example by Aulus Gellius (12. 9). The *pharmakon* is notoriously drug, cure, poison, and spell. It can even
be used of paints, artificial colours which deceptively produce *simulacra* ('images'). It is more than usually difficult
to find the nearest Latin equivalent to *pharmakon*, but the
hippomanes and the *herbae* ('grasses') of vv. 100–1 are descriptions of *pharmaka*, while *philtra* (vv. 105–6) cover a
similar although not identical semantic range. Could *philtra*

---

[48] Cf. e.g. 1. 377 *scilicet id falsa totum ratione receptumst*, 3. 523, 540, 754 *illud
enim falsa fertur ratione, quod aiunt*, 4. 481–5, 764.

[49] It is a feature of Derridean style to centre a discussion around one signifier
which is invested with programmatic significance.

nocent ('drugs do harm') be a variation on the Homeric phrase, κακὰ φάρμακα ('harmful drugs', *Od.* 10. 213 etc.)?

κακὰ φάρμακα: *Love, Poetry, and Magic*

Under the sign of the *pharmakon*, the discourses of love, poetry, and magic blend into one. The metaphorical connection between love and magic, and actual pharmacological practice in erotic matters, constitute a well-developed, though elusive, tradition in literature when they are appropriated by Roman elegy. A full treatment of *medicina amoris*, the range of metaphor and practice associated with magic and medicine in erotic discourse, would be an enormous task and is beyond the scope of the present work.[50] My intention here is simply to discuss a few key passages in the history of erotic magic (and medicine), particularly those Ovidian or programmatically elegiac passages which may be aids to the interpretation of our poem.

First, however, we must note one more strand in our conceptual nexus: medicine. Love the *pharmakon* is both cure and disease. A magic spell, a medicinal remedy, a harmful poison. It is important to remember that the language of love is deeply involved with that of medicine, a subject more closely related to magic in ancient thought than is easily recognized. (See Luck 1985: 3–17.) Strict demarcation between science and magic is often sought by

---

[50] See Tupet (1976). Fauth (1980) discusses the connection in Augustan poetry between the disease of love (caused by Eros) and the use of magic rites and remedies: his article is appropriately entitled '*Venena Amoris*'. *Venenum* and *Venus* are etymologically connected through *ueneror*. *OLD ueneror* suggests an original meaning of *uenus* as 'propitiatory magic', whence Venus. Tibullus may hint at the connection: *quidquid habet Circe, quidquid Medea ueneni* | . . . | *et quod, ubi indomitis gregibus Venus adflat amores,* | *hippomanes cupidae stillat ab inguine equae,* | *si modo me placido uideat Nemesis mea uultu,* | *mille alias herbas misceat illa, bibam* (2. 4. 55–60). Concentrating firstly on Dido, Fauth explains the physical and mental symptoms of her passion in terms of disease, and points out that while Virgil uses Apollonius' Medea as a model for Dido, he exploits the pharmacological connection by having Dido turn to magic only *after* she has begun to suffer from the disease of love (see esp. 265). The connection between erotic enchantment and medicinal magical practice in Tibullus (esp. 1. 2) is also treated in detail (Fauth, 271). See also Ross (1975: 66–8, 91), Gow (1952) on Theocr. *Id.* 2, Nisbet and Hubbard (1970) on Hor. *Carm.* 1. 27. 21, Murgatroyd (1980) on Tib. 1. 2. 59, Dodds (1951: 194–5), for binding spells including those for use in love, also Luck (1985). On love as magic see Segal (1989), esp. pp. 10–12, and Winkler (1990) esp. his ch. on erotic magical spells, pp. 71–98.

modern society: witness the comment by the *OCD* on Nicander. 'We find in his poems absurd errors due to popular superstition alongside exact descriptions of plants and medicinal prescriptions so detailed and precise that the remedy could be made up today.' The essential connection between magic and medicine in ancient thought can be seen most simply by a glance at the several thousand recipes for drugs and remedies given by Pliny in his *Natural History* (Books 20–32), which include some concocted by *magi*. The boundaries between what we would call scientific, folk, and magical drugs are so nebulous as to be almost indistinguishable, particularly from the viewpoint of our culture, which tries to make rigorous distinctions in these fields. (See Luck 1985: 38–9, Lloyd 1979 and 1983: esp. 201–17.) Where, for example, do aphrodisiacs like those mentioned by Ovid (*Ars* 2. 415–24) fit as between medicine and magic? Answer: they are *pharmaka*.

Among the earliest of well-developed literary examples of the tradition of erotic magic is Sophocles' *Trachiniae*. The *pharmakon* around which the action is centred, although it is hidden away in the secret recesses of the house for most of the play, is steeped in ambivalence from its beginning. It is formed, the reader will remember, from the blood (or occasionally the semen) of the Centaur, Nessus (an ambiguous 'man'), drawn by Hercules in anger at Nessus' attempt to rape Deianeira, and is mingled with the poison of the monstrous Hydra. Already the fusion of eros and violence constitutes its substance. The Centaur deceptively gives it to Deianeira as a supposed cure for Heracles' potential infidelity. Years later, it is administered to the hero by his wife, both innocently and deceptively. At once a poison and a cure, it works by burning Heracles up. (Love notoriously burns.) As a near-equivalent of *pharmakon*, Ovid uses the term *philtron*. This word for a love-potion is rare in Latin, particularly in poetry and before Ovid.[51] Hyginus uses the word (*Fab.* 34) precisely for the poison given to Deianeira by Nessus as a love-potion, which she then innocently uses on Hercules. This itself directly or indirectly refers back to Sophocles (*Trach.* 584, with which compare 1142):

[51] It occurs at Laevius *poet.* 27. 1, and after Ovid at Juv. 6. 611 *hic Thessala uendit philtra, quibus ualeat mentem uexare mariti.*

φίλτροις δ' ἐάν πως τήνδ' ὑπερβαλώμεθα
τὴν παῖδα καὶ θέλκτροισι τοῖς ἐφ' Ἡρακλεῖ

But if somehow with potions I might conquer
that girl and with spells upon Heracles . . .

Love, magic, and medicine form a conceptual triangle
which is given one of its clearest representations by Plato.
Aristophanes in *Symp.* 189d describes Love as man's ἰατρὸς
τούτων, ὧν ἰαθέντων μεγίστη εὐδαιμονία ἂν τῷ ἀνθρωπείῳ
γένει εἴη ('doctor of these things, through the healing of
which the greatest happiness would come to the human
race'). A few paragraphs earlier, Eryximachus the physician
describes bodily health in terms of the principles of love at
work in the body (186). In this case, love is nothing less
than the ordering force of the universe, akin to the power
which the *pharmakeus* (very roughly, 'magic-worker') controls. In *Ars* 2, the medicinal aspects of the *pharmakon*
surface again at the end of the first half of the book,
vv. 319–36: what to do when your mistress is ill. A golden
opportunity is presented for the lover to display his devotion. He is to weep (as long as the mistress sees it), and to
be indefatigable in his attentions (*Ars* 2. 327–30):

> multa uoue, sed cuncta palam, quotiensque libebit,
> quae referas illi, somnia laeta uide.
> et ueniat quae lustret anus lectumque locumque,
> praeferat et tremula sulphur et oua manu.

Make lots of vows, but all openly, and as often as you like
see auspicious dreams which you can relate to her.
And have an old woman come to purify the bed and the room,
and let her bring sulphur and eggs with trembling hand.

The false divination again stands on a nebulous boundary
between science and magic, as does the witch-like doctor
(with whom compare Tib. 1. 5. 11–12). The *pharmaka* she
applies are treated ironically. For the lover (after v. 99) they
are, of course, hollow; but for the mistress they remain
gratae uestigia curae ('evidence of welcome concern', v. 331).
Finally, in v. 335, the lover is advised to avoid giving *amari
pocula suci* ('cups of bitter juice'), since this remedial *pharmakon* would be poison to his design, the mistress's favour.
That sort of drug the rival—who does not have the advan-

tage of Ovidian control of the erotic *pharmakon*—should apply.

The magical medicine of love is most overtly highlighted in Ovidian poetry with the *Remedia Amoris*, both generally and, in vv. 249–90, specifically. Again Ovid claims that no cure is to be found for love through magic, only through *Remedia* = cure = *pharmakon* (= magic = love). The rejection is problematized by the essential connection between magic and medicine, the drug which could be a spell or a cure. The unhappy lover will be saved by *sacro carmine* ('sacred song(-spell)', v. 252), not by *infami carmine* ('nefarious spell(-song)', v. 254). The two are only as different as the two sides of the pharmacological coin—the beneficent poison. The same canonical exempla are used: Medea and Circe. This time the Circe example is extended, making a second Calypso of the original first detainer. Where does her magic end and her non-magical fascination begin? She is said to have tried all sorts of magic, and to have attempted *detinuisse* (v. 272) Ulysses *his . . . uerbis* ('to have held back Ulysses with these words', v. 271). Is her beguiling speech a spell or not? But at v. 287 she *adsuetas . . . decurrit ad artes* ('rushed to her accustomed arts'): the *ars* of words having failed she tries the *ars* of spells. They are not so very different.

Love elegy constantly poses as trying to create an opposition between magic and love (and between magic and poetry, on which see below), an opposition which is always already collapsed into an identification. Indeed, one might say that the point of the pseudo-opposition is to construct the identification, and the lover's (any lover's) weakness in the face of that identification. 'It's not magic, it's love' is another way of saying 'love is magic, and I am under its spell'. This pharmacological cure, which is also the disease, reflects that ambiguity of love of which its bitter-sweetness is a telling cliché.[52] The metaphor of the harbour is a simpler manifestation of the paradox. The harbour can be ambiguously either a stable relationship or contentment out of love—and it is not easy to tell which. The *pharmakon* is both the cure and the poison. Love itself is both symptom

---

[52] See Carson (1986) for a sensitive discussion of 'sweet-bitterness' in ancient erotic discourse.

and cure. Derrida, examining the 'painful pleasure' of the *pharmakon*, describes it as like relieving an itch by rubbing (Derrida 1981: 99). For the lover, consummation is the cure of his passion (suffering), but, like the supposedly curative drugs of Plato's *Timaeus* (22b) (Derrida 1981: 100), it serves only to aggravate the disease. Since the *Ars Amatoria* is written in counterpoint to the traditions of elegy, it will be useful to look briefly at some key passages of elegiac erotic magic.

The deceptive *pharmakon*, unstable in signification, desirable in its instability, stands at the founding moment of the Propertian corpus—and therefore, for us, of elegy as we know it (Prop. 1. 1. 1–2):

> *Cynthia prima suis miserum me cepit ocellis*
> *contactum nullis ante cupidinibus.*

> Cynthia was the first to capture with her eyes my unhappy self,
> infected previously by no desires.

Cynthia cast a binding spell on the poet with her eyes, those notoriously magic features, when previously he had been free from this contagion (vv. 2, 26), which now turns him mad (vv. 7, 26).[53] Slipping easily between magic and medicine, the poet constructs his love as a spell of which Cynthia is both essence and agent. Then suddenly (v. 19), he poses as attempting—rather weakly—to create an opposition between the magical female world of love, spells, and witches (Prop. 1. 1. 19–24):

> *at uos, deductae quibus est fallacia lunae*
> *et labor in magicis sacra piare focis,*
> *en agendum dominae mentem conuertite nostrae*
> *et facite illa meo palleat ore magis!*
> *tunc ego crediderim uobis et sidera et amnis*
> *posse Cytaeines ducere carminibus.*

> But you, who own the deceit of the moon drawn down,
> and whose task is to perform rites in magic hearths,
> come now, convert the mind of my mistress,
> and make her more pale than my own face.
> Then I will believe that you are able to draw
> the stars and rivers with your Colchian spells.

---

[53] See Tupet (1976), esp. pp. 333–5, for madness as an effect of magic.

and on the other hand the male world of friendship, rationality, and scientific medicine (Prop. 1. 1. 25–8):

> *et uos, qui sero lapsum reuocatis, amici,*
> *quaerite non sani pectoris auxilia.*
> *fortiter et ferrum saeuos patiemur et ignis,*
> *sit modo libertas quae uelit ira loqui.*

> And you, my friends, who [too] late recall the fallen,
> seek aid for an unhealthy heart.
> Bravely I will suffer both iron and savage fires,
> if only I may have the freedom to speak what anger
> wishes.

Both sides of the opposition are doomed, however, as the erotic pallor requested for Cynthia is reflected in the lover's own face,[54] and the curative operations which he claims to be willing to undergo in order to escape his love merge into the servile punishments which are so common a signifier of erotic pain and which are alluded to in the Milanion exemplum which forms the central panel of poem 1. 1. Love, the poem proclaims, is magic and pain, but a pain and a spell which, in the end, the lover does not want to avoid. The exhortation *hoc . . . uitate malum* ('avoid this evil', v. 35) is not so much an expression of the lover's altruistic concern that others should not suffer as he does, but a warning to keep off the poet's territory—his persona as lover.

In the opening poem of Propertius' second book, magic is again programmatic. In order to construct his generic persona in erotic elegy, Propertius, as is well known, opposes epic to Callimacheanism, and political encomium to elegy and the life of love. In opposition to the political discourse of 'dying for the fatherland', Propertius proclaims the value of erotic 'death'. Undying devotion is signified by a proclaimed willingness to swallow poison, as long as the lover's funeral procession can start at the beloved's house (Prop. 2. 1. 51–6):

> *seu mihi sunt tangenda nouercae pocula Phaedrae,*
> *pocula priuigno non nocitura suo,*

---

[54] The couplet will be discussed further below.

seu mihi Circaeo pereundum est gramine, siue
  Colchis Iolciacis urat aena focis,
una meos quoniam praedata est femina sensus,
  ex hac ducentur funera nostra domo.

Whether I must touch the cups of stepmother Phaedra,
cups which were not to harm her stepson,
or whether I must perish by the grass of Circe, or
whether the Colchian [Medea] boils pots [for me] on
  Thessalian hearths,
since one woman has preyed on my senses,
my funeral procession will be led forth from that house.

The supposed opposition between the drugs of witches and
the love of Propertius collapses into an identification. It is
precisely these *pocula*, the *pharmaka* of love, which cause
and constitute the lover's erotic 'death', and the subtext is
exposed by the *excursus* which describes them: these
pocula ('cups') were not to *nocere* ('harm') the object of
Phaedra's erotic-magical attentions, Hippolytus.[55] In that
they, directly or indirectly, caused his death but did not
make him fall in love (cause erotic death), they did and they
did not harm him—in all the senses of 'harm'. They are
love-spells.

Mirroring the first poem structurally, poem 2. 1 now slips
into the discourse of medicine, proclaiming love as a disease,
but a unique one (Prop. 2. 1. 57–8):

omnis humanos sanat medicina dolores:
  solus amor morbi non amat artificem.

Medicine heals every human pain:
only Love does not love a curer [art-worker] of its disease.

Various mythological heroes have been cured, by a mixture
of homoeopathic medicine and magic, but not love. Love,
claims the lover, does not love an *artifex* of its *morbum*. The
cure for love is sex (like the homoeopathic cures of the
heroes), but homoeopathy for sex (more sex) creates more
desire (more sex, more of the disease). As soon as the
pharmakon-cure is applied, the other side to its ambivalence
sets in immediately and the *pharmakon* becomes the

---

[55] The erotico-magical connotations of *nocere* will be discussed below. A
similar exposure of erotic *pharmaka* occurs at Tib. 2. 4. 59.

disease—desire.[56] A *pharmakon* brought Propertius' love
on: a *pharmakon* is sought to assuage it, but if anyone were
able to take away this complex of desire and failed homoeopathy, he would be intervening in the natural order—giving
fruit to Tantalus (vv. 65–70). Destroying the schema of
tantalization would destroy the fabric of the erotic world.
The receding fruit, the constantly outpouring water, the
forever regrowing liver: these are the symbols of desire. To
assuage them would be the end of eros. Only by 'dying' can
you (a lover) live the life of love; only by forever seeking
the cure-spell can you do what you really want to do—
experience the disease-spell.

Posturing innocent credulity, Tibullus exposes himself to
the deceit of the *pharmakon*. He has a magic potion, he
claims, which will blind Delia's husband to her relationship
with the poet (1. 2. 41–58), even if he catches them in bed. It
was provided for him by a witch, who even performed
magic rites to rid him of his love, only he sabotaged them
by praying instead for mutual love. On whom are these
pharmaka working? Whom in this poem does love really
make blind? Similarly in 1. 5 Tibullus has trustingly sought
the aid of a witch, who is also a witch-doctor, to cure the
sick Delia in the hopes of putting her in his debt. When
describing his impotence with other women, the poet attempts to set up an opposition between magic, which might
so naturally have this effect, and the charms of his mistress,
which he claims as the true source of his impotence.[57] But
of course these charms are magic also, and are even supplied
with a witch to perform the magic: not, of course, the
beloved herself, but a vicarious witch, a *lena* ('procuress'),
onto whom the lover's sexual fears and hatred can be
displaced (1. 5. 47–58).

Both cause and cure, the erotic *pharmakon* is deceptive,
ambivalent, and unavoidable in the discourse of elegy.
Sophisticated poetry treats love, and poetry, as magic, and
works because it sees how what might be called primitive
superstition is a metaphorical reflection or expression of a

[56] A verbal echo between Prop. 2. 1. 57 and 1. 2. 8 underlines the ambiguous
beneficence of the *pharmakon*. 2. 1. 57 *solus amor morbi non amat artificem*: 1. 2. 8
nudus Amor formae non amat artificem.

[57] A similarity in the treatment of Marathus' love will be discussed below.

psychological reality. (See Fauth 1980: 274.) The charm to make someone fall in love is probably as old as human society, and it is only a small step to seeing Love itself as the spell which does the damage; and only another from there to seeing love as a disease whose poison is a cure and whose cure is poison.[58]

Enchantment, Eros, and Elegy

The seductive, magical power of *poetry* is a theme as old as Homer, and perhaps finds its epitome in the myth of Orpheus.[59] Witches *lunam deducunt* ('draw down the moon'), poets *carmen deducunt* ('draw out a song'), and Orpheus *solebat | cantando rigidas deducere montibus ornos* ('used by singing to draw down hard ash-trees from the mountains', Virg. *Ecl.* 6. 70–1). As early as Homer, the *pharmakon* of poetry manifests itself in the effect on audiences of the tales of Demodocus, for example, and of Odysseus himself. Likewise, the magic of the Sirens' singing is seductive, dragging the listener away from his right mind towards abandonment and enthralment.[60] The pharmaceutical effect of words is realized in the *Odyssey* by the real *pharmakon* which Helen uses to spice her words.[61]

Love is magic, poetry is magic, charming, drawing, enchanting, enticing, fascinating, poisoning, and curing. It is the case of magical poetry connected with magical love that concerns me here. Perhaps the *locus classicus* for the associa-

---

[58] See Luck (1985: 92 and 96) for texts of love charms, which are remarkably violent in expression. See also Winkler (1990), esp. p. 81. In Plutarch's *coniugalia praecepta*, an accusation of the use of drugs in erotic matters is overturned with the statement that the accused 'has drugs in herself' (*Mor.* 141b–c). See also Lucian *D. Meretr.* 8.

[59] See Warden (1982: 8 and 45) on Orpheus; Segal (1989: 1–35, 'The Magic of Orpheus'); Dodds (1951: 140), and Luck (1985: 11–12), who are concerned with the place of poetry in the sociology of magic; Walsh (1984), who traces the theme of poetic enchantment from Homer to Euripides. See also Nisbet and Hubbard (1970) on Horace *Carm.* 1. 32. 15 for examples of the curative powers of poetry.

[60] Pucci (1979) reading the Sirens as, in a sense, '*Iliadic*' Muses seeking to flatter Odysseus into stopping ship and changing poem, points to the associations between the Sirens and Circe: 'Circe, the sensual magician, who possesses the same destructive power of θέλγειν (*Od.* 10. 213, 291, 318, 326) that she attributes to the Sirens, emerges as a saviour of Odysseus against powers who are so similar to herself ... Circe has already characterized the Sirens' pleasing song as a powerful incantation' (p. 128).

[61] Bergren (1981) examines the ambiguous effectiveness of Helen's drug and the power of words to affect minds and feelings.

tion of the magic of love and of words is Plato's *Symposium*. At 197e Agathon speaks of ᾠδῆς . . . ἦν (Love) ᾄδει θέλγων πάντων θεῶν τε καὶ ἀνθρώπων νόημα ('song which Love sings, casting spells on the minds of all gods and men'). When his turn comes, Socrates relates the story of his instruction in love from a very witch-like *magistra amoris*, but the true *pharmakon/pharmakeus* is Socrates himself (Derrida 1981: particularly 117–28) who draws Alcibiades almost against his will and brings him into a state of frenzy. He compares him with Marsyas, the erotically suggestive flute-playing satyr who bewitches mankind with his playing (215c–d).

The double-edged spells (potions and poems) which are cure and symptom, cure and poison in erotic discourse, are central to the understanding of Theocritus *Idyll* 11, where Polyphemus finds a *pharmakon* for his love in singing about it. Many commentators have made of this *pharmakon* a remedy pure and simple,[62] but Goldhill (1986: 31–5) shows how the *pharmakon* must be seen as ambivalent between love-philtre and love-cure, with the implication that the reader also, while reading this example of the cure of love, is in fact also 'shepherding' his love like Polyphemus. As in our passage, according to my suggestion, so too in the *Idyll* we watch the addressee watching the inset story and also shepherding his love, and again the same applies to us. A similar reading is possible for the *medicina amoris* which Gallus seeks in *Ecl.* 10 (60). Although he proposes to seek his cure through hunting, and claims that there is no longer any pleasure in poetry, in fact his song is also shepherding his love. The *renuntiatio amoris* poems (Catul. 8; Hor. *Epod.* 15, *Carm.* 1. 5; Ov. *Am.* 3. 11) also revolve around this principle. The rejection of love is part of the discourse of love—it *is* love. The poems are performatively

---

[62] Dover (1971: 174): 'by persisting in singing he eventually found a remedy that he could not have found in any other way.' DuQuesnay (1979: 47): the poem allows the reader 'no room to doubt that the Cyclops has been successfully cured'. Griffiths (1979: 81) realizes that the song is not only the 'major symptom' but also 'contributing cause of Polyphemus' amorous distraction'. But he too seeks a solution: 'What we see in *Idyll* 11, then, is a weak sort of wit befuddling itself with erotic commonplaces (19–71), then singing itself out of them as well (72–9).'

self-confuting, for it is only when it is not true that a speaker says 'I'm not in love', as Ovid himself realizes (*Rem.* 648):

> *qui nimium multis 'non amo' dicit, amat.*
>
> He who tells everyone 'I'm not in love', is.

Love and poetry are both intimately connected with magic: the *Ars* is love, is poetry, is magic. Even as he explicitly rejects its *use*, Ovid employs its *metaphor* covertly to display (so to speak) the spell which he is brewing, the seduction his art is planning, for the passage under consideration in this chapter is shot through with the language of magic. On the surface it says 'don't trust to magic', while the magical subtext subverts the simple message by the ambivalence of the *pharmakon*. The ambivalence hinges around the polysemy of *carmen*, alluded to above in connection with the *Remedia Amoris*. With its roots in the atavistic magical power of words, a *carmen* is a spell as well as a song, an ambiguity which is essential to ancient understanding of the enchanting power of poetry.[63] Love cannot be maintained by *carmina*, but what is the *Ars* itself but a *carmen*?[64] The impetuous Reader might well be deceived by the ambiguity of *carmen*, but the reader is alerted by it. We know that the magic spell which is a drug (poison) and cure can seduce even the most rational and detached of beings into love. Love certainly can be kept by a *carmen*—so watch out for this one![65]

---

[63] For *carmen* meaning a spell see e.g. Virg. *Ecl.* 8. 67–70 *nihil hic nisi carmina desunt* | . . . | *carmina uel caelo possunt deducere lunam* | *carminibus Circe socios mutauit Ulixi*; Tib. 1. 2. 45–56, esp. 53–4 *haec mihi composuit cantus, quis fallere posses:* | *ter cane, ter dictis despue carminibus*; 1. 5. 11–12 *ipseque te circum lustraui sulpure puro,* | *carmine cum magico praecinuisset anus* (note this as a specifically medicinal piece of magic), 1. 8. 17–21 *num te carminibus, num te pallentibus herbis* | *deuouit tacito tempore noctis anus?* | *cantus uicinis fruges traducit ab agris,* | *cantus et iratae detinet anguis iter,* | *cantus et e curru Lunam deducere temptat* (note the incantatory repetition, which will be discussed below); Prop. 2. 28. 35; Ov. *Am.* 3. 7. 31.

[64] It is specifically so called in its proems, *Ars* 1. 2, 2. 3, and in references to it in exile, *Tr.* 2. 207, *Pont.* 1. 1. 30, 3. 3. 37.

[65] On the other hand, if love cannot be kept by song, then it cannot be kept by the *Ars*. How could the *Ars* really teach you how to keep a girl? Ovid humorously undercuts the strength of his erotodidaxis, by suggesting that love, particularly in its elegiac manifestation, is so flighty that it cannot be held down. Cf. *Ars* 2. 164 for a similar joke. In the face of the rich rival, Ovid gives up: *cedimus, inuentis plus placet ille meis.*

Poetry which speaks about magic *carmina* cannot help but reflect on itself, and all the more so in elegy, where a central and programmatic purpose of the song is the opening of doors. Drawing on the old Roman magico-religious significance of the threshold, the elegiac obsession with the act of gaining entry focuses attention on the mistress's door, also symbolizing her body. The song of the locked-out lover is a spell to open the door, but it is a spell which, with the recurrent ambivalence of the *pharmakon*, is potentially most effective on the self-absorbed lover himself. Ovid makes explicit the interconnections of door-magic, love-magic, and poetic magic in *Am.* 2. 1. 17–28, to which I shall digress for a moment in order to elucidate the claim that elegy (including the *Ars*) is a magic spell. In this programmatic poem (*Am.* 2. 1), the mistress's closed door makes it impossible for Ovid to write anything but elegy. Elegy is a *carmen*, the argument goes, *carmina* have magic powers, so elegy must have that power (*Am.* 2. 1. 23–8):

> *carmina sanguineae deducunt cornua lunae*
> *et reuocant niueos solis euntis equos;*
> *carmine dissiliunt abruptis faucibus angues*
> *inque suos fontes uersa recurrit aqua;*
> *carminibus cessere fores, insertaque posti,*
> *quamuis robur erat, carmine uicta sera est*

Songs draw down the horns of the bloody moon
and call back the snow-white horses of the moving sun;
by song snakes split open with burst jaws
and springs run backwards with their streams reversed;
doors have yielded to songs, and the bolt inserted in the door-
      post,
although it was made of oak, has been conquered by song.

Elegy is the *carmen* with the power to open the door.[66] Being a *pharmakon*, it also has power over the lover-singer, power to make him love. The lover (Reader and reader) is seduced.

To return to the passage in hand (that starting at *Ars* 2. 99): the magic powers which are opposed to Ovid's own

---

[66] See also Pease (1935) on Virg. *Aen.* 4. 487; Copley (1942) and (1956), *OLD carmen* 1b.

(and rejected) are described, in answer to the question *quas per artes* ('through which arts') love can be kept, as *Haemonias . . . artes*. This must allude to a possible didactic title not so different from the *Artes Amatoriae—Artes Haemoniae*.[67] The phrase *ars magica* was not uncommon,[68] and occurs in a passage in the *Remedia Amoris* which is very closely parallel with ours (*Rem*. 249–50):

> *uiderit, Haemoniae si quis mala pabula terrae*
> *et magicas artes posse iuuare putat.*

> He'll soon see, anyone who thinks that the evil grasses of Thessaly
> or magic arts can help.

Many spell-formulae such as survive in the magic papyri are written as instructions (like a recipe), and it seems likely that magic was the subject of actual didactic poems.[69] What certainly does occur as didactic material is the related subject of medicine. Nicander's *Theriaca* and his *Alexipharmaca* describe remedies for various poisons, while the *Theriaca* and even more the *De Herbis* of Ovid's friend Aemilius Macer may well have covered material to which the term *ars magica* could be applied. Ovid's point is clear: *Ars Magica* cannot keep a girl in love, only *Ars Amatoria*. Opposition is about similarity: the *Ars Amatoria* is both the opposite of *Ars Magica* and the same thing. While purporting to reject the use of magic in love, Ovid in fact highlights the very indissolubility of the charms of magic and of love and of poetry, and thus problematizes his rejection. If the *Ars Amatoria* is a *carmen*, it is itself a magic spell. The *Ars Amatoria is*, of its nature, an *Ars Magica*. If Ovid is the *pharmakeus*, then he is also the seducer: he is the *magus* of love as well as its *magister* ('mage and master'), who uses the charm of his poetry to seduce Readers and readers.

[67] In the exile poetry Ovid often refers to the *Ars* in the plural. For the association of Haemonia/Thessaly with witches see e.g. Nisbet and Hubbard (1970) on Hor. *Carm*. 1. 27. 21.

[68] See *TLL* 2. 665. 34.

[69] Ovid does not mention magic as a didactic subject in his catalogue in *Tristia* 2, but neither does he mention Tib. 1. 4 specifically, nor the earlier erotodidactic tradition, so this does not mean that such poems did not exist.

In order to see the seductive deception being practised on us, we should look again at vv. 99–107:

> *fallitur, Haemonias si quis decurrit ad artes*
> *datque quod a teneri fronte reuellit equi.*
> *non facient, ut uiuat amor, Medeides herbae*
> *mixtaque cum magicis nenia Marsa sonis:*
> *Phasias Aesoniden, Circe tenuisset Ulixen,*
> *si modo seruari carmine possit amor.*
> *nec data profuerint pallentia philtra puellis;*
> *philtra nocent animis uimque furoris habent.*
> *sit procul omne nefas! ut ameris amabilis esto.*

Anyone who has recourse to Haemonian arts, and gives
that which is torn from the brow of a young horse
is deceived. The grasses of Medea will not make
love live, nor the Marsian chant mixed with magic noises.
The Phasian [Medea] would have held the son of Aeson,
and Circe Ulysses, if love could really be kept by a song-spell.
Nor do pallid potions applied to girls bring profit; potions
are harmful to minds and contain the violence of madness.
Begone, all evil! In order to be loved, be lovable.

Already with the opening word the apparently straightforward message rests on a deceptive surface. The impersonal form of the verb, the lack of immediate or clear gender specification, the programmatic emphatic opening-position of the operative word combine to define the passage: deception is going on here! But who is being deceived? The word itself is open to ambiguity. 'He is deceived who has recourse to Haemonian Arts.' A judgement, this, but also a statement of fact. He who uses magic is deceived into believing it can help him, and deception is also the *result* of exposure to magic,[70] being in the essence of the *pharmakon*. Moreover, seduction is itself a form of deception. The epithet *doloploke* ('deceitful, weaving wiles') is applied to Aphrodite, for example by Theognis (1386) and Sappho (1. 2). We might usefully compare the seductive deception of the following: Cupid's seduction of Dido into love with Aeneas is described in terms of pharmacological deceit, *occultum inspires ignem fallasque ueneno* ('breathe in hidden fire and deceive

---

[70] Cf. Hor. *Epod.* 3. 6–8 *num uiperinus his cruor | incoctus herbis me fefellit, an malas | Canidia tractauit dapes?*

her with poison', *Aen.* 1. 688); Tib. 1. 9. 37 *at non ego fallere doctus* ('but I not skilled in deceit'), 83 *fallaci ... amore* ('deceitful love'); Ov. *Am.* 1. 8. 85 *nec, si quem falles, tu periurare timeto* ('if you are in the process of seducing/deceiving someone, don't be afraid to perjure yourself'), 3. 14. 42; *Her.* 2. 63 *fallere credentem non est operosa puellam | gloria* ('it is no hard-won glory to deceive a trusting girl'); *Ars* 1. 457 *littera Cydippen pomo perlata fefellit, | insciaque est uerbis capta puella suis* ('the letter borne on the apple deceived Cydippe, and all unknowing the girl was captured by her own words'), 3. 443 *nec coma uos fallat liquido nitidissima nardo* ('let not hair shining with liquid nard deceive you'); *Rem.*350 *fallit enim multos forma sine arte decens* ('for beauty, attractive without art, seduces/deceives many'). The charm of love is just as deceptively alluring as a love-charm. Poetry deceives, love deceives, magic deceives. Since the 'Haemonian Arts' bear affinities with Ovid's own Art, deception and therefore seduction might also be the result of exposure to the *Ars Amatoria*. The hint of downward movement in *decurrit*[71] in this same line is significant: the young man (or anyone else) who is deceived when he falls in with witches is very like the girl (or anyone else) who fell (*decidit*) into the trap in the opening couplet of this book, and like Icarus, who fell (*decidit*, v. 91) out of the sky when he was lured into the trap of the heavens.

The *pharmakon* makes one stray from one's natural and normal path. Detour, deviation, delinquency—*decurrit* adds a further twist to the journey imagery which proceeds through the poem, for there is now the possibility of side-tracking and of going a different way from that prescribed by Ovid.[72] The lover's first thought is 'straight to magic', but the catch is that anyone who takes that path is in for a surprise, for at its end he will find the master himself. In the very act of drawing us away from one sort of magic, Ovid (covertly) attracts us to another.

[71] See *OLD decurro* 1b, and e.g. Sil. 1. 359 *ad terram caelo decurrens ignea lampas*.

[72] Compare *Ars* 2. 425 *docta, quid ad magicas, Erato, deuerteris, artes?* The same word (*decurrit*) is used of Circe taking speedy recourse to her magic (*Rem.* 287): *adsuetas Circe decurrit ad artes*.

2f Magic Spells—Love

As has been noted above, the rejection of love is part of erotic discourse and is therefore love poetry. In a similar way, the rejection of magic here is part of the discourse of magic, and so is, so to speak, magic poetry. In fact, it is couched in incantatory language which subverts the simple message of condemnation of incantation. The style (incantatory) is in tension with the overt sense (rational). The text does and does the opposite of (and so inverts) what it says. In this section I shall attempt to expose in detail the magical subtext of our passage.

The m, n, and s sounds in v. 102 have an incantatory effect, with the word order reflecting the sense, in that *nenia Marsa* ('Marsian incantations/dirges') are within the *magicis . . . sonis* ('magic sounds'), all mixed in like a magic brew. The droning sound and meaning of *nenia* attract onomatopoeia.[73] The m alliteration plays **M**edeides herbae ('grasses of Medea') against *nenia* **M**arsa, making a Graeco-Roman magic mix. A similar tension exists between *Marsa* (Italian) and *magicis* (latinized Persian). This section is full of Greek noises (*sonis*) like *PHasias AesonidEN* (self-referentially echoing *sonis—AeSONIden*), and the repeated *philtra* in the next couplet, where the Latin 'f' in *furoris* answers the Greek *sonus* ϕ. The double periphrasis in *Phasias Aesoniden*, the obliquity of Phasias,[74] the *hapax legomenon* name-derived adjective *Medeides*,[75] could be the Hellenistic *doctrina* of the sophisticated scientist, but their alliteration and precious obscurity sound incantatory. This makes a Graeco-Roman *mixta* of this potion of poetry. This incantatory style becomes even more marked in the admonition about *philtra* in vv. 105–6. The p, ph,[76] f and t alliteration, the repetition of

[73] Cf. Hor. *Carm.* 2. 1. 38, 2. 20. 21.

[74] The term Phasias comes from the river Phasis mentioned at Hes. *Theog.* 340, and is used as a periphrasis for Medea at Ov. *Her.* 15. 347, *Ars* 2. 382, 3. 33, *Met.* 7. 298. See Bömer (1976) on *Met.* 7. 6.

[75] So *TLL Onomasticon* 2. 237. Cf. *Rem.* 261 *quid te Phasiacae iuuerunt gramina terrae?*, 263 *quid tibi profuerunt, Circe, Perseides herbae?*; *Met.* 6. 139 *sucis Hecateidos herbae.*

[76] For the pronunciation see Allen (1965: 26–7, 131–2).

philtra, and syllabic play *PALLentia PHILtra PUELLis* (the *PHILtra* making the *PUELLae PALLentes?*—'potions making the girls pale'?) all create an incantatory effect, with five consecutive words starting with a bilabial voiceless plosive, two of them being aspirated. The repeated plosives suggest apotropaic spitting (on which see Murgatroyd 1980 on Tib. 1. 2. 53). Repetition, of sound and word, is a well-known incantatory feature,[77] while the epanalepsis is stressed by *nec . . . profuerint . . . nocent* ('and they do not profit . . . they do harm').[78] Incantatory language in an injunction *against* incantations? And the very word repeated signifies the very thing condemned. Surely this must problematize the condemnation, since it makes the poem itself into a counter-spell to the spell it rejects. There *is* a place for magic in love, but only Ovid has the right formulation.

The *pharmakon* is contagious: entering the discourse of magic, the text necessarily involves itself with magical practices and persons. *Nenia Marsa* is rejected, but still involved in the text. *Nenia*, originally the funeral dirge, stands for spells in (for example) Hor. *Epod.* 17. 29 *caputque Marsa dissilire nenia* ('to split the head with a Marsian spell'); Ov. *Fast.* 6. 141–2 *seu carmine fiunt | naeniaque in uolucres Marsa figurat anus* ('or whether [owls] come about by an incantation, and a Marsian spell shapes old women into birds'). The spirits of the dead, particularly those who had died young, violently, and unjustly, were believed to be sources of magical power. Canidia (Hor. *Epod.* 5) aims to make her love-potion more powerful by its association with the boy's death, but the same event puts power into his curse. (See Luck 1985: 29 on Hor. *Epod.* 5.) The inborn capacity for magic among the Marsians is described by Gel. 16. 11. Like Medea and Circe, the Marsians are part of the expected

---

[77] Cf. e.g. Theocr. 2. 23 Δέλφις ἔμ' ἀνίασεν. ἐγὼ δ' ἐπὶ Δέλφιδι δάφναν | αἴθω, 28–9 τάκω, | ὥς τάκοιθ', 30–1 δινεῖθ' . . . δινοῖτο, 43 ἐς τρὶς ἀποσπένδω κῆς τρὶς τάδε, πότνια, φωνῶ; Virg. *Ecl.* 8. (chorus) *ducite ab urbe domum, mea carmina, ducite Daphnin*, 69–70, 73–5, 77–8, 80, 83, 85, 96–8, 104; Tib. 1. 2. 54 *ter cane, ter dictis despue carminibus.*

[78] These two terms occur together at *Am.* 3. 12. 13 *an prosint dubium, nocuerunt carmina certe.*

vocabulary of magic.[79] 'The Marsi, a tribe or nation of central Italy, maintained their identity until the late second century BC, it seems. Their civilization apparently was just different enough from the Roman one to make them look somewhat bizarre. Hence, Marsian magicians (perhaps priests of some of their local deities) enjoyed a great reputation in Rome: they were especially famous for curing snakebites' (Luck 1985: 6). The medicinal nature of their magic power connects them with the shadow didactic poem, the *Ars Magica*, which lurks beneath the apparently rational surface of the scientist of love.

The same couplet also rejects the herbs of Medea.[80] The collocation of 'herbs and incantations' becomes itself a magic formula.[81] A drug (medicine and spell) is sought to keep love truly *alive*, but not by the ambivalent power of Medea's life-and-death-giving magic, which was applied efficaciously to Aeson, and both efficaciously and inefficaciously, indeed deceitfully, to Pelias.[82] That is the problem with magic herbs: their effects are unreliable. The herbs become specifically *philtra* in vv. 105–6, perhaps the nearest Ovid comes to the word *pharmakon*, and are defined by another magic feature, pallor.[83] Magic is connected with death and fear, and the evil eye which causes illness and impotence.

[79] See Hor. *Epod.* 5. 75 *nec uocata mens tua | Marsis redibit uocibus*; Virg. *Aen.* 7. 758 *Marsis quaesitae montibus herbae*; Ov. *Med.* 39 *nec mediae Marsis finduntur cantibus angues.*

[80] For the magic plants of the archetypal witch cf. Ap. Rhod. 3. 528–30 κούρη τις . . . τὴν Ἑκάτη περίαλλα θεὰ δάε τεχνήσασθαι | φάρμαχ', ὅς' ἤπειρός τε φύει καὶ νήχυτον ὕδωρ; Tib. 1. 2. 51 (with Murgatroyd 1980) *sola tenere malas Medeae dicitur herbas*; Ov. *Her.* 6. 83 (Hypsipyle of Medea) *nec facie meritisque placet, sed carmina nouit | diraque cantata pabula falce metit*; *Rem.* 261–2; *Met.* 7. 224, with Bömer (1976) ad loc. For the efficacy of herbs in magic cf. e.g. Theocr. 2. 1; Virg. *Ecl.* 8. 95; Tib. 1. 2; Ov. *Med.* 35.

[81] Cf. Virg. *Aen.* 7. 757–8 *neque eum iuuere in uulnera cantus | somniferi et Marsis quaesitae montibus herbae*; *Georg.* 3. 283 *miscerunt . . . herbas et non innoxia uerba* (hippomanes was described in the previous three lines as an additive to the herbs and incantations); Hor. *Sat.* 1. 8. 19–20; Tib. 1. 2. 60, 1. 8. 17, 23; Ov. *Her.* 12. 167, *Met.* 10. 397, 14. 20, 357, 15. 326, *Fast.* 2. 425–6; Grat. 405; Luc. 6. 492, 682–3, 768, 822; Stat. *Theb.* 9. 733–5; Sil. 8. 497.

[82] It is ineffective in that it does not succeed in rejuvenating Pelias, but of course it is efficacious from Medea's point of view, which is to kill him.

[83] Pallor is associated with magic at e.g. Hor. *Sat.* 1. 8. 25–6 *pallor utrasque | fecerat horrendas aspectu*; Tib. 1. 8. 17–18 *num te carminibus, num te pallentibus herbis | deuouit . . . anus* (with which Murgatroyd 1980 compares Pers. 5. 55 *rugosum piper et pallentis grana cumini*).

Naturally, words have central importance in many spells, which depend on getting the phrasing exact and on the use of special words of power. (See Luck 1985: 20.) Now, *neniae* are also 'trifles', and the word can be used specifically of literature.[84] Magic spells are *carmina*, but trifling ones, because they are not artistic. The spells which are also trifles are mixed with magic sounds, inarticulate noises. In contrast, Ovid's is the only *artistic* spell, the only one to get the words exactly right for holding on to love.

The pseudo-opposition between medium and message is maintained in the apotropaic formula *sit procul omne nefas!* ('keep away, all evil!').[85] The pious stance of horror at the crime of such violence is, of course, disingenuous, for it is itself a piece of verbal magic, self-referentially banishing the discourse of magic for the closely related discourse of seduction. That pseudo-opposition culminates in the second half of the line just quoted: *ut ameris, amabilis esto* ('in order to be loved, be lovable'). It is not magic which will enable you to sustain a relationship: it is the lesson you will learn from reading the *Ars*. That 'lesson' (be lovable) is telling, both of the nature of the *Ars* and of the involvement and function of magic in this passage. Since a work entitled *Ars Amatoria* lends itself to such jingles on *amo*,[86] in the contextual ambience of magic, the anaphoric jingle becomes the spell which is the *Ars Amatoria*. It is placed in the tradition of wisdom literature by its association with the proverb, *ut ameris, ama* ('in order to be loved, love').[87] Frécaut (1972: 75) mentions on this passage the statement of Hecato of Rhodes, a pupil of Panaetius, reported by Seneca (*Ep.* 9. 6), *ego tibi monstrabo amatorium sine medicamento, sine herba, sine ullius ueneficae carmine: si uis amari, ama* ('I will show you a way of love without medicine, without herbs, without the spell of any witch: if you want

---

[84] Cf. *OLD nenia* 5b and Phaedr. 3. pr. 10.

[85] The exclamation belongs to liturgical language. Cf. Catul. 63. 92 *procul a mea tuos sit furor omnis, era, domo*; Virg. *Aen.* 6. 258 *procul, o procul este, profani* (with Norden's 1916 note and Ovid's parody, *Am.* 2. 1. 3 *procul hinc, procul este, seueri*); Tib. 2. 1. 11 *uos quoque abesse procul iubeo*, 2. 5. 88; Ov. *Am.* 1. 14. 41, *Ars* 1. 31, 2. 151, *Fast.* 2. 623, 4. 116, *Met.* 2. 464, 7. 255, 15. 587 *'procul, a! procul omnia' dixit 'talia di pellant'*.

[86] Cf. *Ars* 2. 267–8 *adferat aut uuas aut quas Amaryllis amabat | at nunc castaneas non amat illa, nuces*.

[87] See Mart. 6. 11. 10, Otto (1962) 17.

to be loved, love'). Seneca's context discusses friendship, which of course can only exist man to man. The formulation of the quotation is very similar to our line: potions, herbs, spells, and a jingle on *amor*.[88] Ovid's slight but significant deviation from the norm condenses the whole work into half a line: not 'love' but 'be lovable'. For success in both the Reader's erotic relationships, active (known) and passive (unknown), he must be lovable, a state which he can achieve through submission to Ovid. The injunction *ut ameris, amabilis esto* is the precise wording of the didactic spell, of which the whole work is a longer formulation.

The most powerful erotic drug—most powerful, that is, in its role in discourse—is hippomanes, rejected (and thereby introduced) in a periphrasis in v. 100.

> *datque quod a teneri fronte reuellit equi.*
>
> and gives
> that which is torn from the brow of a young horse.

Ovid will not write *hippomanes* ('horse-madness'), but with *equi* ('horse') here and *furoris* ('madness', v. 106) he *almost* says *hippomanes*. Hippomanes may be involved in the ambiguity of the rejection of the *Haemonias . . . artes* (v. 99). Since another *Haemonia ars* is horse-raising (cf. Prop. 2. 10. 2). At *Ars* 2. 136, within sight of this line and therefore lending contextual support, the horses of Achilles have the same adjective: *Haemonios dum uigil optat equos* [*Dolon*] ('when Dolon as a spy desires Thessalian horses'). *Haemonia ars*, then, is knowledge of hippomanes. One who uses Haemonian arts is deceived many times over, by the use of magic, by the effect of the aphrodisiac hippomanes, and by the instability of significance in *Haemonia ars*. The rapacious violence of this drug, which is torn from the soft and tender young foal (cf. v. 106), combines with the hint of blood in *Haem-onias*. Since *soni* are at issue here, we may be intended to hear a hint of *HippoMaNeS* in *HaeMoNiaS*, just as we hear *HaeMONIaS* in *MINOS HOMINIS* (in the preceding line), with a play, perhaps, in the match of

---

[88] The proverb is found with erotic and pharmacological associations e.g. at Eur. *Andr.* 207–8 φίλτρον δὲ καὶ τόδ' οὐ τὸ κάλλος, ὦ γύναι, | ἀλλ' ἀρεταὶ τέρπουσι τοὺς ξυνευνέτας.

Latin h (*hominis*) and Greek breathing (*Haemonias*, and the non-existent but ever-present *hippomanes*).

Hippomanes is a well-known aphrodisiac, which comes in three forms: (1) a plant, as in Theocr. 2; (2) a discharge from the mare, usually after intercourse, as in Virg. *Georg.* 3. 280, Tib. 2. 4. 58, Prop. 4. 5. 17; (3) as here, a piece of flesh, possibly the caul, taken from a foal just after birth.[89] Why does Ovid choose apparently the least erotic and therefore least appropriate variety of hippomanes for his aphrodisiac? The other elegists, and Ovid himself at *Am.* 1. 8. 8, employ the discharge variety, the efficacy of which has to do with the mare's own wild sexuality; the plant is neutral (except perhaps through the erotic suggestiveness of picking flowers); but in the case of the caul, the aphrodisiac's efficacy is explained as working because it makes the mother love her foal. That explanation comes from Servius *ad Aen.* 4. 515, which runs

> *quaeritur et nascentis equi de fronte reuulsus*
> *et matri praereptus amor.*

> Love is sought which is torn from the forehead of a
>   new-born horse
> and stolen from its mother.

We have love here all right, but a completely different sort of love from the eros with which the *Ars* is concerned. Ovid chooses the caul-hippomanes precisely because its supposed efficacy depends on an amatory mistake. Describing Dido's attempts at erotic magic, Virgil referred to the *amor* torn from the calf's head. The wording of our passage suggests a deliberate allusion to Virgil's. The phrase *fronte reuellit equi* echoes *equi de fronte reuulsus*, although Ovid refuses to write *amor*—following Virgil—here to match his *artes* in the previous line. But Virgil/Dido's is the wrong sort of potion, the wrong *pharmakon*, the wrong love. Only Ovid has control of the pharmacological forces of love.

---

[89] For which see Gow (1952) on Theocr. 2 and Pease (1935) on Virg. *Aen.* 4. 515. Cf. also Hor. *Carm.* 1. 25. 13–14 *cum tibi flagrans amor et libido,* | *quae solet matres furiare equorum* | *saeuiet circa iecur ulcerosum*, with Nisbet and Hubbard's note on hippomanes, (1970) ad loc. They quote Arist. *hist. an.* 527^a8. See Tupet (1976) 76–80.

In discussion of the Nireus and Hylas exempla, I suggested that the apparently straightforward points of comparison carry more poetic weight than simply as paragons of
male beauty. Likewise in this discussion of the effectiveness
of amatory magic, the most obvious examples of loving
witches are duly rolled out. The four mini-exempla together
constitute a series of deliberately misleading paradigms,
through which the Reader is further deceived and the
reader, when he takes the point, is further enlightened—
and 'deceived', that is, seduced. At first sight, these famous
witches who were deserted by men they loved are perfect
paradigms for the inefficacy of magic in love. For the
impetuous Reader, fine. But the careful and cunning reader
should look more carefully. Firstly, the signifiers are *women*
holding on to *men*, whereas the supposed signified is a man
holding a woman. A small point, perhaps, but its relevance
will be seen retrospectively as we become more suspicious
about the question of who is holding whom. This sort of
retrospective re-reading is part, I submit, of our total response to a text, particularly one such as this, which constantly engages with the activity of re-reading.

Secondly, in some sense these two witches did in fact
succeed in holding their men: Circe kept Ulysses from his
journey for a year and, according to the canonical Homeric
account, he only left on the insistence of his men; and
Medea spent some years as Jason's wife. They might not
have done so directly by open magic, and indeed that very
point makes the exempla still less appropriate, but their
magical power highlights the enchantment of their physical
attractions. Part of Medea's *charm* for Jason was the spells
she used to help the Argonauts win the fleece and escape.
In this instance, the collocation 'Circe/Medea' should
make us think 'Homer/*Argonautica*', rather than 'Homer/
tragedy', an opposition between archaic and Hellenistic
epic which informs also the Nireus and Hylas exempla, and
in Apollonius Medea's magic is successful. She could use
her drugs to keep Jason alive (Hor. *Epod.* 3. 12), although she
could not keep his *love* alive by direct pharmacological
action. Medea's magic is *almost* life-giving. As witch she
does not have the spell quite right (not having read the *Ars*

Amatoria), but as woman she has charming erotic fascination. As for Circe, Luck (1985: 10) comments: 'But even Hermes cannot protect Odysseus from Circe's physical charms; when Circe realizes she has no power over Odysseus, she offers him her bed, they become lovers, and he stays for a while.' So although a male lover cannot expect to put a straightforward spell on his girl to make her stay, there is a hint that the girl might put another, more overtly erotic sort of spell on *him* and have him in her power. Does Ulysses seduce Circe—or Circe Ulysses? (The same question will be asked later of Calypso.) Love *can* be held by a *carmen*, and the lover is himself being seduced by the beloved's charm to stay in the relationship and the poet's charm to read the book.

Having engaged in the ambiguous significance of the *exempla*, we may be alerted to pharmacological ambiguity in the *philtron* of the succeeding couplet (vv. 105–6):

> *nec data profuerint pallentia philtra puellis;*
>   *philtra nocent animis uimque furoris habent.*

> Nor do pallid potions applied to girls bring profit; potions
> are harmful to minds and contain the violence of madness.

The simplest meaning of this—the Reader's meaning—is that there is no advantage in giving a love-potion to your girl, understanding *puellis* ('to girls') with *data* ('given, applied'). To understand *puellis* with *profuerint* ('profit'), however, allows two simultaneous and partially contradictory readings. When the potion is a poison, as it always already is, it might have the result of making the girl frigid (a result like that inflicted on Tibullus by his estranged mistress's charms in 1. 5. 39–44). The suggestion of frigidity/impotence is picked up more forcefully in *nocent*, a word which is common for the harmful effects of magic, including impotence.[90] Some examples from elegy specifically link *nocere* with erotic magic (real and metaphorical). Tibullus says (1. 5. 47) that the charms of Delia, supposedly non-magical but described in terms of magic, *nocuere mihi* ('have harmed me'), that is, have made him so much in love

---

[90] As e.g. at *Met.* 14. 403 (Circe) *illa nocens spargit uirus.*

as to be impotent. In *Amores* 3. 7, where Ovid is playing
around with the idea of his own impotence, *nocere* has come
to mean 'cause to be impotent' (*Am.* 3. 7. 27–8):[91]

> *num mea Thessalico languent deuota ueneno*
> *corpora, num misero carmen et herba nocent.*

Surely my body does not languish, cursed by Thessalian poison,
surely spells and herbs do not harm wretched me.

In contrast, for Marathus the opposite, yet somehow similar
'harm' is done (Tib. 1. 8. 23–6):

> *quid queror heu misero carmen nocuisse, quid herbas?*
> *forma nihil magicis utitur auxiliis:*
> *sed corpus tetigisse nocet, sed longa dedisse*
> *oscula, sed femori conseruisse femur.*

Alas, why do I complain that a spell and herbs have harmed the
   poor boy?
Beauty uses no magic aids,
but to have touched her body, to have given long kisses,
to have entwined his thighs with hers—these things harm him.

Nocere here means 'cause to feel overwhelming desire'.
Love, the remedy which can be a poison, aggravates the
disease. The *pharmakon* could in fact do more harm than
good to your mistress's sexual interest in you, or it could
make her flare up with desire. Alternatively, if the potion
were given to the lover by the girl, it might well profit the
girl, for she would wield the power of the *pharmakon* and
he would be under its spell, be it in desire or in impotence.
One side of the ambiguity picks up the *exempla* of v. 103,
that love the *pharmakon* is a trap for the lover; the other the
instruction of v. 99, that magic is harmful. So, what is
'doing (you) some good' in this poem? What might be
called 'harm' might also be erotically useful. Love is a risky
business.

   The same ambiguity arises in the first poem of Propertius,
a work which has featured at a number of points in this
discussion, where witches are exhorted (Prop. 1. 1. 22–3)

---

[91] Cf. *Am.* 3. 7. 37 *huc pudor accessit facti: pudor ipse nocebat;* | *ille fuit uitii
causa secunda mei.*

> *en agedum dominae mentem conuertite nostrae*
> *et facite illa meo palleat ore magis.*

> Come now, convert the mind of my mistress,
> and make her grow more pale than my own face.

Propertius' wish is for his mistress to grow pale with love, for here, as in our passage, the pallor of the love-potion is transferred from the erotic topos of the lover's pallor; but his phraseology allows for the witches to interpret it differently and make her pale for another reason—illness, death, sexual failure. The elusive *pharmakon* needs artful control.

Is the *pharmakon* useful, didactically, erotically? Love-potions have the 'force' or 'meaning' of madness.[92] Φίλτρον spells (!) *furor*. But is *uis furoris* what we should shun or seek in love? The term *uis* in elegy often suggests rape.[93] Keeping a girl involves not just physical power over her body, but a more subtle power over her mind, so to use a love-potion would be a kind of mental rape. Madness is the risked side-effect of the use of a *pharmakon*. But on the other hand the use of force was advocated in certain circumstances in Book 1.[94] And Love, as is well known, is a form of madness.[95] In Theocritus 2. 51, Delphis is to come back to the magic-using speaker μαινομένῳ ἴκελος ('like a madman'). The word *furor* for the madness of love (and poetry) gains programmatic force for love poets from Prop. 1. 1. 7 *et mihi iam toto furor hic non deficit anno* ('and now this madness has not failed me for a whole year'), followed by Ov. *Am.* 1. 2. 35 *Blanditiae comites tibi erunt Errorque Furorque* ('Blandishments will be your companions, and Error and Madness').[96] In *Ars* 1, *furor* is the overwhelming sex-drive of women (1. 341–2):

---

[92] For *uis* meaning the meaning or significance of words see *OLD uis* 18.

[93] Cf. Ov. *Her.* 5. 131 *uim licet adpelles et culpam nomine ueles*, 16. 21, 186 *ui mea rusticitas excutienda fuit*; *Ars* 1. 673 *uim licet appelles: grata est uis ista puellis*, 679, 699, 703; *Fast.* 2. 613, 5. 205.

[94] Ovid treads the dangerous ground of the tenuous boundaries between courtship, seduction, and rape, perhaps summed up in the incongruity of the injunction (1. 667) to be careful, when using force, of hurting the girl's lips!

[95] The metaphor is very common: see *TLL* 6. 1631. 74. Cf. Catul. 64. 94, 68. 129; Prop. 1. 5. 3, 1. 13. 20; Ov. *Rem.* 119, 497, 581.

[96] Pichon (1902: 157) comments, 'Ac saepissime *furor* pro ualido ardentique amore ponitur, tamquam potenti ut eum, quasi mente capti regere non possint amantes.'

> *omnia feminea sunt ista libidine mota;*
> *acrior est nostra plusque furoris habet.*

> All these things are caused by female lust;
> it is fiercer than ours and has more madness.

Note the echo between this line and ours: *furoris habet/
habent* in the same *sedes*. At *Ars* 2. 487, the *furias* into which
the mares are driven reflect both the reaction of the girl to
discovery of her lover's infidelity, and that passionate wild-
ness in her nature which provides the opportunity for the
lover's reception.[97] The desired result is precisely *uim . . .
furoris*. So if *philtra* do harm to minds in the sense of
afflicting the subject with overwhelming love, and have the
power of wild love, then they might be considered very
useful indeed! The *Ars* itself is a *philtron* with this power.

2g Narrative Seduction

The precise formulation of the spell to *tenere* a relationship
is *amabilis esto* (v. 107), make yourself lovable—by reading
the *Ars*. The precept is illustrated (ostensibly) by the story
of Ulysses and Calypso. In this section, I shall analyse the
exemplum's contribution to the complexities of erotic and
poetic seduction. This narrative (*Ars* 2. 123–44) is often
admired as a classic piece of Ovidian story-telling. (See
Hollis 1973.)

> *non formosus erat, sed erat facundus Ulixes,*
> *et tamen aequoreas torsit amore deas.*
> *o quotiens illum doluit properare Calypso*   125
> *remigioque aptas esse negavit aquas!*
> *haec Troiae casus iterumque iterumque rogauit;*
> *ille referre aliter saepe solebat idem.*
> *litore constiterant; illic quoque pulchra Calypso*
> *exigit Odrysii fata cruenta ducis.*   130
> *ille leui uirga (uirgam nam forte tenebat),*
> *quod rogat, in spisso litore pingit opus.*
> *'haec' inquit 'Troia est' (muros in litore fecit),*
> *'hic tibi sit Simois; haec mea castra puta.*
> *campus erat' (campumque facit), 'quem caede Dolonis*   135
> *sparsimus, Haemonios dum uigil optat equos.*

[97] This passage will be considered further in the final chapter.

> *illic Sithonii fuerant tentoria Rhesi;*
> > *hac ego sum captis nocte reuectus equis—'*
> *pluraque pingebat, subitus cum Pergama fluctus*
> > *abstulit et Rhesi cum duce castra suo;*   140
> *tum dea 'quas' inquit 'fidas tibi credis ituro,*
> > *perdiderint undae nomina quanta, uides?'*
> *ergo age, fallaci timide confide figurae,*
> > *quisquis es, aut aliquid corpore pluris habe.*

Ulysses was not beautiful, but he was eloquent,
and yet he tortured sea-goddesses with love.
How often Calypso grieved at his hurrying away
and denied that the sea was suitable for rowing!
She used to ask for the fall of Troy again and again;
he used often to tell the same story in different ways.
They had stood together on the shore; even there lovely Calypso
demands again the cruel fate of the Thracian leader.
With a light stick (for as it chanced he was holding a stick),
he draws a picture of what she asked in the dense sand.
'This' he says 'is Troy' (he made the walls on the shore),
'let this be Simois to you; consider this my camp.
There was a plain' (he makes a plain), 'which we splattered
with the blood of Dolon, while as a spy he seeks Haemonian
   horses.
There were the tents of Sithonian Rhesus;
here I rode at night on captured horses—'
he was continuing to paint, when a sudden wave took away
   Pergamum
and the camp of Rhesus with its general.
Then the goddess says 'do you see what great names those
   waves,
which you trust for your departure, have destroyed?'
So then, only fearfully trust deceitful figure,
whoever you may be, or have something of more value than body.

Stylistic ring-composition marks vv. 99–144 out as a section. The generalizing, ungendered address *quisquis* (v. 144) echoes *si quis* (itself echoing the opening of Book 1) in v. 99. Both appellations point to the confusion of addressee and the slippage between seducer and seduced at issue in the passage. The foregrounding of the poet as teacher in both couplets links them, as does the echo of *fallitur* ('is deceived', v. 99) in *fallaci* ('deceptive', v. 143). As is often the case, the transition out of the mythological episode is facili-

tated and signalled by emphatic didacticism, with this
teacher's exhortation—*ergo age*—reminiscent of Virgil.[98]
The use of a moralizing, rounding-up maxim is reminiscent
of Lucretian practice, and emphasizes the didactic nature of
the preceding exemplum and the succeeding *praecepta* on
the formal level. On the thematic level, however, 'therefore'
acts as a challenge to the reader: does this moral follow
obviously from the preceding illustration? The ostensible
point of the exemplum is that eloquence is a useful aid
in keeping a girl, and the paradigm is apparently straightforward. The lover is to identify with Ulysses, the arch-
deceiver, the *polumētis* one ('person of many wiles') who
always achieves all his goals, the clever speaker and hero
who has nymphs and goddesses begging him to be their
lover, and a faithful wife waiting nineteen years for his
return. So far, so good, and after the disturbing inappropriateness of the exempla in the last paragraphs, the final
illustration, an extended one, seems comfortingly clear.

[98] Cf. *Georg.* 1. 63, 3. 42 *en age*, 2. 35 *agite*, 4. 149 *nunc age*, 329 *age*. See
Kenney (1958) 203. The imperatives *confide* and *habe* contribute to the didactic
atmosphere of the transition, as does the quasi-formulaic *quisquis es*. Smooth
transitions should not be expected from didactic style, since it employs abrupt
changes of tone and even subject matter to enliven what might otherwise become
a monotonous series of precepts. In particular, Lucretius' *De Rerum Natura* is full
of sudden transitions and changes of direction. The line of the argument turns
back and forth in an almost labyrinthine meander which drives the poem into a
state of flux—the medium is the message. See Thury (1987), who argues that
'elements repeated in shifting contexts serve as illustrations of the poet's meaning'
(pp. 285, 291–2), and that the sudden transitions are an effort to jolt us into
sudden understanding of the message. A few examples of Lucretian sudden
transition will illustrate: at 1. 265 he calls his readers to attention with the didactic
phrase, *nunc age*, and moves from expounding the doctrine that nothing can be
reduced to nothing to a lesson on the invisibility of atoms; 329 jumps from atomic
theory to discussion of the void; 830 plunges suddenly into the *Homoeomeria* of
Anaxagoras; 921 breaks off for a reflection on the poet's own art; 951 turns to the
infinity of space and matter. The idea that Body and Void are mutually exclusive
occurs at 430, and then reappears at 503, after the argument had moved through
discussion of the first beginnings of things. From his rhetorical standpoint as the
'Lucretius of love', Ovid calls his pupils to attention at significant points in the
lecture. Abrupt transition is facilitated by pointedly didactic language and formulaic phrases. For Lucretius it is often *et* (or *sed*) *quoniam docui*, *nunc age*, *adde
quod*, *principio*, etc. Grattius also makes use of didactic formulae at transitions,
beginnings and ends. See Hollis (1973: 91). Ovid often prepares for the transition
in the previous couplet, as at the end of the Daedalus story, with the authorial
obtrusion which is a hallmark of didactic poetry, thus drawing attention to the
status of mythological exempla and other *excursus* in didactic poetry.

But all is not so simple. Even on the simplest level, the exemplum said 'be a good talker', and the moral says 'don't trust to beauty'. The connection is tenuous, and demands attention. A small point undermines the illustrative clarity of the story: in the previous passage the young man was to learn how not to be *left*, as Medea and Circe were; and we saw that one point of incongruity in the Hylas exemplum was that it was Hercules who was *left*. Here, by contrast, Ulysses is threatening to go, and if he succeeds it will be Calypso, ostensibly signifying the beloved girl, who will be left. We are supposed to be learning how to *keep* a girl, not leave her.

I have suggested previously that in this story Ovid is working closely with the Homeric original,[99] and gives us clear hints that he has set the scene within the last few days of their relationship, while Ulysses was making his boat in order to leave—or at least attempting to. The *uirga* ('twig, rod') which Ulysses uses to depict his exploits is part of the raft which he is trying to build. His work is hampered, however, by Calypso's skilful manipulation of Ulysses' own love of talking. Indeed, those 'last few days' which were soon over in Homer, in Ovid are extended into anything up to seven years—the implication from the phrases *o quotiens* ('how often!' v. 125), *iterumque iterumque* ('again and again', v. 127) and *ille referre aliter saepe solebat idem* ('he used to tell the same story often in different ways', v. 128) is of a considerable passage of time. The means of seduction which Calypso used even when Ulysses had all but gone had been, we surmise, in constant use throughout his stay. Who is seducing whom now? While Ulysses' eloquence was bewitching to Calypso, she was able to throw the spell back at him, and use his own love of talking to charm him into staying a bit longer. With the argument for the dating of the scene in mind, together with the inappropriateness of the illustration suggested above, we see that Calypso has at least her fair share of control over the situation. Words have the power to bewitch, but it may be the speaker on whom they cast their spell.

---

[99] I give here a very brief summary of my 1987 article.

Now, if Calypso is doing the seducing, whom does she represent metaphorically? The girl, or Ovid? The answer, I suspect, is both. Ovid, who throughout the book manipulates the Reader's feelings and his self-image, has already eroticized his didactic relationship with his pupil. Now even a *female* lover, especially one who is playing so active a role, as a goddess courting a mortal, can reflect in an active manner on the poet–reader relationship. But Calypso also stands for the girl, in that Ovid is seducing the young man not only into following his advice, but further into involvement in a relationship with a mistress. The girl is the charm which draws him, even while he thinks he is playing a detached game. And as we look down in amusement at his false sense of his own detachment, we have to see that the metaphor applies to us also. We are no more detached from the text than the pupil is.

The *Ars* is the trap into which we fall. The moralizing epigram with which the section ends subliminally warns us of its own deceit, while further entrapping us (*Ars* 2. 143–4):

> *ergo age, fallaci timide confide figurae,*
> *quisquis es, aut aliquid corpore pluris habe.*

Come therefore, only fearfully trust deceitful figure,
whoever you are, or have something of more value than body.

Do not trust a *fallax figura* ('deceitful figure'). In two words the whole work is contained, in a perfect example of Ovidian economy! The surface meaning in the phrase is the instruction not to trust to your own looks in trying to keep a girl, for they are subject to erasure by time's wave: rather you should make use of artistic eloquence. But the *fallax figura* is also the beauty of Calypso: at *Od.* 7. 245 Odysseus describes her as δολόεσσα Καλυψώ ('deceitful Calypso').[100] The only other occurrence of the word δολόεσσα in exactly

---

[100] Do we hear an echo of this in *doluit* (v. 125)? A possible play between *dolus* and *dolor* is suggested by Virg. *Aen.* 1. 669 *et nostro doluisti saepe dolore* (Venus instructing Cupid to make Dido fall in love). The undercurrent of deception in our version of the story was highlighted unwittingly by Ulysses and intentionally by Ovid by his mention of the Dolon episode, whose very name bespeaks deceit, as Ovid shows at *Her.* 1. 39–40 *rettulit et ferro Rhesumque Dolonaque caesos,* | *utque sit hic somno proditus, ille dolo.*

this form in the *Odyssey* is at 9. 32—of Circe. The masculine form is used at 8. 281, of the chains with which Hephaestus caught Ares and Aphrodite. Δολόεσσα Καλυψώ, then, means 'Calypso the Trapper'. Her *figura* seduces Ulysses, and she is additionally *fallax* in her ability to keep him (talking) without his notice. Secretly, Ovid warns us of the dangers of his subject.

Fallax could also be a Latin gloss for *polumētis*, as it is overtly at *Met.* 13. 712 *fallacis Ulixis* ('deceitful Ulysses'). (See Bömer 1982: ad loc.) The deceitful Ulysses' famous attribute recoils on himself, and he is deceived by his love of *figurae*—physical and rhetorical. A *figura* can be a figure of speech (*OLD figura* 9c, 11), particularly when it is a form of speech departing from the straightforward.[101] So the rhetoric of Ulysses is deceptive (seductive)—to Calypso and to himself. But *fallax figura* can hardly fail also to refer to Ovid's story, which was also not what it seemed to be, and is deceiving (seducing) the lover as speech (and Calypso) deceived Ulysses. Moreover, the *Ars* itself is a *fallax figura*, a deceitful thing which is imaginatively fashioned. But this is a cheating loveliness and cheating rhetoric, for *figura* is derived by Varro from *fingo*: *fictor cum dicit 'fingo', figuram imponit* ('when a *fictor* (maker) says "I fashion", he puts a shape/figure on an object', *L.* 6. 78: at the same time he derives *facies* from *facere* and *forma* from *formare*). Now a *figura* is also an etymological formation.[102] So it is a *fallax figura* because a *figura* is something imagined/ fashioned—usually falsely—and the etymology is *fallax* because you think the word is semantically safe ('beauty') but in fact it will deceive you and turn out also to refer to the exemplum that ostensibly illustrates it. This is the spell cast over the critical reader.

---

[101] Cf. *Laus Pis.* 95 *exornata figuris . . . sententia*; Quint. *Inst.* 9. 1. 14 *figura sit arte aliqua nouata forma dicendi*; Sen. *Con.* 7. 1. 20 *qui non . . . palam dicerent, sed per suspiciones et figuras*.

[102] Cf. Gel. 3. 12 *auidum bibendi . . . noua et prope absurda uocabuli figura 'bibosum' dictum*.

2h From *pharmakon* to *pharmakeus*

In purporting to tell us that magic is 'bad' (harmful, dangerous, deceptive, seductive), Ovid is also telling us about—
and demonstrating—his own *magical* Art, 'harmful, dangerous, deceptive, seductive' as it is. Magic, like art, is both
good and bad; it both succeeds and fails. Through the
images of magician and pederast he creates a persona for
himself, an all-powerful Doctor Love, who controls the
minds and destinies of his unwary readers.

The *magister amoris* is of his essence a character of power
and magic—a *pharmakeus*. The Old Nurse is a stock character who advises her charge in erotic matters, and is so often
portrayed as having knowledge of magic that witch-like
characteristics become an integral part of anyone who has
erotic influence. We should recall Socrates' erotic instruc-
tress, Diotima (*Symp.* 201d), whose accomplishments included the highly pharmacological act of postponing the
plague at Athens for ten years. The nurse to whom Phaedra
turns for amatory advice in Euripides' *Hippolytus* also professes knowledge of the arcane. Perhaps the best-developed
example of this image of woman is the elegiac bawd who
attempts to separate the poet and his beloved and who is
therefore excoriated as an awful old hag and a witch. The
magister, or more often *magistra*, *amoris* must be a witch
because she or he has knowledge of the Power—Love the
pharmakon. The imputation of magical interference in erotic
matters to women, particularly older women, is part of the
fear of the female, particularly the female control of
sexuality.[103]

Ovid's thirsty bawd in *Amores* 1. 8, Dipsas, may be taken
as representative of the long tradition of witch-like *magistrae
amoris*. She knows magic arts and Circe's spells (*carmina*,
v. 5); how to turn rivers in their course (v. 6), a common

[103] See Halperin's essay 'Why is Diotima a "Woman"', in Halperin, Winkler,
Zeitlin (1989). Winkler (1990) claims that the imputation of erotic magic to
women is a literary conspiracy, that in reality the overwhelming majority of
providers of magic spells were men, and that erotic magic is a sign of male
violence towards women. This may be right, although I would want to expand his
'literary' category to include a broader cultural spectrum, since the witch with
erotic influence is a figure of sub-literary folk-tale as well as literary genres.

magical feat which, in its seductivity and the power it represents over nature, may be connected with that mythical *shaman*, Orpheus; the effectiveness of herbs (v. 7); and hip- pomanes (v. 8); has power over the elements (vv. 9–12); power to change herself (vv. 13–14); flashes from her eyes (vv. 15–16); can bring forth ghosts (vv. 17–18). Equal to all these powers is her ability to control the mind of Corinna, like the witches on whom Propertius calls in 1. 1. 21–2. Ovid's poem is dramatically staged, with the poet hiding behind *duplices fores* ('double doors': themselves perhaps covert signifiers of the interpretation I shall suggest), until he is betrayed by his own shadow. The reader, particularly the re-reader who returns to the *Amores* after the *Ars* (a type of reading given authorial sanction by the second edition), may suspect that the *umbra* ('shadow') is a sign to Dipsas herself, Ovid's shadow or counterpart. For one should notice how like Ovid himself Dipsas is, both in her magical power and in her advice. She too works *arte* ('by art', v. 6). How apt a description of Ovid himself would be that of Dipsas (vv. 19–20):

> *haec sibi proposuit thalamos temerare pudicos;*
> *nec tamen eloquio lingua nocente caret.*

She has proposed to herself to violate respectable bedrooms;
nor is her tongue lacking in harmful eloquence.

Compare her opening seductive flattery with *Ars* 2. 113; note the didactic gerundives in *Am.* 1. 8. 34 and 38; the use of exempla to prove a point (vv. 39–40), a point made by Ovid at *Ars* 3. 121–2. Compare *Am.* 1. 8. 42 *at Venus Aeneae regnat in urbe sui* ('but Venus rules in the city of her Aeneas'), with *Ars* 1. 60 *mater in Aeneae constitit urbe sui* ('his mother has stopped in the city of Aeneas'); and *Am.* 1. 8. 36 *si simules, prodest* ('if you were to pretend, it is of advantage') with *Ars* 2. 313 *si latet, ars prodest* ('if it is hidden, art is of advantage').[104] Ovid is a Dipsas. The

---

[104] The list continues: even a fairly cursory reading will show parallels and echoes, verbal and thematic, in almost every couplet of Dipsas' speech. (*Am.* 1. 8 first) 44—1. 277; 47—2. 355; 49–50—2. 113, 3. 59–60 esp. 65; 51—3. 91–4; 52—3. 80; 53—2. 113; 55–6—3. 419; 57—2. 273; 59—2. 493-4; 61—2. 279; 63—2. 276; 69—1. 45 (263), 2. 345; 71—1. 615, 2. 311; 73—3. 473, 2. 455; 75—2. 339;

comparison must problematize, if not undercut, his rejection of magic. When Dipsas applies the type of persuasion
to Corinna which is normally applied by pleading lovers
(flattery, reminders that youth is short, mythological justifi-
catory exempla, self-praise), and when Ovid uses similar
techniques in his seduction of the Reader, then each teacher
of love is exposed as a seducer as well as a wielder of the
power of the *pharmakon*, both sex and speech.

Light is thrown on the affinity between Ovid and Dipsas
by comparison with Propertius' *lena* poem, 4. 5. His witch,
Acanthis, is treated far more violently than Ovid's, her
physical features and timely death described in gruesome
detail. Her rhetoric, although employing common topoi of
the persuasion, is not very persuasive. She starts from an
imputation of greed in her audience, in contrast with
Dipsas' flattery and arousal of interest in a handsome young
gentleman. Only gradually does Dipsas insinuate the notion
of material gain (particularly if, in this very dramatic poem,
Am. 1. 8. 28 may be considered an aside). Although Ovid the
subjective love-poet purports to be hardly able to restrain
himself from strangling the witch, unlike his Propertian
counterpart he ends on a light note, cursing her finally with
no worse than the perpetual thirst which plays on her name
and characteristic. Ovid the erotodidactic poet is on the
same side as Dipsas—a seducer and a witch.

The referent of this metaphorical story of magical and
pederastic seduction is us, the reader, seduced into reading
the book. By following the instruction we obey it. Even
when we feel convinced that the seduction is happening to
the Reader, the young man with whom we seek with varying
degrees of success *not* to identify (or, indeed, not!), it is also
happening to us. The reader who tries to be detached is
always already under the spell, and is drawn further into its
web. The pleasure resides in the indeterminacy we invade:
the readings are *ours*.

77—2. 523; 78—2. 427–54; 79—2. 373–80; 81—2. 455; 85—1. 633; 89—2. 255;
93—1. 417, 429; 95—2. 435; 97—3. 593; 100—2. 266; 107—openings of Books 1
and 2, ends of Books 2 and 3.

3

Amor Artis: The Daedalus Episode

Twenty-one lines into Book 2, Ovid employs the didactic strategy of using an exemplum to illustrate the difficulty and importance of the task on which he has embarked—to keep a girl (keep a reader). The exemplum is the story of Daedalus, the archetypal artisan who escaped from his imprisonment in Minoan Crete by flying on wings which he had created. His son, Icarus, was also equipped with wings, but the boy flew too high, the sun melted the wax on his wings, and he fell into the sea. Although dead, he gained eternal fame through the sea which took his name, the Icarian Sea.

The tale of Daedalus and Icarus is a key passage in the study of Ovidian poetry. What is a general phenomenon in the Ovidian corpus and in Ovidian criticism is here particularly evident and arouses strong reactions by being thrown into sharp relief; for this episode provides an apparently pure case of 'excess', 'irrelevance', 'narcissism', 'self-indulgence', 'vacuity', the standard accusations levelled against Ovid, and so is a locus of contestation for the value of Ovidian poetry. This chapter offers a close reading of the exemplum as a paradigm for our understanding of the *Ars Amatoria*, and has implications for the reception of 'Ovid' generally.[1] Reading Ovid involves situating his writing, his artistry, his writing on artistry against a complex web of great predecessors' writings on the same subject as well as against his own earlier and subsequent treatments of the same material. This intertextuality is particularly traceable here, in a story placed in the tradition of two of the great masters of Latin Poetry, Virgil and Horace, and one which

[1] By 'Ovid' I mean the texts which have come down to us as being authored by him, together with ancient, medieval, and modern responses to the man and the works.

Ovid will treat again.[2] How the Daedalus of Virgil and
Horace is to be understood is therefore of central importance to the Ovidian *character* (Daedalus) and the *Ovidian*
Character (the nature of his poetry). This classic case of
repetition provides a specific paradigm for an overall understanding of the nature of Ovidian poetics, for it shows how
to *referre aliter idem* ('say the same thing in different ways'),
and in so doing it may be seen imagistically to confront the
weight of Ovidian criticism of the last two centuries, which
has been in the tradition of the supposed censure: *nimium
amator ingeni sui* ('excessively in love with his own cleverness', Quint. *Inst.* 10. 1. 98).[3]

Self-referentiality is hard to resist: my chapter, like the
exemplum it examines, is 'excessively' long, and perhaps
labyrinthine. Perhaps an itinerary would be useful: I begin
by attempting to expose the expectations which reference to
this classic myth of artistry would arouse for an ancient
audience, and then broaden out this analysis of expectations
to link it on the one hand with other examples in Ovid of
the preoccupation with artists, and on the other hand with
common metaphors for artistry. The scene is then set for
examination of the specific story of Daedalus in Virgil and
Horace. These sections, including the not inconsiderable
space given to the readings of various critics, are crucial to
my discussion of the reception of Ovid's text, both 'then'
and 'now', in that they display the extent to which reading
takes place within the context of readings. After a brief
review (in Section 3*f*) of Daedalus' metaphoric power after
Ovid, the rest of the chapter deals in detail with the passage

---

[2] This passage is the first of many appearances by Daedalus in the Ovidian
corpus. In some sense, however, it is almost already a repetition from Book 1.
There (vv. 289–326), Ovid told the story of Pasiphae as a paradigm for the
extreme passion of women. Although Daedalus is not specifically mentioned in
connection with the deceit of the cow (vv. 325–6), his complicity is an established
part of the myth, which is, as Ovid says (v. 297), a well-known story. The
reference in our passage, at 2. 23, to Daedalus shutting away the Minotaur,
reminds us how he shut away Pasiphae in the wooden cow.

[3] Cf. Quint. *Inst.* 10. 1. 98 *Ouidi Medea uidetur mihi ostendere quantum ille uir
praestare potuerit si ingenio suo imperare quam indulgere maluisset*, Sen. *Con.* 2. 2.
12, on *Ars* 2. 24. The conventional interpretation finds what it seeks and reads
Seneca's comments as strictures. Gamel (1985) argues, however, that this is a
misrepresentation.

in *Ars Amatoria* 2, including its relation to the Daedalus story in the *Metamorphoses* (Sections 3*l* and 3*m*). The exilic appearances of Daedalus are introduced in Section 3*k* as indications of the poet's own re-reading of his earlier work. My analysis reads Daedalus and (differently) Icarus as metaphors for the artistic process, but slippery metaphors which cannot be tied down to one-to-one analogy.

The story of Daedalus and Icarus is the longest mythological interlude in the *Ars* (seventy-six lines illustrating a proem of twenty lines). The story's length and, at first sight, questionable relevance have contributed to leading some to believe that the longer myths are told by Ovid just for the fun of the telling, and have very little bearing on the work as a whole. Galinsky's comment (1975: 42) is among the most outspoken, and may stand for a highly influential strand in the tradition of criticism of the *Ars*: 'Other stories, especially that of Daedalus and Icarus (2. 21–98), illustrate that Ovid could still get carried away with telling a story without much regard for proportion and purposeful function.' (See also Myerowitz 1985: 152–3 and 218 n. 38.) Hollis (1973: 108) tends to this opinion in his defence of the Daedalus episode: 'We may think the Daedalus and Icarus episode . . . far-fetched—Minos could not confine Daedalus, so to control the winged love-god will prove even more difficult—but Ovid goes out of his way to make it plain.'[4] Such interpretations perhaps privilege the beginning and end of the exemplum, while passing over its main thrust, which is concerned with the creation of the wings, the flight, and the fall. Ovid is indeed a great story-teller, but we do an injustice to the poet and to the didactic tradition if we do not look more carefully at the function of all the mythological episodes in the *Ars*. With its implications of a hierarchy of textual elements, the term 'digression' itself suggests the criticism of self-indulgence and irrelevance. An 'interlude', it may seem, is a passage which may safely be excised from the text, and one which is out of proportion with the 'proper business' of the 'main text' is therefore a bad thing. One important point to note, however, is that

---

[4] The last statement refers to vv. 97–8, a couplet which under Hollis's interpretation is a weak apology for the digression—with which, at one level, I would agree.

since didactic poetry generically includes digressions, such digressions are therefore, by their very generic appropriateness, in some sense not digressive from the business of being a didactic poem. There is a respectable, if not unanimously accepted, tradition in classical scholarship of functional readings of mythic insets.[5] This is how people read, and how, I suggest, the *Ars* should be read.

In addition to its position in an important literary tradition, the passage is also foregrounded by its position as a hinge in this poem. As the second proem of the *Ars* it is tailor-made for reflection of and reflection on the poetry of Ovidian verse. It is at the beginning of this book, the middle book of the whole work. The middle of a work is a sensitive position in poetic structure, and that taken by the Daedalus story in Virgil. *Aeneid* 6, although not the exact centre, is the turning-point of the work: it is marked off as an interlude from the main narrative, for example by Aeneas leaving and rejoining his companions at start and finish, with little *obvious* difference or furtherment to the main thread. In the *Metamorphoses*, Daedalus also appears in the middle book.[6]

My hypothesis is that the story is told as a conscious comment on the nature of art, and primarily on the work of the poet within this poem. There are many faces to the metamorphic Daedalus' artistic and poetic suggestiveness. Just as Minos could not tie him down to the land of Crete, so the poets do not and the critic cannot restrict him to one simple metaphoric pattern. (The boundaries between complexity and confusion are, of course, nebulous!) I shall suggest that Daedalus is a metaphor for the poet in many ways. This is most simply expressed in his creation of hybrids, the man-bull and the bird-man, reflecting the hybrid nature of this new artistic endeavour, a fusion of didactic and elegiac poetry. But first a word about vocabu-

---

[5] See e.g. Fowler (1991) on the theory of integrated ekphrasis. Crabbe (1977) exposes the complex interconnections between the Aristaeus/Orpheus episode and Catullus 64, both in frame and in inset. After Virgil's Aristaeus, the didactic daedalic inset epyllion is necessarily dependent on Catullus 64, whose mythic and poetic nexus is paradigmatically daedalic.

[6] See Crabbe (1981) for an argument for the symmetrical centrality of Book 8 to the *Metamorphoses*. Daedalus and Icarus are treated at 2280–4.

lary. The passage is overdetermined with words which have poetic, rhetorical, and literary connotations. The use of such vocabulary foregrounds the discourse of poetics and provides supportive evidence for my argument that the issue of poetics is at stake here. The argument from vocabulary develops cumulatively. No one point or word is intended to be decisive, and indeed not all points carry equal weight, but they are offered as possible contributions to the overall hypothesis.[7]

Metaphorical and symbolic readings of this passage are not unknown. For McLaughlin, 'Minos is the type of the unsuccessful lover who expects to retain affections by sheer fiat, while Daedalus is that of the successful lover who realizes that love can only be retained by art and subtlety.' (McLaughlin 1975: 75. See also Canter 1933, Renz 1935.) Weber (1983: 121) makes a very similar suggestion. Both scholars see Daedalus as *magister* ('master'), *artifex* ('artist'), and *praeceptor* ('teacher'), particularly in relation to Icarus. Myerowitz (1985: 154–67) takes up the idea of Daedalus as the paradigmatic *artifex* ('artist'), and expounds the passage as a paradigm for 'the limits of art or the artist'. Her interpretation, while useful, is to some extent tailored to fit her scheme for the *Ars* as a serious opposition between *cultus* ('culture/sophistication') and *rusticitas* ('boorishness'). Ahern (1989: 291–5) also discusses the relationship between Daedalus and Ovid as poet, interpreting the story as an exemplum of the exhilaration of poetic composition and its resultant danger of 'enjoying escapism too much'. My interpretation does not seek to supplant these readings, or at least, not simply so, but rather to incorporate them in a tradition of response to the story and particularly the Ovidian story of Daedalus, which has regard to its significance for the representation of artistry.

3*a* Early History of the Myth

Narrative and pictorial artists throughout the history of Western civilization and most critics who have reflected on

[7] Cairns (1984*b*: 91) introduces his discussion of programmatic elements in Theocritus 1, with a similar claim.

the story of Daedalus have responded to his mythic significance as archetypal artist, and hence as paradigm for all
artists and for the place of art in the history of culture. Kris
and Kurz (1979: 66), in their enlightening study of the
image of the artist in sociological reception, show how
Daedalus and his divine double, Hephaestus, provide the
archetype for a recurrent motif in the anecdotal biography
and hence the social understanding of artists. Daedalus
made living, moving statues by a sort of artistic magic, so
like nature as to deceive the comprehension. The mythological situation becomes in history a metaphor: people mistake
the artist's representation for reality. They include (75–6)
the theme of the painter who seeks to restore life to or
memory of a dead child through his art, to make a substitute
by representation, as Daedalus attempts in Virgil's version
of the story.

Outside the Augustan poets, our main sources for the
story of Daedalus are the prose mythographers.[8] The earliest literary appearance of the myth is in Homer, at *Il.* 18. 590.
There Hephaestus' creation of the arms for Achilles is
compared with Daedalus' creation of the dancing floor for
Ariadne at Cnossos. A reference to the Icarian sea at *Il.* 2. 145
provokes a frustratingly interesting comment from the Scholiast: 'Philostephanus tells this story, as does Callimachus
in the *Aetia.*' The Callimachus passage in question could
be *Aet.* fr. 23. 3, which makes a very brief mention of the
Icarian sea, a potentially promising candidate since it provides prime *aition* material, or 43. 48–9, which mentions the
murder of Minos, but neither seems sufficient as it stands
to justify the Scholiast's comment. It is not unlikely, therefore, that a vital link in the Daedalus tradition has been
lost.[9] Philostephanus, a pupil of Callimachus, wrote geo-

[8] Diod. 4. 30. 1, 4. 76–79. 4; Arr. *An.* 7. 20. 5; Apoll. *Lib.* 3. 15. 8, *Ep.* 1. 12;
Hyg. *Fab.* 39–40; Paus. 1. 21. 4, 7. 4. 4; Plut. *Thes.* 15, 19; Strabo 14. 1. 19;
Lucian *Gall.* 23. For more on the myths see also Servius and Norden (1916) on
Virg. *Aen.* 6. 14–33; Bömer (1977) and Hollis (1970) on *Met.* 8. 183; *RE* 4. 1994–
2007; Knaak (1902); Rose (1928: 182).

[9] See Pfeiffer (1922: 116) for discussion of *Aet.* fr. 23. 3. *Supplementum
Hellenisticum* 287. 19 provides another connection with Daedalus, from a comment
in Schol. Vet. Aristoph. *Nub.* 508 p. 114 Holwerda, but the context of Hecale
bewailing her life is not likely to be the full story referred to by the Homeric
Scholiast.

graphical works interwoven with marvellous tales, a likely place indeed to find the Daedalus myth in some detail, perhaps from material provided by the master. Apart from such sketchy hints it appears that there was a wealth of drama, now lost, deriving from the myth. Frontisi-Ducroux (1975: 18), in a major study of the Daedalus myth, mentions plays by Sophocles, Aristophanes, Plato, Philippus, Eubulus, all called *Daidalos*, those by Antiphanes and Alexis called *Minos*, a *Pasiphae* of Alcaeus (Comicus), *Theseus* and *Cretans* by Euripides, *Camicians* by Sophocles, and *Cocalus* by Aristophanes, any of which are likely to have dealt with the myth to some extent.

But we may learn more about the background of our hero by considering his anthroponymous status than by catching at the straws of extant Greek versions. Frontisi-Ducroux traces the various possibilities in the multi-faceted words based on *daidalos* of which Daedalus is the anthroponym.[10] The term *daidalos* is attested as Mycenean (Frontisi-Ducroux, 25) and is apparently older than the hero. Frontisi-Ducroux's tables of the usages of *daidalos* etc.[11] in Homer and Hesiod aid our understanding of this difficult word (pp. 29–34). Of particular interest is the connection with Hephaestus. The word occurs seven times during the visit of Thetis to Hephaestus and the forging of the arms of Achilles in Hom. *Il.* 18, until finally the god is compared to Daedalus himself at 18. 590–2. This 'establishes a parallel between the art of Hephaestus and the competency of his mortal rival' (Frontisi-Ducroux, 38).[12]

As a brief summary of the possible range of meaning in *daidalos* I quote (in my translation) Frontisi-Ducroux's definition (p. 43): 'The shape of the domain of representa-

---

[10] See particularly Frontisi-Ducroux (1975: 35) for Daedalus' anthroponymous status. Becatti (1953–4) also sees Daedalus as archetypal artist, a symbolic figure showing the cultural and intellectual ambience of the beginnings of ancient art at Athens. His flight from the Labyrinth is expressive of geometric art and symbolizes the passage from the Minoan artistic world to the Greek.

[11] The adjectives *daidalos* and *daidaleos* both mean 'cunningly wrought'. A *daidalma* is a work of art; *ta daidala* are statues; *daidallō* means to work cunningly.

[12] The association of Hephaestus and Daedalus is treated also by Delcourt (1957), and again by Frontisi-Ducroux at p. 62. See also *RE* 4. 1335, Kris and Kurz (1979: 68).

tion to which the notion of *daidalon* pertains is becoming visible. A great number of artistic objects, of technical terms, the names of specific divinities, and of certain heroes with particular functional reference [that is, it applies to gods heroes who tend to do certain things, like Daedalus, Hephaestus, Athene, Odysseus], the vocabulary of light and of resemblance, that of ruse and illusion, such are the major indications of contexts in which *daidalon* appears.' She finds that the word is particularly applied to adornment, to the embossing of metal on wood, engraving, and weaving. On the shields of Achilles and Heracles it comes to mean the actual representations, the images of life (Frontisi-Ducroux, 74). The *Ars* passage too is a daedalic picture woven into the main thread of the book, or embossed on it as the precious adornment on the plain wood of didactic instruction. Daedalus, as myth and maker, as creator of artefacts and (in literature) created as artefact, is both signifier and signified in the discourse of art. Likewise both what he makes (the wings) and what he does (flies) are metaphors for the artistic process. Like Ovid's *Ars*, the word *daidalon* has seductive illusion. Frontisi-Ducroux, describing as daedalic deceptive illusions the shining fictions of poets, quotes Pindar (*Ol.* 1. 29): δεδαιδαλμένοι ψεύδεσι ποικίλοις ἐξαπατῶντες μῦθοι' ('cunningly wrought stories which seduce with intricate deceptions'). The *Ode* provides the first extant occurrence of a direct association between *daidalos* and poetry. At v. 105 Pindar uses the same vocabulary to express the poet as master craftsman.

κλυταῖσι δαιδαλωσέμεν ὕμνων πτυχαῖς.

I shall craft with glorious folds of song.

3*b* Ovidian Artists

In the ancient understanding of art there was a basic correlation between all forms of artistic production. Architecture, sculpture, painting, weaving, carpentry, and poetry were viewed in antiquity as different aspects of one creative process, and it is this omnipresence of the language and thought of art which makes Daedalus so poetically suggestive a character. (See Frontisi-Ducroux 1975: particularly 24–5, 56–7, and 61.) A philosophy of poetry which expressly emphasizes art and skill, as the Callimachean poets did, is particularly receptive to such considerations.

The particular position of artists in Ovid has been recognized for some time, especially in the *Metamorphoses*. There are as many dimensions to the metamorphic Daedalus of the *Metamorphoses* as there are to its creator: Daedalus' flight *creates* a new dimension to experience. As this again is a subject which has aroused authoritative resistance, it seems necessary to sketch out the position. Leach (1974) takes the story of Arachne as her main example, and argues that it is to some extent a paradigm of Ovid and the *Metamorphoses*. Lateiner (1984) takes it as a premise that certain stories about artists in the *Metamorphoses* were invented or elaborated by Ovid in order to illustrate the primacy of art and its 'spiritual' value. He makes a major contribution to our understanding of Ovidian art by his explanation that the artists change the whole nature of the original story, appropriately in the *Metamorphoses*, the poem of change. (Daedalus is treated on p. 17.) Wise (1977), concentrating on the stories of Phaethon and Daedalus, suggests that the artefact by which they fly is a metaphor for the artistic process, and that particularly in the case of Daedalus, who constructs his own flight vehicle, the creation of the wings mimes the mimetic aspect of artistic creation (53). The flights as literal transitions in geographic space dramatize the literary transitions from story to story within the poem (58). Wise also argues for a similarity between on the one hand the artistic process in which Phaethon and Daedalus are engaged, and on the other hand metamorphosis. One might add that the connection between artistry and metamorphosis is apparent for Daedalus on the more obvious level that while many characters in the poem are turned into birds by another's (usually a god's) agency, he succeeds in turning himself into a 'bird', so to speak, a particularly well-controlled metamorphosis in that the process is reversible.[13] The essential feature of this tale as a metamorphosis is that Daedalus is a bird-man, retaining his mind unchanged (like Apuleius' Donkey). It would be uninteresting if he *just* turned himself into a bird permanently; and it would be mere magic if he physically became bird-shape for a while. It should be remembered that the semantic range of *daidalos* includes metamorphosis.

Artists, then, we may say, are Ovidian. But how much more so when the book in which they appear is called the *Ars Amatoria*! It is an interesting fact about Book 2 that the words *amor* ('love'), together with its derivatives, and *ars* ('art') are the two most common cardinal words in the book. *Amor* occurs 28 times in some form, and *ars* 23 times, besides lots of synonyms for both words.[14] For *amor* this is hardly surprising, since the subject of instruction is love. But the frequency of *ars* and the centrality of the idea of art makes any reference to the word a reflection of the work as a whole. That is not to say that every time Ovid uses the word *ars* we could substitute *Ars Amatoria* and it would still make perfect sense; but rather that whenever Ovid uses the word he is reminding us that this is a work of Art. The poem is art, and is about art. Ovid is the craftsman imparting his art to his apprentices through the medium of art. Ovid loves the art of the synonym, the metonym, the synecdoche: this is his *amor artis* ('love of art').

3c Poetic Metaphors

Flight is a common metaphor for poetry.[15] We will see two excellent examples in Horace, in *Odes* 2. 20 and 4. 2. A simple extension of this metaphor sees the poet as a bird, or some other flying creature. Such must be something of the force of the common Homeric phrase ἔπεα πτερόεντα, winged words. Birds both fly and sing; poets both sing and fly. Perhaps the most famous exponent of this metaphorical family is Pindar.

[13] Crabbe (1981: 2281) brings out the metamorphic properties of Daedalus' and Icarus' flight in the *Metamorphoses*.

[14] The next most common is *puella* ('girl'), at 21 occurrences.

[15] For more on the flight metaphor see Bowra (1964: 9); and Nisbet and Hubbard (1978) on Hor. *Carm.* 2. 20; Becker (1937: 76); Lefkowitz (1969: 53–7); Ruck (1972: 167–8).

μαθόντες δὲ λάβροι
παγγλωσσίᾳ κόρακες ὣς ἄκραντα γαρύετον
Διὸς πρὸς ὄρνιχα θεῖον.   (*Ol.* 2. 86–8)

Mere learners babble, the pair of them,
and like crows chatter vainly against
God's holy bird.   (trans. C. M. Bowra)

ἔχω γονάτων ὁρμὰν ἐλαφράν.
καὶ πέραν πόντοιο πάλλοντ᾽ αἰετοί.   (*Nem.* 5. 20–1[16])

I have a light spring in my knees.
Eagles swoop even across the sea.   (trans. C. M. Bowra)

The idea is used also by Bacchylides (5. 16), Alcman (fr. 26), Theognis (237) where flight is used to describe the celebrity conferred by his poems, and by Pratinas (708. 5P). Euripides fr. 911 may also be using the idea, but the precise context is unknown.[17]

The twin ideas of flight as poetry and as fame feature in a celebrated example of the metaphor by Ennius.

nemo me lacrimis decoret nec funera fletu
faxit. cur? uolito uiuus per ora uirum   (fr. 125 Vahlen (1903))

Let no one honour me with tears nor perform my funeral with
   weeping.
Why? I fly living over the lips of men.

Virgil imitates Ennius in a sentence which is particulary significant for our passage. In the prologue to Book 3 of the *Georgics*, Virgil makes a rare authorial intrusion into the text, to consider his status as poet, his quest for originality, and his hope of fame. (*Georg.* 3. 8–9)

temptanda uia est, qua me quoque possim
tollere humo uictorque uirum uolitare per ora

A way is to be sought (attempted), by which I also may be able
to rise up from the earth and, as victor, fly over the lips of men.

Ovid/Daedalus echoes Virgil's vocabulary and his thought,

---

[16] Cf. also *Nem.* 3. 80–2.

[17] Stoneman (1976) argues against what he calls the 'standard doctrine that Pindar often describes himself as an eagle, and that Bacchylides "imitates" the notion in his fifth ode' (188), and argues that it is the *encomiand* who is the subject of the flight. Goldhill (1983), however, stresses that we should not reduce the complex imagery to any single association of the eagle with either encomiast or encomiand (69). The triangular relations of poet—patron/encomiast—exemplum/hero are important for our reading of myth-narratives.

when he considers the need for a new path, a new direction for his artistic creation: that is, flight for Daedalus, elegiac didactic for Ovid (*Ars* 2. 37).

> *restat iter caeli: caelo temptabimus ire.*[18]

> There remains the path of the sky: through the sky we will strive to go.

The two passages are further tied by the fact that each occurs in a prologue to a didactic book. Although it was Daedalus who made the attempt on the new path, it will turn out to be Icarus who achieves the Ennian and Virgilian posthumous fame.

But for our passage perhaps the most interesting example of the flight metaphor comes from Callimachus, *Aetia* fr. 1. 32:

> ἐγὼ δ' εἴην οὐλαχύς, ὁ πτερόεις.

> But I would be the little, the winged one.

This comes towards the end of the programmatic proem, the most influential passage of Greek literature for Augustan poetics. No longer an eagle, the poet wants to be the delicate winged one, the cicada—not much of a flier. Like Ovid's Daedalus, Callimachus flies, but avoids the heights.

The flight/bird metaphor itself is an extension of the even more common journey metaphor for poetry, whether it is by sea (ship) or by land (chariot) or, in the case of prose, on foot as in *sermo pedestris* ('pedestrian conversation' = prose). The chariot image especially has particular programmatic significance for the Augustans after its appearance in Call. *Aet.* fr. 1. 25–8. It is intimately connected with the motif of originality, when the poet claims to be undertaking a trail-breaking poetic journey. For example, and there are many, it was used by Virgil in the prologue to *Georgics* 3, mentioned above. (*Georg.* 3. 17–19)

> *illi uictor ego et Tyrio conspectus in ostro*
> *centum quadriiugos agitabo ad flumina currus.*

> For him, I, as victor, conspicuous in Tyrian purple,
> will drive a hundred four-horsed chariots beside the rivers.

---

[18] For *temptare* in poetic contexts see Hor. *Ep.* 2. 1. 258–9 *nec meus audet | rem temptare pudor quam uires ferre recusent*; *Ars* 222; Prop. 2. 3. 19 *Aeolio cum temptat carmina plectro*; Stat. *Theb.* 12. 816.

In the same tradition, the journey metaphor is *the* programmatic image in the *Ars*. Ovid embarks on the poem with a parallel between ship- and chariot-driving and the control of Amor (1. 3–4):

> *arte citae ueloque rates remoque mouentur,*
> *arte leues currus: arte regendus Amor*

Through art swift ships are moved by sail and oar;
through art, light chariots: through art Love is to be controlled.

This is echoed less overtly in the opening of the second book. The two exempla for the triumph of Ovid and/or the lover are Paris (ship) and Pelops (chariot) (2. 5–8):

> *talis ab armiferis Priameius hospes Amyclis*
> *candida cum rapta coniuge uela dedit;*
> *talis erat qui te curru uictore ferebat,*
> *uecta peregrinis Hippodamia rotis.*

Such was Priam's son, when, a guest, he spread his shining sails
from arms-bearing Amyclae, with the stolen bride.
Such was he who carried you in his victorious chariot,
Hippodamia borne on foreign wheels.

The poetic ship progresses as the lover and Ovid are engaged on a journey through the poem and the affair (cf. 2. 9–10). Because the poem (love poetry) and love are inextricably linked, an erotic ship has sailed alongside the poetic one, sometimes merging with it and sometimes distinct.[19] It is no accident, then, that Daedalus describes the wings metaphorically as ships in his instruction to his son. Or rather, he calls them 'keels', signifying ships by poetic metonymy. *Carina* ('keel'), in the conceit of the ship of poetry, has a parallel at the end of the *Remedia Amoris*, the

---

[19] Cf. *Sed non, cui dederas a litore carbasa, uento | utendum, medio cum potiere freto* (vv. 337–8), and *nam modo Threicio Borea, modo currimus Euro; | saepe tument Zephyro lintea, saepe Noto* (vv. 431–2). In this case the poem uses the image to effect a change of direction, from advising the lover to hide his infidelities to suggesting he publish them. But lovers can be compared with a ship tossed by different winds, usually signifying involvement in more than one simultaneous affair; cf. *Am.* 2. 10. 9–10 *erro, uelut uentis discordibus acta phaselos, | diuiduumque tenent alter et alter amor.* It is a poetic and erotic ship. Myerowitz's (1985) discussion of the progress image in the *Ars* comes to similar conclusions. See particularly pp. 82–5, 94–6, and her notes 20, 26, and 39 (pp. 208–9).

final resting place for the ship of the *Ars*.[20] Ovid uses Daedalus' poetic image to tie exemplum to *illustrandum* (*Rem.* 811).

> *hoc opus exegi: fessae date serta carinae!*

I have completed this work: give garlands to the exhausted ship!

Since the journey metaphor is a seminal signifier of the poem, the vocabulary of movement and journeys applied to Daedalus supports the suggestion that the story should be interpreted symbolically. Movement is the driving force of Daedalus' art.[21] When he teaches that art to Icarus it is in terms of movement (*monstratque moueri*: 'shows him how to move himself', v. 65). It is perhaps not surprising to find journey-words in a story about a journey, but the extent of such vocabulary is probably worth noting.[22] This mobility is opposed by a contrasting vocabulary of closure and enclosure, which represses or attempts to repress art. Minos *praestruxerat omnia* to his guest ('had put every obstacle in his way', v. 21); Icarus ceased to fly when he was enclosed by the sea and covered by the land.

> *clauserunt uirides ora loquentis aquae*   (v. 92)

The green waters closed his mouth as he spoke.

> *ossa tegit tellus, aequora nomen habent*   (v. 96)

Earth covers his bones, the seas have a [his] name.

---

[20] Cf. also Ov. *Tr.* 2. 469 *qua tot iere carinae* (referring to the poetry of Tibullus and Propertius), *OLD carina* 2b.

[21] For moving a song cf. Virg. *Aen.* 10. 163 *pandite nunc Helicona, deae, cantusque mouete*; Ov. *Am.* 3. 1. 6 *quod mea, quaerebam, Musa moueret, opus*; 37 *inparibus tamen es numeris dignata moueri*; *Met.* 10. 149 *carmina nostra moue.*

[22] Here is a list: *effugio* ('flight', 21), *uiam* ('way', 22), *modus exilio* ('an end to exile', 25), *agitatus* ('driven', 27), *reditum* ('return', 29), *egressus* ('way out', 32), *fugae* ('flight', 36), *iter* ('journey'), *ire* ('to go', 37), *adfecto* ('to make for', 39), *fugiam* ('I may flee'), *uia* ('way', 40), *iter* ('journey'), *transnabimus* ('we will swim through', 41), *mouent* ('they move'), *uias* ('ways', 44), *adeunda* ('to be approached', 51), *effugiendus* ('to be escaped', 52), *aera rumpe* ('break through the air', 54), *sectare* ('follow'), *praeuius ibo* ('I will go in front', 57), *sequi* ('to follow'), *me duce* ('under my leadership', 58), *ibimus* ('we will go', 60), *mobilis* ('mobile', 62), *uola* ('fly', 63), *uela . . . dato* ('set sail'; with *secunda*, in the hinted sense of 'following' (57–8), 64), *moueri* ('to be moved/ move oneself', 65), *iter* ('journey', 68), *uolaturus* ('about to fly', 69), *fugae* ('flight', 72), *mouet* ('moves', 73), *cursus* ('course', 74), *iter* ('journey', 75), *uolat* ('flies', 76), *iter* ('journey', 84), *quatit* ('flaps', 89), *decidit* ('falls', 91). Icarus' involvement in this vocabulary will be considered further in Section 3*j*.

The two obstructions, by Minos and by the natural world, frame the exemplum, enclosing its flight. In his apology to Jupiter for the hybris of flying, Daedalus explains that no other path is open to him.

> *nec tellus nostrae nec patet unda fugae*   (v. 36)
> Neither land nor wave lies open to our flight.

In doing so, he is using a Greek lyric motif of poetic programme where the poet speaks of many paths of song being open to him.[23]

> Ἔστι μοι θεῶν ἔκατι μυρία πάντᾳ κέλευθος.   (Pind. *Isth.* 4. 1)
> By grace of the gods
> I have an endless path
> On every side.   (trans. C. M. Bowra)

Bacchylides uses a similar image at 5. 31 (Campbell):

> τὼς νῦν καὶ ἐμοὶ μυρία πάντᾳ κέλευθος
>   ὑμετέραν ἀρετὰν
> ὑμνεῖν

> Even so for me now are there paths ten thousand every way
> to praise your prowess.   (trans. J. M. Edmonds)

This comes after the use of the metaphor of the eagle's flight for his poetry, and the claim that neither earth nor sea can stop the poet (Bacch. 5. 24–30, trans. Edmonds):

> οὔ νιν κορυφαὶ μεγάλας ἴσχουσι γαίας
>   οὐδ' ἁλὸς ἀκαμάτας
> δυσπαίπαλα κύματα. νωμᾶ-
>   ται δ' ἐν ἀτρύτῳ χάει
> λεπτότριχα σὺν ζεφύρου πνοι-
>   αῖσιν ἔθειραν ἀρίγνω-
> τος μετ' ἀνθρώποις ἰδεῖν.

> No stay to him [the eagle] are the summits of the great earth
> nor yet the steepy billows of the unwearied brine,
> but in a void unabating sped by a breeze from the west,
> plies he his glossy plumage conspicuous to the eye.

---

[23] See Becker (1937). I am grateful to Desmond Schmidt for pointing this out to me.

Ovid uses this motif of the open paths of song again in exile (*Pont.* 1. 1. 35):

> *fert liber Aeneaden, et non iter omne patebit?*

> A book carries a descendent of Aeneas [Augustus], and will not ry path be open?

The journey metaphor evolves its manifestation in flight by association with a related metaphorical group of terms for poetic style, that of orientation—up and down. It is abundantly clear that ancient literary theory used the metaphorical language of orientation to reflect on style. Pseudo-Longinus' treatise περὶ ὕψους (*On the Sublime*) is by its very name an indication of this, and throughout his work the critic uses terminology of elevation. For example (*On the Sublime* 36), sublime writers are said to rise above the human level and to be carried up to proximity to the mind of god—τὸ δ' ὕψος ἐγγὺς αἴρει μεγαλοφροσύνης θεοῦ ('the sublime raises one near to divine greatness of mind'). Horace makes explicit as literary critic what he has practised as poet: there is a risk for the poet (he is speaking specifically of the tragic persona) that *dum uitat humum, nubes et inania captet* ('while he is avoiding the earth, he may catch at clouds and void', *Ars* 230). Ovid himself clearly uses terms of rising to apply to epic poetry. In his inaugural poem the hexameter stands for epic: *cum bene surrexit uersu noua pagina primo* ('when a new page has risen up finely with the first verse', *Am.* 1. 1. 17), *sex mihi surgat opus numeris, in quinque residat* ('let my work rise up with six feet, and fall back with five', *Am.* 1. 1. 27).[24] Furthermore, *surgens* ('rising up, swelling up') is applied to the *Metamorphoses* at *Tr.* 2. 559. The term *humilis* ('humble, associated with the earth'), as used in our passage (v. 61), represents low stylistic level. The following constitute a selection of examples: Cic. *Orat.* 91 (describing the 'middle style') *uberius est aliud ... quam hoc humile ... summissius autem quam illud de quo iam dicetur amplissimum* ('the other is richer ... than this humble style ... but less elevated than that most full-blown style about which I shall speak

---

[24] The *opus*, as ever in Ovid, is sex as well as poetry. For an excellent discussion of the poetic and erotic connotations of Ovid's vocabulary see Kennedy (1993: 58–60).

now'); Virg. *Ecl.* 4. 1–2 *paulo maiora canamus!* | *non omnis arbusta iuuant humilesque myricae* ('Let us sing subjects which are a little greater! Shrubs and humble tamarisks do not please everyone'); Prop. 2. 10. 11 *surge, anima, ex humili; iam, carmina, sumite uires* ('rise up, my soul, from the ground; now, songs, take up your powers').[25] Since in our passage we are concerned with the question of how far to rise to find the level of didactic poetry, an example of the metaphor at the end of the *Eclogues* is of particular importance. Kennedy (1983) has rightly argued that '*surgamus* [*Ecl.* 10. 75] implies not only rising from the position characteristic of the pastoral singer . . . it also presages the poet's move from a genre avowedly humble . . . to something more elevated.'

In this apparently digressional discussion of metaphor, I have sought to elucidate the metaphorical resonances of the Daedalus story, by suggesting that just as it is difficult to 'govern' without metaphorically 'steering' (a ship), or to fly without sailing, or to be a poet and not fly, so it is difficult to fly and *not* be a poet.

3d Virgil, Virgilian Readers, and the Self-Representational Artist

I stressed at the beginning of this chapter that a reading of Daedalus in the *Ars* begs a reading of Daedalus in Virgil and Horace: it also requires a reading of readings of Daedalus, since these passages have thrown into relief a crucial question about reading.[26] I shall discuss contemporary responses to the Daedalus story in Virgil, not only for their contribution to my own reading of Virgil and therefore of Ovid, but also, and in some cases more importantly, with

[25] See also Porphyrion's comment on Hor. *Sat.* 1. 10. 6 (which contrasts mimes and fine poems) *humilis et in uerbis et in conceptionibus materia* ('humble material both in vocabulary and in ideas'); Serv. on *Ecl.* praef. 2. 1, on *Aen.* praef. 4. 9. Examples abound: see *TLL* 6. 3. 3108. 73.

[26] Of course it is possible to read the *Ars Amatoria* without ever even having heard of Virgil. It would be a very different reading, but it would still be a meaningful activity in some situations. When I say that Ovid cannot be read without a consideration of his predecessors, there is a level at which this is a rhetorical move which is not true.

an eye to *the way people read*, to the near-universal attraction towards symbolism which the Daedalus story provokes. Ancient intertextuality is crucial to our reading of Daedalus in the *Ars*: since the symbolism of Daedalus has cast so powerful a spell over Western culture, the modern intertextuality of Daedalian criticism must also be considered. Just as the symbolic Daedalus works differently, within the mythic framework, for different classical poets, so it does for different classical scholars.

The story of Daedalus occurs in the central book of *the* central literary monument in Roman culture.[27] Book 6 is the lynch-pin and turning point, the time for reflection on the nature of Aeneas' mission and on the *Aeneid*.[28] In considering the hinge position of *Aeneid* 6 and its Daedalus episode, the similar Janus-like function of *Ars* 2 and *its* Daedalus should be borne in mind.

In the middle of his *magnum opus*, Virgil writes a Hellenistic epyllion on the story of Daedalus (*Aen.* 6. 14–33):

> *Daedalus, ut fama est, fugiens Minoia regna*
> *praepetibus pennis ausus se credere caelo*   15
> *insuetum per iter gelidas enauit ad Arctos,*
> *Chalcidicaque leuis tandem super astitit arce.*
> *redditus his primum terris tibi, Phoebe, sacrauit*
> *remigium alarum posuitque immania templa.*
> *in foribus letum Androgeo; tum pendere poenas*   20
> *Cecropidae iussi (miserum!) septena quotannis*
> *corpora natorum; stat ductis sortibus urna.*
> *contra elata mari respondet Cnosia tellus:*
> *hic crudelis amor tauri suppostaque furto*
> *Pasiphae mixtumque genus prolesque biformis*   25
> *Minotaurus inest, Veneris monimenta nefandae,*
> *hic labor ille domus et inextricabilis error;*
> *magnum reginae sed enim miseratus amorem*

---

[27] I discuss Virgil before Horace, although the *Aeneid* was published after *Odes* 1–3, because within the hierarchy of genres the *Aeneid* takes precedence. Although it would be rash to make dogmatic statements about direct allusion between Horace and Virgil, it seems eminently likely that each was acquainted with the other's work prior to publication.

[28] Boyle (1972) also sees the book as thematically central, the turning point in Aeneas' psychology, as does Segal (1965: 644): 'It is important that this theme of flight should open the book which definitively shifts the fulcrum from Aeneas' past to his future and Rome's.'

Daedalus ipse dolos tecti ambagesque resoluit,
caeca regens filo uestigia. tu quoque magnam   30
partem opere in tanto, sineret dolor, Icare, haberes.
bis conatus erat casus effingere in auro,
bis patriae cecidere manus.

Daedalus, as the story goes, fleeing the kingdom of Minos,
daring to entrust himself to the sky on straight-flying wings,
swam to the chill North by a novel path
and at last lightly stood above the Euboean citadel.
Returning to land here first, he dedicated to you, Phoebus,
the oarage of his wings, and founded a huge temple.
On the doors, the death of Androgeos; then the people of Cecrops
ordered (for grief!) to pay the penalty with seven bodies
of their children every year; the urn stands there when the lots
   have been drawn.
On the opposite side corresponds the land of Crete, raised up
   from the sea:
here the cruel love of the bull and Pasiphae furtively mated
and the Minotaur, mixed species and two-formed child, is there,
a monument of unspeakable love.
Here is that famous task, the house and the ineluctable bind.
But pitying the great love of the royal woman,
Daedalus himself resolved the tricks and untied the twists of the
   building,
guiding blind footsteps with a thread. You also
would have had a great part in such a work, Icarus, if grief
   allowed.
Twice he tried to fashion the fall in gold;
twice the fatherly hands fell.

The passage is constructed as an epyllion in a number
of ways. Firstly, much of the narrative is presented
through the device of an ekphrasis, the most famous Latin
Hellenistic example of which is of course the story of
Theseus and Ariadne (a story belonging to the same
mythic cycle as Daedalus and Minos) inscribed on the
bedcover of Peleus and Thetis in Catullus 64. Secondly,
the compression of the narrative (particularly in *Aen.*
6. 20–30) is canonically Hellenistic. Lots of stories are told,
but many of them are only hinted at, in accordance with
the Hellenistic device of covert allusion. Instead, the
concentration is on feeling (*miserum!*, *crudelis amor*,

miseret, sineret dolor: ('for grief!', 'cruel love', 'pitied', 'if grief allowed'), and on pathological eros. The fall of Icarus is alluded to by the briefest mention and one which is potentially ambiguous—*casus*—but is covertly signified by the *fall* of Daedalus' hands.

It might be worth noting that Virgil's Daedalus is *leuis* ('light')—that most blatantly programmatic signifier of Callimachean poetics. This Callimachean epyllion, then, is in direct opposition to the great work which frames it. But oppositions are about similarities as well as differences, and the Daedalus episode acts as a kind of mirror image for the *Aeneid*. The huge temple (*immania templa*) which Daedalus builds is a metaphor for the *Aeneid*. Virgil has previously used the metaphor for epic poetry of engraving on temple doors (*Georg.* 3. 26–7):

> *in foribus pugnam ex auro solidoque elephanto*
> *Gangaridum faciam uictorisque arma Quirini*

> On the doors I shall make the battle of the Ganges,
> from gold and solid ivory, and the arms of victorious Quirinus.

Here the decoration of a story on to temple doors quite openly stands metaphorically for the writing of epic or at least encomiastic poetry.[29] That image belongs to the proem to the third *Georgic*, which we have already seen to be important for Ovid's Daedalus through the conceits of the flight (and to a lesser extent the chariot-journey) for poetry and poetic fame. Along with both the *Georgics* passage and the ekphrasis of Book 6, we should remember the first ekphrasis of the *Aeneid*, the pictures on the doors of Dido's temple of Juno in Book 1 (456–93). Apollo's temple is the echo and opposite of Juno's, for there the 'poem' engraved on the doors was martial epic, a 'little' (?) *Iliad*.[30] As the artist of the ekphrasis, that is the pictures on the doors of the temple of Apollo through which Aeneas will achieve his *katabasis* (his journey to the Underworld, as described in

---

[29] Wilkinson (1969: 68) points out that Virgil is here following the Pindaric treatment of architecture as a metaphor for poetry (*Ol.* 6. 1, *Pyth.* 3. 113, 6. 5, *Nem.* 1. 8). Thomas (1983) demonstrates that the metaphor was mediated through Callimachus.

[30] Here I would refer the reader to the discussion of poetic 'size' in the opening sections of Ch. 4.

Aeneid 6), Daedalus acts symbolically for Virgil himself.[31]
The artistry of the doors acts as a metaphor for the whole
work, and especially for the particular artistry of this strange
central book. The engraving (or embossing: *effingere in
auro* (v. 32) is ambiguous) on the doors is daedalic, Daedalus'
action reflecting his anthroponym, which in turn reflects
Virgil's own poetic action. Virgil tells an engraved story
within the story of the life of Daedalus, and Book 6 itself is
also an adornment, an embellishment, philosophical and
ideological gold on the plain wood of the martial epic.

It is interesting in all the mutually reinforcing and cumulatively amplificatory interpretations, which I shall discuss
shortly, that both what Daedalus is himself, and what he
creates, are paradigms for Aeneas and for the book. The
character seems inherently to lend itself to a partial or total
overlap, and a potential, latent, or actualized identification
between what he is and what he does. This overlap figures
in a series of ambiguities in the line of Virgil's narrative
thread in the episode. We slip almost imperceptibly from
an account of the pictures seen by Aeneas to the story of
Daedalus himself, and back to the gaping Aeneas interrupted by the Sibyl.[32] The door-pictures can be read as a
commentary on both Book 6 and the entire work. The
artificer Daedalus representing his own life is both commentator and commentary on the life of Aeneas, the *Aeneid*.
Likewise Ovid's Daedalus is a commentary on one of the
main characters of the poem, the narrator, the teacher, the
poet, Ovid; as Virgil's Daedalus represents Virgil as commentator on the *Aeneid*. The metaphorical and analogical
richness of Daedalus evolves precisely from his mythic
status, and his paradigmatic status within the corpus of
myth, as the classic paradigm of the mythic artist, art(ist) as
myth, myth as art(istry). The gaps between signified, signifier, signification, significance are fudged, even partially

[31] Ekphrasis—adornment, embossing—connects with the daedalic character.
For Virgilian ekphrasis and particularly the contribution of Daedalus see DuBois
(1982: 35–40).

[32] Commenting on *miserum* (v. 21), Putnam (1987: 178) says that 'for one
verbal moment, even in the most "detailed" segment of Daedalus' tale, narrator,
characters, and audience are united in empathy'. Boyle (1972: 117) makes a
similar point.

fused in the anthroponym, allowing the artist to act as
embosser and embossed, commentator and commentary,
signifier and signified, poet and poetry. Myth is an art-
form; Daedalus both makes and is an art-form. As in our
passage, Daedalus is both creator and created, and as there
we see both the making of the wings and the finished
product of the flight, so too in Virgil's story the clear
distinctions between poet and production are broken
down.[33] The force of a master-representer's self-representation within the impersonal genre of epic representation is
irresistible when the all-powerful artist's hand fails to *objec-
tify* what is *subjectively* most important, his dead son, the
obliteration of his future identity guaranteed by the continuation of his *gens* ('family'). The dichotomy of objective/
subjective collapses in self-representation.[34]

Turning to Virgilian readers: Virgilian Daedalus is read
by Putnam (1987) as 'a metaphor for the progress of any
artist'. He suggests that as Daedalus cannot finish his great
work—the image of Icarus—so Virgil leaves *his* great work
generically 'unfinished', which is, in a sense, a way of being
finished. An analogous relationship between Daedalus and
Virgil has also been suggested, albeit tangentially to his
main thesis, by Segal (1965: 644). 'In this failure of Daedalus, this futility of the artist to convey what is closest to
him, there is perhaps an intimation of the final gesture of
Virgil himself, wishing on his deathbed to negate his own
artistic creation.'

More common in recent criticism, however, is analogy
between Daedalus and Aeneas—and thereby the *Aeneid*.
Boyle deals in depth with the symbolism and parallelism
between Daedalus and Aeneas, and believes that 'the specifi-
city and precision [of the parallels] render a non-functional
approach to the Daedalus reliefs untenable'. (Boyle 1972:

---

[33] Cf. Fitzgerald (1984: 55–6): 'The labyrinth is to the cruel monstrosity
pictured on the doors what the doors themselves are to Daedalus' past, for the
temple frieze *is* a labyrinth, whose pattern and balanced symmetry baffle the eye
that would trace a narrative line through its contents . . . The apostrophe to Icarus
. . . both continues the story of Daedalus *and* tells us about the production of the
work on which it is represented; frame and content can no longer be
distinguished.'

[34] Cf. Fitzgerald (1984: 53): 'here, possibly for the first time in ancient
literature, an artistic work is described in which the artist represents his own
story.'

118.)[35] A similar view was voiced by Anderson (1969*a*: 55–6), who speaks of 'several tantalizing details which encourage one to pursue the search for relevance'.[36] No one would deny the lack of *obvious* connection between the episode and the narrative it apparently interrupts. As Fitzgerald says (1984: 53), in a comment which could well be applied to our passage: 'Indeed, the lack of *direct* connection between the digression and the main narrative seems to allow one to work as a prism on the other.' Other scholars have seen connections between Daedalus and Aeneas. Jackson-Knight (1929: 212–13) investigated the significance of the labyrinth as a religious symbol in the *Aeneid*. For Pöschl (1962: 150), the relationship between Daedalus and Icarus reflects that between Aeneas and Anchises. Segal (1965: 642–5) sees both Daedalus and his creation as a reflection of Aeneas' past life, particularly his personal life, and as an aid to his break with the past. The failure of art is intimately connected with the Daedalus myth. In most versions it is to some extent embodied in the fall of Icarus, but for Virgil it is very much the failure of Daedalus, the fall of his hands, which cannot for grief make the representation of the Fall of Icarus. Rutledge (1967: 311) sees Virgil's Daedalus as the type of the creative man, 'a recurrent figure, or motif, on various levels of significance, throughout Virgil's poetry', and hence as a reflection of Aeneas, in creation and in loss.[37]

---

[35] Boyle (1972: 116) maintains that 'it seems reasonably certain that one of their (i.e. the pictures) functions (but by no means the only one) is to represent symbolically Aeneas' recent past and, in the case of the final panel, his imminent future.'

[36] Exile, devotion to Apollo, the labyrinth, which is significant for Aeneas both as a 'spiritual labyrinth' where he fights his own 'psychological monsters', and as a reflection of his wanderings since Troy and of the approaching trip to the Underworld.

[37] For Boyle (1972: 118), the theme of loss and failure 'portends the prospective failure of Aeneas'. Daedalus attempts to compensate for his son's death by immortalizing him in gold. According to Boyle, the failure for Aeneas is his loss of Pallas and of his *humanitas* in his murder of Turnus—because empire does not make up for human loss. Both failures are linked with gold; the gold which should have been fashioned into the story of Icarus on the doors, and the gold studs on the belt of Pallas (10. 499) which 'blind Aeneas to all thoughts of *humanitas* and pity' (119); the substance which is so intimately connected with the representational art of Daedalus—embossing, particularly when deceptive. This oversimplifies the complexity of the *Aeneid*'s philosophy: Aeneas' empire is worth something, as is Daedalus'/Icarus' fame.

The narration of Daedalus' creation of the doors, where Daedalus is both narrator and story, acts as a reflection on the *Aeneid*. Fitzgerald (1984: 54) says: 'In the first part the frieze is described as a finished work of art, but in the second it becomes the narrative of Daedalus, unfrozen and released into history. It is no coincidence that the narrative thread picks up at the very point where Daedalus provides Ariadne with the thread that solves the puzzle that he himself has constructed, for the central theme of this ekphrasis is Daedalus' relation to his own constructs, and more particularly those that involve his own relation with the past.' The episode thus reflects the twofold nature of the *Aeneid*, the severance of past and future undergone by book and hero. Moreover, the ekphrasis' commentary extends specifically to the very climax of the work. 'When Aeneas emerges from the labyrinth of his pursuit of Turnus, his final defeat of his enemy can no more be accommodated into the projected structure of preparation and fulfillment than can Icarus' death be contained on Daedalus' memorial.' (Fitzgerald 1984: 61.)

There has been resistance to symbolic reading. Prescott (1927: 266) sees essentially no function in the episode. The argument has been continued more recently by Kinsey (1986), who maintains that there is no symbolism in the pictures, and states that the only purposes of the passage are 'scene-setting by giving a foundation story and at the same time describing a work of art, two things he is fond of doing', and to typify Aeneas' career so far in that he is only interested in the stories, in his own and his country's misfortunes, not much with the end product (Rome), and has to be distracted by the Sibyl. It is not my business to decide which of these many readings is 'right', but rather to present something of the field of response to Virgil's Daedalus.

As I have sought to stress in this section, Ovid necessarily writes within the intellectual forcefield of Virgil's great monument, just as reading Ovid (and Virgil) necessarily occurs within the intellectual forcefield of other readings. Ovid's awareness of this intertextuality is shown by a number of echoes of Virgil's Daedalus in the *Ars*. Firstly, the Virgilian Daedalus *dares* to fly (*Aen.* 6. 15):

> *ausus se credere caelo*
>
> daring to trust himself to the sky

Likewise, the Ovidian Daedalus finds a *daring* path through the skies (*Ars* 2. 21):

> *audacem pinnis repperit ille uiam*
>
> He discovered a daring path on wings.

In each case, the *novelty* of the undertaking is stressed:

> *insuetum per iter*   (*Aen.* 6. 16)
>
> by a novel path

sunt mihi naturae iura nouanda meae   (*Ars* 2. 42)

the laws of my nature are to be made new for/by me[38]

> *nouae . . . artis*   (*Ars* 2. 48)
>
> of the new art

> *nouum . . . iter*   (*Ars* 2. 75)
>
> the new journey

I shall later deal in more detail with the related themes of novelty and daring. But perhaps the closest link between the two passages is in the metaphor of oars to signify the wings.

> *tibi, Phoebe, sacrauit*
> *remigium alarum*   (*Aen.* 6. 19)
>
> he dedicated to you, Phoebus, the oarage of his wings.[39]

> *remigium uolucrum*   (*Ars* 2. 45)
>
> oarage of birds

Again, this will be discussed further later. At the moment, the main point I wish to establish is the inevitable connection between the Daedaluses of Virgil and of Ovid.

---

[38] Depending on whether you take *mihi* to be dative of the agent or of advantage. Ovid was not of course bound or indeed able to choose between them.

[39] See Putnam (1987: 176 n. 4) on this line .

3*e* Daedalian Horace

In Horace, Daedalus appears in three very difficult passages, all connected with poetry: *Odes* 1. 3, 2. 20, and 4. 2.
Some of the problems of these poems are explained by a
consistent reading of the nature of Icarus, for 2. 20 and 4. 2
both see Icarus as a metaphor for the dangers of poetic
production and the resulting glory considered in the framework of Callimachean art. Neither Horace nor the Daedalus
story can, of course, be forced into one simple model of the
philosophy of art. I repeat that it is important for our
understanding of Ovidian intertextuality to examine in some
detail the story of Daedalus in the poet laureates who were
Ovid's older contemporaries, the modern readings of the
story, and the resistance to those readings, for there have
been strong comments on both sides of the argument.

Odes 1. 3

After the opening addresses to Maecenas and Augustus, the
third poem of Horace's *Odes* is addressed to the greatest
contemporary poet. *Odes* 1. 3 is a propemptikon to the ship
of Virgil. According to Donatus (*Vit. Virg.* 35), Virgil made,
towards the end of his life, a journey to Greece to research
for the *Aeneid*, but it cannot be this journey to which the
Ode refers, because of the relative chronology. Virgil may
well have made some earlier trip, or the journey may be
metaphorical. Whichever is the case, the conceit of the ship
of poetry is so well established that I submit that any
poetically-minded contemporary would be unable to consider a real-life journey of Virgil without also thinking of
the poem's composition.[40] Despite this, however, many
modern scholars have resisted reading any symbolism into
Virgil's voyage.[41] The main objection to the poetic interpre-

---

[40] Lefkowitz (1981) demonstrates that the ancient biographies can be considered to set out readings of the poems in metaphorical narrations of the poet's
circumstances of composing. For arguments in favour of the poetic interpretation
see Lockyer (1967: 42), Cairns (1972: 235), and Basto (1982).

[41] Nisbet and Hubbard (1970) do not mention the possibility; nor does Syndikus (1972), although he deals in some detail (64–5) with the theme of hybris; nor
Quinn (1980), who reads this as a case of 'one poet showing another what he can

tation of 1. 3 is based on the apprehension that Horace is hardly unequivocal in his praise of the venture. Generic considerations can aid us here, however, for, true to the topoi of the genre 'propemptikon' (see Cairns 1972: 8, 120–4, and on this poem 55, 231–5, 280), Horace complains at the folly and madness that takes his friend away on his dangerous voyage. Daedalus provides an example of the folly of attempts to transgress the bounds of man's nature. The invention of *sailing* (the subject of the poem) at the end of the Golden Age was another such ambiguous transgression.

> *expertus uacuum Daedalus aera*
> *pennis non homini datis* (*Carm.* 1. 3. 34–5)

> Daedalus made trial of the empty air on wings
> not given to man.

Daedalus is coupled here with Prometheus and Hercules.

> *audax Iapeti genus*
> *ignem fraude mala gentibus intulit.* (vv. 27–8)

> The daring offspring of Iapetus brought fire to the nations
> by a wicked trick.

> *perrupit Acheronta Herculeus labor.* (v. 36)

> The labour of Hercules broke through Acheron.

Nisbet and Hubbard (1970) comment on the Daedalus line, '[n]o doubt criticism of Daedalus was conventional in the diatribe.' This poem is, however, primarily and essentially a (propemptic) lyric, in the tradition of the lyric, particularly the encomiastic lyric of Pindaric and Bacchylidean epinicia, where *tolma*, heroic pioneering, Herculean enterprise, Argonautic and Promethean invention which push back the boundaries of civilization and humanity are standard themes, the very themes being used by Horace. The whole interpretation turns on the nature of ancient encomium, and the ancient understanding of the ambiguity of progress. Horace reminds us (vv. 29–33) that Prometheus' theft of fire brought about the end of the Golden Age, but we cannot forget that it also brought the beginning of civilization. The ambiguous status of Prometheus as transgressor and benefac-

do by grafting a mock-solemn diatribe against the wrongness of progress . . . onto a propemptikon'.

tor, sinner and hero, is essential to an understanding of the ancient construction of heroes. There is no heroism without excess. In the discourse of lyric encomium, praise of a hero can be achieved by hints at the risk of hybris which the hero runs because of his greatness. For this, we must remember that hybris does not equate with our 'pride' but can signify excess in many forms. Heroes are ambiguous. They may reach that status through suffering (Hercules) or transgression (Prometheus, and possibly also Hercules). So if an encomiast says to the encomiand 'you are transgressing the boundaries of man', he is not or not only saying 'you are a sinner' but 'you are great'. Even to say 'I don't want to be like you, because it is dangerous' is a way of saying 'you are great'. This kind of praising is one which is precisely designed to offset the risks of hybris. If the encomiast 'overshoots the mark' in his praise, then he may attract damaging envy (*phthonos*) towards the encomiand. But the very mention of *phthonos* is itself a form of praise, for fame comes through *phthonos* (*inuidia*). There is no greatness without envy.[42] I suggest that *Odes* 1. 3 should be seen in this tradition of veiled encomium, veiled, that is, but still apparent. This great undertaking is beyond the normal bounds of mankind; it is very dangerous; by implication only the very brave and very skilled could hope to undertake it successfully. It is leaving the accepted safe shallows of Augustan Callimachean poetics for the high seas of epic. A Herculean labour.

The *Ode* ends with a reflection on the crime of climbing the heavens, which Nisbet and Hubbard (1970) rightly interpret as a reference to Gigantomachy. The attack by the giants was the ultimate example of hybris, and as such is a natural metaphoric cousin to the Daedalus story. Now, the attack of the giants on the gods was unambiguously sinful, and becomes a symbol for hybristic presumption by man-

---

[42] Cf. e.g. the picture of *Inuidia* fearing the tortures of hell in Virg. *Georg.* 3. 37–8, in response to both the military success of Augustus and the poetic success of Virgil; *Ecl.* 7. 26; Prop. 3. 1. 21 *at mihi quod uiuo detraxerit inuida turba,* | *post obitum duplici faenore reddet Honos*; Hor. *Carm.* 4. 3. 16. The motif is Pindaric, as at fr. 94a Snell παντὶ δ' ἔπι φθόνος ἀνδρὶ κεῖται | ἀρετᾶς, *Nem.* 8. 20–3; *Isth.* 2. 43; and Callimachean, as in the βασκανίη of the *Aetia* prologue and *Ep.* 21, *Hymn* 2. 105. See also Wilkinson (1969: 170–1).

kind. When it becomes a symbol, however, ambiguities enter the picture. Progress, the attempt to push back the boundaries of human civilization; transgression, which attempts to burst the boundaries of human nature and the condition of man: these are two-sided coins, acts of ambivalent moral value. 'Seeking the stars' is both sinful presumption and also deification through virtue—*per ardua ad astra*. Virgil uses the motif in encomium of Augustus (*Georg.* 4. 562):

> *Caesar . . . uiam . . . adfectat Olympo.*
>
> Caesar seeks a way to heaven.

With this passage at the end of *Odes* 1. 3 we should compare a very similar one at the end of the very first *Ode* (*Carm.* 1. 1. 35–6):

> *quodsi me lyricis uatibus inseres,*
> *sublimi feriam sidera uertice*
>
> If you will insert me among the lyric bards
> I shall strike the stars with my lofty head.[43]

The parallel is surely a significant contribution to the case for the poetic reading of *Odes* 1. 3.

Moreover, Gigantomachy is the theme which above all others epitomizes martial epic, which is the most daring of literary exploits and exactly that attempted by Virgil. Gigantomachy epitomizes the ultimate in poetic audacity, the most quintessentially epic of epics, the polar opposite of Callimacheanism.[44] Since the theme of Gigantomachy will play a part in my argument, it seems worth while to rehearse its programmatic significance here.

Gigantomachy, embracing both battles and gods (see Innes 1979: 195), provides an exact opposite for the slender

[43] See Nisbet and Hubbard (1970) ad loc. for parallels for this proverbial expression. In his epilogue to the *Metamorphoses*, Ovid uses a similar image to prophesy that his epic will win him immortality in demi-god status: *parte tamen meliore mei super alta perennis | astra ferar* (15. 875–6).

[44] I am particularly indebted to Stephen Hinds here. See Wimmel (1960: 31), commenting esp. on Propertius 2. 1; Nisbet and Hubbard (1978) introduction to Hor. *Carm.* 2. 12 and note on v. 7; Innes (1979); Hinds (1987: 129–32, 165 n. 30); Hardie (1986: 85). For the subject in general see also Hom. *Od.* 7. 59, 206; Hes. *Theog.* 185, 617–735 (with West 1966); Apoll. *Lib.* 1. 6. 1; Fontenrose (1959: 239–41), Vian (1952), Hardie (1986: 85–156).

Muse of the Alexandrian. Gigantomachy was already paradigmatic for hackneyed themes in literary polemic in Xenophanes 1. 19–21 West. This was picked up by Callimachus
(see Innes 1979: 166, Wimmel 1960: 31), who refers to it in
his programmatic prologue to the *Aetia* (fr. 1. 20):

> βροντᾶν οὐκ ἐμόν, ἀλλὰ Διός
>
> It is not mine to thunder, but Zeus'.

It is with this background that the theme becomes a motif
of Augustan–Callimachean programmatic refusal to write a
certain sort of poetry, which we call a *recusatio* (see Hardie
1986: 86), as epitomizing what Innes calls 'the most extreme
example of the "thundering" style opposed to that of the
slender elegance of Callimachus' (166) and Hinds 'the very
sternest kind of martial epic that there is' (129).[45] The
opening poem of Propertius' second book makes most explicit the opposition between Gigantomachy and Callimacheanism (Prop. 2. 1. 39–40).

> sed neque Phlegraeos Iouis Enceladique tumultus
> intonet angusto pectore Callimachus.

And Callimachus with his narrow breast would not thunder
the Phlegraean battle of Jove and Enceladus.

In this and in many other occurrences of the theme, there
may be implied encomium in the *recusatio*. At Prop. 3. 9. 47–
8 the motif performs a similar function; again contributes
to a standard *recusatio* at Hor. *Carm.* 2. 12. 7; and is encomiastic at 3. 4. 42. (See Hardie 1986: 87.) Ovid's contribution to
the motif goes so far as to suggest that he had actually
written such a Gigantomachy (*Am.* 2. 1. 11–12):[46]

> ausus eram, memini, caelestia dicere bella
> centimanumque Gyen (*et satis oris erat*).

[45] Hinds is discussing the song contest reported by Calliope in *Met.* 5. 300. His
comment could perhaps also be applied to our passage. 'The fact is that to any
reader with an ounce of Callimacheanism in his make-up this theme more than
any other stands for the sort of unacceptable pomposity repudiated in the *Aetia*
prologue' (129).

[46] Owen (1924) on *Tr.* 2, p. 63 believes that Ovid did actually begin, but not
finish, such a poem, but this view is not generally accepted, although the theme
does get a treatment, albeit highly Callimachean, at *Met.* 1. 151–62. For arguments
against, Reitzenstein (1931) and Innes (1979: 167).

I had dared, I remember, to speak of heavenly wars
and hundred-handed Gyges (and I had enough voice).

This is a programme for a book of elegies, where Gigantomachy cannot aid the lover (*Am.* 2. 1. 17–22).

> *clausit amica fores: ego cum Ioue fulmen omisi;*
> *excidit ingenio Iuppiter ipse meo.*
> *Iuppiter ignoscas: nil me tua tela iuuabant;*
> *clausa tuo maius ianua fulmen habet.*
> *blanditias elegosque leuis, mea tela, resumpsi:*
> *mollierunt duras lenia uerba fores*

My girlfriend shut the door: I dropped the bolt along with Jove:
Jupiter himself fell out of my mind.
Forgive me, Jupiter, your weapons did not help me at all;
a closed door has a bigger bolt than yours.
I took up again blandishments and light elegies, my weapons:
smooth words have softened hard doors.

Here we see the equation between the writing of Gigantomachy and the battle itself which I shall suggest for the
Ovidian Daedalus.[47] Clearly, here Gigantomachy is being
programmatically opposed to elegy.

Since Gigantomachy signifies martial epic, the parallels
between Horace's diatribe and Virgil's great work are quite
precise. Horace celebrates Virgil's poetic achievement by
reminding the reader of the artistic risks which such an
endeavour entails. If, as has been suggested, Virgil is to be
identified with Daedalus in *Aeneid* 6, it is possible that
Horace recognizes the identification and pays tribute to it.
The *Aeneid* was a flight of poetry never before encountered
by man. Virgil achieves hero status through his exploit.

Odes 2. 20

Before studying the function of Icarus in *Odes* 2. 20, we
must first note the prominent position of the poem in
relation to our passage. *Odes* 1–3 constitute an important
structural predecessor to the *Ars*, as a major example, along
with the *Amores*, of a work in three simultaneously published but developing books, assuming the 'second editions'

---

[47] Cf. also *Met.* 10. 150, *Tr.* 2. 333–8; Manil. 3. 5; Sen. *Ag.* 332; *Culex* 27.

of the Ovidian works.[48] *Odes* 2. 20 closes the central book; *Ars* 2. 21–98, as an illustration, supposedly, of the prologue, opens Ovid's. But 2. 20 also heralds *Odes* 3, signalling Horace's metamorphosis into the Pindaric *uates* ('bard') of the *Roman Odes*. It looks both ways, being the geographical equivalent of the temporally-inflected *Odes* 3. 30, where the future of the œuvre is linked with that of Rome. In each case, *Roma Aeterna* ('Eternal Rome') is *imperium sine fine* ('rule without end').[49]

Odes 2. 20, particularly the third strophe, has aroused a great deal of scholarly argument as to its seriousness and good taste.[50] I argue that it is both humorous *and* a serious poetic statement. The bizarre metamorphosis of poet into bird, even down to the feathers sprouting from the man's limbs, humorously offsets the hybris actually or potentially incurred by the extravagance of the poem's claims.[51] The poem is perhaps the most brilliant and developed example of the conceit of flight as a metaphor for poetry.[52] Horace prophesies that he will become a *biformis . . . uates* ('two-formed bard') and rise above the world, envy, and death. Even now he is turning into a bird. More famous even than Icarus, he will fly over the whole world, and the whole world will know him. Because of his fame, he will not truly die, so there should be no mourning at his funeral. Horace

---

[48] Porter (1987) sees the structure of *Odes* 1–3 as constituting a series of rises and falls, climaxing in 2. 20 and the *Roman Odes* to fall back at 3. 7 and climax again, without the excess, at 3. 30. On 2. 20 he says that 'its very image of Icarian flight provides an important clue to the overall shape of the collection. That shape . . . is one that alternates between flying low and flying high . . . the whole collection might . . . be seen as Horace's quest for the *aurea mediocritas*' (220). In this interpretation 1. 3. 34 and 2. 20. 13 represent the two extremes. What he does not consider, however, is the possibility of a positive value to be ascribed to excess, and that Horace says nothing about Daedalus' low-flying caution in 1. 3: he is concerned only with innovation.

[49] It is also the fitting conclusion to the book opened and presided over by Pollio, historian of the collapse of Rome in civil war. Geography is a metaphor for history: the ends of the earth will one day become provinces, just as Gaul and Spain have.

[50] Armstrong (1964: 124–5), Johnson (1966: 272–5), Kidd (1971: 5–16), Pascal (1980: 98–9), Porter (1975: 202–3), Silk (1956: 255–63), D. J. Stewart (1967: 357–61), Syndikus (1972: 480–9), Tatum (1973: 4–25), G. Williams (1968: 570–4).

[51] The studies of Silk and D. J. Stewart suggest that the idea of a poet turning into a bird is not so unprecedented as is generally believed.

[52] On which see Section 3c.

is transformed into a bird, a poet in flight. The metamorphosis has distressed some modern scholars,[53] but the metaphoric possibilities of the poem can be further developed by turning the flying poet into a book.[54] *Pellis* ('skin') can mean 'parchment'.[55] The *pellis* in this case is *aspera* ('rough'): we may remember that Catullus says his book (the physical book as well as the poetry) has been *expolitum* ('polished', 1. 2). The *leues ... plumae* ('light feathers') might conceivably be pens. The image is bizarre, but so is the poem! Through this brilliant three-way imagery the relatively obvious flight metaphor becomes the basis for a subtle equation of the poet and his work, describing himself turning into a book, or himself and his poetry as the same thing, a book-man-bird. The metamorphosis is particularly appropriate for a poet connecting himself with the Daedalus myth, since metamorphosis is one aspect of the myth's anthroponym. The adjective *daedala* is used of Circe, who metamorphoses the sailors into animals, by Virgil (*Aen.* 7. 282); the metamorphic significance of the transformation of raw materials into works of art lurks always within the anthroponym. (See also Frontisi-Ducroux 1975: 62.)

The connection with Daedalus comes in v. 13 (*Carm.* 2. 20. 13–16):

> *iam Daedaleo notior Icaro*
> *uisam gementis litora Bosphori*
> *   Syrtisque Gaetulas canorus*
> *   ales Hyperboreasque campos.*

> Now, more famous than Daedalean Icarus
> I shall see the shores of groaning Bosphorus
> and the African sands
> and the far-northern fields
> as a tuneful bird.

Discussion of v. 13 is problematized by the textual difficulty, but my reading can admit any of the variants since it is the

---

[53] For example, Fraenkel (1957: 301) describes the detail of the metamorphosis as 'repulsive or ridiculous, or both'.

[54] This idea derives from an original insight of A. G. Lee's, developed by J. R. G. Wright and J. G. W. Henderson, and communicated to me by John Henderson.

[55] Cf. Mart. 14. 184. 2, 14. 190. 1.

comparison with Icarus which is important. I personally favour *notior*, with Nisbet and Hubbard (1978), Quinn (1980), and Syndikus (1972), because the theme of the poem is poetic fame.[56]

This time it is Icarus who signifies the poet. The problem scholars find in the association of Horace and Icarus seems to stem from the supposed ill omen of Icarus' death. Alternatives to *notior* ('more famous') such as *fortior* ('stronger, braver'), *cautior* ('more cautious'), *tutior* ('safer'), etc., which seek to offset the bad connotations of the association, risk destroying Horace's point by apologizing for it. If he had written *cautior* the comparison with Icarus would still be there. Since Icarus fell into the sea and died, a comparison for Horace's poetry with his flight has seemed inappropriate. But the metaphorical parallels are much more precise. Icarus did not wholly die but in some sense was metamorphosed into an ocean after his death;[57] Horace (man and book) will not wholly die but will be metamorphosed into a poetic bird after his death. Icarus metaphorically becomes the Icarian Sea just as much as Horace (the poet) 'becomes' 'Horace' (the book/the poetry). Horace here applies the double-sided encomiastic coin—humorously, engagingly—to himself. The hybris of the claim to a greatness which bursts the boundaries of human nature is offset when the poet implicates to himself precisely those ambiguities which were discussed in the previous section. (It is further offset by the very absurdity of the *reductio* to which the flight-metaphor is subjected.) Icarus signifies both failure and fame. The ambivalence of the attribution to oneself of specifically Icarian fame adheres to the rules and refinements of politeness, for it is also a hint at *my* failure and so is caught up in the rhetoric of the disclaimer.

[56] For the textual argument see Carrubba (1982), who posits *motior*. Other variants include the well-attested but unmetrical *ocior* (β/E), *tutior* (Bentley), *fortior* (Delz), *cautior*. The last strikes me as totally inappropriate to this extremely *incautious* poem. For *notus* in specifically poetic contexts cf. Hor. *Ars* 346 *hic* [*sc. liber*] *longum noto scriptori prorogat aeuum*; Ov. *Tr.* 2. 464 *Tibullus . . . te principe notus erat*. (Possibly cf. also Virg. *Ecl.* 5. 43 *Daphnis . . . hinc usque ad sidera notus*; Stat. *Theb.* 4. 714 *ille alta per auia notus audiri*.)

[57] In the *Metamorphoses* version of the story (*Met.* 8. 183–235), the transformation of Icarus into the ocean (like his and Daedalus' previous transformation into birds) is just one of many hidden metamorphoses.

The self-deprecating joke is a *captatio benevolentiae* which allows the poet to temper his poetic claim into acceptability.

It is this connection between flight and daedalic fame in a poetic context which makes *Odes* 2. 20 particularly important source-material for our poem. Fame, eternal life in memory, comes through poetic achievement. In a poem where the distinction between the poet and his work is very tenuous, what we are told to remember is not only that Icarus plunged to his death through his flight but also that he has an eternal name—the Icarian sea. The comparison with Icarus, then, constitutes a claim to poetic fame. But can the metaphor be pushed further? As I suggested above, the poem heralds Horace's transformation into the Pindaric *uates* of the *Roman Odes*. It may be, then, that Icarus in this poem is involved in the contrast between Callimacheanism and Pindaricism (I use the terminology advisedly—I do not mean 'the contrast between Callimachus and Pindar') which I shall suggest in the next section. 'Look at me!' says Horace, 'I'm being Icarus. I'm going to go over the top poetically.' This is a way of saying 'I'm going to write elevated poetry' while engagingly laughing at one's own pomposity.

Apart from the obvious Icarian connection between this poem and our story in the *Ars*, the passages are linked by the theme of overcoming the Styx. Horace, as Icarian bird, will transgress/exceed the fundamental principle of human nature by the fact that he will not die (*Carm*. 2. 20. 5–9):

> *non ego pauperum*
> *sanguis parentum, non ego quem uocas,*
> *dilecte Maecenas, obibo*
> *nec Stygia cohibebor unda.*

I, the offspring of poor parents,
I, whom you call [send for: Nisbet and Hubbard (1978)],
beloved Maecenas, shall not die,
nor will I be constrained by the Stygian wave.

The Ovidian Daedalus tries to ameliorate the impiety of his forthcoming flight through the heavens by offering to undertake an opposing journey across the Styx, if only such a way were open to him (*Ars* 2. 41–2):

> *per Styga detur iter, Stygias transnabimus undas;*
> *sunt mihi naturae iura nouanda meae.*

> If a path through the Styx were given, we would swim through Stygian waves;
> laws of my nature are to be made new for me.

A journey *to* the Styx is an absolutely natural part of the human condition: it is the return trip that is only for heroes. Ovid's Daedalus will find another way to change his nature, but a *per Styga . . . iter* is exactly what Icarus gets when he flies too high.[58] The journey which Icarus takes through the Styx does not wholly stop his return, because he achieves immortality through his name.

When considering this theme in the Daedalus-stories of Horace and Ovid, it should be remembered that the Daedalus of Virgil introduced and mirrored the story of Aeneas' own journey through the Styx and back: an epic feat of heroic daring bordering on impious hybris,[59] and one achieved by the great heroes of legend, Hercules and Theseus. Poetic fame, for Horace and for Icarus, involves transgressing the bounds of man.

Odes 4. 2

Daedalus and Icarus appear again, albeit somewhat elliptically, in Horace's reflection on Pindaric imitation, *Odes* 4. 2. The brevity of the allusions to the myth in Horace (particularly 2. 20 and 4. 2) is itself indication of the accessibility of the symbolism. As in *Odes* 2. 20, it is again Icarus who signifies the poet, but this time the comic possibilities of the metamorphosis are replaced by concentration on the carefully wrought, daedalic waxen wings. The artistic history of *daidalos* is thrown into sharper relief for us if we read, for a moment, lower-case 'd' in *ope daedalea* ('with much-wrought aid'). There is an essential correlation between Daedalus' creation of the wings and the laborious

---

[58] Brandt (1902: ad loc.) also reads this as foreshadowing the death of Icarus, as does Rudd (1988: 63).

[59] Cf. Virg. *Aen.* 6. 391 *corpora uiua nefas Stygia uectare carina.*

production performed by the Horatian bee (*Carm.* 4. 2. 29–32), discussed below.

> Pindarum quisquis studet aemulari,
> Iule, ceratis ope Daedalea
> nititur pennis uitreo daturus
>   nomina ponto.   (*Carm.* 4. 2. 1–4)

Whoever seeks to emulate Pindar, Iulus,
depends on wings of made wax by the aid of Daedalus,
destined to give his name to the glassy sea.

The danger in imitating Pindar was that he was a great raging river (4. 2. 5–8):

> monte decurrens uelut amnis, imbres
> quem super notas aluere ripas,
> feruet immensusque ruit profundo
>   Pindarus ore.

Like a river running down from a mountain,
which the rains have fed beyond its accustomed banks,
huge Pindar seethes and rushes with his deep mouth.

Pindar was great, but, the poem seems to say, 'un-Callimachean'. Is he therefore to be avoided as a model? The poem surely cannot reject imitation of Pindar out of hand, although it is amusing that it initially appears to reject a major part of Horace's lyric stance: rather, I suggest, it considers the problem of imitating the 'non-Callimachean' Pindar in a Callimachean manner. It would be wrong, of course, to see any simple opposition between Pindar and Callimachus, since Callimachus owes an enormous debt to the earlier poet, and this is why I have put inverted commas around the designation 'un-Callimachean'. There are Callimachean epinicia, the *Victoria Berenices* in particular; there is what we might call a 'widow's mite' principle in Pindar too, in his unabashed praise through the notions of *phthonos* ('envy'), *hybris* ('excess') etc. On the other hand, Horace's sapphics play their part, like Callimachus' elegiacs in the *Victoria Berenices*, in undercutting and lightening their Pindaric-style encomia. One might perhaps say, rather, that Horace constructs an 'opposition' between his two predecessors as a strategy for his own self-definition as a lyric poet.

It is part of that strategy—an ironic part—that the opposition is itself deconstructed by the scale of the poem and by
Horace's own lyric stance elsewhere in the collection.

The opposition, such as it is, is brought out in the
seventh and eighth stanzas (4. 2. 25–32):

> *multa Dircaeum leuat aura cycnum,*
> *tendit, Antoni, quotiens in altos*
> *nubium tractus: ego apis Matinae*
>   *more modoque*
>
> *grata carpentis thyma per laborem*
> *plurimum circa nemus uuidique*
> *Tiburis ripas operosa paruus*
>   *carmina fingo.*

A lot of air holds up the Dircean swan,
Antonius, whenever he makes for the high tracts of the clouds:
I, in the way and manner of the Apulian bee
plucking welcome thyme with a great effort
around the groves and banks of wet Tiber,
am little and fashion much-wrought songs.

The flight-metaphor for Pindar was the high soaring of
some great bird. *Olympian* 2. 86–8 comes particularly to
mind.

> σοφὸς ὁ πολλὰ εἰδὼς φυᾷ.
> μαθόντες δὲ λάβροι
> παγγλωσσίᾳ κόρακες ὣς ἄκραντα γαρύετον
> Διὸς πρὸς ὄρνιχα θεῖον.

He knows, whose blood tells him much;
Mere learners babble, the pair of them,
and like crows chatter vainly against
God's holy bird.   (trans. C. M. Bowra)

Whatever exactly one believes about the identity of the duet
of crows,[60] there can be little doubt that the subject under
discussion is the pre-eminence of natural powers over what
is merely learnt, of *phusis* over *technē*,[61] and that the high

---

[60] Cf. e.g. Kirkwood (1981); Ruck (1972: 167): 'the crows are obviously poets.'

[61] Bundy (1972: 90 n. 113) seems to me to simplify the question in Pindar.
'Thus, Pindar's *phua* has nothing to do with the natural, unschooled, unconscious
genius of the eighteenth and nineteenth centuries, but denotes schooling by
experience in the truth of words and actions in a living tradition; the "learning"
he speaks of in these passages is mere rote imitation of things not understood.'

soaring of the eagle is a metaphor for inspired Pindaric poetry. Horace contrasts himself with Pindar by describing himself as a meticulous bee, a low-flying creature. At this point, we should remember Callimachus' contribution to the flight motif, in the *Aetia* prologue (*Aet.* fr. 1. 32):

> ἐγὼ δ᾽ εἴην οὐλαχύς, ὁ πτερόεις
> I would be the little, the winged one.

Horace's 'little bee' equates with Callimachus' cicada.

It might seem that the poem's programme condemns the imitator of Pindar to poetic disaster. Some scholars have found in this a distressing inconsistency with *Odes* 2. 20. (See particularly Pascal 1980, Tatum 1973.) Certainly the two poems act as prisms on each other. Note, for example, that Horace dissociates himself from the Pindaric swan in a poem (4. 2) which refers back to another (2. 20) which metamorphosed him *into* a swan. But the references to Icarus at 2. 20. 12 and 4. 2. 2 are not as inconsistent as Pascal seems to suggest. He describes Icarus in 4. 2. 2–3 as 'a metaphor for poetic disaster' (Pascal 1980: 100). Perhaps so, yet Icarus signifies not only death, but also fame. I suggest that, rather than simply opposing Callimachean to Pindaric values, the subject of *Odes* 4. 2 is as much the connection as the opposition between Pindar and Callimachus. Moreover, it discusses the difficulties and dangers of imitating Pindar *as* a Callimachean poet while still adhering to the poetic values of delicacy and littleness. Who is indicated by the opening *quisquis* ('whoever')? The person who desires *Pindarum . . . aemulari* (to 'emulate', as well as to 'imitate', 'Pindar') is as much Horace as it is Iulus Antonius, and of course it is also Callimachus. An imitator of Pindar has only the delicate work of Daedalus to sustain him; but Pindar himself was supported by *multa . . . aura* (v. 25), a lot of/a large breeze. The anti-Callimachean weighting of the *multa . . . aura* is obvious. To that extent, then, I suggest that the delicate Daedalian work which upholds the imitator (Horace, Callimachus) is, quite precisely, the set of literary values expounded by Callimachus. It is precisely these resources on which the flight of Daedalus and Icarus in the *Ars* will rely. Daedalus says

of the carefully crafted wings that they will escape from
Minos *hac . . . ope* ('with this aid', *Ars* 2. 52). The poet
who dares the dangerous task of imitating Pindar relying
on such resources is worthy of great renown, an eternal
name. He is going to fly high even while he flies low.
Even when referring to Icarus' death, Horace emphasizes
his eternal fame.

3*f* Daedalus as Metaphor

Such is the Daedalus whom Ovid inherited, a character
whose entire history is rich with artistic and poetic suggestiveness. The metamorphic Daedalus cannot be tied down
to one neat metaphorical pattern. In *Odes* 1. 3 Daedalus'
invention signified the daring of epic poetry; in 2. 20 Icarian excess hinted at elevation; in 4. 2 father and son were
combined to create a statement about the relationship between elevated poetry and Callimachean art. In Virgil,
Daedalus signified, by opposition almost, the writing of
epic poetry, but was himself highly Callimachean. Let it
not be thought, incidentally, that there is a simple opposition between Callimacheanism and epic or other elevated
poetry.[62] What is important here is that the Augustans
used a hint at such an opposition, in all its ambiguities,
in their discourse of poetics. In Virgil's *Aeneid* and
Horace's *Odes* we have *the* central monuments of Roman
literary culture, in that within the socio-political ambience
in which they were written, and in the classical tradition,
they have achieved canonical status. As works of the political and social establishment, as well as of great literary importance, they are considerable, indeed inescapable influences
on all contemporary and subsequent writers of Latin
verse. Ovid *inevitably* writes within the intertextual forcefield of their works.

But before we examine the Ovidian Daedalus in more
detail, it would be worthwhile to mention briefly the later
fortunes of the myth. What happens to Daedalus later in

---

[62] See Sections 3*h* and 3*j*.

the Ovidian corpus I shall consider below in Sections 3*k* and 3*l*. I mentioned above that part of my purpose in examining in some detail the ancient and modern textuality surrounding Daedalus was to foreground the powerful attraction towards symbolism which the myth inspires. In the Middle Ages, the myth became an allegory for the dangers of presumption and of progress.[63] An example of the myth which is particularly telling for the way it was read in later antiquity, however, comes from Ausonius. In *Epistle* 23, the writer thanks his pupil (they speak in terms of an honorific father-son relationship) for sending him a poem of his creation dealing with the 'three books of Suetonius which he devotes to the kings'. The poem was clearly in the high style. Ausonius quotes the lines *audax Icario qui fecit nomina ponto | et qui Chalcidicas moderate enauit ad aras* ('daring was he who made a name for the Icarian Sea, and he who swam carefully to the Euboean altars'),[64] which Ausonius interprets as follows:

quid enim aliud agunt [these lines] *nisi ut tu uegetam et sublimem alacritatem tuam temeritatem uoces, me uero, et consultum et quem filius debeat imitari, salutari prudentia praeditum dicas? quod equidem contra est. nam tu summa sic adpetis, ut non decidas. senectus mea satis habet, si consistat.*

For what do these lines mean, but that you call your vigorous and lofty zeal rashness, but you say that I, being both cautious and one whom a son should imitate, am endowed with wholesome prudence? Indeed the matter is to the contrary. For you seek the heights in such a way as not to fall. My old age has enough if it may stand still.

For Ausonius, and presumably for the addressee, his pupil Paulinus, the flight denotes, allegorizes even, different stylistic levels for poetry. This may well suggest that such an interpretation was part of the accepted heritage of the legend.

---

[63] See Ashton (1941), who shows how Icarus was used in the Middle Ages and Renaissance as a paradigm for the ambiguity of progress: hybris or benefaction? See also Rudd (1988) and the other essays in that book.

[64] The reference to Virg. *Aen.* 6. 14 is clear. Cf. also Hor. *Carm.* 4. 2. 4 *nomina ponto*.

The search for a straightforward allegory from the Daedalus myth is doomed to failure. As the metamorphic properties of his name suggest, the symbolism of the myth changes in different circumstances (although each instance reflects on every other instance) and cannot be reduced to simple formulae. Horace, as we saw, offers us at least three models; Ovid offers us several, even within one telling of the story. I suggest that the paradigm is about writing/reading the *Ars* and reflects in a number of different but not unconnected ways on the poem. Similes are, of course, about differences as well as similarities. It is a reflection on poetic fame, the artistic process, stylistic levels, and Callimachean artistry. My argument derives not only from the history of the myth, but also from the wealth of subliminal programmatic hints to be found in the passage.

3g Hybrids and Other Couplets

Daedalus is a metaphor for the *Ars*. One element of the Daedalus story's poetic symbolism for the *Ars* is the question of stylistic level, a question of exceptional importance in the case of this strange new hybrid poem. Neither subjective elegy nor didactic epos, at times it uses the most comic and low-level aspects of elegy and the most elevated aspects of didactic, not serious, and yet somehow serious, never quite straight satire yet forever undermining everything, including itself, and always very conscious of itself and its mixed parentage.

The generic mix-up of the poem is signified metaphorically by the hybrid nature of the protagonists in the exemplum. Daedalus effects his own and his son's metamorphosis into bird-men. The two beings who embark on the flight are twofold bodies (v. 72):

> *monte minor collis, campis erat altior aequis*
> *hinc data sunt miserae corpora bina fugae*

There was a hill less than a mountain, more lofty than the plains,
From here the two bodies are given over to pitiful flight.

The phrase *corpora bina* suggests not only two, but twofold:

half man, half bird.[65] Most interestingly, *binus* is used in the context of hybrids by Lucretius (5. 878–80):

> *sed neque Centauri fuerunt, nec tempore in ullo*
> *esse queunt duplici natura et corpore bino*
> *ex alienigenis membris compacta.*

But there have never been Centaurs, nor at any time
could things exist with a double nature and twofold bodies,
fitted together from limbs generated in different places.

The double nature of the bird-men is reflected by the grouping of the words in the pentameter in twos: *Monte MinOR Collis, CampIS erat AltiOR AEquIS*. As I shall discuss further below, the double nature is a novel nature, and so proclaims imagistically the originality of Ovid's fusion of elegy and didactic.

Daedalus' most famous production of a hybrid was that of the bull-man,[66] the Minotaur, which was the offspring of Pasiphae and the bull through Daedalus' contrivance. The artist constructed a wooden cow in which Pasiphae was enclosed in order to achieve consummation with the bull,[67] just as he later enclosed the fruit of that union in the labyrinth (vv. 23–4):[68]

> *Daedalus, ut clausit conceptum crimine matris*
> *semibouemque uirum semiuirumque bouem*

Daedalus, when he has shut up the thing conceived by the
crime of its mother
the half-bull man and half-man bull . . .

Whatever credence one may give to the story of Seneca (*Con.* 2. 2. 12) that the pentameter of this couplet was one of three lines which Ovid particularly wanted to keep, while his critics wanted it removed, the line was clearly as famous

---

[65] The distributive makes perfectly good Latin (cf. Kühner and Stegmann 1966: 1. 659), although sufficiently unusual to be effective. Kühner and Stegmann (1966: 1. 661) also give examples of *binus* meaning 'a pair of'.

[66] Putnam (1987: 176) describes Daedalus in relation to Pasiphae and the bull as 'the inventor of hybrid objects that cater to the furtive in their recipients and in their turn create further hybrids—a fake beast enclosing a true human . . . that begets a man-animal—the Minotaur'.

[67] Diod. 4. 77. 1; Apoll. *Lib.* 3. 1. 4; Servius on Virg. *Aen.* 6. 14.

[68] Apoll. *Lib.* 3. 1. 4; Diod. 4. 77. 4; Servius on Virg. *Aen.* 5. 588; Hyg. *Fab.* 40.

and infamous in antiquity as it is today. Wilkinson (1955: 84) here calls Ovid a 'juggler with words', while Fränkel (1945: 183) says that 'it was not the playful ring of the words alone that caused him to give his verse the shape to which his critics objected', but that it 'indicates ... a monstrous combination of two natures, both of which had an equal claim on his (i.e. the Minotaur's) identity'. In content the line is a *reductio ad absurdum* of the many attempts to express the twofold nature of the Minotaur.[69] An additional twist is given to this line by the suggestion of Rusten (1982), that Ovid is directly imitating lines from Empedocles Περὶ φύσεως, fr. 446 Kirk and Raven. Here the poet describes an intermediate stage in the world's development in which parts of different animals were found combined into various monstrous forms, and uses two phrases which are close to Ovid's, βουγενῆ ἀνδρόπρωιρα ('man-faced bull-child') and ἀνδροφυῆ βούκρανα ('man-born bull-head'). The allusion is appropriate to the wide-ranging didactic background to the poem.

In form, this artistic line (v. 24) is a *reductio ad absurdum* of the elegiac couplet, with its love of balance and antithesis, and its possibility for metrical interchange. The couplet as a whole is programmatically elegiac. The hexameter is common to epic and elegy—and v. 23 is a very serious and awe-inspiring hexameter; but the pentameter is unique to elegy—and v. 24 is an ultimately light and witty example. The harsh alliteration in the hexameter, the spondaic centre to the line, the periphrastic reference to the Minotaur all build up an effect of mystery and monstrosity—to be dispelled suddenly in the delightfully ridiculous pentameter. This is the generic mix-up nature of the *Ars*. I should make it clear what I am proposing. The hybrids in the exemplum reflect metaphorically two not unconnected features of the work: first, the mixture of genre (elegy and didactic), and secondly, more generally, the very nature of the elegiac couplet. Daedalus becomes a fake man-animal when he flies like a bird. The double nature of the bull-man reflects the bird-man Daedalus, the hybrid unit of this verse, that is the

[69] Cf. Eur. fr. in Plut. *Thes.* 15. 2; Plat. *Phaed.* 58b; Virg. *Aen.* 6. 25; Ov. *Her.* 2. 70, 10. 102, 127; *Met.* 8. 156, 169.

elegiac couplet, and the hybrid subject of this work, that is didactic love elegy.

The elegiac couplet combines the hexameter—the powerful metrical unit of high didactic as well as epic, with its smooth succession of feet—with a softer, weaker, deviant poetic line, with its jerking, almost awkward division into two sets of two and a half feet. Ovid similarly plays with the nature of the elegiac couplet in *Am.* 1. 1, where Cupid steals one foot from each couplet and stops the poet writing serious epic, and where the elegiac interplay between strong and weak, male and female, active and passive is programmatically at issue. The Ovidian obsession with the *genus impar*, 'limping Elegy', is explicit about its connection with and distinction from epic, in the discussion of the association between Venus and Vulcan, the 'deified' *puella* and the 'slave' lover, the hexameter and the pentameter (*Am.* 2. 17. 22):

> *iungitur herous cum breuiore modo.*
> The epic verse is joined with a shorter one.

It is the pentameter which gives us clues to the particular nature of the elegiac couplet. Cunningham (1958) argues that Ovid subscribed to the theory of the pleasant or appropriate fault, and applied it to the elegiac couplet. This is a good point: elegy is less than epic, but the *uitium* ('vice', 'fault') is a *causa decoris* ('cause of attractiveness'). In order to counter the contention of Heinze that *Metamorphoses* passages inspire pity and fear while elegiac passages inspire pity only (obviously too narrow a contention), Little (1970: 80) uses the example of the myth of Io, told in *Her.* 14. 89–92 and *Met.* 1. 637–41. 'Here we must believe that *et conata queri mugitus edidit ore* ['and trying to complain she gave forth lowing from her mouth'] (*Met.* 1. 637) is designed to arouse pity and fear, while *conatoque queri mugitus edidit ore* ['she gave forth lowing from her mouth which was trying to complain'] (*Her.* 14. 91) is designed to arouse only pity.' But if we look at what follows these two almost identical lines, we find two lines very similar in content but very *different* in form.

pertimuitque sonos propriaque exterrita uoce est. (*Met.* 1. 638)

and she feared the sounds and was frightened by her own voice.

territaque est forma, territa uoce sua. (*Her.* 14. 92)

she was terrified by her form and terrified by her voice.

The pentameter again exhibits the characteristic balance and antithesis of elegy, although the hexameters could almost be interchanged.

A prime example of the programmatic use of this forte-piano characteristic in the elegiac couplet comes in the description of Daedalus' creation of the wings (vv. 45–6). I shall discuss that couplet in detail later. A couple of couplets in Daedalus' instruction to Icarus stretch the programmatic signification of elegiacs, by reflecting together what one couplet normally does (vv. 59–62):

> *nam, siue aetherias uicino sole per auras*
> *ibimus, impatiens cera caloris erit;*
> *siue humiles propiore freto iactabimus alas,*
> *mobilis aequoreis pinna madescet aquis.*[70]

For if we go through the upper air, near the sun,
the wax will not endure the heat;
but if we toss our wings low down, near the sea,
the mobile feathers will grow wet from the waters of the sea.

The first couplet is *high*, the second is *low*. The first is full of light, fire, air, and heat, the highest elements, having natural affinity with the divine and the philosophical language of the soul.[71] The second, however, is heavy with

---

[70] Note the construction of these lines: *aetherias . . . per auras* is picked up by *aequoreis . . . aquis* (62), enhanced by the anaphora of *siue*, stringing the four lines together as a sub-set. *Vicino sole* (59) is echoed by *propiore freto* (61), which is itself picked up again in *deo* (*sole*) *propiore* in 85. Note the sound of line 60, with i and m sounds in the first half, and c and r sounds in the second. Then in the next couplet (63–4) the chiasmus of *uola uentos | aurae uela* in the middles of the lines is enhanced by the balance of *quoque . . . quaque*; note the assonance in *naTE TImeto* and *secunDA DAto*, in *uENTos . . . ferENT*, and in *uenTOs . . . timeTO*.

[71] Nisbet and Hubbard (1970) on Hor. *Carm.* 1. 28. 5 say that *aetherius* is 'appropriate where the mortal body is contrasted with the immortal soul'. *Aetherias . . . per auras* is a very poetic phrase: cf. e.g. Lucr. 3. 405 *uiuit et aetherias uitalis suscipit auras*; Virg. *Georg.* 2. 291–2 *quae quantum uertice ad auras | aetherias, tantum radice in Tartara tendit*; *Aen.* 4. 445–6, 7. 557; Ov. *Met.* 5. 512; Manil. 1. 149; Stat. *Theb.* 6. 857. *Aura* is a possible symbol for poetic inspiration (e.g. Hor. *Carm.* 3. 4. 8).

sluggish water and, by the implication of *humiles*, earth. The following couplet opens with an instruction *inter utrumque uola* ('fly between the two'). A flight-path *between* those two couplets is the right one for the *Ars*. Icarus' mistake (to be considered further later) was that he did not fly between the two, but flew up to the heights of pure hexameter.

The elegiac couplet, then, does in microcosm what the whole poem does in macrocosm. You need Daedalus *and* Icarus to make a statement about this poem.

3h *inter utrumque uola*: Daedalus as Poet

Another question addressed by the exemplum is: what is the correct stylistic level for didactic poetry, as opposed to epic on the one hand, and prose instruction on the other? It would be nice to be able to draw a simple distinction between flying low (but not too low), little poetry done by art, and Callimacheanism, on the one hand, and flying high, great poetry, epic, *ingenium*, and anti-Callimacheanism on the other. But although like all simplifications this has an element of truth, the texts do not admit so simple a dichotomy. There *is* no simple formula for good writing, for poetic artistry and success; you can win by breaking all such formulae. As a man who flies but sets a middle course, Daedalus becomes an awkward metaphorical paradox, but one exactly suited to the multi-resonance of Ovid's poetic statement. Firstly, flight is a metaphor for poetry, and Ovid's didactic poem, the exemplum states, really is *poetry*. It is higher up in the hierarchy of genres than subjective elegy. Furthermore, a second point made by the exemplum is that didactic poetry generally and Ovid's own hybrid didactic erotic poem especially, espousing as it does avowedly Callimachean values, must not fly too high, or it will become ridiculous, unable to sustain its own weight. As has been suggested in a number of places, 'Callimacheanism' in the Augustan poets and particularly in Ovid cannot be pressed into one simple formula.[72]

Daedalus sets a middle course. This, I suggest, is the

---

[72] A similar point has been made by Thomas (1986: 113).

course of the *Ars*. It is possible that Ovid has actually reshaped the myth to fit his scheme. Although the warning against flying high is central to the myth as a metaphor for hybris, I have not been able to find mention of avoiding a low course before Ovid. Virgil and Horace are interested in the high flying and the fall, but have nothing to say about avoiding the sea, while the early mythographers are equally quiet. Strabo, a near contemporary of Ovid's, specifically mentions (14. 1. 19) the melting wax but says nothing about going too low. Diodorus (4. 77. 9) says that Daedalus deliberately kept close to the sea to keep his wings moist. The report of Apollodorus (*Epit.* 1. 12) does include an injunction against flying too low lest the wings be detached by the damp, but this belongs to the first or second century AD. Although it would be rash to posit active influence from Ovid to Apollodorus, it is also impossible to be sure that the mythographer is following a source earlier than our passage. Our modern view of the story comes to a considerable extent from the Ovid-influenced Middle Ages. If the notion of the middle way exists here, or even came into existence, solely for the purposes of Daedalus' rhetoric, with the force of contextuality it comments on the nature of this work, steering as it does a middle course between epic and elegy. The language of the middle way, an Aristotelian value subsumed into popular morality, was extensively used by Horace, most famously in the *auream . . . mediocritatem* ('the golden mean', *Carm.* 2. 10. 5). After Horace it is difficult to talk of middle ways without his influence.

There is one particular kind of sublimity which Daedalus rejects in our passage—climbing to heaven to attack the gods, or writing Gigantomachy. Daedalus' second speech, addressed first to himself and then to Jupiter, bears the hallmarks of a programmatic didactic proem, complete with *recusatio* (vv. 33–42):

> quod simul ut sensit, 'nunc, nunc, o Daedale,' dixit
>   'materiam qua sis ingeniosus habes.
> possidet et terras et possidet aequora Minos: 35
>   nec tellus nostrae nec patet unda fugae.
> restat iter caeli: caelo temptabimus ire.

> da ueniam coepto, Iuppiter alte, meo.
> non ego sidereas adfecto tangere sedes;
>   qua fugiam dominum, nulla nisi ista uia est.   40
> per Styga detur iter, Stygias transnabimus undas;
>   sunt mihi naturae iura nouanda meae.'

When he realized this, 'Now, Daedalus, now,'
he said, 'you have material for your talent to work on.
Minos possesses both land and sea:
neither earth nor wave lies open to our flight.
There remains the path of the sky: by the sky we will attempt to
    go.
Forgive my essay, great Jupiter.
I do not strive to touch the starry seats;
there is no other way but this by which I may escape my master.
If a path through the Styx were given, we would swim through
    the Stygian waves;
the laws of my nature are to be made new for me.'

As soon as Daedalus realizes that no normal human means
of escape is open to him, that his artistry is being blocked
and his expression repressed, he finds an outlet for and
through his technological talents from the challenge to his
intellect. Just as there previously existed no way out for
Daedalus, so there is no room for development in classic
subjective elegy for Ovid. Three components are needed
for any artistic production: the *materia*, provided here by
the necessity of the situation, be that for Daedalus to get
out of Crete or for Ovid to keep the girl in love (that is, to
write erotic didactic poetry); the *ingenium*, the inspired
intellect which allows the worker to make use of the *materia*;
and the *ars* which the worker applies to his idea to create a
finished product.[73] In describing his artistic inspiration in
the next few lines, Ovid has Daedalus use language redolent
of poetics. The first pentameter is thick with literary connotations. Daedalus reminds himself that he has *ingenium*, and
points out that he now has *materia* in the form of a challenge. His *ars* is of course an essential part of his anthroponymous status.[74] *Materia* and *ingenium* are coupled elsewhere

[73] Cf. *Met.* 8. 159 *Daedalus ingenio fabrae celeberrimus artis.*

[74] For *materia* cf. Cic. *Inv.* 1. 7 *materiam artis eam dicimus in qua omnis ars et ea
facultas quae conficitur ex arte uersatur*; Cic. *de Orat.* 1. 10; Hor. *Ars* 38–9 *sumite*

by Ovid in overtly literary contexts.[75] Particularly to be compared is *Tr.* 5. 1. 27–8:

> *non haec ingenio, non haec componimus arte:*
> *materia est propriis ingeniosa malis.*

We have composed these things not by intellect, not by art: the material is creative through its own misfortunes.

The two words in question are in the same position in the pentameter in the *Ars* and *Tristia* passages, while the thought that trouble brings inspiration is reminiscent of that expressed less than ten lines later in our passage (v. 43):

> *ingenium mala saepe mouent*

Misfortunes often provoke the intellect.

The request *da ueniam* ('forgive') occurs at *Tr.* 5. 1. 65 and *Ars* 2. 38, and *ingeniosus* occurs again in the same pentameter position at *Tr.* 5. 1. 74, parallels which give further contextual support for the connection. By these later self-allusions, Ovid directs us towards a metaphoric, poetic reading of his earlier work.

The thought that the only path open to this artistic endeavour is the sky prompts Daedalus to a nervous apology to the sky-god, great Jupiter. Poets, also, often 'start from Zeus', most significantly at the opening of Aratus' *Phaenomena*, which, as a Hellenistic didactic poem, is an important literary predecessor to the *Ars*.[76] When Daedalus asks forgiveness for violating Jupiter's territory, the vocabulary he uses makes this also a prayer (Ovid's) for literary indulgence. The word *uenia* ('forgiveness'), often found with the prayer *da*, is frequently used of literary indulgence.[77] Daeda-

---

materiam uestris, qui scribitis, aequam | uiribus, 131; Ov. *Am.* 1. 1. 2, 1. 1. 19, 3. 1. 25, 3. 1. 42; *Rem.* 387; *Met.* 12. 160; *Tr.* 1. 5. 56, 2. 70, 321, 336, 382, 516, 4. 3. 73, 5. 1. 6, 28, 5. 5. 50; *Pont.* 1. 10. 24, 2. 5. 26, 2. 5. 32, 3. 4. 40, 3. 9. 47, 4. 8. 71, 4. 10. 72, 4. 13. 23, 46; *Priap.* 68. 19; Mart. 5. 53. 3, 8.0. 7, 12.0. 11. The word is rare in poetry before Ovid, except in the scientific sense in Lucretius. For *ingeniosus/ingenium* cf. e.g. Hor. *Ars* 295, 323; Prop. 1. 7. 22, 2. 1. 4, 2. 24. 23, 2. 30. 40, 3. 3. 22, 3. 9. 52, 4. 6. 75; Ov. *Am.* 1. 15. 2, 2. 1. 18, 2. 17. 34, 2. 18. 11, 3. 1. 25, 3. 8. 3, 3. 12. 8, 16; *Met.* 8. 534, 15. 146; *Fast.* 1. 18, 24, 2. 123, 3. 310; *Tr.* 2. 342, 5. 1. 74; *Pont.* 2. 5. 64; [Ov.] *Ep. Sapph.* 84, 194.

[75] *Am* 3. 1. 25; *Tr.* 5. 1. 28; *Pont.* 2. 5. 26, 4. 13. 46, etc.
[76] Cf. also Theocr. 17. 1; Virg. *Ecl.* 3. 60.
[77] Cf. Hor. *Sat.* 1. 4. 105; *Ep.* 2. 1. 78, 170; *Ars* 11, 264, 267; Prop. 2. 25. 4; Ov. *Tr.* 1. 1. 46, 1. 7. 31, 3. 14. 51, 4. 1. 104, 5. 1. 65; *Pont.* 1. 8. 9, 3. 4. 16, 3. 9. 55, 4. 2. 23; Stat. *Silv.* 1.pr. 13; *Priap.* 68. 2; Quint. *Inst.* 10. 1. 72.

lus seeks this indulgence for his *coeptum*, this thing which he begins, his invention, flight/poetry. *Coeptum* (often in the plural) frequently signifies a poetic invention, and frequently occurs in programmatic proems, as its derivation suggests it should.[78]

Since by this time the reader's sensitivity to multiple significance should be well aroused, and since the prayer is subliminally parading itself as a programmatic proem, the address to Jupiter may hint at a facetious reference to Augustus. It is by now a well-established conceit to speak of the emperor in deificatory terms.[79] The prayer thus becomes a disingenuous declaration of innocence, and sets in motion a subliminal *recusatio*. When Daedalus tells Jupiter that he does not plan to *attack* the heavens, the implication of a reference to the attack on the gods by the giants is impossible to resist. No one would deny, then, that this is 'a reference to Gigantomachy'.[80] But does 'Gigantomachy' signify only 'the battle of gods and giants' or also 'writing poetry about the battle of gods and giants'? I submit that with the force of contextuality the latter is inevitable. Ovid's Daedalus is keen to take up the positive value of progress (the invention of flight—in the metaphor the invention of erotic didactic poetry) but to excise its sinful connotations. The ultimate example of hybris was the attack on heaven by the giants, an act of audacity which, it appears, Daedalus assures Jupiter he does not contemplate in his celestial journey. So he

[78] Cf. Lucr. 1. 418; Virg. *Georg.* 1. 40 *da facilem cursum atque audacibus adnue coeptis*, 2. 39; Hor. *Ars* 14; Ov. *Ars* 1. 30, 771; *Rem.* 704; *Fast.* 6. 652, 798; *Met.* 1. 2 *di, coeptis . . . adspirate meis*; *Tr.* 2. 555; *Pont.* 2. 5. 30, 3. 1. 159; Manil. 3. 36; *Culex* 41. Seven of the passages cited are prayers for inspiration for didactic poetry.

[79] Cf. Hor. *Ep.* 1. 19. 43; Ov. *Ars* 3. 115–16; Rudd (1976: 25). See also Scott (1930) for emperor worship in Ovid. His study is somewhat uncritical, but is useful in showing the part played by poetry in deification.

[80] *Adfecto*, rare in poetry (cf. *TLL* 1. 1181. 2), occurs in a number of contexts pertaining to ascent to heaven, or specifically to Gigantomachy. Cf. Ov. *Am.* 3. 8. 51; *Fast.* 3. 439–40 *fulmina post ausos caelum affectare Gigantas | sumpta Ioui*; *Met.* 1. 152–3 *adfectasse ferunt regnum caeleste Gigantas | altaque congestos struxisse ad sidera montis*, 2. 58 of Phaethon attempting an Icarian flight; *Pont.* 4. 8. 59 *adfectantes caelestia regna Gigantas*. The word occurs nine times in Ovid. Cf. also *Am.* 1. 1. 13–14 *sunt tibi magna, puer,* [sc. *Cupido*] *nimiumque potentia regna: | cur opus adfectas ambitiose nouum?* The jingle *sidereas . . . sedes* is echoed in the attack on the abode of Jupiter by the Giants in *Met.* 5. 348: *aetherias ausum sperare Typhoea sedes*, where *sedes* is in the same metrical *sedes* as here.

denies association with the Giants; and Ovid denies the place
of the very highest kind of poetry in his didactic poem.

In the context of our passage, which is thick with subliminal poetics, the simple apology for hybris takes on the
characteristics of a *recusatio*: the way of the *Ars* is not
bombastic epic but Callimachean delicateness, and it is not
martial epic but didactic. 'I will go through the sky,' Daedalus says (v. 37), 'but not too high—not to the heavens.'
'This will be poetry,' Ovid says under the metaphor, 'but
not the highest kind of poetry there is.' The well-known
conceit of the poet 'doing what he says' has amusing implications here. On the level that this line simply means 'I will
not attack heaven with my flight' we might assume 'Jupiter'
(whomever that may indicate) to be pleased; but on the
level that it means 'I am not going to write an encomium of
your victory (over the Giants or anything else)' it is not
quite so satisfactory to the god. An association with Augustus as victor in Gigantomachy could lurk beneath the surface.[81] In a Callimachean-style *recusatio*, the poet proclaims
that he will not write a certain type of poetry, often epic or
panegyric, because he subscribes to the Callimachean philosophy of art and considers 'smaller' genres 'better'.[82] He
couches his refusal as a deprecation of his own poetic
powers, which, he claims, are insufficient to the weight of
the task. But with the Callimachean value placed on terms
like 'smaller' and 'weight', the apparent self-deprecation is
necessarily also a self-proclamation.[83] When Daedalus tells
Jupiter that he will not attack the heavens, this is also Ovid
saying that he is not writing martial epic or encomium of
Augustus and that he subscribes to Callimachean poetic
values—although not necessarily telling us what that
means!

Daedalus is the paradigmatic inventor. His invention of
flying is more than a technological advance: it is the creation
of a new nature and so a bursting of the boundaries of the

[81] For the encomiastic equation of Augustus with Jupiter as conquerer of the
Giants see Wimmel (1960: 31).

[82] These metaphorical terms will be discussed further in the next chapter.

[83] Generalizing is always problematical. I do not intend to suggest that this is
the way *recusationes* always work.

human condition. Daedalus ends his dedicatory speech by inserting himself into the discourse of the ambivalence of inventiveness:

sunt mihi naturae iura nouanda meae.

The laws of my nature are to be made new for/by me.

The wings which he gives to himself and to Icarus are not given to men by nature. *Pinnis . . . datis* ('with wings given', v. 57) forcefully echoes *pennis non homini datis* ('wings not given to man') in Horace's first daedalian *Ode* (1. 3. 35). Going beyond the laws of his nature was man's primal sin—or his great glory. Ovid draws on this theme from the diatribe against inventiveness, making a pretence at pious scruples; but by making new the laws of his nature, Daedalus is sharing in Horace's daedalic metamorphosis into bird-nature in *Odes* 2. 20. Daedalus' 'bird-nature', Ovid's 'erotic didactic', is more than simply a grafting of wings on to a man, didactic style on to elegiac subject matter: it is the creation of a new nature. Two subliminal hints in the passage reinforce the 'bird-ness' (so to speak) of the post-metamorphic Daedalus. First, the mother-bird simile (v. 66). It is not surprising that Ovid uses the image of a bird to describe Daedalus teaching Icarus to fly, but that fact should not blind us to the closeness of the link between simile and *illustrandum*. Secondly, the new nature of the bird-man is foreshadowed at the very opening of the exemplum (v. 21):

hospitis effugio praestruxerat omnia Minos

Minos had built obstructions in the way of his guest's escape.

This is the only occurrence in Ovid of the fairly rare word *effugium*. The word is often used in the context of flight (see Bailey 1947: on Lucr. 1. 975, 1. 983), and may be intended, by Ovid, to foreshadow Daedalus' flying escape. It is used by Cicero to describe how nature has provided for the birds (*alias habere effugia pinnarum* 'others have flight on wings', *ND.* 2. 121),[84] but Daedalus is to take on a new,

---

[84] The only other occurrence in Cicero is at *Ver.* 5. 166. At *Met.* 5. 288 the Muses escape the violence of Pyreneus: *sumptis effugimus alis.*

foreign, and dangerous nature (v. 42), alien to that of man
—a bird's. Silius Italicus makes the pseudo-metamorphosis
plain: *nouus exterruit ales* ('the new bird was terrified',
Sil. 12. 95).

Daedalus, as I said, is the paradigmatic inventor (v. 22):

> *audacem pinnis repperit ille uiam.*
>
> He discovered a daring path on wings.

In this opening couplet, the verb signifying Daedalus' invention (*repperit*) gives him almost the status of a πρῶτος εὑρετής
('first founder').[85] The greatest of such heroes were hon-
oured, even deified, for the benefaction to mankind brought
about by their inventions. If the poet here hints at his
poetic invention, claiming equal originality and glory, he
has didactic authority for portraying his teaching as such
beneficent inventions, since Lucretius used the concept for
philosophical findings, those greatest of benefits to mankind
(1. 136):[86]

> *nec me animi fallit Graiorum obscura reperta*
> *difficile inlustrare Latinis uersibus esse*
>
> I am under no delusions about the difficulty
> of illuminating in Latin verse
> the hidden discoveries of the Greeks.

A way which is *audax* is daring but great: given the daedalic
contextualization, we may compare the use of audacity in
contexts of literary endeavour and literary fame.

> *da facilem cursum atque audacibus adnue coeptis*   (Virg. *Georg.* 1. 40)
>
> Give me an easy course and nod assent to my daring attempt.

> *sanctos ausus recludere fontis,*
> *Ascraeumque cano Romana per oppida carmen.*   (*Georg.* 2. 175–6)[87]

---

[85] Cf. Lucr. 3. 1036 *adde repertores doctrinarum atque leporum*; Var. *R.* 1. 2. 19
libero . . . repertori uitis; Virg. *Aen.* 7. 772 *repertorem medicinae talis et artis*; Prop.
2. 33. 27 (of Bacchus); Ov. *Her.* 5. 151; *Am.* 1. 3. 11 *uitisque repertor*; *Rem.* 76;
Fast. 2. 329 *repertori uitis pia sacra parabant*, 3. 762 (again a reference to
Bacchus); *Met.* 8. 246 *serrae repperit usum* (of Perdix inventing the saw). For
poetic versions cf. Tib. 2. 5. 112; Hor. *Ars* 278–9 *post hunc personae pallaeque
repertor honestae | Aeschylus*.

[86] Cf. Lucr. 1. 732 *praeclara reperta* (of Empedocles), 5. 2; and also Virg.
Georg. 2. 22 *quos ipse uia sibi repperit usus*.   [87] Cf. Virg. *Georg.* 4. 565.

. . . daring to open up the holy springs,
and I sing a Hesiodic song through Roman towns.

> *seu per audaces noua dithyrambos*
> *uerba deuoluit*   (Hor. *Carm.* 4. 2. 10)[88]

whether he rolls out new words in daring dithyrambs . . .

> *pictoribus atque poetis*
> *quidlibet audendi semper fuit aequa potestas*   (Hor. *Ars* 9–10)[89]

the same power has always been given to poets and painters
of daring whatever they like

> *non ideo debet pelago se credere, siqua*
> *audet in exiguo ludere cumba lacu.*   (Ov. *Tr.* 2. 329–30)[90]

Any skiff which dares to play about in a little lake
ought not therefore to trust itself to the sea.

In the last of these examples, the poet uses the metaphor,
made poignant by his exile, of the open sea representing
high poetry and the safe shallows representing Roman/Hel-
lenistic art. Now it is the skiff-driver in the little lake who
is daring, rather than the expected tempter of the high seas.
It can, ironically, be called 'daring' to attempt the 'safety'
of Callimacheanism. The question arises at this point: to
what extent is Daedalus 'daring'? He invites his son to
burst through the boundaries of human nature as he bursts
through the air (v. 54):

> *inuentis aera rumpe meis.*

> Break through the air on my invention.

But Icarus himself will cap his father's invention. Is Daedalus signifying Callimachean caution opposed to epic excess?
This question will be considered later. First we must look
at Daedalus' creation.

As I have suggested before, Daedalus' peculiar status as
signifier and signified allows his creation (the wings), as
well as his action (the flight), to act symbolically. The
creation of the wings mimes the creative and mimetic aspects of the artistic process (vv. 45–8):

---

[88] Horace is referring to Pindar, and alluding to elevated endeavours, with the
resultant artistic risks.

[89] See Brink's note on *audendi* (1971: ad loc.).

[90] Cf. also Hor. *Ep.* 2. 1. 166, 182, 258; *Ars* 382; Prop. 4. 6. 45.

> *remigium uolucrum, disponit in ordine pinnas*
> *et leue per lini uincula nectit opus;*
> *imaque pars ceris adstringitur igne solutis,*
> *finitusque nouae iam labor artis erat.*

> He disposes his feathers, oarage of birds, in order
> and weaves together a light work with bindings of linen;
> the lowest part is tied with wax melted by fire,
> and now the task of the new art was finished.

The careful, Callimachean-style crafting of the *Ars* is mirrored in that of the wings; the hybridization of the poem is mirrored in that of the very description of the act of creation. The hexameter of the first couplet is very poetic, almost martial epic, but in the pentameter the bonds are of linen, a work of delicate fragility, the liquid sounds in the pentameter aiding the sense. The description opens with a very poetic phrase. Already in Homer the metaphor of wings is applied to ships' sails or oars (*Od.* 11. 125):

> τά τε πτερὰ νηυσὶ πέλονται
> which become wings for ships

The image is powerfully used by Aeschylus in an eagle simile (*Ag.* 52):[91]

> πτερύγων ἐρετμοῖσιν ἐρεσσόμενοι.
> driven by their oarage of wings

Most significantly, as mentioned above, it occurs in Virgil's version of the Daedalus story (*Aen.* 6. 19), in which Daedalus, arriving at Cumae, dedicates his *remigium alarum* ('oarage of wings') to Apollo. Ovid's line begins in close allusion to the epic phrase, the elevated style being maintained through the hexameter with a flash of a military metaphor in the phrase *disponit in ordine* ('disposes in order').[92]

As Daedalus disposes his feathers, so Ovid disposes his words. *Disponere* is a technical term in the context of rhetorical/poetic organization of material, as for example at

---

[91] West (1978), commenting on the same metaphor in Hes. *Erg.* 628, says it is an established epic metaphor. Cf. also Eur. *Ion* 161; Ap. Rhod. 2. 1255; Lucr. 6. 743; Virg. *Aen.* 1. 301; Ov. *Met.* 5. 558, 8. 228; Sil. 12. 98.

[92] See *TLL* 5. 1. 1423. 13 for *disponere* and *OLD ordo* 2, 3, and 13c.

Cic. *Inv.* 1. 9 *dispositio est rerum inuentarum in ordinem distributio* ('disposition is the placing in order of ideas'); *de Orat.* 2. 79 *inuenire quid dicas, inuenta disponere* ('to invent what you may say, to dispose what you have invented').[93] As the *ordo uerborum* ('order of words') reflects, Ovid has arranged epic material in high-style poetry—but then tied together a light work as the couplet dissolves into Hellenistic littleness.

The *leue . . . opus* which Daedalus ties together out of his epic material is a light, Callimachean work, for the programmatic connotations of *leuis*, associated as it is with *leptotēs* ('fineness, delicacy'), make it one of the classic terms of Roman Callimacheanism. A *leue opus*, then, is the epitome of artistry, particularly in the sphere of Callimachean poetics. Appropriately to the context, Daedalus *ties* the work together (*nectit*). The word suggests the skilled and delicate twisting of poetry,[94] particularly in the Callimachean tradition. Virgil uses the image most famously at the end of the *Eclogues* (10. 70–1):

> *haec sat erit, diuae, uestrum cecinisse poetam,*
> *dum sedet et gracili fiscellam texit hibisco.*

This will be enough, goddesses, for your poet to have sung,
while he sits and weaves a basket with a slender mallow-reed.

Servius' comment is worthy of repetition: *allegorice dicit. significat composuisse hunc libellum tenuissimo stilo* ('he speaks allegorically, meaning that he has written this little book with the most slender pen [style]'). The weaving metaphor for writing poetry is used by Pindar (fr. 169 Bowra):

> ὑφαίνω δ' Ἀμυθαονίδαισιν ποικίλον
> ἄνδημα.

I weave an intricate binding for the children of Amythaon.

A related image is that most characteristic of Augustan

---

[93] Cf. Cic. *de Orat.* 2. 179–80, [Cic.] *Rhet. Her.* 1. 3, 3. 16; Hor. *Ars* 35, 41; [Ov.] *Ep. Sapph.* 13. For *ordo* in similar contexts see Cic. *de Orat.* 2. 179 *qui ordo tibi placeat . . . et quae dispositio argumentorum*; *Brut.* 276; Hor. *Sat.* 1. 4. 58–9 *et quod prius ordine uerbum est | posterius facias*; *Ep.* 1. 19. 29; *Ars* 41 *nec facundia deseret hunc nec lucidus ordo*; Petr. 6. 2; Quint. *Inst.* 7. 1. 1, 9. 3. 91.

[94] Cf. Ov. *Pont.* 4. 2. 30 *nec numeris nectere uerba iuuat*; Sen. *Ben.* 1. 4. 5; Stat. *Theb.* 5. 36, 8. 636.

metaphors for poetry, *deducere carmen* ('to spin out a song').[95]

It is with such delicate wings that Icarus seeks to fly to the heavens. We are reminded of their Callimachean metaphorical weakness by a suggestion of a word-play, as Icarus falls out of the sky (v. 86):

> *nec tenues uentos bracchia mota tenent.*

and his moving arms do not hold on to the thin breezes.

Ovid hints at a connection between *tenuis* ('slender', another powerful Callimachean signifier) and *teneo* ('I hold', a major signifier for this second book of the *Ars*).[96] The derivation would be by antiphrasis: *tenuis a non tenendo* ('thin from not holding') perhaps, like *lucus a non lucendo* ('grove from no light getting through').[97] Propertius also hints at the play (1. 11. 11):

> *aut teneat clausam tenui Teuthrantis in unda*

or [the water] might hold you shut up in the slender wave of Teuthras.

How could something flimsy *hold* something? But that is just what the poem does: it is a delicate Hellenistic work which holds girls (and readers) enthralled. The bonds of love, and of the *Ars*, and of *ars* are *tenues* ('thin'). They may be only *uincula lini* ('bonds of linen'),[98] but they are immeasurably strong.

In the second couplet of the description there is more vocabulary of poetics. The feathers are joined together with wax which has been melted by fire, a description which

[95] For the weaving metaphor cf. Bacch. 5. 9; Lucr. 1. 418, 6. 42; Auson. *Mos.* 415; Quint. *Inst.* 9. 4. 17; and esp. Prop. 2. 1. 35; *Ciris* 9 *coeptum detexere munus*, 39; Nemes. *Ecl.* 3. 16.

[96] For the function of *tenuis* in Callimachean programme an easy example is Virg. *Georg.* 4. 6 *in tenui labor; at tenuis non gloria*. For *tenuis* as belonging to plain style cf. *OLD tenuis* 12; Cic. *de Orat.* 3. 212; *Orat.* 29 *si tenui genere uteretur, numquam . . . tonare dictus esset;* Quint. *Inst.* 8. 3. 18 *a sermone tenui sublime* [*uerbum*] *discordat.*

[97] As Isidore explains (1. 37. 24) *antiphrasis est sermo a contrario intellegendus, ut 'lucus', quia caret luce per nimiam nemorum umbram* ('antiphrasis is a word understood from the opposite, as 'grove', because it lacks light through the great shade of the woods').

[98] Cf. Isid. 19. 27. 1 *quod sit molle et lene*, as would be very appropriate to the subject matter.

must foreshadow the fall of Icarus when the sun melts the wax. In Silius' version of the story, the phrase *solutis . . . remis* ('with oars [i.e. wings] undone', 12. 97–8) is used of the fatal melting. At the same time, however, modelling of wax is a metaphor for education.[99] Cairns (1984*b*: 97–8) has argued convincingly that wax was an important *poetic* symbol for Philetas, and that the symbol is picked up by Propertius at 4. 6. 3 *cera Philetaeis certet Romana corymbis* ('let Roman wax contend with the ivy-clusters of Philetas'). The same metaphor occurs in the forming of words into literature,[100] and acts programmatically for poetry through its part in the construction of pipes.[101] In the *Metamorphoses* version of the Daedalus story, the production of waxen pipes acts as a simile for the production of the waxen wings (8. 191–2):

> *sic rustica quondam*
> *fistula disparibus paulatim surgit auenis*

> In such a way, once upon a time, a rustic pipe gradually
> grows with reeds of different sizes.

The programmatic function of the signifier consolidates that of the signified. Making wax pipes (the signifier) is programmatic for poetry and so endorses the programmatic function of the signified (Daedalus making the wings). The artistic construction of the wings reflects both the pedagogic and the poetic aspects of Ovid's Art.

Before the work undergoes Daedalus' programmatic tying, the wax is loosened. The term used for the loosening relates to poetics (*solutis*), for *soluo* can have the sense of breaking up a metrical line.[102] In Horace's last Daedalian

---

[99] Cf. Hor. *Ars* 163 (with Brink 1971); Pers. 5. 40 *artificemque tuo ducit* [*sc. animus Persi*] *sub pollice uultum*; Juv. 7. 237 *exigite ut mores teneros ceu pollice ducat | ut si quis cera uoltum facit*; Plin. *Ep.* 7. 9. 11; Otto (1962: 80).

[100] Cf. Cic. *de Orat.* 3. 177 *sicut mollissimam ceram* [*uerba*] *ad nostrum arbitrium formamus et fingimus.*

[101] Pan pipes are waxen at Ov. *Met.* 11. 154 *et leue cerata modulatur harundine carmen.* Waxen pipes are programmatic for pastoral at Virg. *Ecl.* 3. 25–6 *aut umquam tibi fistula cera | iuncta fuit?* In the story of Pygmalion, wax is again a metaphor for the artistic process: *ut Hymettia sole | cera remollescit tractataque pollice multas | flectitur in facies* (*Met.* 10. 284–6).

[102] Cf. *OLD soluo* 11b; Hor. *Sat.* 1. 4. 60–1 *ut si soluas 'postquam Discordia taetra' . . . inuenias etiam disiecti membra poetae.*

Ode, where it is dangerous to imitate Pindar because he is like a great river rushing down the hillside (4. 2. 11), the great lyricist is described as using *numeris . . . lege solutis* ('unruly measures'), perhaps echoed by *igni solutis* in our line. Ovid starts with a formless mass of loose poetic *materia* and by the application of his *ars* turns it into *Ars*. Ovid's subject matter, whether it is Daedalus, or erotodidaxis, or both, is the stuff of poetry and by the use of *ars* is joined together into the taut (Callimachean) structure of verse.

Suddenly in the pentameter, in a classic example of Hellenistic compressed narrative, the work is complete. If ever there was a programmatically 'short' work (under the 'short is good' metaphor, which will be the main subject of the next chapter), then this is it. It is a *labor nouae artis* ('a task of a novel art'), terms with easy signification of Callimachean poetics, both in the careful artistry of the production and in the originality of the product. The creation of the wings is further linked with the creation of the book by the reminiscence in *iam labor artis erat* ('and now the work of art was . . . ') of the line in Ovid's own proem, *hoc erit artis opus* ('this will be a work of art', v. 14). Daedalus, in making new his nature (v. 42), creates a new art-form which will produce a new form of journey (v. 67); as Ovid creates a new form of poetry. Daedalus' *ars* is Ovid's *Ars*.

3*i* Daedalic Instruction

If Daedalus stands metaphorically for Ovid as poet, it will be no surprise to find him also behaving as teacher.[103] I have already mentioned the hint of education in the wax. There is perhaps also a hint in the *ima . . . pars* ('lowest/ earliest part') at early education, which is formed by the use of wax tablets. Suddenly in the next line the work is over— from infancy to graduation in two lines. A narrator's com-

[103] The parallels between Daedalus and Icarus and the *praeceptor* and his pupil have also been noted by Fyler (1971: 203), Verducci (1980: 37–8), and Myerowitz (1985: 162–30). Ahern (1989) also stresses the ironic inappropriateness of the exemplum, and argues primarily that Daedalus be seen as teacher, Icarus as pupil, and Minos as conservative social custom which would obstruct the erotic adventures of the pupil.

ment on Daedalus' moment of inspiration also signals his status as *magister amoris* ('teacher of love') (vv. 43–4):

> *ingenium mala saepe mouent: quis crederet umquam*
> *aerias hominem carpere posse uias?*

> Evils often move the intellect: who would ever have believed
> that a man would be able to pluck a path on the air?

It is *mala* which move Daedalus' artistry. *Mala* in erotic contexts without further definition are almost always the woes of love.[104] *Mala* shape the mode of the artist's expression, force the elegist to bewail at his mistress's door, Daedalus to fly through the skies, and Ovid to follow the path of the *Ars*. The poet in exile used similar terminology of his own *ingenium* (*Tr.* 3. 14. 33):

> *ingenium fregere meum mala*

> Misfortunes have broken my intellect.

The erotic connotations of *mala* and the ubiquitous presence of the amatory poetry in the exile poetry allow these *mala* to signify not only the poet's sufferings in exile, but also the erotic sufferings (or poems) which caused the exile. Again the poet in exile re-directs our reading of his earlier work.

It is in the speech to his son, however, that Daedalus' didactic tendencies are displayed. This speech stands in the didactic tradition of 'advice to sons', as exemplified by early Wisdom Literature (see West 1978: 3–25), and by Nestor's advice to his son, Antilochus, in Hom. *Il.* 23. 306–48, on how to drive a chariot. The didactic nature of the speech is signalled at its close with the narrator's comment (v. 65):

> *dum monet, aptat opus puero*

> While he is giving this advice, he fits the work to the boy.

Daedalus' advice is signalled as a lecture, *monere* being an overtly didactic term.[105] The *opus*, his *ars*, which Daedalus

---

[104] Cf. e.g. Virg. *Ecl.* 10. 61; *Aen.* 4. 549; Tib. 1. 2. 87, 1. 8. 64, 2. 6. 19; Prop. 1. 5. 28, 1. 7. 14, 1. 9. 18; Ov. *Her.* 11. 33, 20. 53; *Rem.* 138, 526, 768.

[105] Cf. Cic. *Tusc.* 2. 44 *tantum monet Epicurus quantum intellegit*; Tib. 2. 4. 51; Hor. *Ars* 344 *lectorem delectando pariterque monendo*; Ov. *Am.* 1. 8. 21 (Dipsas); *Ars* 1. 459, 2. 427–8 *qui modo celabas monitu tua crimina nostro,* | *flecte iter et monitu detege furta mea*, 509, 548 *quid faciam? monitis sum minor ipse meis* (cf. *Am.* 2. 19. 34), 3. 353, 494, 750; *Rem.* 124, 136, 296, 439, 804; *Tr.* 3. 4. 13 *haec ego si monitor monitus prior ipse fuissem* specifically about the *Ars*.

fits to Icarus parallels the *opus*, his *Ars*, which Ovid fits to the love-god.[106] That, after all, is ostensibly what this *exemplum* is all about. *Monere* can also signify poetic inspiration,[107] which is appropriate since, on one level of the metaphor, what Daedalus is teaching to Icarus is the art of poetry. At one level, Ovid too is teaching his pupil the art of elegiac love—or love elegy (vv. 51–64):

> *cui pater 'his' inquit 'patria est adeunda carinis;*
> *hac nobis Minos effugiendus ope.*
> *aera non potuit Minos, alia omnia clausit:*
> *quem licet, inuentis aera rumpe meis.*
> *sed tibi non uirgo Tegeaea comesque Bootae,*   55
> *ensiger Orion, aspiciendus erit;*
> *me pinnis sectare datis; ego praeuius ibo:*
> *sit tua cura sequi, me duce tutus eris.*
> *nam, siue aetherias uicino sole per auras*
> *ibimus, impatiens cera caloris erit;*   60
> *siue humiles propiore freto iactabimus alas,*
> *mobilis aequoreis pinna madescet aquis.*
> *inter utrumque uola; uentos quoque, nate, timeto,*
> *quaque ferunt aurae, uela secunda dato.*

To him his father says, 'On these keels we must go to our fatherland;
with this aid we must escape from Minos.
Minos can't block the air, although he has blocked everything else:
do what is allowed—burst through the air on my invention.
But you must not look at the Tegean girl and the companion of Bootes,
sword-bearing Orion.
Follow me on the wings you have been given; I shall go first:
let your concern be to follow, you'll be safe under my leadership.
For if we go through the upper air, near the sun,

---

[106] *Aptare* is a word of literary fitting: cf. Hor. *Carm.* 2. 12. 1–4 *nolis longa ferae bella Numantiae . . . mollibus | aptari citharae modis*, 2. 19. 25; *Ep.* 1. 3. 13; *Ars* 81, 195; Ov. *Tr.* 3. 7. 10 *aptaque in alternos cogere uerba pedes*, 4. 10. 25, 5. 1. 17–18. *Aptus* has particular significance for the *Ars.* Cf. 1. 5 *curribus Automedon lentisque erat aptus habenis* (cf. 2. 738), 1. 10 *sed puer est aetas mollis et apta regi* (of Amor), 1. 227–8 *et erunt quae nomina dicas, | si poteris uere, si minus, apta tamen* (cf. 2. 262), 1. 446, 760, 2. 724, 3. 122, 529, 808; *Rem.* 94, 126, 669. The art of love is finding τὸ πρέπον.

[107] Cf. Virg. *Aen.* 7. 41 *tu uatem, tu, diua, mone*; Tib. 1. 6. 50; Ov. *Fast.* 1. 467, 3. 261, 5. 447.

the wax will not endure the heat;
but if we toss our wings low down, near the sea,
the mobile feathers will grow wet from the waters of the sea.
Fly between the two; moreover, my son, fear the winds,
and spread your sails where the breezes bear you.

Specifically didactic vobaculary and syntax are prominent.
The gerundives *adeunda*, *effugiendus*, and *aspiciendus*
present a common grammatical feature of pedagogic style,
the last being enhanced by the address to the didactic 'you'
(*tibi*). The speech is full of imperatives, while the phrase *sit
tua cura* (v. 58) is a didactic formula.[108] With the phrase *me
duce*, which is used a number of times of his own erotodidaxis, Ovid installs Daedalus in the position of teacher,
producing and undermining a military metaphor, as it does
more overtly at *Ars* 1. 382:[109]

> *nec iuuenum quisquam me duce captus erit.*

And under my leadership no young man will be captured.

The whole speech is structured as a lecture: 'this is what
you must do; this is why you must do it; trust me; this is
what will happen if you don't; so do it!'

This is not just a lecture, however: it is also a didactic
poem. As Daedalus instructs his son in the art of sailing
through the air, he would naturally include some advice on
navigation by the stars (vv. 55–6):

> *sed tibi non uirgo Tegeaea comesque Bootae,*
> *ensiger Orion, aspiciendus erit*

But you must not look at the Tegean girl and the companion of
    Bootes,
sword-bearing Orion.

In so doing, he takes on the guise of the teacher of *Phaenomena*. Aratus must be an important didactic predecessor for
the *Ars*, especially if it is true that Ovid himself wrote a

---

[108] Cf. Virg. *Georg.* 1. 51–2 *uentos et uarium caeli praediscere morem | cura sit ac
patrios cultumque habitusque locorum*, 3. 305, 384, 4. 113; Ov. *Ars* 1. 354 *ancillam
. . . nosse . . . cura sit*, 2. 122, 242, 295, 3. 380, 484; *Rem.* 681.

[109] Cf. also *Rem.* 69–70, 253. The phrase is also used for a poetic lead: cf. Lucr.
6. 95 *Calliope . . . te duce ut insigni capiam cum laude coronam*; Prop. 3. 9. 47 *te
duce* [addressing Maecenas—with a certain irony] *. . . Iouis arma canam*; Ov. *Tr.*
4. 10. 119 (in a hymn to the Muse) *tu dux et comes es*; *Pont.* 2. 10. 21, 3. 3. 30.

Phaenomena. In his extreme caution, however, and in trying to protect his son, Daedalus is more informative on what his pupil should *not* do than what he should. 'Don't look at the stars; don't find your own way; just follow.' It is all too easy to get lost among Ovid/Daedalus' constellations, whether as aeronaut, as pupil of love whose instruction has been 'delayed', or as critic—as the reader may see in the following paragraphs.

Daedalus chooses the right stars for a teacher of navigation, or rather for a poet of the stars.[110] Helice and Orion are the standard navigational constellations as recorded by Apollonius (Ap. Rhod. 3. 744–6, trans R. C. Seaton):

> οἱ δ' ἐνὶ πόντῳ
> ναυτίλοι εἰς Ἑλίκην τε καὶ ἀστέρας Ὠρίωνος
> ἔδρακον ἐκ νηῶν.

> and on the sea sailors from their ships
> looked towards the Bear and the stars of Orion.

Helice is specifically the sign for the Achaeans according to Aratus (vv. 37–8, trans. G. R. Mair):

> Ἑλίκῃ γε μὲν ἄνδρες Ἀχαιοὶ
> εἰν ἁλὶ τεκμαίρονται ἵνα χρὴ νῆας ἀγινεῖν.

> It is by Helice that the Achaeans on the sea
> divine which way to steer their ships.

He goes on to remark on the extreme brightness of Helice. Orion is the sign for navigation (Arat. 728–31, trans. Mair):

> ἤδη καὶ Ποταμοῦ πρώτην ἁλὸς ἐξανιοῦσαν
> ἀγὴν ἐν καθαρῷ πελάγει σχέψαιτό κε ναύτης,
> αὐτὸν ἐπ' Ὠρίωνα μένων, εἴ οἴ ποθι σῆμα
> ἢ νυκτὸς μέτρων ἠὲ πλόου ἀγγείλειεν.

> Then, too, can the sailor on the open sea mark the first bend
> of the River rising from the deep, as he watches for Orion
>   himself

[110] For the constellations see Brandt (1902: ad loc.); also Musaeus *Hero and Leander* 213–14; Non. *D.* 38. 336. For Callisto cf. Arat. 41; Ov. *Met.* 2. 401; Paus. 8. 3. 6; Apoll. *Lib.* 3. 8. 2. For Bootes cf. Arat. 91; Ov. *Fast.* 3. 405. For Orion cf. Arat. 322; Ov. *Fast.* 5. 493–544; Hyg. *Astr.* 2. 34. The line's companion piece in the *Metamorphoses* mentions the same constellations: *nec te spectare Booten | aut Helicen iubeo strictumque Orionis ensem* (*Met.* 8. 206–7). Helice is Callisto. See Bömer (1977: ad loc.).

to see if he might give him any hint of the measure of the night or of his voyage.

Orion is very bright (Arat. 323–5, trans. Mair):

> μὴ κεῖνον ὅτις καθαρῇ ἐνὶ νυκτὶ
> ὑψοῦ πεπτηῶτα παρέρχεται ἄλλα πεποίθοι
> οὐρανὸν εἰσανιδὼν προφερέστερα θηήσασθαι.

Let none who pass him spread out on high on a cloudless night imagine that, gazing on the heavens,
one shall see other stars more fair.

So Daedalus acts as an astronomer; and the ubiquitous teacher self-referentially explains that he is not writing the *Phaenomena* now. This is the Art of Love. Daedalus/Ovid both is and is not Aratus.

A difficulty arises, however, when the lecturer refers to Orion as the companion of Bootes. As we read the hexameter, we might posit a learned allusion in *comesque Bootae* ('companion of Bootes') to Callisto's son, Arcas. Callisto, as a bear, was nearly killed by Arcas while he was hunting (*Met.* 2. 496–507). Both were metamorphosed into stars, Arcas becoming part of Bootes. Hyginus (*Astr.* 2. 1–2) shows that there is some confusion of identification over the three. Then (2. 4) he reports that Arcas/Arctophylax (i.e. the son of Jupiter and Callisto) was sometimes called Icarus (to whom Bacchus gave the vine: not to be identified, but possibly to be confused, with our Icarus), and that *complures Icarum Booten, Erigonen Virginem nominauerunt* ('many have called Icarus Bootes, and Erigone the Virgin'). Indeed, this would seem to allude quite neatly to Arat. 91–3 (trans. Mair):

> ἐξόπιθεν δ' Ἑλίκης φέρεται ἐλάοντι ἐοικὼς
> Ἀρκτοφύλαξ, τόν ῥ' ἄνδρες ἐπικλείουσι Βοώτην,
> οὕνεχ' ἁμαξαίης ἐπαφώμενος εἴδεται Ἄρκτου.

Behind Helice, like to one that drives, is borne along Arctophylax, whom men also call Bootes,
since he seems to lay hand on the wain-like bear.

In this case, Ovid/Daedalus would be making a professorial

correction of the confusion, by pointing out that the star, Arcas, is *part* of the constellation, Bootes.

But in the pentameter—*para prosdokian*—it is *Orion* who is the companion of Bootes. A sudden change in the pentameter which forces us to re-read the hexameter differently is very Ovidian, but that does not resolve the oddity. These two constellations are nowhere near each other in the sky, and indeed Orion is rising as Bootes is setting (Arat. 581–9).[111] Burman (1727: ad loc.) notices this problem, but claims that it is not a cause for concern, and quotes V. Flacc. 2. 67–8 *quo sidere uibret | Ensis et Actaeus niteat qua luce Bootes* ('in what star the Sword flashes and with what light Actaean Bootes shines') and less helpfully Prop. 2. 33. Bömer, commenting on the slightly less problematical *Met.* 8. 206–7, also feels that Daedalus/Ovid simply takes the most famous navigational constellations without further functional intention. The charge of carelessness in the choice of constellations is surely belied by a joke in *uirgo*. While the Latin term *uirgo* could signify someone who would not be signifiable by the English term 'virgin', we are probably meant to remember that Callisto was clearly not a virgin when metamorphosed, but that just beneath the feet of Bootes comes the constellation Virgo (cf. Arat. 97). Ovid both displays his *doctrina* in astrology—and gets it wrong. This is deliberate self-irony—the teacher who cannot teach.[112]

This is hardly a satisfactory solution to the problem, nor do I claim to have one.[113] A passage from the *Odyssey*, however, may shed some light on this couplet. Odysseus,

---

[111] *Comes* can be 'applied to a person or phenomenon occurring or existing at the same time as another' (*OLD comes* 6c): cf. Hor. *Carm.* 1. 28. 21–2 *deuexi rapidus comes Orionis . . . Notus*.

[112] At 2. 164, Ovid gives up in the face of the opposition of the rich rival: *cedimus: inuentis plus placet ille meis* ('I give up: he is more pleasing than my inventions'). This is an amusingly, perhaps slightly disturbingly defeatist attitude. But perhaps we should remember that *cedendo uictor abibis* ('by yielding you will depart as victor', v. 197).

[113] Among tentative further explanations for the problem could be that, if we can trust the remaining fragments of Hesiod's *Astronomia*, the first didactic poet treated Callisto, Bootes, and Orion together in that order, in which case Orion would be the *comes Bootae*, the one who follows after. It is unlikely that we can, however.

on his voyage away from Calypso's island, did not sleep but watched (5. 272–4)

ὀψὲ δύοντα Βοώτην
Ἄρκτον θ', ἣν καὶ ἄμαξαν ἐπίκλησιν καλέουσιν
ἥ τ' αὐτοῦ στρέφεται καί τ' Ὠρίωνα δοκεύει

Bootes setting late, and Arctos, who is also called the Wain, and who turns around in the same place and keeps an eye on Orion.

Beneath the didactic stance there may lie a recondite Hellenistic allusion. A passage from Musaeus *Hero and Leander* (203–20) uses terminology similar to Daedalus', when Leander promises that he will cross the wild sea for the sake of Hero's love; he will be a ship of love, and instead of navigational stars he will be guided by her lamp (vv. 213–14, trans. C. Whitman):

καί μιν ὀπιπεύων, οὐκ ὀψεδύοντα Βοώτην,
οὐ θρασὺν Ὠρίωνα καὶ ἄβροχον ὁλκὸν Ἀμάξης

and keeping my watch on that, not on late-setting Bootes,
Nor bold Orion, nor the track of the Wain [= Callisto] untouched
    by the sea.

Musaeus also uses the most famous navigational signs, but similarity between the two passages lies also in the fact that the person is *not* to use these constellations as aids to his journey, and that the 'swimmer' is a young man who will come to a watery end. If Musaeus is following a lost Hellenistic source, as is often believed (see Gelzer's 1975 note, p. 304), then the clue to our passage may lie there also.[114]

The Callisto-Bootes complex and Orion are nearly opposite each other in the sky, hence the passage of Manilius illustrating the unchangeability of the stars (1. 501–5):

iam tum, cum Graiae uerterunt Pergama gentes,
Arctos et Orion aduersis frontibus ibant,

---

[114] A further hint for the coupling of Bootes and Orion may be present in Nonnus *Dionysiaca* 38. 334–7. Lucifer calls out to the careering Phaethon, ἀμφοτέρων δὲ | πλαζομένων πεφύλαξο καὶ ἀπλανέων χορὸν ἄστρων, | μὴ θρασὺς Ὠρίων σε κατακτείνειε μαχαίρη | μὴ ῥοπάλῳ πυρόεντι γέρων πλήξειε Βοώτης. The connection is stronger with the *Metamorphoses* equivalent.

haec contenta suos in uertice flectere gyros,
ille ex diuerso uertentem surgere contra
obuius et toto semper decurrere mundo

Even then, when the Greek peoples overturned Pergamum,
Arctos (the Bear) and Orion went with their brows opposed to
  each other:
she content to turn her circles about the pole,
he to rise up opposite her as she turns from the other side,
coming in her way, and always to run around the whole world.

Isidore also treats the three in that order next to each other
(at 3. 71. 8–10). Through these standard constellations of the
book-learned, Ovid places both himself and Daedalus in
the tradition of great didactic poets. Perhaps the 'mistake'
about Orion being the companion of Bootes is a trap for the
critic . . .

Daedalus' astronomical lecture teaches Icarus that he is
meant passively to follow his father's lead. The habitual
form of *sequi* (v. 57) suggests careful, assiduous following
(cf. Tib. 2. 3. 7); or 'stalking', as at *Rem.* 201 (the only other
instance of the word in Ovid) *nunc leporem pronum catulo*
sectare sagaci ('now stalk the swift hare with a skilled
hunting-dog'). Icarus is told to play follow-my-leader with
his father, never straying from his artistic path, to become
in fact an imitator.[115] The metaphor of *following* is especially germane to didactic writing, where fidelity to authoritative sources (for the teacher) and to the instruction (for
the pupil) is a central aim. The metaphor is most elaborately
expressed by Lucretius (3. 1–30). *Sectare* is followed by
sequi in the next line, and *uela secunda* ('following sails' as
well as 'good-omened') in v. 64, while Daedalus emphasizes
his *active* role through his phrasing: *me . . . ego praeuius . . .*
me duce, but Icarus must passively accept the wings and
follow. The sequence of Me You makes Icarus follow his
father through the couplet: *me . . . sectare . . . ego praeuius*
. . . tua cura . . . me duce . . . tutus eris.[116]

---

[115] For this sense of the word see *OLD* 6; Tac. *Ann.* 16. 22 [*Thrasea*] *habet*
sectatores . . . qui nondum contumaciam sententiarum, sed habitum uultumque eius
sectantur; Gel. 1. 21. 7.
[116] Is there a hint of a play on Daedalus' underlying fear for his son in this
repetition of Me and You *me . . . tu*? See Ahl (1985: 175, 178) for the play on

Daedalus ends his lecture and approaches the flight with extreme caution, even fear. Icarus is told to *fear* the winds; Daedalus tries out the wings *fearfully*; he weeps before they go, and constantly watches his son as they fly. The journey which Daedalus and Icarus are about to undertake places them in the same relational positions as Ovid and the trainee lover on their journey through the poem. Ovid calls out to his pupil (vv. 9–10):

> quid properas, iuuenis? mediis tua pinus in undis
>   nauigat et longe, quem peto, portus abest.

Why do you hurry, young man? Your ship is sailing on the high
  seas
and the harbour which I am making for is far away.

This is what Icarus will do. Icarus stands metaphorically for the wandering boy, Amor, the poem which always threatens to break free from Ovid's poetic control, and the pupil who rushes off heedless of Ovid's didactic control.

3j Icarus: An Epic Failure

Daedalus offers us one artistic model, the model of the cautious Callimachean. Icarus offers us a more *fortis* ('strong') vision of art (vv. 75–84):

> iamque nouum delectat iter, positoque timore   75
>   Icarus audaci fortius arte uolat.
> (hos aliquis tremula dum captat harundine pisces
>   uidit, et inceptum dextra relinquit opus.)
> iam Samos a laeua (fuerant Naxosque relictae
>   et Paros et Clario Delos amata deo),   80
> dextra Lebinthos erat siluisque umbrosa Calymne
>   cinctaque piscosis Astypalaea uadis,
> cum puer incautis nimium temerarius annis
>   altius egit iter deseruitque patrem.

Now the novel journey delights him, and having put aside his
  fear
Icarus flies more strongly with audacious art.
(Someone saw them, while trying to catch fish with a quivering
  reed,

---

metus. Since *me* and *tu* are highlighted in this couplet, the syllables of *tutus* may be laid under contribution: *TUTUs*.

and the task on which he is engaged drops from his hand.)
Now Samos on the left (Naxos had been left behind,
and Paros and Delos loved by the Clarian god),
Lebinthos was on the right and Calymne shaded with woods,
and Astypalaea girt with fishy seas,
when the boy, rash in his heedless youth,
drove his path higher and deserted his father.

As the flight progresses, Icarus begins to enjoy himself, and
to do some adventurous experimentation of his own. As he
turns away from Daedalus he makes real progress, for you
are really learning when you learn independence from your
teacher. At this point (v. 76) we expect to hear about the
fall, but are instead delayed by three couplets of scene-
painting, allowing Ovid/Icarus to build up his soaring
powers.

The vignette of the watching fisherman reinforces the
status of the exemplum as signifier of the poem, particularly
as didactic. Fishing and hunting imagery have been central
to the *Ars*.[117] The instruction on how to find a girl began
with it (1. 45–6):

> *scit bene uenator, ceruis ubi retia tendat;*
> *scit bene, qua frendens ualle moretur aper.*

A hunter knows well where to stretch out his nets for deer;
he knows well in which valley the gnashing boar lives.

The image culminates in the triumphal opening of Book 2
(v. 2):

> *decidit in casses praeda petita meos.*

The desired prey has fallen into my trap.

Aliquis ('someone') in this case becomes an unsuccessful
lover who gives up in amazement on seeing the flight of the
Ars.[118] The phrase recalls Tib. 2. 6. 23 *haec [spes] captat
harundine pisces* ('this [hope] catches at fishes with a reed'),
where he is clearly, if covertly, alluding to the erotic fishing
metaphor. K. F. Smith (1913: ad loc.) points out that *captat*
means 'strive to catch', and not succeed.

---

[117] Fishing and hunting are also some of the classic subjects of didactic poetry.

[118] Pearson (1969) has a slightly different interpretation: the lover is amazed at
seeing his beloved fly out of reach.

The two succeeding couplets display themselves as a nobler form of didactic poetry, on geography, or some learned topic such as were the subjects for Hellenistic scholars; or as a pan-Aegean sweep from epic.[119] Now Icarus metaphorically signals a poet. The young poet begins a little shakily. The first couplet (vv. 79–80) rushes through four islands, all of them two-syllable names with short 'os' endings[120] and only one given any sort of an epithet, while the weird syntax adds up to rather a rocky first attempt. Still under the influence of his father, Icarus' first attempt is not very recondite. Naxos is a very well worked theme, mostly famously, and famously left, in the daedalic inset in Catullus 64; Delos is programmatically over-sung, according to Virgil (*Georg.* 3. 6):

> *cui non dictus Hylas puer et Latonia Delos?*

> Who has not spoken of the boy Hylas and Leto's Delos?

Paros is famous for its marble (e.g. *Met.* 7. 465 *marmoreamque Paron*, in another pan-Aegean sweep), and so is again lacking that edge of subtlety which is the mark of the great poet. Icarus therefore *leaves* (*relictae*) these famous isles behind in the quest for originality.

By the second couplet (vv. 81–2), the new poet has acquired more dexterity. The names are full and rounded, with each ending different, and the two epithets sonorously poetic, while the sweep culminates in an elegant four-word line to describe Astypalaea. The islands are more obscure: neither Calymne nor Astypalaea is mentioned in poetry before Ovid.[121] 'Icarus' (Ovid as Icarus) even attempts word-plays. The first is a relatively easy pun on Delos, derived from *dēlon* ('clear'),[122] and the cult-name Clarius,

---

[119] Cf. Virg. *Aen.* 3. 124–7 *linquimus Ortygiae portus pelagoque uolamus | bacchatumque iugis Naxon uiridemque Donusam, | Olearon niueamque Paron sparsasque per aequor | Cycladas.*

[120] In *Naxosque* the vowel is short although the syllable is long.

[121] See *TLL Onomasticon* and Bömer (1977) on Calymne. For Calymne see Strabo 10. 5. 19. For Astypalaea see perhaps Hyg. *Fab.* 157, where an Astypale is mentioned as bearing Periclymenus and Ancaeus to Neptune.

[122] Cf. Plut. *Fab.* 385c Δήλιος δὲ καὶ Φαναῖος οἷς ἤδη τι δηλοῦται καὶ ὑποφαίνεται τῆς ἀληθείας; Isid. 14. 6. 21.

hinting at *clarus* ('clear').[123] It is appropriate to have a play involving Greek and Latin words in a couplet showing off its bilingual virtuosity. The second play on words is more recondite. *Calymne* is very like *kalumma*, a head-covering or veil (v. 81);

> *siluisque umbrosa Calymne*
> Calymne shaded with woods

So the veiled place is shaded with woods. The two name-plays interact as opposites, the first being about clarity and the second about obscurity. The crescendo climaxes (v. 82) with an island described in full poetic terminology with a hint at Homeric epithets for islands, like *perirrutos* ('sea-girt', *Od.* 19. 173), *amphialos* ('living amid seas', *Od.* 21. 252).

> *cinctaque piscosis Astypalaea uadis.*
> and Astypalaea girt with fishy seas.

The word order of the line does what it says, with *piscosis . . . uadis* ('fishy seas') surrounding *Astypalaea*. With a whole line to describe one island, the narrative slows down, as Icarus builds up his elevated poetic powers.

In addition to his elevation, Icarus' flight-path may be significant. Rudd (1988: 24) discusses the question of the 'aeronauts' route' and destination. As he says, the sequence Naxos, Paros, Delos makes sense as a route from Crete to Attica (he assumes that that is their destination rather than Cumae), but the eastern turn towards Calymne does not. Of course, Icarus has to end up in the Icarian sea.[124] The interesting suggestion has been made to me by Anna Wilson that Icarus has left the path of Daedalus in order to head for Homeric Ionia, perhaps Colophon, the birthplace (or one of the birthplaces) of Homer.[125] His route thus becomes a metaphor for his poetic allegiance to epic. The oblique reference to Colophon through the Apolline epithet *Clarius*

---

[123] Cf. the equation of Tibullus' Delia with Plania.

[124] Rudd's tentative solution is that Icarus originally fell into the sea off Attica, giving his name to the Attic deme Icaria (5km from Marathon). 'When Ionians from Attica colonized [the other end of the Aegean] in the tenth or eleventh century BC, they named it Icaria after the old-country deme, and as a result the legend of Icarus suffered geographical dislocation.'

[125] Cic. *Man.* 33; Hor. *Ep.* 1. 11. 3; Vitr. 4. 1. 4; Liv. 37. 26. 5.

(from Claros, an Ionian town near Colophon) adds contextual support to the suggestion.

This is Icarian poetry. In contrast to that of Daedalus, Icarus' art is characterized by incaution, folly which is part of the daring of a high-soaring poet.[126] When at last he drives his course higher, he has reached elevated style, having flown to the heights of poetry to enjoy a moment of independent glory before he falls.[127] And with that fall, as Icarus' epic flight collapses, the tone of the passage descends into comedy (vv. 85–90):

> uincla labant et cera deo propiore liquescit
>   nec tenues uentos bracchia mota tenent.
> territus a summo despexit in aequora caelo;
>   nox oculis pauido uenit oborta metu.
> tabuerant cerae; nudos quatit ille lacertos,
>   et trepidat nec, quo sustineatur, habet.

The bonds slip and the wax begins to melt in the vicinity of the
  deity,
and the moving arms do not hold on to the thin winds.
Terrified he looked down from the highest heaven to the depths;
darkness rose up over his eyes with panicking fear.
The wax had melted; he flaps naked arms,
and shakes, having nothing to hold him up.

The elegant movement of Daedalean art has become a frantic flapping, as Icarus tries to perform a proverbial adunaton: *sine pennis uola* ('fly without wings'). This is the risk of flying too high—you may become ridiculous. Ovid burlesques Icarus' epic pretensions by a reminiscence of the experiences of the Aeneadae in the first storm scene (*Aen.* 1. 106–7):

> hi summo in fluctu pendent; his unda dehiscens
>   terram inter fluctus aperit, furit aestus harenis

---

[126] For *cautum* and *incautum* in this context cf. Hor. *Carm.* 2. 10. 2–3 *dum procellas | cautus horrescis* (a poem reflecting similar double language of poetry and life); *Ars* 46 *in uerbis etiam tenuis cautusque serendis*, 266–7 *tutus et intra | spem ueniae cautus*.

[127] With *altius egit iter* cf. Cic. *Brut.* 276 *quorum altior oratio actioque esset ardentior*; *Orat.* 192 (describing the middle style) *neque humilem et abiectam orationem nec nimis altam et exaggeratam*; Sen. *Ag.* 327–8 *nil acre uelim magnumque modis | intonet altis*. For *deseruitque patrem* cf. TLL 5. 1. 677. 38 *deserere artem*. It can mean leave the study of literature, or, as here, a particular master.

Some hang on the crest of the swell; for others the gaping wave
uncovers the sea-bed between the swells; the surge seethes with
sand.

Ovid burlesques the *Aeneid* passage also by lifting the scene
to a ridiculously higher level, and substitutes a small boy
(who had pretensions to an Aeneas-like persona at v. 50) for
the warriors of Troy. Even Icarus' fear is of epic propor-
tions. In contrast to the mild vocabulary of fear applied to
Daedalus (*timide*), the darkness which covers Icarus in his
terror has precedents in Homeric fear, for example
(*Il.* 4. 461):

> τὸν δὲ σκότος ὄσσε κάλυψεν
>
> Darkness covered his eyes.

This *is* an epic sea-storm scene, for Icarus got epically
shipwrecked on his poetic journey.

The wax melts and the *leue opus* ('light work') falls apart.
Icarus has nothing *quo sustineatur* ('to hold him up', v. 90),
unlike Daedalus, who knew how to hold his part; that is, he
sustinet cursus ('maintained his course', v. 74). The navigational language gains a new level of appropriateness in that
Daedalus must literally *hold up* his course—altitudinally.
Daedalus characteristically maintains his middle course
(unlike his son, who fails to hold up his course—literally)
and, it is perhaps hinted, his character, for *sustinet* can have
the sense of 'maintain a part or character'.[128] Daedalus
maintains the middle way of Hellenistic littleness. Ovid too
knows all about holding, about *teneo*-ing, however difficult
it may be *detinuisse* ('to have held on to/back') Daedalus,
Amor, the poem, and the exemplum.

When Icarus falls into the sea, the water covers his
mouth and stifles his cries to his father (vv. 91-2):

> *decidit atque cadens 'pater o pater, auferor' inquit;*
> *clauserunt uirides ora loquentis aquae.*

He falls and falling says, 'Father, oh Father, I am being carried
off';
the green waters closed his mouth as he spoke.

---

[128] Cf. Cic. *de Orat.* 2. 251 *naturae ridentur ipsae, quas personas agitare solemus,
non sustinere*; Juv. 3. 93 *cum Thaida sustinet aut cum uxorem comoedus agit*.

The second half of the pentameter is repeated by Ovid in a passage from exile which initially seems unconnected. Ovid, about to be shipwrecked, says (*Tr.* 1. 2. 13–14):

> *uerba miser frustra non proficientia perdo.*
> *ipsa graues spargunt ora loquentis aquae.*

> Unhappy and in vain, I am wasting profitless words.
> The heavy waters splatter my mouth as I speak.

Such an exact quotation should not be ignored. *Tristia* 1. 2 presents Ovid speaking poetry under the dramatized situation of the sea voyage, and his words (his poem) are stopped by the water splashing in his face. The sea voyage as a metaphor for poetic composition has a particular poignancy for the writer in exile, or rather, on his way to exile. This is shipwreck, poetic failure, as he is constantly reminding us in the exile poetry. In the *Ars*, Icarus has been signalling poetry under the metaphor of flight, and is now stopped by the waters closing over his mouth as he ceases to fly. In the previous *Tristia* poem, the *Ars* was Icarus falling to his death and suppression (1. 1. 90). It is impossible to talk with a mouth full of water; it is impossible to write poetry when you cease to fly through the air or over the seas.

Daedalus steers a middle course, but Icarus flies high. One strand in the web of poetic programme here is a sort of an altercation between 'epic' and 'Callimacheanism'.[129] All sorts of problems arise in a statement like this, hence my hedging disclaimers, and indeed in the very act of attempting to understand the passage and to set it straight, we risk destroying some of the resonances and ambiguities of this complex metaphorical system (even calling it a 'system' has that risk). One simple point to note first is that 'epic' can stand for all elevated poetry, and of course 'elevation' depends on the viewpoint of the speaker. Flying high stands for epic: safety stands for Callimacheanism. But safety can be Callimacheanism, and so a sort of poetic success; or

---

[129] It can be part of the polemic to oppose Callimacheanism to epic. On this subject generally see Bundy (1972), although some scholars (for example F. Williams 1978: 86) would say (and I would agree) that the opposition is not so simple.

poetic caution, and so a sort of failure. Daring can be epic, or elevated poetry produced using the canons of Callimacheanism, or even Callimacheanism—you can 'dare to be little'.

By his extreme poetic caution Daedalus risks losing the fame which his son wins to his great cost. He does not seek to touch the stars (v. 39): such a flight of fame is not for him. But Icarus soars to heaven, up into the heights of poetry with only the *leue opus* ('light work') of Daedalus to support him. After a brief moment of glory he falls, and fails, but he wins eternal fame. Despite the positive value laid by Ovid and other Augustans on moderation and Callimachean littleness *as opposed* to high (generally epic) poetry, it is nevertheless also a topos of classical poetic thought that it can be great to be 'great', and even (after Virgil) that it might be possible to be 'Callimachean' while being un-Callimachean. It can be great to be 'great' (un-Callimachean): that is what Horace's Icarus humorously says. In each of the three Horatian *Odes*, elevated poetry, and possibly in some sense un-Callimachean poetry, is at issue. It can be great to be un-Callimachean—Pindar, Ennius, the *Aeneid*, Icarus. What is remarkable about the *Aeneid* is that although we might expect it to belong to the Icarian side of the dichotomy, in fact the commentary on it offered by *Odes* 1. 3 belongs to the discourse not of *nomina ponto* ('names to the sea', that is the Icarian story of fame through flawed greatness and failure) but of Daedalian heroes, for in Horace's reading (which would be endorsed by many modern critics) Virgil in the *Aeneid* manages to be Daedalus (not Icarus) without the poetic caution and without the loss of fame. I am tempted to simplify by saying that Virgil is Callimachean (being Daedalus), as opposed to the Icarian, un-Callimachean Pindar and Ennius. Such oppositions are, however, always already deconstructed.

A number of signals in the passage relate Icarus to the world of epic. I mentioned above that the journey through the Styx connects Daedalus with Horace as famous book-bird, and indirectly with Aeneas in katabasis. The difference is that the journey through the Styx is precisely *avoided* by Daedalus. It is Icarus who will undergo it, and return, in a

sense, through his fame. The heroic and potentially hybristic journey and the still more heroically hybristic relationship with human mortality opposes Daedalus to things epic
and identifies Icarus with them.

During the lecture from his father, Icarus is playing with
the materials (vv. 49–50):

> *tractabat ceramque puer pinnasque renidens*
> *nescius haec umeris arma parata suis.*

The boy played about with the wax and beamed at the feathers,
unaware that these are arms prepared for his shoulders.

The scene itself introduces Icarus' own creative attempts,
as he uses his *ingenium* on the *materia*.[130] Icarus is *nescius*
('ignorant') of *ars*, however, and *nescius* of the significance
of what he handles, as he simply delights in its instrinsic
beauty. In this, he is reminiscent of Aeneas admiring the
arms created for him by Vulcan, who as Hephaestus is the
divine counterpart of Daedalus. *Arma* is rather a strange
word to use of the wings in the context, although acceptable
Latin in the sense of equipment, tools. The unusual use of
arma, together with his ignorance, gives Icarus pretensions
to being an epic hero; and hints at a parody of the Shield of
Aeneas (Virg. *Aen.* 8. 729–31):

> *talia per clipeum Volcani, dona parentis,*
> *miratur rerumque ignarus imagine gaudet*
> *attollens umero famamque et fata nepotum.*

He marvels at such things on the shield of Vulcan,
a parent's gift, and ignorant of the substance he rejoices in the
   image,
lifting up on to his shoulder the fame and fates of his
   descendants.

In so far as there may be an opposition between epic and
Callimacheanism, the old controversy between *ars* and *ingenium* can be pressed into its service. Although literary
polemic cannot be reduced to simple oppositions, the dichotomy between *ars* and *ingenium*, however false, was
manipulated by the Augustans into their Callimachean

---

[130] *Tractabat: tracto* has an overtly literary sense of dealing with a subject,
OLD tracto 9.

poetic manifesto. The ancient critic pseudo-Longinus, on the other hand, valued surges of natural genius, even flawed, above perfection—*ingenium* above *ars*: so he says in a passage where the meticulous 'safe' care of the Alexandrian is deprecated (*On the Sublime* 33–4). The views of pseudo-Longinus should not necessarily be taken to reflect exactly those of the Augustan poets, but it is interesting that he claims that flawed sublimity is better—and particularly will win greater fame—than perfect mediocrity (33, 36). The examples he gives (33) of perfect mediocrity are mostly Hellenistic poets. Flawed sublimity is exactly what Icarus achieves.

'Flawed sublimity' would, I suspect, quite accurately describe the attitude of the Augustans to Ennius, so in this consideration of poetics we might expect the figure of Ennius to appear. Ennius epitomizes, in some senses, the *opposite* of what we might call 'Roman Callimacheanism', a figure against whom a Callimachean poet may define his poetic theory, and yet was a (fallen) hero. He fell into the trap of using *ingenium* before *ars*, so Ovid suggests (*Tr.* 2. 424):

> *Ennius ingenio maximus, arte rudis.*
> Ennius the greatest in intellect, crude in art.

The term *maximus* ('greatest')—a self-referential superlative—is ambiguous: 'bigness' is the opposite of Callimacheanism, but it is also 'greatness'.[131] Ennius is *arte carens* ('lacking in art'), but he will have a *casurum nullo tempore nomen* (*Am.* 1. 15. 19), 'a name which will never fail', or, moreover, fall. Icarus falls, but his name does not. Icarus is signalled as *rudis* ('crude') by the term used for Daedalus' instruction to him, *erudit* ('teaches', v. 66), which was commonly derived from *rudis* (Isid. 10. 81).[132] Icarus, being *rudis*, feels the tug of the epicist. By contrast, Ovid places Callimachus' *ars* above his *ingenium*, in the same poem as the comment on Ennius just quoted (*Am.* 1. 15. 13–14):

---

[131] This will be discussed further in the next chapter.
[132] The word is often glossed as *paideuein*.

> *Battiades semper toto cantabitur orbe:*
> *quamuis ingenio non ualet, arte ualet.*

The child of Battus will always be sung throughout the world.
Although he is not strong in *ingenium*, he is strong in *ars*.

Valet here is given a quasi-paradoxical, Callimachean weighting. Callimachus is famous not despite his lack of weight in *ingenium* but precisely because of it—as a Callimachean.

Icarus is carried away by his new journey (*iamque nouum delectat iter*, v. 75), in terms redolent of the seductive frenzy of poetic inspiration.[133] There is an interesting instance of *delectare* ('to delight') in the exile poetry (*Tr.* 4. 1. 35–6):

> *nos quoque delectant, quamuis nocuere, libelli,*
> *quodque mihi telum uulnera fecit, amo.*

My books delight me, even though they have harmed me,
and I love the weapon which caused my wound.

Within the terms of the metaphor, this is what happens to Icarus. This is the magical, mesmeric effect of Ovid's poetry, to seduce beloved, lover and reader—and author—alike. (Sexual hints lie not far beneath the surface, as so often when Ovid is talking about poetry.) For the poet in exile, this *amor artis* ('love of art') was in a real sense poetic shipwreck, but one which brought him fame.

In his lecture, Daedalus instructs Icarus to be wary of the winds: *uentos quoque, nate, timeto* ('fear the winds, also, my son', v. 63). Daedalus' advice betrays his character as one of extreme caution, in keeping with the canons of Hellenistic art (when it suits the speaker!) and, for that matter, with the ethos of the *Ars*. The student has to learn to love, paradoxically, with his wits about him and with great caution and attention to detail. By contrast, full sails and strong winds are a metaphor for elevated style in poetry and rhetoric.[134] Instead of strong winds, Icarus is to

---

[133] Cf. *Ars* 2. 237; Hor. *Sat.* 2. 1. 28; *Ep.* 2. 2. 59. *Delectare* is fairly rare, particularly in poetry, according to *TLL* 5. 422. 23. Its rarity allows the occurrences more resonance with each other.

[134] Cf. *Ars* 3. 99–100; *Tr.* 2. 547–8 *ne tamen omne meum credas opus esse remissum,* | *saepe dedi nostrae grandia uela rati*, 3. 4. 31–2 *tu quoque formida nimium sublimia semper,* | *propositique, precor, contrahe uela tui.*

use the little *aura* ('breeze') of Callimachean caution. The contrast between *uentus* ('wind') and *aura* ('breeze') is repeated in a poetic progress image at *Ars* 3. 99–100:

> *sed me flaminibus uenti maioris iturum,*
>   *dum sumus in portu prouehat aura leuis.*

> But while we are in port, may a light breeze drive me
> as I am about to go with the blasts of a greater wind.

The *uela* ('sails') which Icarus is to give to these *aurae* are of course in fact wings, wings which are now sails as well as oars (*remigium uolucrum*). It is proverbial to speak of using sails and oars meaning to go with all speed, and this is exactly what Icarus does. When, in the highly programmatic first poem of the *Tristia*, the story of Icarus (= the *Ars*) is used as a warning to the new book not to seek the heights, the same proverbial terminology is used (*Tr.* 1. 1. 89–92):

> *dum petit infirmis nimium sublimia pennis*
>   *Icarus aequoreis nomina fecit aquis.*
> *difficile est tamen hinc, remis utaris an aura*
>   *dicere.*

> While he was making for realms too lofty on his weak wings,
> Icarus made a name for the plain of the sea.
> But it is difficult to say from here
> whether you should use oars or sails.

Clearly it should not use both, as that would be flying *fortius* ('more strongly'), as Icarus does.

Daedalus promises that if Icarus follows his moderate course, he will be safe: *me duce tutus eris* (v. 58). Simple fatherly concern couches Callimachean programme here, for the terminology may remind us that Apollo once told Propertius to avoid the high seas if he wanted to be 'safe' = Callimachean (Prop. 3. 3. 23–4):[135]

> *alter remus aquas alter tibi radat harenas,*
>   *tutus eris.*

> Let one of your oars be in the sea, and the other scrape the sand;
> you will be safe.

With Daedalus as his leader, Icarus will follow Hellenistic

---

[135] For a brief programmatic interpretation of this couplet see my note (1990).

littleness and be safe—but he does not want to be safe. Daedalus' 'safety' is answered by Icarus' fame (*Tr.* 3. 4. 21–2):

> *quid fuit, ut tutas agitaret Daedalus alas,*
> *Icarus inmensas nomine signet aquas?*

Why was it[136] that Daedalus beat safe wings,
when Icarus signed huge seas with his name?

Although Icarus falls by soaring to the heights, there is encomium of his great fame. 'Safety'—poetic or otherwise—was not for him.

So what does all this signify? Is it that 'Daedalus' equals Callimacheanism; 'Icarus' equals anti-Callimacheanism/ epic; Ovid equals Daedalus and rejects anti-Callimacheanism? There may, I suspect, be an element of truth in that, but already it is a false dichotomy. Daedalus is not an unambiguous signifier of Callimacheanism, as *Odes* 1. 3 shows us; nor is Callimacheanism an unambiguous signified. Daedalus can be transgressive or cautious. Callimacheanism can be cautious or transgressive. Icarus is the famous transgressor, but is he 'epic' or 'attempts at elevated poetry in Callimachean style'? A simple dichotomy between Daedalus and Icarus—and their signifieds—is belied by two parallels in the text, which I shall discuss next.

First, Daedalus opens the exemplum with an *audax uia* ('daring way'). His flight-path was both a feat of presumptuous, potentially hybristic daring and a cautious middle course. Icarus later leaves his father and flies *fortius* ('more strongly') with *audaci arte* ('audacious art', v. 76). Is Icarus more *audax* ('daring') than Daedalus, or *audax* in a different way? You can dare to be little and you can dare to be great. Secondly, Daedalus initiates a novel journey, a *nouum iter* at v. 67, which is then re-initiated by Icarus at v. 75. The difference is in the reactions of the fliers. Daedalus treats it *timide* ('fearfully') while Icarus delights in it, *posito timore* ('having put aside fear'). Daedalus and Icarus are both dealing with poetry, but only Daedalus treats it carefully.

If Daedalus is Ovid, then what does it mean to lose

---

[136] We might perhaps give a stronger translation: 'What use was it . . . ?'

Icarus? The loss of the son is after all self-representational failure. We might perhaps say that losing Icarus is writing Callimachean didactic, not heroic epic or high didactic. Is it therefore losing the excess of fame? It is a way of saying 'I'm Callimachean', but is that itself a claim to fame? And is Ovid ever Icarus? Are sons ever their fathers? Icarus is and is not Ovid. The whole story is caught up in the rhetoric of the disclaimer, so that it is up to the *reader* to decide whether Ovid's claim not to be claiming greatness really constitutes a claim to greatness. It is up to the reader to decide whether Daedalus or Icarus is Ovid, whether Daedalus or Icarus is more *audax*. Only the reader can decide the extent of Ovid's poetic fame.

3k *sit modus exilio*: Daedalus and Ovid in Exile

If the myth of Daedalus and Icarus is as functional in the *Ars* as I am suggesting, one might expect it also to be functional elsewhere in the Ovidian corpus. The story of Daedalus' *patrius amor* ('fatherly love') becomes in the exile poetry the story of Ovid's *amor patriae* ('love of the father-land'). In the exile poetry, the myth resurfaces in another prominent and programmatic position, at *Tristia* 1. 1. 89–90,[137] where it illustrates Ovid's advice for his book, to avoid the heights of readership—Augustus.

> *dum petit infirmis nimium sublimia pennis*
> *Icarus aequoreis nomina fecit aquis.*

While he was making for realms too lofty on his weak wings,
Icarus made a name for the plain of the sea.

This and the preceding passage (*Tr.* 1. 1. 81–2) clearly refer to the trouble caused by the Emperor's reaction to the *Ars*.

> *me quoque, quae sensi, fateor Iouis arma timere:*
> *me reor infesto, cum tonat, igne peti.*

I confess that I also fear the arms of Jupiter, which I have felt:
when it thunders I think that I am being attacked by hostile fire.

There is a clear hint at Gigantomachy here. The extent to

---

[137] See Hinds (1985) for the programmatic significance of this poem.

which Augustus' reading of the *Ars* was actually responsible for the poet's relegation is immaterial; the point is that Ovid plays with this idea, or pretence, throughout the exile poetry (*Tr.* 1. 1. 87–8):

> *ergo caue, liber, et timida circumspice mente,*
> *ut satis a media sit tibi plebe legi*

So take care, my book, and look around you with a fearful mind, that it should be enough for you to be read by the masses.

Here Icarus is quite overtly a paradigm for the *Ars* itself (89–90).[138] Now it is the *Ars* itself which dared the heights, dared to be great (poetry); but its daring, like that of the imitator of Pindar, was on the basis of *infirmis pinnis* ('weak wings'), *daedalea ope* ('with daedalic assistance'), Callimachean (equals—metaphorically—good artistic) 'weakness'. Here Icarus' ambiguous fame rests precisely on the weakness of his wings, like the baby bird which Ovid/Daedalus taught to fly (*Ars* 2. 66). Even here, amid the (pose of) gloom and despondency, Icarus retains his ambiguity between fame and death, for the *Ars*, Ovid claims, caused his downfall *because* it achieved such great poetic fame, and Icarus is the ideal paradigm, within the rules of *decorum*, for such ambiguous success.[139] Much of the exile poetry which purports to defend the *Ars* in fact exalts it. *Tr.* 1. 1. 89–90 is the answer to what is on one level the question of *Ars* 2. 21–98, namely, how does one achieve poetic fame? Answer: through flight, risk of failure, and *inuidia* ('envy').

In his prayer to Augustus in *Tristia* 1. 1, Ovid forcefully redirects our reading of the *Ars*-story by a clear echo of Daedalus' prayer to Minos.

> *et, quoniam in patria fatis agitatus iniquis*
> *uiuere non potui, da mihi posse mori.*   (*Ars* 2. 27–8)

---

[138] It is interesting in view of Wise's (1977) hypothesis (that the flights of Daedalus and Icarus and *Phaethon* are paradigmatic for the *Metamorphoses*) that the other boy who fell out of the sky is also paradigmatic for the poetic fate of Ovid: *uitaret caelum Phaethon, si uiueret, et quos | optarat stulte, tangere nollet equos* (*Tr.* 1. 1. 79–80).

[139] For self-deprecation as a polite tempering of a claim for greatness see above, Section 3*e* on *Odes* 2. 20.

And since, driven by an unfair fate, I have not been able to live
in my fatherland, grant that I may die there.

> *ablataque principis ira*
> *sedibus in patriis det mihi posse mori.*   (*Tr.* 1. 1. 33–4)

> and may the removal of the princeps' anger
> grant me to die in my paternal home.

The echo assists a fusion of the two exiles, whose art
brought fame—and loss.

Icarus' ambiguous connection with Ovid's poetic fame
and failure surfaces again at *Tristia* 3. 4. 21–2:

> *quid fuit, ut tutas agitaret Daedalus alas,*
> *Icarus inmensas nomine signet aquas?*

> Why was it that Daedalus beat safe wings,
> when Icarus signed huge seas with his name?

This poem elaborates the ambiguous idea *nomina magna
fuge* (v. 4): 'avoid great friends', or 'avoid great fame'? The
poem advises its addressee not to seek the *heights* in *great*
friends, but to live for himself in obscurity, because fame
results in Ovid's own present predicament. Can we really
believe the poet's contention that it would have been better
to have lived in obscurity when the poem ends in celebration
of his own *nomen*? (*Tr.* 3. 4. 45–6):

> *Nasonisque tui, quod adhuc non exulat unum,*
> *nomen ama: Scythicus cetera Pontus habet*

> Love the name-fame of your Naso, which alone
> is not yet exiled. Scythian Pontus holds the rest.

That celebration is itself a clear reference to the end of our
passage (vv. 97–8),

> *Icare,' clamabat; pinnas aspexit in undis.*
> *ossa tegit tellus, aequora nomen habent.*

> Icarus,' he was calling; he saw the feathers in the waves.
> Earth covers his bones, the seas have his name-fame.

Icarus is dead, but he has achieved great fame: a sea and an
island named after him. The contrast between *ossa* ('bones')
and *nomen* ('name') encapsulates the success and the failure,
the fall and the fame. The sea has a name (Icarian Sea).

The sea has his (Icarus') name, one which has been uttered three times in the last two couplets and one which was in Daedalus' possession until it was appropriated by the sea and he lost the right to the other name, *pater* (*nec iam pater*, 'no longer a father', v. 93). And the sea has fame—of Icarus.[140] The appropriation by the sea of (the name) Icarus is foregrounded by the threefold naming of him, creating the echo *Icare aequora*, with the same metrical pattern and with '*ora*' echoing '*are*'. The structure playfully merges and submerges *Icare* in *aequora*. The simple answer to Ovid's not-so-rhetorical question (of *Tr.* 3. 4. 21–2 quoted above) is—fame. The emphasis thrown on our passage by the fact that in both *Tristia* examples of the myth the poet has one eye permanently on the *Ars* is perhaps the fullest support for a highly functional interpretation of the story.

The passage which begs consideration at this point is the retelling of the Daedalus and Icarus story in the *Metamorphoses* (8. 183–235). The following hypothesis is only tentative. For my argument, the most interesting possibility about the story of Daedalus and Icarus in the *Metamorphoses* is that it was written or revised with knowledge of the exile. Ovid is at pains to remind us that the *Metamorphoses* was not finished when he was exiled (*Tr.* 1. 7. 13–14, 3. 14. 19–24). As a reason to be allowed home, there is of course a *poetic* point in having the poem 'unfinished', while the *magnum opus* may also be generically 'unfinished' in conscious imitation of the greatest of *magna opera*, the *Aeneid*. The exiled poet's frequent references to his desire to burn the manuscript are probably intended to place his poetry and poetic career in the Virgilian tradition. Neither of these poetic points, however, need preclude the claim to be unfinished actually being true. This being the case, it seems eminently plausible that some parts of the poem are written or revised in exile or with knowledge of the sentence. Hinds has pointed out to me (in conversation) that the last book is largely narrated by the exile Pythagoras, in an extended speech which is in a sense the peroration of the work (*Met.* 15. 75–479). Hints in the Actaeon story lead in a similar

---

[140] For famous names cf. e.g. Virg. *Aen.* 6. 776 *haec tum nomina erant, nunc sunt sine nomine terrae*; Feeney (1986) on the great *nomen* of Pompeius Magnus.

direction. The Daedalus story is centrally placed in the *Metamorphoses*; it is one which in the exile poetry proper is certainly used as a metaphor for the poet's fall at the agency of his *Ars*; and in the *Ars* itself it is at the very least the central mythological paradigm. I submit that the story in the *Metamorphoses* actually refers to the *Ars*, to the poem itself, not just to the *Ars* story.[141]

Two phrases in *Metamorphoses* 8 are particularly suggestive. *Damnosas . . . erudit artes* ('he taught damning/loss-bringing arts', *Met.* 8. 215) says Ovid of Daedalus teaching his *ars* (flight) to his addressee (Icarus). This is what Ovid does. As I mentioned earlier, *erudit* is exactly the kind of word to describe the action of a didactic teacher, while in exile the *Ars* becomes a *damnum* for Ovid,[142] and the *Ars* is often referred to in the plural in the exile poetry. Then when Daedalus sees the tell-tale feathers in the sea, Ovid comments *deuouit . . . suas artes* ('he curses his own arts', *Met.* 8. 234). 'Cursing his arts' is exactly the story of the exile poetry. The same word of cursing, *deuoueo*, is used at *Tr.* 5. 7. 31–2:

> *quae me laesisse recordor,*
> *carmina deuoueo Pieridasque meas.*

> I curse my songs and my Muses
> when I remember how they have hurt me.

It occurs again in the following line. If my interpretation is correct, Ovid uses the story of Daedalus in the *Metamorphoses* to reflect on his own *ars*-induced loss—his exile. The exile was the atonement, the price which Ovid paid for his boundary-bursting *Ars*, his famous crime.[143]

There is one further line in *Metamorphoses* 8 which

---

[141] Marchesi (1918: 58) maintains that of all the stories from the *Ars* retold in the *Metamorphoses* only that of Daedalus and Icarus evinces such close verbal parallelism in the two tellings. This likely suggestion of itself, if true, is support for my suggestion.

[142] Cf. *Tr.* 1. 2. 95, 1. 8. 47, 2. 3 *cur modo damnatas repeto, mea crimina, Musas?*, 2. 492 many other didactic poems have been written *quae damno nulli composuisse fuit*, 3. 1. 8, 5. 2. 12.

[143] The involvement with debt and atonement which von Albrecht (1977: 76) sees as central to the *Metamorphoses* version of the Daedalus story is supportive of the suggestion. Von Albrecht also hints at a parallel with Ovid's own later situation.

seems to refer very specifically to poetic composition
(8. 200–1):

> *postquam manus ultima coepto*
> *inposita est*

after the final touch had been put to the work . . .

Ovid uses language of Daedalus' creation of the wings
which he later applies to his own *magnum opus*, the *Metamorphoses* (*Tr.* 2. 555–6):

> *quamuis manus ultima coeptis*
> *defuit*

although the final touch was lacking from the work . . .

This causes some difficulty of interpretation, and perhaps
should not be pressed, but it is not impossible for the story
to reflect simultaneously on the writing both of the *Ars* and
of the *Metamorphoses*. The 'Escape from Exile' which metaphorically 'kills the son' is precisely the Ovidian myth of
his own existence. (See Davisson 1984.)

3*l inter utrumque uola*: *Ars* and *Metamorphoses*

Since questions of stylistic level are examined in this passage, a question in the reader's mind must be the differences
and similarities between this telling of the story and that in
Metamorphoses 8. Stylistic differences between various versions of the same tale as told by Ovid received their first
major treatment from Heinze (1919: 308–403), in a seminal
thesis which was for some time accepted as canonical. He
argued for major differences in narrative style between the
versions of the Rape of Persephone in *Met.* 5. 359 and *Fast.*
4. 417, the former emphasizing divine majesty and power,
the latter gentle sadness and humanity, differences which
he characterized as *deinon* ('terrible') and *eleeinon* ('pitiful'). (Heinze 1919: 322.) He claimed that these distinctions hold good for Ovid's narrative style in epic and elegy
generally, a thesis which was accepted for many years, but
which later produced a strong reaction.[144] Little, in particu-

---

[144] Tränkle (1960); Bernbeck (1967: esp. 127–31); Anderson (1969a: 352–4);
Little (1970); Galinsky (1975: esp. pp. vii–viii); Barsby (1978); Knox (1986).

lar, argues that the generic approach is not even a meaningful way to study the *Metamorphoses*. For this discussion I
am greatly indebted to Hinds (1987, and personally), who,
also arguing from the basis of the Persephone stories, exposes the problem of the false assumption that the presence
of generic inconsistency proves the irrelevance of genre.[145]
The Augustan poets inherited an interest in genre from
Alexandria.[146] *Remedia Amoris* 371–82 is Ovid's own most
overt statement on generic appropriateness, a passage, and
a poem, the appreciation of which 'depends on an awareness
of the fact that it represents a bold marriage of elegiac
norms on the one hand and the norms of didactic epos on
the other' (Hinds 1987: 117). These are statements of great
relevance to our own poem.

In the proem to the *Metamorphoses* (1. 1–4), Ovid poses a
question which continues to tease throughout the poem:
how, or in what sense, is it an epic?

> *In noua fert animus mutatas dicere formas*
> *corpora: di, coeptis—nam uos mutastis et illas—*
> *adspirate meis primaque ab origine mundi*
> *ad mea perpetuum deducite tempora carmen!*

The spirit carries me to speak of forms changed into new
bodies: gods, for you have changed them also, inspire
my attempt and from the first origin of the world
to my own times draw down a perpetual song.

This request immediately places the poem in tension with
Callimachean poetics, for it is seemingly in accordance with
and simultaneously in contradiction of the master's precepts.[147] However 'elegiac' it may be, the *Metamorphoses* is

---

[145] See now also Hinds (1992), where the broader implications of metapoetic
analyses of Ovid are discussed.

[146] Cf. Brink (1971) on Hor. *Ars* 73–85, and Hinds (1987: 116).

[147] See Kenney (1976); Knox (1986); Hinds (1987: 18–22), esp. pp. 19 'in the
very act of repudiating Callimachean principles, Ovid seems to let them in again
by the back door', 121, 132, where he describes the problem as 'the tension which
in some sense informs [Ovid's] whole enterprise'. For *deductum* in Callimachean
poetic theory see Reitzenstein (1931: 25–40); Eisenhut (1975); and J. R. G.
Wright (1983: 154 n. 83). Hinds argues that 'not only when they are being
observed, but also when they are being transgressed, boundaries of genre [are]
essential to the presentation [of the two Rapes]' (p.102). The play works on the
double level of epic = *Metamorphoses* against elegy = *Fasti*, but also against

still generically (ontologically?) epic. Indeed, I would add that generic differences must exist between a narrative poem and a narrative interlude in a non-narrative poem such as the *Fasti* or the *Ars*. There is of course a sense in which these non-narrative poems do have a narrative of sorts, but they are not generically narrative. Discussing this very point, von Albrecht (1977: 78–9) claims that the difference between epic and elegiac narrative is precisely the context, and not the content. The frame for the Daedalus story, he points out, is in the *Metamorphoses* the conflict between Athens and Crete set in the larger context of the History of the World, while in the *Ars* it is separated from its context and unheralded. 'Context' in this context must mean 'mythical context'. This is not to argue that the interludes in elegiac versions are intrinsically irrelevant to the main text but that their relationship is of a *different nature* from that of a passage in a narrative poem to *its* main text.[148]

Commenting on the Daedalus episode in *Metamorphoses* 8, Hollis believes that 'so light is the poet's touch, that one cannot speak of any stylistic difference between the hexameter and elegiac versions' (1970: 58). He is surely right in commenting on the lightness of the *Metamorphoses* treatment, and indeed in pointing out that the relatively light and un-epic nature of Ovid's epic can be seen here by comparison with Silius Italicus' version (12. 89–103). But since Silius' poem is martial epic, the highest form of poetry known to Latin poets, and the vehicle for the *recusatio*, there is still room for a lighter touch in the *Metamorphoses* without total loss of epic status. The question is further complicated by the unusual nature of the *Ars*. Here is a poem which belongs to didactic epos in form, and to love elegy in subject matter and metre. It is poetry with pretensions, satirically undercut, and so is both higher and

Gigantomachy = bad = un-Callimachean epic (p. 129). The argument that the *Metamorphoses* is 'low' epic while the *Fasti* is 'high' elegy is important. With that proviso he nevertheless sees important stylistic differences between the two tellings of the Proserpina story.

[148] Connected with this point is the question of the internal narrator, for which see Due (1974: 80–1); Crabbe (1981: 2292–3); Genette (1972: 225–67) = (1980: 212–62).

lower than its own subject matter. Because in the Daedalus story Ovid writes in the didactic mode of the Aristaeus episode of the Fourth *Georgic*, any comparison of styles between the two tellings is further complicated by the fact that the passage is one of the most elevated in the whole book. With these caveats, however, we should attempt to examine the stories for stylistic differences.

There is no denying that the two tellings of the Daedalus and Icarus story evince close verbal parallels: indeed, the very closeness of the parallels invites, even challenges the reader to compare the versions. Let us take a simple example first. In the Catalogue of Islands, Calymne appears in both poems.

> *siluisque umbrosa Calymne*   (*Ars* 2. 81)
> and Calymne shaded with woods

> *fecundaque melle Calymne*   (*Met*. 8. 222)
> and Calymne rich in honey

By a neat piece of *uariatio*, the same island is graced with a poetic description, but a different one; both have adjective and ablative noun, although with order reversed, but giving totally different descriptions. Is Calymne 'fertile with honey' in the *Metamorphoses* in part because it has now been graced twice in Ovid's poetry—is it 'fertile with the stuff of poetic craft'? The association of honey and bees with poetic programme is most famously developed by Lucretius,[149] but occurs also in a daedalic Horatian *Ode* (4. 2. 27). No obvious difference in stylistic level here, but a straightforward example of difference in sameness.

Following my suggestion above (Section 3*g*) that the basic unit of elegy, the elegiac couplet, is a primary locus for investigation of generic difference, it seems likely that the level of the couplet may be fruitful for analysis of stylistic difference. The building blocks of elegy are sig-

---

[149] Lucr. 1. 936–50 and 4. 11–25 *nam ueluti pueris absinthia taetra medentes | cum dare conantur, prius oras pocula circum | contingunt mellis dulci flauoque liquore | . . . sic ego nunc . . . uolui tibi suauiloquenti | carmine Pierio rationem exponere nostram, | et quasi musaeo dulci contingere melle.*

nalled metaphorically in the Daedalus story by the building
blocks of the wings, feathers (*Ars* 2. 45–8):

> *remigium uolucrum, disponit in ordine pinnas*
> *et leue per lini uincula nectit opus;*
> *imaque pars ceris adstringitur igne solutis,*
> *finitusque nouae iam labor artis erat.*

He disposes his feathers, oarage of birds, in order
and weaves together a light work with bindings of linen;
the lowest part is tied with wax melted by fire,
and now the task of the new art was finished.

The hexameter we saw to be consciously epic, while the
pentameter is programmatically elegiac. The hexameter is
closely echoed in the *Metamorphoses* version of the story
(*Met.* 8. 189–92):

> *nam ponit in ordine pennas,*
> *a minima coeptas, longam breuiore sequenti,*
> *ut cliuo creuisse putes: sic rustica quondam*
> *fistula disparibus paulatim surgit auenis.*
> *tum lino medias et ceris adligat imas,*
> *atque ita conpositas paruo curuamine flectit,*
> *ut ueras imitetur aues.*

For he places the feathers in order, starting from the smallest,
with a shorter one following a long one,
so that you might think them to have grown on a hill.
Thus sometime a rustic pipe grows gradually
with reeds of unequal length.
Then he ties the middle parts with linen and the lowest with
  wax,
and bends the wings composed in this way with a gentle curve,
in order to imitate true birds.

By so close a parallel, the text points to the differences
between the *Ars* pentameter and the line in the *Metamor-*
phoses following that which is parallel with the *Ars* hexameter. The *Metamorphoses* version continues the description
of the feathers drawn up in line, as if for battle, for three
more lines. The inclusion of a simile is an epic touch, and
there is another one to embellish the tying of the wings.
The *Ars* treatment, on the other hand, immediately dissolves into Hellenistic delicateness.

When Icarus plays around with the material of his father's craft, his action is signified with a word, *renideo* ('beam, smile back at'), which occurs in Ovid only here and in the parallel *Metamorphoses* passage.

> *tractabat ceramque puer pinnasque renidens*
> *nescius haec umeris arma parata suis.* (*Ars* 2. 49–50)

The boy played about with the wax and beamed at the feathers
unaware that these were arms prepared for his shoulders.

> *puer Icarus una*
> *stabat et ignarus sua se tractare pericla,*
> *ore renidenti modo, quas uaga mouerat aura,*
> *captabat plumas, flauam modo pollice ceram*
> *mollibat lusuque suo mirabile patris*
> *inpediebat opus.* (*Met.* 8. 195–200)

The boy Icarus was standing with him and, unaware
that he was handling his peril,
with beaming face, now caught at the feathers
which the wandering breeze had moved,
now softened the yellow wax with his thumb and by his game
impeded his father's marvellous work.

We are invited by the word's rarity to compare the two passages. The *Metamorphoses* sentence starts half-way through v. 195 and ends half-way through v. 200. This is the nature of a *perpetuum carmen* ('continous song', *Met.* 1. 4)— one that runs on and on in its metre. The *Ars* version is the standard Ovidian couplet; a complete sentence with a fairly strong sense break between the two halves. For this 'standard Ovidian couplet' we might compare, for example, four couplets of Daedalus' reflection on his art (*Ars* 2. 35–42):

> *possidet et terras et possidet aequora Minos:*
> *nec tellus nostrae nec patet unda fugae.*
> *restat iter caeli: caelo temptabimus ire.*
> *da ueniam coepto, Iuppiter alte, meo.*
> *non ego sidereas adfecto tangere sedes;*
> *qua fugiam dominum, nulla nisi ista uia est.*
> *per Styga detur iter, Stygias transnabimus undas;*
> *sunt mihi naturae iura nouanda meae.*

Minos possesses both land and sea:
neither earth nor wave lies open to our flight.

There remains the path of the sky: by the sky we will attempt to
  go.
Forgive my essay, great Jupiter.
I do not strive to touch the starry seats;
there is no other way but this by which I may escape my master.
If a path through the Styx were given, we would swim through
  the Stygian waves;
the laws of my nature are to be made new for me.

In each of these four couplets the hexameter makes a
statement of the situation or of intention, and the pentameter reflects on the thought of the hexameter. The Daedalus of the *Ars* is highly elegiac in his self-expression, and
self-referentially so. Likewise, in the final couplet of the
prayer to Minos, it seems almost as if everything were to be
sacrificed to elegiac balance (vv. 29–30):

> *da reditum puero, senis est si gratia uilis;*
>   *si non uis puero parcere, parce seni.'*

Grant return to the boy, if you hold cheap a favour done to an
  old man and his thanks;
or, if you don't want to spare the boy, spare the old man.

The rhetorical pathos of Daedalus' speech, culminating in
the selflessness of the prayer that at least his son should be
spared, is undercut by the lighthearted antithesis, while the
alternation between hexameter and pentameter is emphasized by the repeat of *puero senis/seni* ('boy, old man'), first
together then separated at the ends of the pentameter's two
halves, and the anaphora of *parcere parce* ('spare'). The
argument of this paragraph is that the nature of the sentence and its relationship with the metrical line constitute
a difference in stylistic level between the *Ars* and the
Metamorphoses.

Among the most fruitful places for examination of generic
difference is narrative. One way this functions in our stories
is in the considerably greater amount of direct speech given
to the *Ars* Daedalus. In the *Ars*, 33 out of 76 lines are
spoken by Daedalus, while in the *Metamorphoses*, 12 out of
53 lines are in his mouth. In each case I have counted every
line in which Daedalus speaks. The self-representational
nature of Daedalus as artist (actually telling his own story),

throws emphasis on the non-narrative parts of the narrative within this non-narrative poem, while at the same time playing with the slippage of identity of speaker, narrator, and poet. Ovid will rarely be tied down to neat critical patterns, however. As a prelude to the flight, we have in the *Ars* a passage of narrative scene-painting, which does not have a corresponding passage in the *Metamorphoses* version, where, if Ovid acted in a straightforward manner, we might expect it as an epic touch (*Ars* 2. 71–2):

> *monte minor collis, campis erat altior aequis;*
>   *hinc data sunt miserae corpora bina fugae.*

There was a hill less than a mountain, more lofty than the plains;
from here the two(fold) bodies are given over to pitiful flight.

This couplet varies our range of shot, as we stand back, cool off, and get our bearings before homing in for the character's-eye view of the flight.

Expansion of narrative can more easily be seen as an epic touch in the vignette of the fisherman.

> (*hos aliquis tremula dum captat harundine pisces*
>   *uidit, et inceptum dextra relinquit opus.*)   (*Ars* 2. 77–8)

(Someone saw them, while trying to catch fish with a quivering reed,
  and the task on which he is engaged drops from his hand.)

> *hos aliquis tremula dum captat harundine pisces*
> *aut pastor baculo stiuaue innixus arator*
> *uidit et obstipuit, quique aethera carpere possent*
> *credidit esse deos.*   (*Met.* 8. 217–20)

Someone saw them, while trying to catch fish with a quivering reed,
or a shepherd leaning on a staff, or a ploughman on his plough-handle,
and was dumbfounded, and believed that these beings
who could fly through the air must be gods.

A stylistic difference is apparent here, foregrounded by the very similarity of the descriptions, simply from the narrative expansion of the epic version. Moreover, the *aut . . . ue* ('either/or . . . or') expression is characteristic of high style. The epic reaction to this amazing sight is to think of the gods. Whatever might justifiably be said about the stylistic difference between the *Metamorphoses* version and that of Silius Italicus, it should be noted that when Silius' gods tremble at the flying man, it is the *Metamorphoses* version of the story which he is following, where the spectator believed that those who could fly must be gods. The elegiac reaction, by contrast, is to drop the fishing-rod in dumbfounded amazement, a response with which we might usefully compare Paris' reaction to Helen's revealing dress (*Her.* 15. 253–4):

> dum stupeo uisis—nam pocula forte tenebam—
> tortilis a digitis excidit ansa meis.

While I marvel at the sight, the coiled handle—for by chance
I was holding a goblet—fell from my fingers.

Simile is narrative within narrative (within narrative again in the *Metamorphoses* case) and so is narrativity intensified. I described a simile as an epic touch. The treatment of simile is a promising, albeit sometimes a frustrating, vehicle for examining stylistic/generic difference. Brunner (1966: 363) argued that Ovid's long and expanded similes, the use of which is restricted almost exclusively to the *Metamorphoses*, serve to add epic flavour to material basically not of an epic nature. In a later article (1971), he examines in avowedly Heinzian terms the use of simile in the *Metamorphoses* and *Fasti*, and discovers a preponderance of *deinon* in the former and *eleeinon* in the latter. (See also Wilkins 1932.) Is there a discernible difference in the function of simile in our two stories? The two versions use the same point of contrast in a simile illustrating Daedalus teaching Icarus how to fly.

> erudit infirmas ut sua mater aues.   (*Ars* 2. 66)

just as their mother teaches young fledglings.

> uelut ales, ab alto
> quae teneram prolem produxit in aera nido.   (*Met.* 8. 213–14)

just like a bird, which has drawn forth its tender young
from the lofty nest into the air.

The same and different. This is the only simile in the *Ars*

version, and a very short one, made still shorter by the
displaced *ut*, a word-ordering which also facilitates fusion
between Daedalus and the mother bird as the subject of
erudit. In the *Metamorphoses* version the simile is expanded,
while there is another simile, for the making of the wings,
at *Met.* 8. 191–2. While it would be hard to argue for a
difference on the sentimental level between our two similes,
the extreme brevity of the one over the more developed
narrative of the other suggests a deliberate stylistic differentiation, enhanced by the very similarity of the subject
matter.

The *Metamorphoses* story has generally more of the tragic
and ominous—or rather, the tragic and ominous is highlighted more openly: witness Icarus playing with the
feathers:

> *ignarus sua se tractare pericla*   (*Met.* 8. 196)
> unaware that he was handling his peril

> *nescius haec umeris arma parata suis*   (*Ars* 2. 50)
> unaware that these are arms prepared for his shoulders.

In the case of the *Ars* Icarus, his ignorance specifically of
the *danger* is not spelled out. When Daedalus kisses his son
farewell, only in the *Metamorphoses* are the kisses *non iterum
repetenda* ('never to be sought again', 8. 212). That picture
is one which clearly, albeit quirkily, places the story, even
in the *Ars* version, in an epic tradition (*Ars* 2. 69–70):

> *iamque uolaturus paruo dedit oscula nato,*
>   *nec patriae lacrimas continuere genae.*

> and now, about to fly, he kissed his little son,
> and the fatherly cheeks did not check their tears.

Ovid is conniving with Daedalus' sentimentality, for *paruus*
is a word for a very young child. There are two famous epic
precedents for fathers kissing young sons before a dangerous
development: Hector and Astyanax in *Il.* 6. 474, and Aeneas
and Iulus in *Aen.* 12. 440. It is a neat twist that in what is on
one level an examination of different types of poetry, Ovid
should choose to draw on some of the most un-epic passages
of the two greatest epics. A second, more obvious line of

tradition leads back through the *Metamorphoses* Daedalus to the Daedalus story in Virgil.

> *genae maduere seniles,*
> *et patriae tremuere manus.*   (*Met.* 8. 210–11)

The aged cheeks grew wet and the fatherly hands trembled.

> *bis patriae cecidere manus.*   (*Aen.* 6. 33)

Twice the fatherly hands fell.

One might wish to make a case here for extra epicness in the *Metamorphoses* version by noting that, while all these passages are involved in a very tight intertextuality, the *Metamorphoses* version is expanded by the inclusion both of the tears and of the weakness of hands.[150]

In this section, I have attempted to argue for some difference of stylistic level between the *Ars* and the *Metamorphoses*. In the next section, I shall centre this discussion of difference on the characterization, particularly the self-characterization of the two Daedaluses, and end it with some reflections on the significance of such differences.

3m Self-(re)presentation: Daedalus as Orator

One major difference between the epic and elegiac versions is in the character of Daedalus as presented by each. Characterization is considered by Heinze and Hinds as a legitimate subject for the investigation of style: indeed, Heinze claimed that what above all made the *Fasti* story elegiac was its stress on 'grevious lamentation and pity'. (See Hinds 1987: 103.) By the exclusion of the larger mythic context, the less pleasant side of Daedalus' character is suppressed in the

---

[150] Von Albrecht (1977: 76) also notices this difference in the tragic and ominous between the two versions. I cannot agree with his contention that the distinction between epic and elegiac narrative lies *only* in context and form and not in content. Heinze, according to von Albrecht, saw the generic difference to lie in the fact that epic is 'heroic and majestic', while elegy is 'full of feeling and asymmetrical' (whatever that means). The fact that von Albrecht finds epic elements in the *Ars* (for example, Daedalus is found to have a certain dignity and majesty, p. 78) and elegiac elements in the *Metamorphoses* (for example, the emphasis on the feelings of Daedalus—Heinze's 'gefühlvoll'—which is essential to the epicness of foreboding) is hardly sufficient reason to dismiss the value of generic differentiation with regard to content.

Ars. There is no direct mention of Perdix or the reason for the artist's exile, nor of the death of the Minotaur, while the affair of Pasiphae is glossed over, and there is no hint of the death of Minos.[151] The epic Daedalus murders his nephew out of pride in his work. The elegiac Daedalus also loses his son to his pride in his work, but has prepared for his cruel fate by his apologies and explanations. By the suppression of the Perdix, Death of the Minotaur, and Cocalus stories, emphasis is laid on Daedalus as a gentle, oppressed artist, concerned to excuse his sacrilege.

At the very opening of the story, Ovid foreshadows and connives with Daedalus' self-representation with words which characterize him as victim in the oxymoronic juxtaposition, *hospitis effugio* ('the escape of the guest'), oxymoronic, in that a guest is no guest if he cannot leave. Servius *auctus* on Virg. *Aen*. 2. 140 claims for *effugium* a ritual significance, being used of a victim which escapes the sacrificial knife. Daedalus is the victim of Minos' attempts to suppress his creative artistry. Daedalus' first speech, coming early in the narrative, allows him to characterize himself and to represent himself/be represented as an orator, pleading before Minos the judge. Through his peculiar status as signifier and signified, he displays himself as an artist with words as well as with his hands (vv. 25–30):

> *'sit modus exilio,' dixit 'iustissime Minos;*
> *accipiat cineres terra paterna meos,*
> *et, quoniam in patria fatis agitatus iniquis*
> *uiuere non potui, da mihi posse mori.*
> *da reditum puero, senis est si gratia uilis;*
> *si non uis puero parcere, parce seni.'*

'Let there be a limit to exile,' he said, 'most just Minos;
let my paternal earth receive my ashes,
and since, driven by an unfair fate, I have not been able to live
in my fatherland, grant that I may die there.
Grant return to the boy, if you hold cheap a favour done to an
   old man and his thanks;
or, if you don't want to spare the boy, spare the old man.

---

[151] Although on one level these stories, as being part of the mythic corpus, always lurk in the shadows around the actual *Ars* text.

The prayer for the body to rest in one's homeland goes back to Homer (*Il.* 22. 338), and is picked up by Virgil at the end of the *Aeneid* in the words of Turnus (12. 935–6):

> *et me, seu corpus spoliatum lumine mauis,*
> *redde meis*

and return me, or, if you prefer, my body deprived of life
to my people.

In the usual versions of the Daedalus story, Sicily and Cumae are Daedalus' destinations, but Diodorus and Hyginus report variants in which he did actually return to his home in Athens. Ovid refers to the variant, while Daedalus gets rhetorical mileage out of the highly emotive concept of the fatherland.

Like an orator, Daedalus reminds his audience of his sufferings. The 'exile' and the 'unkind fate' to which Daedalus alludes suggest a vague sense of persecution rather than merited punishment, and *exilium* could be applied whether the victim was condemned or not. In true oratorical style, the speaker presents himself as a patriot, who has been forced to wander far from home. This could almost come out of a rhetorical text book. Cicero, as teacher of rhetoric, advises precisely this sort of self-characterization, for example at *Part.* 56:

nam aut caritate mouentur homines, ut deorum, ut patriae, ut parentum, aut amore, ut fratrum, ut coniugum, ut liberorum, ut familiarium . . . ex his et cohortationes sumuntur ad ea retinenda, et in eos a quibus ea uiolata sunt odia incitantur et miseratio nascitur

For men are moved either by esteem, as of gods, fatherland, parents, or by love, as of brothers, wives, children, friends . . . from these, both exhortations that they be retained are derived, and also hatred is evoked against those by whom they have been violated, and pity is born.

Daedalus also uses the well-known but effective ancient technique of arousing pity by bringing in the defendant's children, as Cicero advises (*Orat.* 131):

nec uero miseratione solum mens iudicum permouenda est—qua nos ita dolenter uti solemus ut puerum infantem in manibus perorantes tenuerimus.

Nor for that matter is the mind of the judges to be moved by pity alone—which we are accustomed to use so pitifully that we hold in our arms an infant child in our peroration.

The rhetoric is specious, exaggerating the helpless youth and the age of the two captives. The heavy antitheses of *uiuere . . . mori* ('to live . . . to die', v. 28) enclosing the line, of *puero, senis* ('boy, old man', v. 29), and of *puero . . . seni* (v. 30) aid the rhetoric. Daedalus' plea hints at the formulae of prayer language. Given the context, the high incidence of anaphora cannot be accidental: *paterna/patria, potui/ posse, da/da, puero/puero, si/si, senis/seni, parcere/parce*.[152] Daedalus' self-characterization is gentle and pitiful: there is no corresponding speech or prayer in the *Metamorphoses*. (See also Frécaut 1972: 360 on this point.)

The *Ars* Daedalus is a gentle, victimized artist, transgressing the bounds of his nature only out of necessity and with great concern for his hybris, driven by pious love for his fatherland and his son. At least, this is how he presents himself in a passage where the author allows his character considerable freedom to speak for himself. His *Metamorphoses* counterpart, on the other hand, is a much more confident figure. There is no apology for hybris in the *Metamorphoses*. His dismissal of Minos' power is as offhand as the *Ars* Minos' dismissal of Daedalus' pleas, the two phrases using the same grammatical construction.[153]

> *terras licet . . . et undas*
> *obstruat*   (*Met.* 8. 185–6)
>
> although he may block off lands . . . and seas

---

[152] For anaphora as a feature of prayer formulae see Norden (1916) on Virg. *Aen.* 6. 46 and Nisbet and Hubbard (1978) on Hor. *Carm.* 2. 19. 7.

[153] For discussions of the textual problem see Ker (1958: 225); Kenney (1959: 254); Willis (1972: 146); Hunt (1979: 343). Ker's emendation is almost certainly correct. As he says, it cannot possibly mean 'but he was permitted to say this and much more', which would make the rest of the sentence very awkward. But more than just 'although' it means (paraphrasing) 'but he could say all this and as much as he liked, Minos was not going to let him out.' This use of *licet* + paratactic subjunctive (on which see Leumann, Hofmann, and Szantyr (1965–79: 2. 605); Kühner and Stegmann (1966: 2. 2. 443); *TLL* 7. 1361. 31) appears at least in this type of context to be slightly colloquial. See Brink (1971) on Hor. *Ars* 459; Tränkle (1960: 72).

> sed et haec et multo plura licebat
>   diceret   (*Ars* 2. 31–2)

but although he said this and much more . . .

The *Metamorphoses* Daedalus is sure that the sky is open to him (*Met*. 8. 186):

> at caelum certe patet: ibimus illac!

But certainly the sky is open: we will go that way!

The *Ars* Daedalus is more tentative (*Ars* 2. 37):

> restat iter caeli: caelo temptabimus ire.

There remains the path of the sky: through the sky we will strive to go.

As often happens, two very similar lines show their difference. *Ars* 2. 35 *possidet et terras et possidet aequora Minos* ('Minos possesses both land and sea') expresses depression and desperation in the face of the thalassocrat, and becomes the basis for Daedalus' apology to Jupiter, *qua fugiam dominum nulla nisi ista uia est* ('there is no other way but this by which I may escape my master', v. 40). In the companion *Metamorphoses* line, however, Daedalus almost sounds as if he is answering Minos' challenge (*Met*. 8. 187):

> omnia possideat, non possidet aera Minos.

Minos may possess everything, but he does not possess the air.

Daedalus is almost a brave and confident epic hero. It is certainly true that both Daedaluses *fear* the forthcoming flight, but while the *Ars* Daedalus is generally and perpetually fearful, his *Metamorphoses* equivalent only fears *for his son* (*comitique timet*, 'and fears for his companion', 8. 214). Significantly, the epic Daedalus' fear is expressed in a clear allusion linking him to the greatest Roman epic hero, Aeneas, who, on his departure from Troy, accompanied by his son and carrying his father, is described as *comitique onerique timentem* ('fearing for both his companion and his burden', *Aen*. 2. 729).

I submit, then, that there are indeed observable differences of stylistic level between the epic and elegiac versions. The suspicion that my attempts to make distinctions have been constantly undermined by the twists and generic games of the texts need not invalidate the contrast, however much it may problematize it. Such difference as there may be is offered in support of my claim that one resonance of the Daedalus story in the *Ars* is a programmatic statement that the poem will not fly too high. Being a little less than epic (even Ovidian/Callimachean epic) but a little more than elegy, for it has narrative, expanded mythology, and didactic, almost epic, pretensions, the *Ars* will find fame by a middle path.

A final point on stylistic level: generic inconsistencies are sometimes held to render consideration of genre irrelevant, but it is hard to imagine a piece of literature which is absolutely consistent generically.

3n Doctus Poeta

No one nowadays would, I think, deny that Ovid is a *doctus poeta*, a poet consciously writing in the style and tradition of the scholar-poets of Alexandria—at least in his self-proclamation. Since *doctrina* is a rather woolly critical label which can cover a wide poetic range, it hardly needs arguing that Ovid displays Hellenistic *doctrina*. But because narrativity is at issue in this passage, I am concerned here with the way Ovid uses the vocabulary of his story obliquely to refer to variants or other myths which therefore are and are not part of this story. A myth is, after all, the sum of its variants, which may range very broadly. (Levi-Strauss 1958: 240.)

The Catalogue of Islands is likely to be a fertile ground for examination of *doctrina*. As de St Denis (1935: 358–9) says, Ovid is in fact correct in his placement of the islands. By writing poetry of these islands he is obeying the injunction of his master, Callimachus (*Hymn* 4. 2–3):

> ἦ μὲν ἅπασαι
> Κυκλάδες, αἳ νήσων ἱερώταται εἰν ἁλὶ κεῖνται,
> εὔυμνοι

Indeed all the Cyclades, which are the most holy of islands lying in the sea, are used in beautiful hymns [well-hymned].

Callimachus himself is here writing in a Pindaric tradition
(see the opening of *Isth.* 1). The mixing of Greek words,
particularly names, was highly prized by Roman writers. It
is a favourite device for the teacher of the *Georgics*, found in
the context of catalogues at 4. 334–47 (nymphs) and 4. 367–
70 (rivers). In the final item of the catalogue, there may be
a hint at a little-known myth, present simply for the sake of
displaying Ovid/Icarus' *doctrina* (v. 82):

> *cinctaque piscosis Astypalaea uadis*
> Astypalaea girt with fishy seas.

Astypalaea is the name of the mother of Ancaeus by Neptune. Could the story of his conception be hinted at in the
words *cincta . . . uadis?* The same story is told by Pausanias
(7. 4. 1) in a discussion of Aegean islands. He says that
Ancaeus married a woman called Samia, hence Samos,
which is also present in our passage. For at least some of
this story he claims an authority in 'the poet Asius', presumably the sixth-century poet one fragment of whose work
survives. (See West 1972: 46.) A lost Hellenistic (perhaps
geographical didactic?) source is just as possible for Ovid's
line, however. *TLL Onomasticon* 1. 194 connects this line
with the evidence from Plin. *Nat.* 8. 59 that the island was
famous for its medicinal shells.[154]

The narrative contains many hints at allusions to variants,
and to other parts of the Daedalian mythic system. I have
mentioned above how the suppression of the wider mythic
context aids the characterization of Daedalus. It also effects
the Hellenistic device of almost complete concentration on
one episode of a multifold legend. In the opening couplet,
Ovid produces a paradigmatic example of compressed narrative, of which the rest of the story is, on one level, simply
an expansion (vv. 21–2):

> *hospitis effugio praestruxerat omnia Minos;*
> *audacem pinnis repperit ille uiam.*

---

[154] *TLL Onomasticon* 1. 194 also mentions a popular derivation for Astypalaea
from a Punic/primitive Greek word meaning 'humilis, sc. quasi inter duo editiora
demissum locum occupans'. See also Bömer (1976) on *Met.* 7. 461. Perhaps an
allusion to the *inter utrumque uola*-theme would be a little too obscure.

> Minos had put every obstacle in the way of his guest;
> he discovered a daring path on wings.

In having Daedalus leave before the death of the Minotaur, and while still in open communication with Minos (although sensing an underlying threat of danger), he is moving away from the more common tradition (cf. Apoll. *Epit.* 1. 12, *RE* ad loc.), following lesser known stories related by Diodorus and Hyginus. In contrast, he follows the usual chronology in the *Metamorphoses* version. He is clearly not following the usual tradition, whereby Daedalus and Icarus were locked up in the Labyrinth (cf. e.g. Apoll. *Epit.* 1. 12). There may, however, be an oblique reference to that story in the word *praestruxerat*. According to Diodorus (4. 77. 7), Minos caused all the boats in the island to be searched and promised a reward for information about Daedalus. *Praestruo*, which would well describe the activity of the first great architect (Daedalus himself), is ironically used of attempts to block the artist.

Reference to Daedalus' building of the Labyrinth is certainly present in the next couplet (vv. 23–4):

> *Daedalus ut clausit conceptum crimine matris*
> *semibouemque uirum semiuirumque bouem*
>
> Daedalus, when he has shut up the thing
> conceived by the crime of its mother
> the half-bull man and half-man bull . . .

The elliptical reference to the stories is typical of Hellenistic and Ovidian narrative, and facilitates almost complete concentration in the episode on one particular act of daedalic creation, the winged flight. Less clearly present but still, I think, glanced at, is the story of Perdix, for, according to Apollodorus (*lib.* 3. 15. 8), Daedalus was exiled from Athens for the murder of Perdix, and so the story of his death lurks behind Daedalus' reference to *exilium* and indeed his very presence in Crete. Now, I have claimed above that the story of Perdix is suppressed, in order to characterize Daedalus as the 'gentle, oppressed artist'. This is a prime and quite simple example of polysemy. In Daedalus' telling of the story, Perdix is suppressed, but Ovid—as narrator—

appropriates the speaker-character's vocabulary to wink at the learned reader with a suggestion of a different story. Perdix is and is not present in the text.

Twice Ovid uses Daedalus' words to lean on other myths about Minos. Daedalus' address to Minos as *iustissime* ('most just', v. 25) is for him simple flattery, but for Ovid it refers to Minos' later position as judge among the dead.[155] In the same way, Daedalus' nervous analysis of his situation (v. 35)

> *possidet et terras et possidet aequora Minos*
>
> Minos possesses both land and sea

allows Ovid to remind the reader of the myth of Minos as a ruler of wide territories and the first great sea power.[156] Throughout the passage, Ovid emphasizes the sailing metaphor for flight. This perhaps rather obvious metaphor may serve an additional function, which is to refer obliquely to a rationalistic explanation of the myth, that Daedalus invented sails for ships. The myth is reported by Pausanias (9. 11. 4). (An allusion to this myth in Ovid would of course depend on the mythographer following an earlier source.) Another rationalistic account, reported by Diodorus (4. 77. 5), has Pasiphae provide a ship for Daedalus and Icarus to escape, and Icarus die when disembarking. When Daedalus/Ovid uses the highly poetic image of the keel of a ship as a metaphor for the wings (v. 51), and says that these wings are the 'keels' by which we will escape, he suggests that this, a fantastic flight, is the variant of the story that we will follow, and this, flight, is the poetic image we will use.

Hints at such demythologizing make an ironic self-referential joke when Ovid usurps a narrator's naïve amazement at the rather worrying inventiveness of Daedalus (vv. 43–4):

> *ingenium mala saepe mouent: quis crederet umquam*
> *aerias hominem carpere posse uias?*

> Misfortunes often move the intellect: who would ever have believed
> that a man would be able to pluck a path on the air?

---

[155] Cf. Hom. *Od.* 11. 569; Plat. *Gorg.* 524A; Virg. *Aen.* 6. 432; Sil. 14. 42. He is a great lawgiver in life at Plat. *Min.* 39.
[156] Cf. Herod. 1. 171; Thuc. 1. 4, 1. 8; Apoll. *Lib.* 3. 1. 3.

Of course, no one in contemporary sophisticated society *would* believe the story as it stands. Who would believe Ovid's story? Who would believe a man who said he had flown through the skies? Who would believe a man who said he could keep an elegiac mistress in love? But this is poetry and, as Plato reminds us (e.g. *Rep.* 377D–403C), it is in the nature of poets to make people believe what is not true.[157] As Callimachus says (*Hymn* 1. 64),

> ψευδοίμην ἀίοντος ἅ κεν πεπίθοιεν ἀκουήν.

> May I deceive [speak fiction] in such as way as
> to persuade the listener.

30 All just an Irrelevant Digression?

The ostensible point of this exemplum was to illustrate the difficulty of *imposuisse modum* ('to have imposed a limit/ restraint') on the wings of the flighty love-god (vv. 19–20):

> *et leuis est et habet geminas, quibus auolet, alas;*
> *difficile est illis imposuisse modum.*

> And he is light and has twin wings, on which he can fly away;
> it is difficult to impose a restraint on them.

The difficulty, that is, of keeping Love in a girl (keeping a girl). *Modus*, however, is also metrical order, so the phrase also means 'constrain love in verse'—write erotic didactic poetry. The 'twin wings' of Love are probably the two elements of the elegiac couplet. It is as hard to write poetry as it is to stop Daedalus flying away (vv. 97–8):

> *non potuit Minos hominis conpescere pinnas,*
> *ipse deum uolucrem detinuisse paro.*

> Minos could not restrain the wings of a man;
> I am preparing to hold down a flying god.

Is that *really* the point? Acceptance of it as such makes the final couplet into a feeble excuse for a long, irrelevant, and self-indulgent piece of story-telling. Yes, at one level, it is all an irrelevant digression, and it self-ironizingly jokes

---

[157] Cf. Plin. *Ep.* 6. 21. 6 *poetis mentiri licet.*

about its own irrelevance. But it should first of all be remembered that didactic poetry is supposed—generically—to contain digressions. Part of the purpose of this closing couplet is to foreground the tale's didactic nature. It imitates a very Lucretian practice of ending a section by stating what he has just shown.[158] Ovid, however facetiously, follows this practice.

Moreover, by displaying itself as *blatant* self-indulgence, overkill, and ill proportion, the story questions the criteria being used against it.[159] The exemplum is obsessed with and full of references to its own length. Daedalus' over-expansive lecture, delivering in fourteen lines what his *Metamorphoses* counterpart says in a few words, to which Icarus is not really listening, reflects self-referentially on this macrological exemplum. The flight of Daedalus is a digression from the main business at hand, which is to give erotic advice to the lover. He is sailing on the high sea of love without Ovid's guidance, and is all the more desperate for the instruction to begin. The digression is an *egressus* ('way out') like that which Minos refused to Daedalus (v. 32).[160] It is hard to *imponere modum* on this digression also, which flies off apparently out of control. As Love threatens to fly out of Ovid's control, as Daedalus flies out of Minos' control, as Icarus flies out of Daedalus' control, so the exemplum flies out of Ovid's control (and analysis

---

[158] Examples abound, incl. Lucr. 1. 205, 237, 262–4 *haud igitur penitus pereunt quaecumque uidentur,* | *quando alid ex alio reficit natura nec ullam* | *rem gigni patitur nisi morte adiuta aliena,* answering 215–16 *huc accedit uti quidque in sua corpora rursum* | *dissoluat natura neque ad nilum interimat res,* 328 *corporibus caecis igitur natura gerit res,* 548, 907, 3. 633, 737, 4. 526–40 *corpoream uocem quoque enim constare fatendumst* | *et sonitum, quoniam possunt impellere sensus . . . ergo corpoream uocem constare necessest.*

[159] Myerowitz (1985) 153 also notes the challenge thrown by the exemplum's disjunction from the main text.

[160] An *egressus* can be a digression from one's main theme. Cf. V. Max. 4. 8. 1 *opus pio egressu . . . prouectum in suam ordinem reuocetur;* Tac. *Ann.* 4. 32 *ingentia illi* [earlier historians] *bella . . . libero egressu memorabant; OLD egressus* 2. It is a technical term in rhetoric. Cf. Quint. *Inst.* 4. 3. 12. *Egressus* is a rare word in poetry, particularly before Ovid. Another victim of the Minotaur saga expressed herself in a similar manner at Catullus 64. 185 *nec patet egressus pelagi cingentibus undis.* This could be simple allusion perhaps, or deliberately aligning this passage with what is perhaps the most famous example of the daedalic ekphrastic inset. Was that an *egressus* from my point?

out of the critic's control). As an *egressus*, the very appearance of the story at this point acts symbolically.

Icarian poetry is digression within digression. In the six
lines of cheating of expectation between Icarus starting to
fly *fortius* and actually leaving his father for the fall, Ovid
teases us with digression, appearing to have deserted the
Ars Amatoria for the moment. On this level of reading,
Ovid himself becomes the referent of *aliquis* (vv. 77–8):

> *hos aliquis, tremula dum captat harundine pisces,*
> *uidit, et inceptum dextra relinquit opus.*

Someone saw them, while trying to catch fish with a quivering
   reed,
and the task on which he is engaged drops from his hand.

As well as a fishing rod, a *harundo* can be a pen.[161] Ovid
has been catching at girls/lovers/readers with his reed (pen),
but in enjoyment of this *excursus* he has ditched the *Ars*,
and during this story which on one level is self-indulgent,
the lover is flailing on the high seas without advice. Ovid is
also leaving another *inceptum . . . opus* ('work in hand'),[162]
the *Metamorphoses*, for it is after *uidit et* ('sees and') that
the two versions change.[163]

In the final couplet, Ovid slows the story down with two
big stopping words, *conpescere* ('restrain') and *detinuisse*
('hold down'), speaking of detaining love (Love) by reference to one of the key words of the poem, *teneo*. He is
holding love, the girl, the lover, the reader, keeping them in
suspense to intensify interest in the subject. Throughout
the exemplum, he has been narrator, though still didactic
poet narrating, while at the same time being metaphorically
the subject of his own narration. Like Daedalus, he is
signifier and signified. Indeed, the heavy authorial self-refer-
ence in *ipse . . . paro* ('I myself am preparing') points to the
fusion which is now being undone. The final joke in this
monster simile is its very *in*appropriateness, on one level.

[161] Cf. *TLL* 6. 3. 2543. 62; Var. *Men.* 578 *ponam bisulcam et crebrinodam harundinem.*

[162] With *inceptum* compare *coepto* v. 38, with *opus* the same word in v. 46.

[163] This is not to claim that Ovid was working on the *Metamorphoses* at the same time, but rather that when he came to write *Met.* 8. 219 he also 'rewrote' *Ars* 2. 77–8, in that he caused us to reread it.

By the fact that the exemplum fails to *imponere modum* on itself, by the undermining joke that detaining the love-god after all *is* impossible, Ovid self-deprecatingly dispels the potential hybris of the exemplum's poetic pretensions and pretensions to poetic fame and the *inuidia* potentially incurred by them.

A final joke to dispel the *inuidia* potentially incurred by this macrological exegesis. When Daedalus calls out for his lost son he asks (v. 94)

> *quoque sub axe uolas?*

> Where under the celestial axis/in what region of the sky do you fly?

Now *axis* can denote the axis of a spiral scroll or volute.[164] If the reader is alert to the self-referentiality of this exemplum, s/he might be amused to hear this as a reference to a physical book. Icarus is the poem, 'flying' (that is, metaphorically, being poetry) quite literally under the axis of a scroll.

[164] *OLD axis* 6.

4

Callimachean Apollo and the Long and Short of Art

When Apollo suddenly appears in the poem at v. 493, his presence commands attention, and proclaims the cardinal importance of the scene within the poetic scheme of the *Ars* (2. 493–508):[1]

> *haec ego cum canerem, subito manifestus Apollo*
> *mouit inauratae pollice fila lyrae.*
> *in manibus laurus, sacris induta capillis*   495
> *laurus erat: uates ille uidendus adit.*
> *is mihi 'lasciui' dixit 'praeceptor Amoris,*
> *duc age discipulos ad mea templa tuos,*
> *est ubi diuersum fama celebrata per orbem*
> *littera, cognosci quae sibi quemque iubet.*   500
> *qui sibi notus erit, solus sapienter amabit*
> *atque opus ad uires exiget omne suas:*
> *cui faciem natura dedit, spectetur ab illa;*
> *cui color est, umero saepe patente cubet;*
> *qui sermone placet, taciturna silentia uitet;*   505
> *qui canit arte, canat; qui bibit arte, bibat.*
> *sed neque declament medio sermone diserti,*
> *nec sua non sanus scripta poeta legat.'*

While I was singing this, Apollo, suddenly present,
struck with his thumb the strings of his golden lyre.
Laurel was in his hands, with laurel his holy hair was adorned:
he comes manifestly a bard.
This god said to me, 'teacher of wanton love,
come, lead your pupils to my temple,
where there is the letter celebrated in fame throughout the whole world,
which orders each one to know himself.

---

[1] The most relevant discussions of this passage are by Miller (1983: 32–4), A. A. R. Henderson (1983: 33), and more briefly by Wimmel (1960: 137). See also Lenz (1961: 138–9), Newman (1967: 397–402), and Wilkinson (1956: 237).

Whoever knows himself, alone will love wisely
and will perform his task to his utmost ability:
whomever nature has endowed with beauty, let him be gazed at
    for that;
whoever has a tan, let him often lie with naked shoulder;
he whose speech is pleasing should avoid sullen silence;
he who sings well should sing; he who drinks well should drink.
But let not the eloquent declaim in the midst of conversation,
and let not the mad poet read his writings.'

Ovid acclaims the epiphany, and then counters with a paradigmatic specimen of his own *Ars* (2. 509–12):

> *sic monuit Phoebus: Phoebo parete monenti;*
> *certa dei sacro est huius in ore fides.*
> *ad propiora uocor; quisquis sapienter amabit,*
> *uincet et e nostra, quod petit, arte feret.*

Such was Phoebus' advice: obey the advice of Phoebus;
sure faith is found in the sacred mouth of this god.
I am called to things nearer to hand; whoever loves wisely,
will conquer and will bear off from my art what he seeks.

The passage with which this chapter is concerned goes down to v. 534. It is quoted below, in Section 4*h*.

4*a* 'Callimacheanism' and the Long and Short of Art

I have suggested that one of the many facets to the story of Daedalus and Icarus was to reflect on what it might be like to be a Roman Callimachean poet, and on the strengths and possible pitfalls of contemporary 'Callimacheanism', as we, perhaps rather carelessly, call it.[2] By the time it reaches Ovid, this patchwork tradition is constructed from the poetic theory and practice not only of the master himself, but also of his near-contemporaries, of the neoterics, and finally of the Augustans. In the Callimacheanism of any

---

[2] I must ask the reader's indulgence for my use of inverted commas in this chapter, in particular. I intend the use to indicate the metaphorical and semantically precarious status of these words. I realize, of course, firstly that I, in company with most people, use inverted commas for all sorts of other purposes, and also that the precariousness which I mentioned applies to words generally, but the trope invites us to consider the words it highlights. What happens when an indication of irony is itself ironic?

generation, of any one poet, indeed of any single poem, the contemporary socio-political and poetic views and values are influential in shaping the manifestation of the tradition. Callimachus' poetic theory provides a metaphorical language and a set of images to be refined into any number of personal poetic statements.[3] The 'long/short' dichotomy which so often arises in these contexts is a mast for nailing colours to rather than a scientifically accurate means of measurement, that is, a Persian chain.

Poetic statements in antiquity are frequently couched in terms of a contest. Such is the case for Callimachus and the Telchines in the *Aetia* prologue, for Callimachus and *Phthonos* (Envy) in the *Hymn to Apollo*,[4] and, I shall suggest, for Ovid and Apollo in our passage. My intention is to hypothesize that both in the story of Daedalus and Icarus and also in the Epiphany of Apollo, Ovid alludes to the 'short is good' metaphor in previous and contemporary poetics, and comments that shortness is not an unproblematical category, and that although straightforward shortness *may* be good, there is a risk. Although the *Ars* transgresses a narrow interpretation of the rule of brevity, it is 'Callimachean' in that it is Art. How short is a 'short' lecture? Having few verses is not the only way to be Callimachean. The risk is that if the so-called padding is removed from Ovid's work, the residue is something very like the speech of Apollo—it is missing the *ars* (*Ars*). Expansion and repetition, two of the great charges laid against Ovid, are deliberately exposed as what constitutes his art. The tale of Daedalus, 'Callimachean' though it is in many ways, trangresses the rules of brevity but gives us art; the speech of Apollo, Hellenistically short though it is, artistic though it is in some ways, is nevertheless lacking in that expansion which makes Ovid's Art art. 'Length' is a problematical concept in a poem where the absence of Menelaus from Helen while Paris was visiting was dangerously long, while that of Ulysses from Penelope was—artistically—*breuis* ('short'), just

---

[3] This point is well made by Ross (1975). See esp. 6–7, 18–19, 115, 123.

[4] Bassi (1989) argues convincingly for the unity of *Hymn* 2, basing the case on the 'motifs of exclusion and combativeness' (p. 227) which pervade both the central panel and the framing literary contest.

long enough to arouse her feelings (*Ars* 2. 355–72). The measure of length = art is effectiveness.

Length, or rather the lack of it, is a problematical value in Callimachean poetics. Length is relative. Callimachus begins the *Aetia*, not exactly a short work, with his celebrated attack on the Telchines for expecting long poems (*Aet.* fr. 1. 3–6):[5]

> εἵνεκεν οὐχ ἓν ἄεισμα διηνεκὲς ἢ βασιλήων
> πρήξιας ἐν πολλαῖς ἤνυσα χιλιάσιν
> ἢ προτέρους ἥρωας, ἔπος δ' ἐπὶ τυτθὸν ἑλίσσω
> παῖς ἅτε, τῶν δ' ἐτέων ἡ δεκὰς οὐκ ὀλίγη.

because I have not accomplished one continuous song
or the deeds of kings or heroes of old, in many thousands of
verses,
but I roll out my poetry little by little, like a child,
although the decades of my years are not few.

In the mutilated lines following v. 9, short poems are favourably (v. 16) compared with long (it does not matter for our investigation which poets are referred to):

> ἀηδονίδες δ' ὧδε μελιχρότεραι

but 'nightingales' are sweeter thus.

Poetry should be judged by art, not a measuring-chain (vv. 17–18):

> αὖθι δὲ τέχνηι
> κρίνετε, μὴ σχοίνωι Περσίδι τὴν σοφίην

Forthwith judge poetry by art, not a Persian chain.

Enormously influential as this prologue was, it is nevertheless difficult to ascertain the import of the metaphorical oppositions.[6]

---

[5] I am using the text of Hopkinson (1988) in all quotations from the first fragment of the *Aetia*.

[6] Lyne's (1984) examination of the *Aetia* prologue is useful. He stresses that Callimachean poetic values are aesthetic rather than moral. The 'littleness' which Callimachus expounds, on this reading, means 'slight in content, in moral worth', and as such is an amusing misrepresentation of his critics (Lyne, p. 19). Whether or not this theory adequately explains Callimachus' own practice, in the case of the Augustans it would be impossible to dispense with the moral element in the exposition of poetic values. See also Wimmel (1960: 83–7), F. Williams (1978: 86), Hopkinson (1988: 86).

The metaphorical language of 'big' and 'little' is programmatic, indeed polemical, in the tradition we are considering.[7] The neoterics made a show of taking the metaphor
very literally: for example in Catullus' praise for Nepos'
short history of the world (see Cairns 1969), and attack on
Suffenus' boorish expansion (poem 22) and Volusius' volu-
minousness (poem 36). But it is not simply a question of
the number of verses in a poem; 'length' is also a metaphorical measure of quality. We use the same metaphor in the
terminology of the *opera minora*, the minor poems, or at the
other end of the scale the *magnum opus*, the great work.
Although these terms may well also apply to the actual
length of the works concerned, the metaphor implies lesser
in status as well as physically shorter. For a Callimachean,
however, this positive poetic 'quality' can be expressed in
the metaphorical language of size, as applying to a *type* of
poetry—and this is how for Callimachus metaphorical size
fits with manner. His poems should not be measured with
the Persian chain, but with and by art. The preference for
art over length is as a *means of judgement*. The result is that,
for Callimachus, and Callimacheanism, the overt value-
judgement 'big is great is good' is playfully inverted. Size
becomes a metaphor for manner, and so reintroduces the
value-judgement by the back door. 'Short' poems may be
sweeter (v. 17), but the essence of their shortness does not
depend simply on the number of verses employed: rather,
shortness becomes a metaphor for good artistry—in the
Callimachean manner. How 'long' is a long epigram? How
'short' is a short elegy? Callimachus, at least as interpreted
by Ovid, says, I suggest, not so much that short poems are
good and long poems are bad, but that poems which are
inartistic (by Callimachean standards!) are bad. The argument threatens to become circular. The self-deprecating
joke is that on one level he is quite precisely introducing
this long poem by saying that long poems are bad.

   Is this to say, then, that absolute size is irrelevant to the
question of what makes a poem Callimachean? Not exactly:

---

[7] The image is very well known: a simple illustration of the spread of the
metaphor can be seen in Hor. *Carm.* 2. 16. 37–40 *mihi parua rura et | spiritum
Graiae tenuem Camenae | Parca non mendax dedit et malignum | spernere uulgus.*

although size is (*a*) always relative, to genre, to expectation, etc.; and (*b*) more a matter of metaphorical size than literal number of verses. Rather, what is crucial in the Calli-machean programme is the presentation of size. To take an example at one end of the scale, Lucan *presents* his poem as immense, in conscious and self-displaying reaction to the Callimachean code. Masters (1992: particularly 32–3, 38, 68–70) has powerfully illustrated the way in which the *Bellum Civile* parades its immensity, in opposition to Calli-machean values. What makes the poem so epically excessive is not its length *per se*, but its imagery (part of which might be actual size) and its manner. Epic is big, in all ways: Ovid's poem is not-big.

Callimachus himself exemplifies the tensions in his poetic theory in his *Hymn to Apollo* (*Hymn* 2). I shall suggest that this work is closely alluded to by our passage.[8] The word *megas* ('great, big') occurs three times in the *Hymn*. At v. 85 it is fairly inert: ἦ ῥ᾽ ἐχάρη μέγα Φοῖβος ('Phoebus rejoiced greatly'), but the other two instances are, I suggest, signifi-cant. They are linked by the simple but effective device of ring-composition which produces the frame of this and so many other Hellenistic poems.[9] The good man who receives the epiphany—the poet himself—is *megas* in v. 10. By con-trast, the god does not appear to him who is *litos* ('worthless, paltry, small': the sort of adjective we would normally associate with Callimacheanism, were the metaphor acting straightforwardly). Finally, Apollo, with oracular obscurity, replies to Envy's attack on the poet by contrasting the great dirty river with the pure little stream (vv. 108–12):

> Ἀσσυρίου ποταμοῖο ΜΈΓΑΣ ῥόος, ἀλλὰ τὰ πολλά
> λύματα γῆς καὶ πολλὸν ἐφ᾽ ὕδατι συρφετὸν ἕλκει.
> Δηοῖ δ᾽ οὐκ ἀπὸ παντὸς ὕδωρ φορέουσι Μέλισσαι,
> ἀλλ᾽ ἥτις καθαρή τε καὶ ἀχράαντος ἀνέρπει
> πίδακος ἐξ ἱερῆς ᾿ΟΛΊΓΗ λιβὰς ἄκρον ἄωτον.

> The stream of the Assyrian river is great,
> but it drags a lot of mud of earth and a lot of refuse

---

[8] Koster (1983: 9–21) argues that the *Hymn* is the literary progenitor of the Augustan pose of priest of Apollo (or the Muses), and particularly of the use of that pose for poetic theory. An interesting example he cites is Hor. *Carm.* 3. 1. 1.

[9] See Bassi (1989) for the argument over the unity of the hymn and its frame.

with its waters. But the Melissai do not bring water
from everywhere to Deo, but whatever creeps up
pure and unsullied from a holy spring, a little stream,
the choicest prize.

F. Williams's (1978) complex discussion of the passage understands the *pontos* ('sea') preferred by *Phthonos* as large and
pure (Homeric poetry), the *potamos* ('river') as large and
impure (traditional imitation-epic), and the spray from the
pidax ('spring') as small and pure (Callimachean poetry). It
is clear, I think, that Apollo is praising both the droplets
from the pure spring and also Callimachus' poetry, and that
the spring is contrasted with a raging river, while Callimachus' work is defended from the accusation of not being
long enough, whatever that might mean.[10] I would suggest,
however, that the complexities of *megas* within the poem as
a whole can bear expansion. The stream of the Euphrates
may be *megas*—big, but it is not *megas*—great. The *pidax* is
oligē but *is* great. Does the hymn have a dimension? Is it a
'big' poem? For a Homeric hymn? For a Pindaric hymn? A
Callimachean hymn? If *Phthonos* has noticed it, it must be
'*megas*' (poetically great). Length is a big problem, in discussion of which Callimachus—and Ovid—teases us with
value-laden vagueness.[11] It is by now fairly well accepted
that Callimachus' imagery does not necessarily imply literal
shortness as the main criterion for artistry. What is not so
well accepted, however, is the extent to which Ovid has
engaged with the question of literal and metaphorical
length, together with 'Callimachean' allegiance. I place 'Callimachean' in inverted commas here in order to remind the
reader that the figure, image, even myth of Callimachus is

---

[10] The reading is called 'impossibly devious' by Hutchinson (1988: 68 n. 85).
He does not argue the point beyond noting the insecurity of the reading οὐδ' ὅσα, on
which in fact F. Williams's interpretation is by no means entirely dependent. See
F. Williams (1978: ad loc.) for bibliography.

[11] Here I am in some agreement with Hutchinson's remark (1988: 77) that
Callimachus 'wishes to make [the reader] admire his own work; the aim is not to
write full descriptive criticism or to aid our understanding'. His interpretation of
the end of *Hymn* 2 (his p. 78) is not so very different from that of those critics,
such as myself, who would give a more functional reading of the polemic than
Hutchinson allows.

used by the Augustan poets as a flag, and an authority
which allows them self-deprecating self-display.

4*b* Seduction and Repetition

I propose that the Epiphany of Apollo is self-consciously
placed in a tradition of examination of Callimachean literary
(theoretical) programme; that Apollo's speech is his version
of the *Ars Amatoria*; that the immediate sequel (vv. 511–34)
is Ovid's response, a taste of his own *Ars* (*ars*), expansive
but artistic.

What, then, do this scene and this chapter have to offer
to the present reading of *Ars* 2? Sections 4*c*–*g* offer an
analysis of the Apollo scene, and then its sequel is treated in
4*h*–*i*. This chapter seeks throughout to illuminate Ovid's
particular brand of Callimacheanism, as introduced in the
first two sections of the chapter, and to affirm the value of
Ovidian poetry by exposing the poem's own display of
seduction and repetition. There is both an overt claim to be
'Callimachean', which itself constitutes a claim to poetic
'greatness' without bigness, delivered primarily through the
intertextual associations with Apollo scenes elsewhere; and
also an illustration of that poetic value, in the seductive
game Ovid plays with Reader and reader.

Before discussing the scene in detail, it might be useful to
draw out a little further the elements of seduction and
repetition to be found here. Both 'reader' and 'Reader' are
seduced by the passage. I suggested earlier that the reader
is the victim of Ovid's teasing seduction, which draws him
further and further into Ovid's power. On its simplest
level, this means that whenever we pick up a joke, appreciate
an incongruity, become involved in a complexity of situation, recognize an allusion, detect an inconsistency, or
engage in any of those activities which constitute our response to the text, we are thereby drawn further into the
text, and when we stand back and watch ourselves being
drawn in (not standing back), a further level is added to our
induced appreciation. This applies generally to the act of
reading. Specific to the *Ars*, however, is the muted but self-
conscious display of authorial seduction, facilitated by the

peculiar stance of the didactic poet *vis-à-vis* his audience. The reader is lead on a wild goose chase through a labyrinth of literary allusion, constantly deceived by *paraprosdokian* twists. Just when we think we have caught on to what it going on, the poem twists and slips out of our grasp, and we realize that it is we ourselves who are caught. This is what happens to a responder taking the role of 'sophisticated reader'. For the 'naïve Reader' (the addressee) the case is different. It should be remembered that responding to the text involves both separating and merging these two acts of reading. I shall suggest that Ovid's answer seduces the addressee into continuing the affair and the poem, by offering him a new way of doing the same thing (*referre aliter idem*). Moreover, by encouraging the apprentice to picture himself as a suffering romantic elegiac lover, Ovid seduces him actually into being in love, not just acting as a lover. This is necessary if the following section of the instruction is to have its effect. The next lesson is 'how to cope with your mistress's infidelity'. If this is to be the difficult task as which it is paraded, the lover must be made to be emotionally involved. If his response to being refused entry by his beloved is simply to find another one, all he has to do is to go back to the beginning of the book. And that way he will never reach the study of advanced poetics/erotics.[12] It is not only the beloved who must be manipulated if the affair is to last 'a long time'. The quotation marks around this last phrase are designed to remind the reader that 'length' in this poem and in this discussion is problematical. It is a relative term, depending more on artistic effectiveness than on objective length—if such a thing could exist.

To turn to repetition: both the epiphany of Apollo and the 'painful lover' scene constitute classic cases. Ovid's answer in vv. 511–34 and to a lesser extent Apollo's speech are a recapitulation of an earlier stage in the poem and, in the case of Ovid's version, of the amatory situation of the *Amores*. The passage therefore epitomizes in miniature what Book 2 does as a whole. Ovid has often been accused of repetition. My claim is that repetition is the point (I repeat

[12] This is not to say that the advanced lover is expected to be monogamous. *Di melius!*, as Ovid would say.

myself), for while on one level it is hard to avoid recognizing the repetition of material (indeed we must do so), on another level the *meaning* of that material has changed so that it is functionally quite different. Repetion makes this miniature *Ars Amatoria* into the winning entry in a song contest with Apollo, and manipulates the lover into the right position to learn his next lesson.

4c The Literary History of the Scene, *reuocatio*, and Talking Gods

As has been stressed at a number of points in this book, digressions such as this one on the literary background to Ovid's scene are not digressions, or only in so far as the Daedalus episode constitutes a 'digression', for the relationship between our scene and its literary history is crucial to my reading. Without that history, the words Ovid uses would mean something different.[13] One of the means by which Ovid engages with the question of Callimacheanism and poetic value is by placing his writing within the tradition—perhaps, for him, at the end of the tradition, although that is a position fated to be usurped. This intertextual relationship makes the difference between a reading of the scene as 'scene-painting', or simple *uariatio*, and a reading of it as a complex of poetic statements, or functional *uariatio*, since for a Callimachean poet, an epiphany of Apollo warning the poet to return to the 'correct' poetic track is the ultimate appeal to authority and declaration of allegiance. Although the four most important epiphanies (those to Callimachus himself, Virgil, Propertius, and Horace) are well known, a brief mention of each will set the scene for Ovid's contribution.

Callimachus enlists divine authority for his programmatic poetic defence against the Telchines with the introduction of the god of poetry (*Aet.* fr. 1. 21–4):

καὶ γὰρ ὅτε πρώτιστον ἐμοῖς ἐπὶ δέλτον ἔθηκα
γούνασιν, Ἀπόλλων εἶπεν ὅ μοι Λύκιος

---

[13] As ever in these sorts of discussions, we are faced with the problem of the ignorant reader. For him/her, the text just does mean something different.

... ἀοιδέ, τὸ μὲν θύος ὅττι πάχιστον
θρέψαι, τὴν Μοῦσαν δ᾽ ὠγαθὲ λεπταλέην.

For when I first put a writing-tablet on my knees,
Lycian Apollo said to me, '. . . poet, feed the victim as fat as
     possible,
but, my friend, keep the Muse slight.'

This polemical epiphany-scene in possibly the most programmatically charged position in Hellenistic poetry, the
prologue to the *Aetia*, and so to the collected works of
Callimachus (see Parsons 1977: 49–50, Trypanis 1958: 13),
begins a chain of such scenes at significant moments.

For Virgil it is at *Ecl.* 6. 3–5, where it is involved in the
Augustan apologetic *recusatio*.[14] From this point on, the
disclaimer acquires a potential political as well as a poetic
force.

> *cum canerem reges et proelia, Cynthius aurem*
> *uellit et admonuit: 'pastorem, Tityre, pinguis*
> *pascere oportet ouis, deductum dicere carmen.'*

While I was singing of kings and battles, the Cynthian [Apollo]
     plucked my ear
and admonished me: 'it is right, Tityrus, for a shepherd
to fatten up rich sheep, but to sing an attenuated song.'

Wimmel states (1960: 133) that Virgil's originality within
the tradition is shown through the fact that both poets are
interrupted, but whereas Callimachus was preparing simply
to write, Virgil was preparing to write specifically about
kings and battles—panegyrical epic. It should be noted that
reges et proelia ('kings and battles', *Ecl.* 6. 3) correspond to
the *basileōn* and *hērōas* ('kings and heroes') on whom
Callimachus did not write (*Aet.* fr. 1. 3 and 5), but Callimachus does not pretend to any intention of ever writing epic,
and Apollo's advice (anterior to the scene with the
Telchines) was simply as to the style of his poetry. Virgil,
on the other hand, takes the possibility of epic quite

---

[14] So Wimmel (1960) 133. His discussion of the motif (pp.135–141) centres on
the *Eclogue*. As well as the central passages (including our own) he also collects
variants which bear an obvious generic similarity to the original but which may,
for example, have a different advising god, or advise a less overtly 'Callimachean'
change of direction.

seriously, and Apollo's advice is more specifically concerned with his subject matter. Despite the attempt I have just made, it is unwise to define dogmatically the differences and similarities between the two scenes. The fact that the import of Apollo's warnings to the two poets is and is not the same (that is, that Virgil both quotes and adapts Callimachus) shows in miniature how Ovid uses his sources. On the one hand he *is* doing the same thing as Callimachus and (differently) Virgil, and on the other he is doing something very different from either of them.

Propertius introduces Apollo into another programmatically charged scene, the dream on Helicon.[15] The tradition makes its way to Propertius through the poetic initiation of Gallus in Virg. *Ecl.* 6. 63–73, two disparate parts of which Propertius conflates, as well as of the *Aetia*. A separate but interrelated tradition from Hesiod through Ennius also contributes to Propertius' poem. Wimmel shows throughout his discussion how the Roman poets conflate various aspects of Callimachean literary polemic into their epiphany scenes, a fact which will bear upon the conflation by Ovid of the Delphic, Delian, and Lycian Apollo, which we will see later.

> *cum me Castalia speculans ex arbore Phoebus*
> *sic ait aurata nixus ad antra lyra:*
> *'quid tibi cum tali, demens, est flumine? quis te*
> *carminis heroi tangere iussit opus?'* (Prop. 3. 3. 13–16)

> . . . when Phoebus, spying me from the Castalian wood,
> speaks thus, leaning on his golden lyre by the caves:
> 'Madman, what does this river have to do with you?
> Who ordered you to touch a work of heroic song?'

For Horace, the *reuocatio*-epiphany maintains its political nuance. Notably, the scene occurs in the very last *Ode* (*Carm.* 4. 15. 1–4):

> *Phoebus uolentem proelia me loqui*
> *uictas et urbis increpuit lyra,*
> *ne parua Tyrrhenum per aequor*
> *uela darem.*

---

[15] Hes. *Theog.* 22–35; Call. *Aet.* fr. 2. See Fedeli (1985: ad loc.) and his introduction to this poem, esp. pp. 111–12.

Phoebus twanged his lyre at me, when I wanted
to speak of battles and conquered cities, chiding me not to
spread my little sails over the Etruscan sea.

With such a famous background, the import of Ovid's
epiphany is immediately clear. He even draws attention to
his predecessors by verbal reminiscences. The opening
phrase, *haec ego cum canerem* ('while I was singing this'),
besides setting the scene for the poet to be interrupted,
echoes Virgil's *cum canerem reges et proelia* ('while I was
singing of kings and battles', *Ecl.* 6. 3); *inauratae . . . lyrae*
('of his golden lyre', *Ars* 2. 494) echoes *aurata . . . lyra* ('on
his golden lyre') in Prop. 3. 3. 14, in both cases the adjective
and agreeing noun coming before the main caesura of the
pentameter and at its end respectively, in true elegiac fashion;[16] the god striking his lyre to get the poet's attention
(*Ars* 2. 494) reminds the reader of Horace's *Phoebus . . .
increpuit lyra* ('Phoebus twanged (with) his lyre',
Carm. 4. 15. 1–2). The opening line of Apollo's address to
the poet strongly echoes other admonitory poetic epiphanies. There is a vocative: *praeceptor amoris* (*Ars* 2. 497),
aoide (Call. *Aet.* fr. 1. 23), *Tityre* (Virg. *Ecl.* 6. 4), *demens . . .
Properti* (Prop. 3. 3. 15 and 17). There is (not surprisingly) a
word of speech: (in the same order) *dixit* (497) *eipen* (22),
admonuit (4), *ait* (14). The Virgilian *admonuit* ('admonished') is echoed twice in Ovid's acclaim of the epiphany
(v. 509):

> *sic monuit Phoebus: Phoebo parete monenti.*

Such was Phoebus' advice: obey the advice of Phoebus.

Ovid has placed himself firmly in a poetic line of descent
from Callimachus, through Virgil, Propertius, and Horace.
The connection with Virgil's Apolline epiphany is particularly enlightening, for, through this, specific allusion is
made to a scene which both in itself and in its embedding is
highly conscious of its part in a poetic tradition. Ross
(1975: 27) and Elder (1961: 175–6) describe *Eclogue* 6 as

---

[16] Rhyme occurs in this position in about 20% of pentameters in Roman elegy.
90% of these are between substantive and agreeing adjective. Platnauer (1951:
49), whose statistics I have quoted, believes this form of rhyme to be
unintentional.

Virgil's 'poetic genealogy' and his 'House of Inspiration'
respectively, through which the poet includes himself in the
company of other great inspired poets, Apollo, Linus, Orpheus, Hesiod, Silenus, Gallus. (Their discussions treat the
whole poem rather than its introductory epiphany.) Already
Ovid has appropriated the *Eclogue*'s central theme of poetic
descent, and, with amusing presumption, Virgil's poetic
genealogy.

Such is one strand in the literary ancestry of the Apollo
scene. When eventually Apollo makes his pronouncement,
however, it is not as the literary 'Lycian' god (by which I
intend a shorthand for the tradition of warning epiphanies
which stem from Callimachus), but under the auspices of
his Delphic temple and its famous maxims. Miller's discussion (1983: 33) shows the conflation of two Callimachean
Apollos. Apollo was often an interlocutor and giver of
information in the aetiological parts of the *Aetia*, and it is
the descendent of *this* Callimachean manifestation of the
god who actually speaks in our passage, although it is
Apollo's 'Lycian' (literary) version who appears in our
poem. At *Aet.* fr. 114, *Delian* Apollo explains aspects of his
own cult, which is what Ovid's Apollo does here (Miller
1983: 33). The golden statue of Apollo at Delos gives the
aetion for the fact that he (the statue) holds the Graces in
his right hand and the bow in his left, probably by reference
to the Delphic maxim μετανόει ἁμαρτῶν ('repent of your
faults'), as is convincingly argued by Pfeiffer (1952: 21–2).
Although not 'Callimachean' in the sense we expect, the
actual speech of Apollo relates more closely to that other
Callimachean tradition of 'the god explaining an aspect of
his cult', for Ovid has his Apollo 'explain' the maxim
γνῶθι σαυτόν ('know thyself'). The passage thereby finds a
new way of placing itself in the tradition of the master.

The speaking Apollo here stands in the tradition of informative deities in the aetiological elegy—another branch
in the didactic tradition, perhaps—as exemplified in Callimachus and by Ovid in the *Fasti*. On the erotodidactic side,
the entire instructive section of Tibullus' '*ars*', 1. 4, is spoken
by the god Priapus. Ovid follows this tradition again with
the theophany of Venus in *Ars* 3. 43–56 and that of Cupid

in *Rem.* 555–76.[17] Ovid's choice of informative god here is important. From Priapus one is unlikely to hear profound wisdom; from Vertumnus or Horus one will learn the History of Rome; but from Apollo—particularly a composite Apollo—one receives the wisdom of the world.

Ovid twists Virgil's hint of substituting Cynthian Apollo for Callimachus' Lycian Apollo, by introducing the god of Delphi. Although he begins ostentatiously in the Callimachean-Lycian tradition, the substitution creates in its actual realization a very different scene from the norm. The interrelation between Callimachus, Virgil, and Ovid facilitates a further play with literary allusion. Clausen (1976) has shown that Virgil's replacement of Callimachus' Lycian Apollo with the appellation 'Cynthius' consolidates his statement of allegiance to Callimachean poetics. In extant literature, 'Cynthius' as applied to the god (as opposed to the mountain on which he was born) is first used by Callimachus, at *Hymn* 4. 9–10, *Aet.* fr. 67. 5, 114. 8.[18] Virgil therefore replaces Callimachus' more obvious 'Lycius' (which is 'as old as Pind. *Pyth.* 1. 39') with a cult-name which is specifically an invention of the master's.[19]

This kind of play with cult-titles was prevalent in Callimachus. One famous Callimachean story, that of Acontius and Cydippe, hints at the three cult-titles: Delian, Delphic, and Cynthian. At *Aet.* fr. 67. 5, Callimachus addresses Apollo as 'Cynthius', when introducing the story. Now, it was on Delos that the affair began, while it was Apollo's Delphic oracle which provided the solution (*Aet.* fr. 75. 20–37). This technique of covert, abstruse allusion to cult-titles is imitated and further refined by Ovid. Since Ovid subliminally refers to all three manifestations of Apollo, and the term 'Cynthius' is a coinage and rare in Callimachus, he may be recalling the Callimachean practice of introducing unusual cult-names, even specifically referring to some or all of the passages just cited. Ovid thus uses his synthesis of the

---

[17] On didactic theophanies in general see Prinz (1914: 41–4) (he is mostly concerned with the epiphany of Cupid).

[18] This point is modified slightly in a later article (1977). The term also appears in a poem of Posidippus, but it is Callimachean none the less.

[19] Virgil's other use of the term comes at *Georg.* 3. 36, another highly 'Callimachean' context. See Parsons (1977: 1–3).

Callimachean and Virgilian epiphanies, together with allusion to the Delphic and Delian manifestations, to allude to yet another Callimachean passage.

There are many variants in the tradition of the *reuocatio*. A further link in the chain leading up to our passage is the variant Apollo scene in *Amores* 1. 1, where Cupid usurps the god's poetic function (1. 1. 1–4):

> *Arma graui numero uiolentaque bella parabam*
> *edere, materia conueniente modis.*
> *par erat inferior uersus; risisse Cupido*
> *dicitur atque unum surripuisse pedem.*

Arms in heavy measure and violent wars I was preparing
to give forth, material in harmony with metre.
The second line was equal; Cupid is said
to have laughed and to have stolen one foot.

This passage is echoed in the *Metamorphoses*, the first erotic adventure of which is caused when Cupid has usurped another of Apollo's functions, archery (*Met.* 1. 452–73). Note the similarity between Ovid's and Apollo's indignant exclamations:

'*quis tibi, saeue puer, dedit hoc in carmina iuris?*' (*Am.* 1. 1. 5)
'Who gave you, savage boy, this right over songs?

'*quid'que 'tibi, lasciue puer, cum fortibus armis?*' (*Met.* 1. 456)
'What, wanton boy, do strong arms have to do with you?'

The result, for both Ovid and Apollo, is to be shot by an erotic arrow. For Apollo, the usurpation of his province of archery is confirmed by the accuracy of the shot; for Ovid, the overturn of his poetic intentions is confirmed by the type of poetry he goes on to write, as is the usurpation of Apollo's poetic role. The parallel in the *Metamorphoses* reiterates the replacement of Apollo by Cupid, and makes his theft of the foot into a double theft—that of epic poetry and of Apollo's poetic authority.

In this founding moment of his corpus, then, Ovid covertly refers to a tradition, the Apolline or pseudo-Apolline *reuocatio*, which he will later use overtly, ostentatiously even. The less obvious version (*Am.* 1. 1) of the tradition makes the traditional point, while the easily accessible, self-advertising version (*Ars* 2) appears to be employed for a purpose unconnected with that tradition. Again this structure of allusion has parallels in Virgil's *Eclogues*. In the middle of the book, Virgil makes clear and unmistakable allusion to the Callimachean epiphany tradition. J. R. G. Wright (1983: 123) has argued that the oracular response of *Ecl.* 1. 44–5 directs the poet towards pastoral poetry, and thus is a covert allusion to the same tradition. Both Virgil and Ovid begin with a covert allusion to the *Aetia* tradition, using a variant advising deity, and then produce an obvious allusion part-way through the work, or, in Ovid's case, the corpus of amatory poetry.[20]

Ovid's technique in manipulating the corpus of ancient literature in the production of his text highlights a major constituent feature of Callimachean literary polemic which we might perhaps call the 'topos of originality'. The phrase recreates an amusing paradox in the tradition, whereby each poet makes a claim to be the first to write in a particular way. The substance of the claim may be true and the poetry original, but the essence of the claim is conventional. Propertius (for example) can speak of pure springs and untrodden paths, and we are to recognize the allusion *as* an allusion, while at the same time accepting the accuracy of the claim to be genuinely original. The very concept of originality expounded by the Augustans in particular itself belongs to a complicated tradition of intertextual allusion. No text exists in isolation. An ancient poet not only of necessity writes within a tradition, but actively parades the traditionality of his work, creatively drawing on other texts as source material. This is not to say that there cannot be an unoriginal ancient poet, but that assumptions about what constitutes originality may be harmful to the reading of ancient and indeed other texts. The entire system of classical allusive technique depends on this intertextual relationship.[21] With Ovid, in this passage, the *idea* of origi-

---

[20] I am not suggesting that *Ars* 2. 493 is pointedly half-way through that corpus: the point is that it is not at the beginning.

[21] That technique receives perhaps its best ancient formulation in Horace's dictum (*Ars* 128) *difficile est proprie communia dicere*. The *magnum opus* on the

nality, if not the topos, takes on a new perspective. Ovid begins his scene with heavily underscored conventionality, which ostentatiously places the scene in a Callimachean polemical tradition. But the epiphany develops in quite a different way, which in fact relates to *other* Callimachean traditions (the god explaining an aspect of his cult). The scene is and is not a warning-epiphany, is and is not original.

So far we have seen the Callimachean *reuocatio* and the tradition of informative deities as formative influences on our passage. Another important intertext is Callimachus *Hymn* 2, which may represent a wider tradition of programmatic Hymns to Apollo, to which I turn in the next section.

4d Hymns and Ritualism

Along with Apollo's redirectory appearance in Callimachus' *Aetia*, the other foundation text in the history of Callimachean Apollo is Callimachus' hymn to the god, *Hymn* 2. I propose that our scene is written consciously, even ostentatiously in the light of that *Hymn*, thereby aligning itself with, and defining itself against, what is also a foundation text for the metaphor 'short is good'. It is one aim of this section to argue for ritual and hymnic elements generally in our passage, as well as for specific connection with the Callimachean hymn, in order both to suggest that Apollo is more than just a 'variant speaker' and that this is a section markedly different from its surroundings, and also to support the argument for a poetic interpretation of the scene.

The programmatic *Hymn to Apollo* may be representative

subject in modern criticism is G. Williams (1968). Many critics, fighting against the background of Romantic criticism, have contributed to the study. DuQuesnay's discussion (1976: 37) of 'creative writing within a tradition' is helpful in stressing that the *use* of tradition was actually considered correct and indispensable by the Romans. Or as Ross puts it: 'these poets saw themselves not as isolated innovators, but as the latest representatives of a purposefully selected succession of antecedents, giving new life and purpose to an established inheritance' (1975: 3). Wimmel (1960: 133) hints at this paradox, although he does not overtly make the point, in his use of the phrase, *'primus'*-Motiv, and in his discussion of the epiphany in *Eclogue* 6: 'Trotz des Wegsymbols im Aitienprolog ist Vergils Verbindung von Apollszene und *'primus'*-Motiv origineller, als man denkt.' Wimmel goes on to show how the originality motif is developed in the later history of the scene.

of a tradition wider than that which has come down to us. Kennedy (1980) has suggested that Gallus may possibly have written a hymn to Apollo, including *reuocatio* material of the type I have been discussing. Ross (1975: 121) brings out the Gallan significance of Propertius 3. 3, a poem in the tradition of Apolline warning-epiphanies. Again, Propertius' model could be the hypothesized hymn. If Gallus did write such a hymn (and the poetic genealogy of *Eclogue* 6 supports the possibility), then a link is missing from our chain of allusion. F. Williams (1978), commenting on Callimachus' claim that it was the Delphians who invented the cry ἰὴ ἰὴ παιῆον during the god's fight with the Python (*Hymn* 2. 97), mentions Pfeiffer's view (on fr. 88) that Apollonius' version of the story (2. 705–13), a hymn to Apollo sung by Orpheus, was an imitation of Callimachus' treatment of the subject in *Aetia* 4. F. Williams suggests, taking support from the argument in the hymn between Apollo and *Phthonos*, that the *Aetia* passage was one singled out for particular criticism by Callimachus' enemies. We are now entering the realms of speculation, but since both the *Aetia* prologue and the *Hymn* are source material for our passage, then the fight's status in Callimachean polemic adds another link to the chain of allusion in our passage. Ovid's Epiphany of Apollo is thick with ritual motifs.[22] As well as specifically alluding to Callimachus' *Hymn*, the passage may perhaps glance at the Apolline prophecy-scene in Virgil *Aeneid* 3, and the epiphany of Apollo at the opening of *Aeneid* 6, as source texts for primitive ritualism.

Ovid's Apolline game with his reader must be considered in relation to Callimachus'. Callimachus' *Hymn* 2 begins with ritual motifs. Although the material is traditional, there is no surviving earlier example in literature of 'such a mimetic presentation of an epiphany ritual'. (See F. Williams 1978: ad loc., Weinreich 1968: 67–74.) Most importantly, the Homeric hymns do not display such dramatic presentation. The game which Callimachus plays with the Homeric hymns and with his own sophisticated persona is to adopt a pose of greater naïve religiosity and ritual primitiv-

---

[22] Koster (1983: 21), in a discussion centring on Callimachus *Hymn to Apollo*, describes our passage as 'a travesty of the hymn'.

ism than do the archaic hymns. 'Can't you see?' he asks
innocently, for Apollo appears only to the good, or great,
man (*megas*, 'great', v. 10). Ovid is playing the same game,
but goes one better in pseudo-naïve amazement. 'Look,'
says Callimachus, 'Apollo is about to come. Can't you see?'
'Look,' says Ovid, 'Apollo really has come. Can't you see
him? I can. (I must be *megas*.)'

It is in the opening lines and the closing couplet that the
ritual motifs can most easily be seen. This itself reflects the
structure of the *Hymn to Apollo*, where, as often in a
Callimachean hymn, the main central panel is framed by a
highly ritualized, and in this case highly programmatic
beginning and end. I shall now explore the ritual elements
in the *Ars* passage, in connection with those of Callimachus'
hymn (*Ars* 2. 493–6):

> *haec ego cum canerem, subito manifestus Apollo*
> *mouit inauratae pollice fila lyrae.*
> *in manibus laurus, sacris induta capillis*
> *laurus erat: uates ille uidendus adit.*

While I was singing this, Apollo, suddenly present,
struck with his thumb the strings of his golden lyre.
Laurel was in his hands, with laurel his holy hair was adorned:
he was manifestly a bard.

Soundplay—anaphora, assonance, alliteration—is a feature of ancient ritual language.[23] In the sophisticated literary manifestations of the discourse, the device is particularly, albeit subtly present. Koster (1983: 15) finds a play
on Apollo's name at Call. *Hymn* 2. 69 ὤπολλον πολλοί (*ōpollon
polloi*, 'Apollo, many . . .'). F. Williams (1978) notes the
effect of the alternation of long and short *o* sounds in the
first line. Donnet (1983: 221–7) treats in detail the interweav-
ing soundplay, especially in the prologue (1–8). In the first
line, the final syllable of δάφνινος (*daphninos*, 'laurel', the
word whose Latin equivalent is involved in the Ovidian
play discussed below) echoes that of τὠπόλλωνος (*tōpollōnos*),
itself the closure of the first hemistich, while its vowel
sounds look forward to those of the word which closes the

---

[23] DuQuesnay (1976) 82 notes that this device was a feature of the style of the
Sibylline oracles, and of the oracular part of *Eclogue* 4.

second line, ἀλιτρός (*alitros*, Donnet 221). ἀλιτρός plays chiastically with ὅστις (*hostis*), and with τὸ μέλαΘΡΟ-ν (*to melaTHRO-n*) (*aliTROS* and *melaTHRON* end each half of the line), which itself plays rhythmically with τὰ θύρετρα (*ta thuretra*), in the following line, the final syllable of which joins in the play of ἀλιTPΌs (Donnet 221–2). In vv. 6–8 the dental (or alveolar) plosives *t d* and velar plosives *k g* interplay with each other (see Allen 1965: 3), reinforced by the initial anaphora, αὐτοὶ αὐταὶ (*autoi autai*, Donnet 223–4). φοῖνιξ (*phoinix*) in v. 4 echoes Φοῖβος (*Phoibos*) in the previous line, reinforced by the preceding syllables, ποδὶ (*podi*) and τι (*ti*), while its final ξ, ending the line, echoes the final sound of the first line, ὄρπηξ (*horpēx*), and the first consonant of the next line, ἐξαπίνης (*exapinēs*). Similar soundplays are found in vv. 32–41 and vv. 58–62.

Ovid also makes sophisticated use of this primitive ritualistic feature.

> *inAURatae . . . LYRae . . . LAURus . . . LAURus*
> *APOLLo POLLICe CAPILLIs fILa ILLe*

One line of play works mainly through the lyre and the laurel, a second mainly through Apollo, his thumb, and his hair, both plays being reinforced by the alliteration of 'l' throughout this introductory passage. *LYRae* works both ways, playing off against both *LAURus* and *polLIce fILa*. More simply, the god's speech is acclaimed at the end with a chiastic double anaphora (v. 509):

> *sic monuit Phoebus: Phoebo parete monenti*

Such was Phoebus' advice: obey the advice of Phoebus.

The suddenness of a theophany is often expressed, for example in the two *Aeneid* passages mentioned above.[24]

> *tremere omnia uisa repente*   (*Aen.* 3. 90)
> Suddenly everything seemed to tremble.

> *uentum erat ad limen, cum uirgo 'poscere fata*
> *tempus' ait; 'deus ecce deus!' cui talia fanti*
> *ante fores subito non uultus . . . mansere*   (6. 45–7)

---

[24] Cf. *Fast.* 2. 439, 2. 501, 4. 17; and see Norden (1916) on Virg. *Aen.* 3. 90 for more parallels.

They had come to the threshold, when the virgin said
'Time to request the fates; the god, lo, the god!' As she spoke
before the doors suddenly her expression changed . . .

and in a scene from Phaedrus which derives from that in
Aeneid 3 (Phaed. A. 6. 3):

> *subito sacratae uatis horrescunt comae*
> Suddenly the holy hair of the prophet bristled.

Most importantly, the motif occurs in Call. *Hymn* 2. 4–5:

> ἐπένευσεν ὁ Δήλιος ἡδύ τι φοῖνιξ
> ἐξαπίνης
> Suddenly the Delian palm nods pleasantly.

Apollo is *manifestus*. This word provides us with two
possible etymological plays, one 'primitive', the other
'sophisticated'. Cassiodorus (*in psalm.* 49. 3) suggests the
link with liturgical practice: *manifeste dicitur, quasi a mane
dies festus* ('something is said to be "manifest", as if [from]
a festal day in the morning'). The morning is particularly
associated with omens at, for example, Juv. 6. 601. The
OLD, by contrast, derives the word from *manus* ('hand')
and *festus* ('festal'). Could this hint that Apollo has fallen
into Ovid's hands, appearing as suddenly in the book as
he does to the poet? Contextual verbal support for this
may be derived from the next pentameter, *in manibus* ('in
the hands'), where the first and final syllables of the operative word play against those of *manifestus*. The import
of *manifestus* is most closely paralleled in the *Hymn to
Apollo* by the reminder that ὡπόλλων οὐ παντὶ φαείνεται
('Apollo does not appear to everyone', v. 9) but only to
the good man (poet)—such as Callimachus, or Ovid. The
scholiast on v. 12 says that the prologue to the *Hymn*
stresses the presence of Apollo because 'it is said in the
case of prophetic gods that the deities are sometimes
present, sometimes absent, and when they are present the
oracles are true, when absent false.' The ancients laid
great stress on the clarity of a vision to emphasize its

authority.[25] Ovid begins and ends his epiphany by (ironically
—or not . . .) stressing its prophetic authority as well as its
literary pedigree.

The detailed description of the god's appearance maintains this emphasis on the clarity of the vision, which is
summed up with *uidendus* ('to be seen, to seem') in v. 496.
Again we may compare examples in *Aeneid* 3 and 6: *tremere
omnia uisa repente* ('everything suddenly was seen/seemed
to tremble', *Aen.* 3. 90), and *maiorque uideri* ('to seem [be seen
as] greater', 6. 49) of the Sibyl coming under the influence
of Apollo. We might compare particularly *Aen.* 2. 589–91:

> *cum mihi se, non ante oculis tam clara, uidendam*
> *obtulit et pura per noctem in luce refulsit*
> *alma parens.*

> . . . when to me my kindly mother, never previously so clear
>   before my eyes,
> gave a vision of herself and shone in pure light
> through the night.

Virgil emphasizes the clarity and genuineness of the appari-
tion, since it is through Venus' words that Aeneas sees the
cosmic scale of events, and learns to accept his own part,
desertion of his city. We should perhaps not push for a
specific allusion here, but rather see this as supporting
evidence for the claim that the *Ars* passage is involved in
the tendency of ancient sacral language to stress the clarity
of a vision as a guarantee of its genuineness.

The underscored visual vividness of Apollo's appearance
may perhaps be intended to evoke some actual representation of the god, perhaps his statues in the Palatine temple.
The two famous statues, one outside the temple carved by
an unknown artist, and one inside by Scopas, both depicted
the god as a citharode, and are the subject of a poetic
description by Propertius, at 2. 31. 5–6 and 15–16. (See
Cairns 1984a: 151–3.) Cairns suggests that Prop. 4. 6. 69–70

[25] Pease (1935) on Virg. *Aen.* 4. 358 describes *manifestus* as belonging to
visions and theophanies. Cf. Virg. *Aen.* 3. 148–51 *penates . . . uisi ante oculos astare
iacentis | in somnis multo manifesti lumine*, 4. 358 *ipse deum manifesto in lumine uidi*;
Ov. *Pont.* 1. 1. 63. (For the phrase *manifestus Apollo* cf. *Ep. Sapph.* 23 *sume fidem
et pharetram: fies manifestus Apollo*, a 'true Apollo', then, just as Ovid claims
here.)

also refers to the Palatine statues (probably that of Scopas),
as does Tib. 2. 5. 2–10 (the inauguration of Messalinus as a
quindecimuir in the Palatine Temple). All three passages,
sometimes in considerable detail, describe Apollo as a citharode. A number of factors link our passage with the three in
question: for example, gold, which will be discussed further
later. Although gold is not specifically connected with the
statues themselves in any of the passages, Propertius 2. 31
opens *aurea Phoebi | porticus* ('golden colonnade of Phoe-
bus'); the god('s statue) is *seen* by the poet, *uisus mihi
pulchrior ipso* ('seemed to me/was seen by me more beautiful
than his own self', Prop. 2. 31. 5, perhaps Propertius is also
hinting at an epiphany), just as our Apollo is *uidendus*; his
lyre and its adjective are in the same *sedes*, in Prop. 2. 31 at
v. 6 *tacita . . . lyra* ('with silent lyre'), and in our passage at
v. 494 *inauratae . . . lyrae* ('with golden lyre': with this
compare Prop. 3. 3. 14 *aurata . . . lyra*, in the *reuocatio*-scene
there); then at Prop. 2. 31. 15 the god is again a citharode.
Another link with the Propertian statue-poems is forged by
the fact that Prop. 4. 6. 69–70 performs a programmatic function similar to that suggested (though not realized) by our
passage:

> *bella satis cecini: citharam iam poscit Apollo*
> *uictor et ad placidos exuit arma choros*

> Wars I have sung enough: now Apollo demands his lyre
> and as victor takes off his arms for peaceful dances.

Here again Apollo is a poet whose lyre is specifically mentioned, as in our passage he is specifically a *uates* with a
lyra. In Tibullus 2. 5, Apollo is to come with lyre and songs
(v. 2); in the following line he is asked to play in a phrase,
nunc te uocales impellere pollice chordas | . . . precor ('now I
pray you to pluck the singing strings with your thumb'),
closely echoed by Ovid's description, *mouit inauratae pollice
fila lyrae* ('struck with his thumb the strings of his golden
lyre'); the god is to comb his hair both in Tibullus (v. 8) and
in Ovid (v. 495); he is to bring his own laurel, as he did
when singing triumph-poems for Jupiter in Tibullus (vv. 5
and 9–10), in Prop. 4. 6. 70 (where he is *uictor*), and in *Ars*
2. 495–6, a line which may also suggest the Triumph. On
Apolline holy days it was common practice to wreath his

statues in laurel. (See Amandry 1950: 126.) Our Apollo comes dressed, not surprisingly, in laurel.

Allusions to the statues bring us *ad mea templa* (that is, to the temple or temples of Apollo) and provoke a liturgical atmosphere in which Ovid, following Callimachus, can employ the ritual motif of stress on the clarity and genuineness of a vision in a pose of pseudo-naïve amazement. Pseudo-naïve, of course, because the intertextuality with both written and visual art-works is highly sophisticated. The opening word of the next line works in a similar way. The demonstrative *is* was largely avoided in poetry, according to Axelson (1945: 70–4). Ovid uses the vivid deictic to *point* to the god (cf. *ille* in the previous line), playing the same game as Callimachus. Piously he stresses the oracle's reliability by emphasizing the presence of the god. Subliminally he attacks the reader: '*There* he is! Anyone who cannot see what is going on here poetically is *litos* ('worthless').'

Apollo announces his arrival with a chord on the lyre. The sound of the lyre heralds the arrival of the god in other epiphanies also.[26] When Tibullus prays for an epiphany, he asks (2. 5. 3)

> *nunc te uocales impellere pollice chordas*

Now [I pray] you to pluck the singing strings with your thumb.

Noise is commonly one of the signs heralding an epiphany. It occurs in our main source text (Call. *Hymn* 2. 5):

> ὁ δὲ κύκνος ἐν ἠέρι καλὸν ἀείδει

The swan in the air sings beautifully.

at Virg. *Aen.* 3. 92:

> *mugire adytis cortina reclusis*

The cauldron rumbles as the shrine is revealed.

and at Phaed. A. 6. 4:

> *mugit adytis Religio*

Religion rumbles in the shrine.

[26] Cf. Hor. *Carm.* 4. 15. 1–2; Ov. *Rem.* 705 *Phoebus adest: sonuere lyrae, sonuere pharetrae*; Lygd. 4. 39–40 *hanc (lyram) primum ueniens plectro modulatus eburno | felices cantus ore sonante dedit (Phoebus)*; *Culex* 13 *recinente lyra*; and Kennedy (1980: 43).

Since these liturgical passages have been brought to mind, the word *mouit* in our passage also creates a verbal link with another sign of an epiphany, that of movement or trembling. The *Hymn* also opens with trembling laurels and shrines, although a specific verbal link is hard to establish. More likely is a glance at (*Aen.* 3. 90–2):

> tremere omnia uisa repente,
> liminaque laurusque dei, totusque moueri
> mons

Suddenly everything seemed to tremble,
both the threshold and the laurel of the god, and the whole mountain to move.[27]

and (Phaed. A. 8. 4):

> tripodes mouentur . . . tremuntque lauri.

The tripods move and the laurels tremble.

Moreover, *mouere* can perform another ritual function, that of the movement of sacred objects during a liturgy.[28] The semantic range of *mouere* in sacral discourse allows it to contribute to the general ritual atmosphere beyond the straightforward meaning of the line.

The god's famous symbols accompany him. The celebrated golden lyre of Apollo[29] featured also in Callimachus' *Hymn*, in a passage heaped up with golden attributes (*Hymn* 2. 32–4):

> χρύσεα τὠπόλλωνι τό τ᾽ ἐνδυτὸν ἥ τ᾽ ἐπιπορπὶς
> ἥ τε λύρη τό τ᾽ ἄεμμα τὸ Λύκτιον ἥ τε φαρέτρη,
> χρύσεα καὶ τὰ πέδιλα. πολύχρυσος γὰρ Ἀπόλλων.

Golden is Apollo's tunic and his cloak,
his lyre and his Lyctian bow and his quiver,
and golden are his sandals also. For Apollo is rich in gold.

F. Williams (1978) says that 'the motif of the deity being

---

[27] Cf., in an epiphany of Isis, Ov. *Met.* 9. 782–3 *uisa dea est mouisse suas—et mouerat—aras,* | *et templi tremuere fores.*

[28] Cf. Hor. *Carm.* 3. 21. 6 *moueri digna bono die*, on which G. Williams (1969) claims sacral overtones for *moueri*. This quasi-middle use of *mouere* seems to be common in liturgical contexts.

[29] On which see Call. *Hymn* 2. 33; Prop. 3. 3. 14; and Bömer (1977) on *Met.* 8. 15.

clothed in gold, and equipped with golden accoutrements is frequent in epic, the underlying concept being that "gold is the stuff of radiance . . . and imperishableness" . . . Adjectives formed from χρυς- are very frequently applied to Apollo . . . and the motif is of course particularly apt if Apollo is identified with the sun.'[30]

With the lyre comes the laurel. The famous branch proclaims Apollo even without corroboration.[31] The tree was closely connected with Delphi from earliest times, when oracles there actually issued from the laurel.[32] In the *Hymn* also, the shaking laurel is the first sign of the approaching epiphany. The shaking laurel is frequently mentioned in Apolline appearances (as at Virg. *Aen.* 3. 91, Phaed. A. 6. 5), and is regarded as another guarantee of the genuineness of the oracle. According to F. Williams (1978), it is not always clear in what form the laurel is envisaged. Since our epiphany is so unexpected, Ovid has the god bring his symbols with him, as Tibullus prays (2. 5. 5–6):

> *ipse triumphali deuinctus tempora lauro,*
> *. . . ad tua sacra ueni.*

> With your brow crowned with triumphal laurel
> come to your rites.

Sacred persons (gods and priests) frequently carry their sacral emblems, as does Apollo's own priest earlier in the book,[33] and 'authorities from the beginning of the fourth century refer to the Pythia or Apollo as shaking the laurel'. (Parke and Wormell 1956: 26.) It remains, however, slightly odd that the god is holding laurel and playing the lyre at

---

[30] See also Kennedy (1980: 109–10) on *Culex* 11 *aurea proles*. Ovid's description echoes that of his female opposite and counterpart, Dipsas, in *Am*. 1. 8. 59 *ipse deus uatum palla spectabilis aurea | tractat inauratae consona fila lyrae*. For her, Apollo's only interesting attribute is the material value of the gold.

[31] As a young John Henderson (1976: 360) put it (on Phaed. A. 8. 5): 'the Apolline phytomorph was omnipresent assistance for the autosuggestion of numinous presence.' For the connection between Apollo and the laurel see Ovid's aetiological tale at *Met*. 1. 559 (with Bömer 1969). It was this event which was sparked off by Cupid's appropriation of Apollo's province of archery.

[32] For the association of the laurel with Delphi see Amandry (1950) 126–34, and Parke and Wormell (1956: 26).

[33] *Ars* 2. 401–2 *audierat laurumque manu uittasque ferentem | pro nata Chrysen non ualuisse sua*.

the same time! How many hands does he have? From
here we are returned to one of our key texts, Call. *Aet.*
fr. 114, the interlocuting Delian Apollo explaining the fact
that his cult-statue holds the Graces in his right hand
and the bow in his left. The question of what Callimachean Apollo has in his hands is always apposite. The
hint of burlesque implied in the incongruity of holding
lyre and laurel together is in keeping with the precarious
balance of the scene between the elevated and the comic-
ally inane.

Last comes Apollo's famous hair.[34] Again it is paralleled
in the *Hymn to Apollo* (2. 38–40):

> αἱ δὲ κόμαι θυόεντα πέδῳ λείβουσιν ἔλαια.
> οὐ λίπος Ἀπόλλωνος ἀποστάζουσιν ἔθειραι,
> ἀλλ' αὐτὴν πανάκειαν.

> His hair pours forth fragrant oil on the ground.
> The hair of Apollo does not distil oil,
> but panacea itself.

F. Williams (1978) suggests an allusion in this line to the
Apolline title *akersekomēs* ('long-haired'). Whether or not
Ovid is consciously alluding to the title, the introduction of
the god's famous attributes suggests hymnic style.

Most of the god's most famous attributes are presented
or hinted at: golden lyre, laurel, hair, prophecy, wisdom,
poetry, healing, if the reference to Apollo's Paeanic powers
through his grandson Machaon in v. 491 may be laid
under contribution to our scene. Only archery is missing,
perhaps because Cupid, while usurping Apollo's poetic
function in *Am.* 1. 1, is portrayed as an archer. A related
feature of hymnic style is accumulation of titles for a
god.[35] Since this passage is involved in so complex a web
of intertextual allusion, which lays the other texts under
contribution to the production of its own meaning, we
can, I suggest, see the hinted presence of a great many
cult-titles for Apollo.

---

[34] See Nisbet and Hubbard (1970) on Hor. *Carm.* 1. 21. 2 *intonsum, pueri,
dicite Cynthium* (note that this again is in a liturgical context); Tib. 2. 5. 8;
Murgatroyd (1980) on Tib. 1. 4. 38.
[35] See Men. Rhet. Fr. 3. 334 Spengel; Heyer (1933); Norden (1913: 168–76).

Through the power of his very clear echoes, Ovid has hinted at Lycian Apollo (through Callimachus), Cynthian (through Virgil), Delphic (overtly), and Delian (through the 'god explaining an aspect of his cult'), Paean (through v. 491). I suggest that there is a glance also at Palatine Apollo. A possible reference to the Palatine statues I have mentioned above. In addition, when the god invites Ovid to bring his pupils 'to his temple', we may for a moment imagine that Apollo is referring to the temple dedicated by Augustus on the Palatine on Oct. 9, 28 BC, with its adjoining libraries for Greek and Latin books. (See *CAH* 10. 119 and Dio 50. 3.) That is clearly where the talking book of *Tristia* 3. 1. 60 is going:

> *ducor ad intonsi candida templa dei.*
> I am led to the bright temple of the unshorn god.

This hypothesis gains support from the clear fact that more than one manifestation of Apollo is involved in this passage, and from the suggestion of allusion to the statues in the temple and the literary reflections of them.

There may perhaps be a hint, in the emphasis on the clarity of the vision and particularly in the word *manifestus*, at the cult-name Clarius, by means of the word-play on *clarus* ('clear') which was mentioned in the previous chapter. Yet another of Apollo's titles is *hekaergos* ('he who works from afar'). The title occurs in the *Hymn* at v. 11, and Callimachus plays on the name at v. 7: ὁ γὰρ θεὸς οὐκέτι μακρήν ('for the god is no longer far away'). F. Williams (1978: on v. 11) quotes etymologies for the title from Eustathius (138. 28, as the bowman and the sun), which stress Apollo's remoteness. The Apollo who appears in our poem hails from Greece, from the centre of the world at Delphi. Finally, another title used in the *Hymn* is *euorkos* ('he who keeps his oaths', v. 68). Throughout our passage there is ironic emphasis on Apollo's reliability, culminating in the proclamation that (v. 510)

> *certa dei sacro est huius in ore fides.*
> Sure faith is found in the sacred mouth of this god.

Certa . . . fides ('sure faith') echoes and may allude directly to the epithet *euorkos*.[36]

On the level of pseudo-religiosity, the acclaim alludes to that of Apollo's oracle to the Aeneadae in *Aeneid* 3. 188:

> *cedamus Phoebo et moniti meliora sequamur*

Let us yield to Phoebus and with his advice follow the better path.

Ovid ironically calls his pupils to obey the great god of prophecy like the *pius Aeneas*, the servant of Fate. When in the next line Ovid draws attention to the redirection he has undergone at Apollo's hands, he may again be alluding to the god's redirection of the Aeneadae in Virgil's passage.

> *ad propiora uocor*   (*Ars* 2. 511)

I am called to things nearer to hand.

> *quo Phoebus uocet errantis iubeatque reuerti.*   (*Aen.* 3. 101)

Where Phoebus calls the wanderers and orders them to return.

I have used the language of irony and burlesque in discussion of Apollo's reliability. When Apollo appeared he looked like a *uates*, a prophet and a poet, that is, with divine authority. It is Ovid himself, however, who is the true *uates* of this poem.[37] His pious acclamation of the divine message is undercut by the close parallel between what he says of Apolline authority and of his own.

> *Phoebo parete monenti*   (v. 509)

Obey Phoebus' advice.

> *uati parete perito*   (*Ars* 1. 29)

Obey the skilled bard.

That claim comes in a context, the prologue to the whole work, which explicitly denies the poetic/erotic authority of

[36] On Apolline oracular truth generally see Parke and Wormell (1956: 1, 2, and n. 1); Virg. *Aen.* 3. 434 *animum si ueris implet Apollo*; 6. 343, where Aeneas believes (wrongly) that the usually reliable Apollo has deceived him, and on which Norden (1916) quotes Aesch. *Choeph.* 559 ἄναξ Ἀπόλλων, μάντις ἀψευδὴς τὸ πρίν. F. Williams (1978) says on Call. *Hymn* 2. 68 that this 'suggests that an ancient oracle was fulfilled', and gives examples of passages where the veracity of a prophecy's source is stressed.

[37] So he claims at vv. 11 and 739.

Apollo in the poem, rejecting Apollo in favour of *usus*. (See Ahern 1990.)

> *non ego, Phoebe, datas a te mihi mentiar artes,*
>   *nec nos aeriae uoce monemur auis*   (1. 25–6)

I shall not tell lies, Phoebus, about my arts having been given by
   you,
nor am I advised by the voice of a bird of the air.

> *usus opus mouet hoc: uati parete perito*   (1. 29)

Experience is the inspiration for this work: obey the skilled bard.

At the opening of our book, Ovid usurps Apollo's victory cry (vv. 1–3):

> *Dicite 'io Paean' et 'io' bis dicite 'Paean':*
>   *decidit in casses praeda petita meos.*
> *laetus amans donat uiridi mea carmina palma*

Cry 'io Paean' and twice cry 'io Paean':
the desired prey falls into my trap.
The happy lover presents my songs with a triumphal crown.

The *phoinix* ('palm') may shake for Apollo in Callimachus' *Hymn*, but in Ovid's poem it is the poet himself who receives the *palma*, a crown now, not just a palm.

It is a Lucretian practice to apply the language of oracular truth to his poetry (5. 110–12):

> *Qua prius adgrediar quam de re fundere fata*
> *sanctius et multo certa ratione magis quam*
> *Pythia quae tripodi a Phoebi lauroque profatur*

Before I begin to pour forth my oracular responses on this
   matter,
more sacredly and with much more certain reason than
that which the Pythia says from the tripod and laurel of
   Phoebus . . .

Ovid, following this practice, again usurps Apollo's authority to tell the ultimate truth in his instruction to women in the art of sex (*Ars* 3. 789–94):

> *sed neque Phoebei tripodes nec corniger Ammon*
>   *uera magis uobis quam mea Musa canet;*
> *si qua fides, arti, quam longo fecimus usu,*
>   *credite: praestabunt carmina nostra fidem.*

> sentiat ex imis Venerem resoluta medullis
>   femina

But neither the tripods of Phoebus nor horned Ammon will sing
more truth than my Muse;
if you have any faith, trust to my art, which I have made
through long experience: my songs will show my trustworthiness.
Let a woman feel the pleasure of sex, resolved from her very
  depths.

This precept, incidentally, is, in the nature of oracles,
undercut a few lines later, when women are advised to fake
(*Ars* 3. 797–8). Ovid's intertextual relationship with the Lucretian practice is underscored by the fact that his avowed
independence of Apollo reflects Lucretius' theology of the
non-involvement of the gods—yet each usurps the gods'
prophetic powers.

Perhaps most significantly, Ovid again claims prophetic
authority for his erotodidaxis immediately after the passage
which I have described as the poet's answer to Apollo's
poetic challenge (vv. 535–42):

> quid moror in paruis? animus maioribus instat;
>   magna cano: toto pectore, uulgus, ades.
> ardua molimur, sed nulla, nisi ardua, uirtus;
>   difficilis nostra poscitur arte labor.
> riualem patienter habe: uictoria tecum
>   stabit, eris magni uictor in Arce Iouis.
> haec tibi non hominem sed quercus crede Pelasgas
>   dicere; nil istis ars mea maius habet.

Why do I delay in minor matters? My mind drives towards
  greater things.
I sing a major prophecy: attend, ye masses, with your whole
  mind.
Hard is the path we strive along, yet there is no
virtue which is not hard.
A difficult task is demanded by my art.
Be patient of a rival: victory will stand with you,
and you will be victor in the citadel of great Jupiter.
Believe that it is not a man who says this to you
but the Pelasgian oaks; my art has nothing greater than this.

The ritual atmosphere again builds up magnificently for
this great precept. It is not Apollo's advice which will *tenere*

a girl/lover/reader, but Ovid's. Ovid's claim might be dramatized thus: '*I* am the Apollo of this work; it is I who hold the keys of wisdom, poetic and erotic.'

4e The Thread of the Book

Suddenly Apollo entered. Although, in the nature of epiphanies, Apollo usually arrives *suddenly*, the very *position* of the scene here contributes to its surprise tactics, since it performs no obvious programmatic function. In the other main representations of the scene, the stage is poetically set. This is most obvious in Callimachus, the scene occurring in the programmatic prologue to his *magnum opus*; Virgil's version is also in a prologue—to the first poem of the book's second half—significantly to a poem which will push back the boundaries of pastoral poetry; Propertius introduces Apollo into the third poem of a book which even more overtly than previously reflects on itself, and creates the poetic atmosphere by the programmatically charged dream-scene; perhaps most importantly, Horace's Apollo enters the very last *Ode*. Ovid's version, however, does not appear to be especially significant in positioning. It does occur about half-way through the adultery theme, dividing it into 'how to manipulate her reactions' and 'how to control your own', but since almost anything could be at the beginning, the middle, or the end of *something*, the position should not be made to bear weight unless it contributes to reading. In this case, the position alone of the Apollo scene does not make so great a contribution to reading as to be the sole justification for the placement. It is not a beginning, it is not a restart; it is a misplaced and very funny scene which does none of the things we feel it should.

What has this done to the structure and quasi-narrative thread of Book 2? To consider this question we need a brief overview of the book's progress. In this section, I attempt to contextualize my reading of the Apollo scene by grounding it in the book as a whole. Such contextualization will require a 'digression' on what was just called the 'quasi-narrative' of the book; but, like all Ovidian digressions, it is in fact crucial to the entire reading. I argue that the scene is functional both for the poetic statement of the poem and also for the construction of Ovid's persona as teacher.

The book begins with the extended programmatic prologue, including the story of Daedalus and Icarus; even when at last we think the instruction is about to begin, we are further delayed with the section telling us how important it is to read the *Ars* (vv. 99–144) and to 'be lovable'; then the rest of the first half (vv. 145–336) is taken up with instructions on pleasing your mistress; after a restart at v. 337, most of the second half deals with infidelity in all its forms, how to cope with faults, moral and physical, and then climaxes in instructions on the act itself. It has been noted before that all three books divide into two main sections dealing with different stages of the affair's development.[38] In Book 2, this reflects the double seduction of the girl by the apprentice-lover and of the lover by Ovid, for the first half is concerned with keeping the girl in love, while the second expends a lot of its force in keeping the *lover* himself interested in love. The relationship is given new dimensions by adultery—so the lover does not lose interest too soon and simply go back to the beginning.

And now in more detail. Prior to the entry of Apollo, we have been learning how to deal with the mistress's distress (contrived by the lover) at the lover's double-dealing (vv. 459–60):

> *oscula da flenti, Veneris da gaudia flenti:*
> *pax erit; hoc uno soluitur ira modo*[39]

Give her kisses as she is crying, make love to her as she is crying: there will be peace; in this way only anger is resolved.

The creation myth, with sex as the great civilizing force, serves as an illustration of this dictum, and the section is rounded off with the Doctor assuring us of the efficacy of his prescription (vv. 489–92). And then in comes Apollo.

We have seen previously, in Section 2g on Narrative

---

[38] See Weber (1983) 113. Kling (1970) discusses the thematic structure of Book 2. He also mentions the division between the two halves of the book.

[39] This, incidentally, was also the prescribed means to avert the mistress's suspicions, in the case where infidelity is to be kept secret: *sed lateri ne parce tuo; pax omnis in uno est; | concubitu prior est infitianda Venus* (vv. 413–14) Ovid keeps his student hard at work!

Seduction, how Ovidian transitions are both deliberately abrupt, in the didactic manner, and at the same time subliminally prepared, by verbal and thematic foreshadowing and echo, by twists of thought and meaning sometimes hinging on a double meaning in a single word. The introductory word *subito* ('suddenly') is a powerful signifier of this feature of didactic style, for it can be used to effect a complete change of direction, the classic example being the sudden rain in *Fast.* 4. 385 which cuts short Ovid's conversation with his informant, and with which we should compare the sudden wave which interrupts Ulysses' epic and Ovid's exemplum in *Ars* 2. 139. The suddeness of the epiphany both does and does not perform such a change of direction here. Against this background we now need to see both why the epiphany is a surprise, and why it is not.

The first of these conditions is easy enough to fulfil and has been alluded to already. Even allowing for the inherent surprise of an epiphany, the position of the scene is unusual. Then, having accepted the epiphany, we fully expect Ovid to be redirected on to the correct path of the *Ars*, away from the philosophical didactic epos he had slipped into. Inasmuch as this *is* what Apollo does, Ovid has developed the tradition to the point where the poet not only claims he was 'about to write epic' or 'dreamt he was doing so' when the god interrupted, but actually *has* done so. So strong are the allusions to the warning epiphany that the poem very nearly performs this function—but then tantalizingly withdraws. I mean that Ovid deliberately encourages us in the expectation of a standard Apollo scene, and so in some sense really does give us what we expect.

But even if we read it as a redirecting answer to the heavy cosmology of vv. 467–80, we had already got back on the track with vv. 489–92. I do not entirely agree with Watson (1984: 395) that these four lines are a 'complete non-sequitur, for we are asked to believe that the very cause of the mares' *furiae* (i.e. sex) may be employed as the cure for anger and as the producer of *requies*'. Although (deliberately) an apparent non-sequitur, the very lack of smoothness makes the point and so is a sort of smoothness, for it is precisely the violence of the mares' desire (or the girl's, induced by artistic infidelity) which facilitates the production of *requies* ('rest, relief, peace'). This is the nature of the erotic *pharmakon*: the 'cure' is that which causes the 'disease'. To simplify—the *desire* is *furor* ('madness') while the *fulfilment* produces *requies* ('peace'). The greater the *furor* the more satisfactory the *requies* produced; but that itself produces more *furor* and so the opportunity for the artistic production of more *requies*.

In some sense, Apollo does redirect the poem, since Ovid counters with a show-piece of his own art, but that section (vv. 511–34) is itself misplaced, having more in common with the early *Ars* than with the theme of adultery which surrounds it. Apollo has in fact sent Ovid off course, and it takes him a whole section and two apparently abrupt transitions to return to the right path. The first of these occurs as part of the acclaim of the epiphany (vv. 511–12):

> *ad propiora uocor; quisquis sapienter amabit,*
> *uincet et e nostra, quod petit, arte feret.*

I am called to things nearer to hand; whoever loves wisely, will conquer and will bear off from my art what he seeks.

The opening phrase of this couplet recurs at *Fast.* 6. 83, where Hebe uses it to move her narrative suddenly from the Labours of Hercules to Romulus' arrangement of the people according to age. This parallel might suggest that the phrase is simply a device for changing direction. Such a change does indeed occur, as the poem leaves 'Apollo' and moves to 'the trials of love'. The appearance of a redirectory phrase here, however, must remind us of the Lycian Apolline function (which we had expected from the epiphany) of warning the poet to return to the correct poetic track. Has Apollo fulfilled our expectation after all? He has, in that the sequel to his epiphany is vintage *Ars Amatoria*, overtly and pointedly drawing on the traditions of Roman love poetry and thereby standing in opposition to the high-didactic cosmology section which in our expectation provoked the god's entry. But he has *not* set the poem back on course, in that the 'own subject' on which Ovid was pontificating before he was interrupted was adultery, and it is not until v. 549 (with its two preceding couplets) that he returns to that subject. It takes almost thirty lines more for the poem to recover from Apollo's redirection. In these three lines (vv. 509–11) Ovid is playing the part of the priest responding to and interpreting the oracle, but his 'interpretation' maintains oracular ambiguity. The phrase *ad propiora uocor* describes the effect of the epiphany, since if Ovid does obey Apollo he will 'know himself' and return to his own sphere, that is, the *Ars Amatoria*, as exemplified in the next section. But from where? The return to relevance is just as much from the Apollo scene itself as from the cosmology which preceded it. Is Apollo the agent of redirection, then, or the detour away from which the redirection occurs? Ovid has broken Apollo's enigmatic order of vv. 507–8, by declaiming this scene *medio sermone*—in the middle of the *Ars*. The second transition (v. 535) is initially prepared by the ascending tricolon, rising up through the couplet from the lover's base position at his mistress's feet, at the end of v. 534. Then in v. 536 the liturgical language echoes that of the Apollo scene.[40] Finally, even once the epiphany is under way, it continues to cheat our expectations at every turn.

A first and simple hint at why the epiphany might not be so unprepared after all comes from the conclusion to the previous section. Sexual relations are *medicamina* which surpass *Machaonios . . . sucos* ('the drugs of Machaon') in efficacy (v. 491). Machaon, along with Podalirius, was a son of Asclepius (Hom. *Il.* 2. 731–2), himself a son of Apollo (Pind. *Pyth.* 3, although not in Homer). He was the healer of Menelaus at *Il.* 4. 200–1, and of Philoctetes at Soph. *Phil.* 1333. A cult of Machaon at Gerenia is attested by Pausanias (3. 26. 9). In a typical display of Callimachean abstruse learning, Ovid alludes to Apollo's Paeanic powers not through his son, the predictable Asclepius, but through his lesser-known grandson, Machaon, and so effects a subliminal link to the Apollo scene.

The oddity of the Apollo scene is, as has been hinted, mitigated to some extent if it is read as an answer to the preceding cosmology section. In order to illustrate his claim that the female of the species naturally desires sex, Ovid

---

[40] It is a telling comment on the problems of selection that Murgatroyd (1982) omits vv. 511–34.

diverted into a Lucretian-type pseudo-scientific history of creation, where sex is the great civilizing force.[41] The link between the two passages can be developed, although the findings increase the level of surprise with one hand while explaining it with the other. Apollo is to be seen in his heavily Callimachean guise as warning Ovid *away* from cosmology (philosophical epic). But in the midst of the multi-textual allusion to the tradition stands Virgil's Sixth *Eclogue*, in which the Callimachean Apollo directs Virgil *towards* cosmology—the Song of Silenus. Z. Stewart (1959: 183) has argued convincingly for an interpretation of the Song as 'a survey of types of poetry, especially—perhaps solely—types for which Rome had inherited a taste from Alexandria'. Cosmology, and scientific poetry generally, thus becomes the first in a list of topics or genres eminently suited to treatment by a Roman Callimachean poet.[42] Although Apollo could still tell Ovid to 'get on with the *Ars*', his normal Callimachean function is problematized by the fact that he warns Ovid away from the very subject towards which he directs Virgil.

A further subliminal link between the sections comes through the association of Apollo with the Golden Age. The scene for vv. 471–80 was set in the pre-civilized Golden Age, and Apollo, in his prophetic manifestation, is associated with the return of that time.[43] Nisbet (1978: 59 and 62) explains *Ecl.* 4. 10 *tuus iam regnat Apollo* as meaning '[provided that Lucina helps the birth . . .] your Apollo is as good as reigning'. This is evidence that Apollo's reign is not prior to the return of the Golden Age but is identified with it, the idea being expressed in contemporary, non-Hesiodic terms. A neo-Pythagorean view assigned the last

---

[41] See Miller (1983: 32). A further, less direct link with Lucretius is supplied by the didactic history of sex-mad mares. The obvious *Georgic* allusion to mares is itself intertextually involved with the proem to the *De Rerum Natura*, where, under the influence of Venus, the mares *rapidos tranant amnis* (Lucr. 1. 15).

[42] Z. Stewart claims that both *Ars* 2. 467–73 and *Met.* 1. 5–88 show signs of Empedoclean and Orphic/Stoic/Neo-Pythagorean philosophy as well as Lucretian.

[43] DuQuesnay (1976: 76) suggests the possibility of a Sibylline oracle announcing the coming of a new saviour-king and a new Golden Age. Sibylline prophecies played a major role in the celebration of the *Ludi Saeculares* in 17 BC and subsequently.

age to Apollo, but, perhaps more relevantly, the Sibyl assigned it to the Sun. This, Servius explains ad loc., means Apollo. So the cosmogony section in our poem foreshadows Apollo and prepares the ground for his entry.

To sum up, then, the epiphany of Apollo at this point in the poem both is and is not an oddity: that is, it is a complete surprise which has also been subtly prepared. It has deliberately and artistically used Apolline redirection to confuse the quasi-narrative thread of the poem.

The argument which I am opposing is that Apollo does not interrupt the thread of the work, because the scene is merely an artistic embellishment necessary to avoid monotony in what is essentially a monotonal genre. But I have reservations about Miller's comment (1983), that these precepts could ('with very little alteration') have been spoken by Ovid '*in propria persona*', by which he presumably means in Ovid's erotodidactic persona. Likewise when Wimmel (1960: 140) sees the theme employed for mere scenic enrichment, it may indeed be part of the gradual degeneration of the epiphany's poetic-apologetic character which he detects (140). But both critics find traces of the Apolline prohibition in v. 507, which must undercut an interpretation of the passage as straightforward wit; particularly in Wimmel's case, since his argument was that the epiphany is simple scene-painting because it does *not* contain a poetic message. Although Apollo's words themselves might seem in keeping with Ovid's own advice in general (passing over for the moment the element of parody, particularly in v. 506), Apollo cannot be *just* an amusing variant speaker here (although he is that too), because the precepts are so out of touch with the current state of the Art. We have already learned about pleasing the girl in the first book and in the first half of the second, where these precepts would really belong. We are learning that everything has its proper moment and that artistry depends on appropriate timing. In taking us back to the beginning, Apollo fails the test of appropriateness, and in so doing opens his pompous pronouncements to burlesque.[44]

---

[44] On Ovid's ironical treatment of addresses to gods in the *Ars* see Frécaut (1972: 224–5).

Moreover, Ovid, in his answering section, continues in a vein which although tangentially connected with adultery, also seems to fit better into the *seruitium amoris* ('slavery of love') of the first section of Book 2. The section which I have labelled 'Ovid's answer' may be an amusing variation on his erotodidaxis, but within the quasi-narrative scheme of Book 2 it is an intruder, for it is on one level a separate section, about the nature of Ovid's art/Art. He only returns to his main theme at v. 535 *quid moror in paruis?* ('Why do I delay in minor matters?'). The *parua* are the precepts suited to an earlier stage of the affair and poem (*seruitium amoris*, paraclausithyron, etc.), in contrast with the more advanced study of the artistic stage-managing of adultery. In fact Apollo has steered Ovid *away* from his correct path. On the other hand, the very incongruity of the scene makes it—artistically—perfect for this position.

4f The Reader as Victim

With the advent of Apollo, the authorial seduction of the 'sophisticated reader' is foregrounded. Ovid provides us with a heavily advertised allusion. Despite its easy celebrity, the status of the scene in Callimachean poetics gives it an authority in the field of *doctrina* which flatters us into feeling learned for spotting it. The accessibility of the allusion might seem to negate the prerequisite of abstruse learning, were it not for the polemical charge of the scene, which acts like a password to the select club of esoteric Callimachean literati. We are encouraged for a moment to include ourselves in that élite, and for five or six lines the manipulation is not undermined, as we become more and more certain that Apollo will tell the poet to keep his work light, perhaps warning him away from the heavy cosmology of the previous section (vv. 467–80).[45] Again, to paraphrase the thought: 'You are not Lucretius,' we expect him to say; 'get back to the *Ars*.' But our expectation is spectacularly cheated. Looking for literary polemic from Lycian Apollo, we find Delphic Apollo explaining an aspect of his cult, and thereby offering some advice to lovers—his own *Ars Amato-*

[45] Miller (1983: 32) also notes that the cosmology could be expected to be the cause of Apollo's entry. See also Watson (1984: 389).

ria.[46] When, after eight lines, we finally learn that Apollo has not come to do a *reuocatio* (vv. 499–500), we are amused—embarrassed—to see our mistake, but even as the binding-spell is undone it works another, for the trick played on us draws us even closer into the text than a standard and by now well-worked Lycian warning would have done.

Now that we are confident that the epiphany after all has nothing to do with poetics, but is simply an amusing variant way of giving erotic advice,[47] Ovid casts another net around us. Apollo ends on a decidedly literary note (vv. 507–8):

> *sed neque declament medio sermone diserti,*
> *nec sua non sanus scripta poeta legat.*

> But let not the eloquent declaim in the midst of conversation,
> and let not the mad poet read his writings.

This is indeed a problematic injunction from the god of poetry![48] Not only does this seem to take us full circle back to Callimachus' Lycian Apollo, but also it is a hint, with Apollo as an unwitting mouthpiece, towards a poetic level in the epiphany, which I will suggest in the next section. And the advice to 'know oneself', which we thought applied simply to the lover, is in keeping with the topoi of Augustan *recusatio*. We were sure at the outset of the section that the poem was talking about poetry, then realized it was simple erotic instruction, but we end up being forced retrospectively to notice that Apollo's basic precept, 'know yourself', reads in this context as a virtual equivalent of the literary warning we originally expected to hear. The topos of self-awareness in poetic and particularly Callimachean theory is exemplified by Apollo's advice in his epiphany to Propertius

---

[46] The idea that Apollo's speech is Ovid's version of Apollo's version of Ovid's poem is analogous to the suggestion of Elder (1961) 115 that Virgil's Song of Silenus in *Eclogue* 6 is to be seen as originally Apollo's song.

[47] Miller (1983: 33): 'Indeed, with minor changes Apollo's speech could easily have been spoken by Ovid *in propria persona*'; Wimmel (1960: 137): Ovid employs the Apollo theme as 'bloßen szenischen Bereicherung'.

[48] Miller (1983: 32) understands the couplet as belonging to the tradition of the instructing Apollo, taking *non sanus poeta* as equivalent to *demens* in Prop. 3. 3. 15. 'Here Apollo is no doubt obliquely pointing to Ovid himself, who in the previous section (467–92) discoursed at some length on cosmogony and natural history, topics more appropriate for a philosophical epic, it is perhaps implied, than for the erotodidactic mission at hand.'

(3. 3. 15–24), and by the Apollo-substitute, Horus, in the *reuocatio* at Prop. 4. 1. 71–4. Outside the 'Lycian' tradition, the idea is expressed perhaps most significantly in Horace's instruction (*Ars* 38–9):

> *sumite materiam uestris, qui scribitis, aequam*
> *uiribus.*

> Writers, take up material
> equal to your powers.

The joke on Apollo and on us is that the pearls of wisdom from the great god of Delphi are at some level little more than pompous expansion of the injunction to make the most of your good qualities. At another level, however, the precept of self-awareness and appropriate exploitation of one's abilities really is great wisdom, and as such is appropriate to the *Ars*. That is the problem with oracles: they are ambiguous, as Virgil comments of the Sibyl *obscuris uera inuoluens* ('veiling truth in obscurity', *Aen.* 6. 100). Indeed, much of the effect of this passage hangs on the notorious ambiguity of prophecies and their problematic relationship with (helpful) truth. In another famous Apolline epiphany, that at *Aen.* 3. 90–9, the god literally redirects his petitioners, quite correctly, but with the result that the Aeneadae are, or think they are, thrown off course and delayed in their mission. But what was the 'right' course for their journey to Italy? The quickest, or the one by which they achieve, through trial, the necessary metamorphosis into proto-Romans? The false understanding of Apollo's true information produces the 'true' result. Virgil has exploited the natural ambiguity of oracles to great effect in his notoriously difficult, indeed indecipherable *Eclogue* 4.[49] Likewise Apollo's advice here is stupid or brilliantly witty—or both.

Perhaps the best example of the ambiguity of signifiers in this oracular passage comes in the ritualistic description of Apollo's appearance (v. 496):

[49] As Nisbet (1978: 64) comments on the *Eclogue*: '[ambiguities] may be accepted in oracles ... even when one meaning seems more obvious than the other', and compares (p. 74 n. 65) Enn. *Ann.* 179 *aio te, Aeacida, Romanos uincere posse*, where the 'natural' interpretation is the wrong one.

> *uates ille uidendus adit*
> He was manifestly a bard.

Vates is an exceptionally appropriate word in the context. The figure of the *uates* as a poetic speaker with divine, prophetic, even priestly authority was subsumed by the Augustans into their poetic persona. Newman (1967: 29) traces its development through the period, and shows how Virgil connected it specifically with Apollo.[50] By describing Apollo in these terms, Ovid appears to place the god firmly in his now-traditional role as the inspiring deity of Augustan poetry. The eventual very different result of the passage burlesques that role and the image of the *uates* itself. Moreover, the double sense of *uates*—poet and prophet—exactly fits the double function of Apollo in the passage. He first *appears* as the Callimachean/Lycian god who gives poetic advice (a poet), but then metamorphoses into the god of the great oracle at Delphi (a prophet). Ovid picks up the motif of the clarity of visions and twists it to aid the fudging ambiguity which we must retrospectively apply to *uates*. He looked like a *uates* ('poet'), but in fact he was a *uates* ('prophet').

The deceit that this is going to be a Lycian-type warning epiphany is maintained by the form of the first line of Apollo's speech, which, as mentioned, strongly echoes other *reuocationes*. The address *lasciui ... praeceptor Amoris* ('teacher of wanton love') is exactly what we might expect Apollo to use when about to admonish the poet for not adhering to his programme, the title having acquired programmatic force from Ovid's self-proclamation in the first prologue (*Ars* 1. 17):

> *ego sum praeceptor Amoris*
> I am the teacher of Love.

There is a reminiscence of this in Ovid's first exile poem, when the book itself is told to disclaim any such title (*Tr.* 1. 1. 67):

[50] Unfortunately, the *Ars* only receives the briefest mention (p. 113).

> *'inspice' dic 'titulum: non sum praeceptor amoris'*
> 'Look at the title,' say, 'I am not the teacher of love.'

So far, so good. The text holds off the unbinding of the spell to the last moment.

An ancient text would probably have preserved an ambiguity not open to the modern editor. Despite the tenuous distinction between Amor and *amor*, it seems appropriate to print *Amor* here, to emphasize the teacher/pupil conceit between Ovid and Love.[51] Heldmann (1981) mentions our line in his discussion of AMOR (the ambiguity between the god and the metonym) in the proem to Book 1 (*Ars* 1. 7–10):

> *me Venus artificem tenero praefecit AMORI;*
> *Tiphys et Automedon dicar AMORIS ego.*
> *ille quidem ferus est et qui mihi saepe repugnet;*
> *sed puer est, aetas mollis et apta regi.*

Venus has put me, being an artist, in charge of tender LOVE;
I shall be called the Tiphys and Automedon of LOVE.
He indeed is wild and often fights against me;
but he is a boy, an age which is soft and malleable.

He rightly stresses (p. 162) that a contemporary audience could easily have perceived the 'witty double meaning' of AMOR, and argues that when reading forwards, we must understand *amoris* in *Ars* 1. 8 with a lower-case *a*—for the poet is here *artifex*—but when in the following line we meet the boy Love, we must retrospectively add a second meaning to 1. 8, and read an upper-case *A*. On our line he says (p. 165 n. 10) that although the pentameter demands the reading *praeceptor amoris* (teacher of, i.e. about love), since the teacher is stated to have pupils (in the plural), who are presumably lovers, we can understand 'an ironical-polysemous allusion to the Proem'. By the very nature of the metonymic use of the names of gods, it is clearly impossible to state dogmatically whether Apollo (or Ovid) is addressing Ovid as the person who teaches Love or the person who teaches about love. The adjective *lasciuus* ('wanton') is quite frequently applied to Love, and is especially apt when

---

[51] See Hollis's instructive note (1977) on *Ars* 1. 7, on the conceit of the poet as the teacher of the boy-god, Love.

Love is envisaged as a cheeky schoolboy.[52] Although aware of the ambiguity, for the moment we see Ovid as the teacher of one wayward student, Amor, his poetic subject matter. We expect the god's admonition to relate to the poet's handling of his material: we expect a *reuocatio*.

Despite the change of number, that expectation is not entirely dispelled in the pentameter:

> *duc age discipulos ad mea templa tuos*
> Come, lead your pupils to my temple.

Although the plural comes as something of a surprise, Latin syntax certainly does not use number in the same way as English and the examples quoted in the last note show that Cupid may be envisaged as plural. The word *discipulus* only occurs four times in Ovid. At *Fast.* 3. 830 it is found in the real world of pupils and their *magistri* in the context of their patron goddess Minerva. The remaining two occurrences come within two lines of each other, and the word occurs twice, connoting either the love-god in the context of the *Ars*, or the *Ars* itself:

> *discipulo perii solus ab ipse meo*   (*Pont.* 3. 3. 46)
> I alone have perished because of my pupil.

> *haec te discipulo dona magister habet.*   (*Pont.* 3. 3. 48)[53]
> Your master has these things as gifts from you, his pupil.

Lucretius and Virgil do not have the word, although it might seem a likely description of the didactic addressee. Ovid has developed the pedagogic possibilities of didactic, not only by making his subject matter into his pupil, but also by his elaborate construction of a teacher/pupil relation-

---

[52] Cf. Ov. *Am.* 3. 1. 43 *rustica sit sine me lasciui mater Amoris*; *Met.* 1. 456, where Cupid is called, by Apollo incidentally, *lasciue puer*; *Pont.* 3. 3. 47 *dum te, lasciue, docemus* (clearly continuing the metaphor of *Ars* 1. 17). Compare also Prop. 2. 29. 7 *quorum [Cupidinum] lasciuior unus . . . inquit*; Tib. 1. 10. 57 *lasciuus Amor rixae mala uerba ministrat* (where Amor is a mischievous practical trickster but also standing metonymically for the effects of the emotion); Sil. 11. 410; Sen. *Phaed.* 277. In examples like Hor. *Carm.* 2. 11. 7 *pellente lasciuos amores canitie* and Ov. *Ars* 3. 27 *nil nisi lasciui per me discuntur amores* the metonymical reading must gain ground.

[53] Note that *Pont.* 3. 3. 47 was quoted in relation to the previous line in the *Ars*.

ship with his recipient. The normally singular addressee, the 'young friend' for whom the advice is constructed, and the reader, perhaps, alone with the text, has become in this most dramatic scene a flock of disciples sitting at the master's feet. A difficulty is to decide whether the 'pupils' are primarily to be seen as Love or the lovers. (One cannot pronounce definitively, of course.) In Apollo's intention they must be the student-lovers for whom he is planning a miniature lecture: but the atmosphere contrived by the hexameter, reminiscent as it was of the conceit of the first prologue, suggests that *we* are intended on first reading to understand Apollo as summoning Ovid along with his poetry to be rebuked and returned to the path of his programme. The later occurrences of *discipulus* in Ovid and the other uses of the word seem to confirm this misapprehension, since it is precisely *not* a signifier of the didactic addressee. Deciding dogmatically between 'Love' and 'the lovers' in this line is like trying to tie down Daedalus—it is not the way to read the *Ars*.

I have suggested above that there may be a hint of the Palatine temple in this couplet. If so, then it forms part of the deception of the reader, since we are still expecting some poetic admonition. Perhaps it would not be pushing the reader's credulous susceptibility to Ovidian manipulation too far to read the next line also as being applicable to Palatine as well as Delphic Apollo (v. 499):

> *est ubi diuersum fama celebrata per orbem*

. . . where there is [the letter] celebrated in fame throughout the
   whole world.

Rome, too, vaunts itself on its world-wide fame. If Ovid at first appears to connect the epiphany with the Palatine temple, but then cheats our expectation by clear reference to Delphi, he may be intending jokingly to correct an element in the theology of Virgil's *Aeneid*. Paschalis (1986) has argued that Virgil introduced Apollo into the Aeneas legend as an oracular deity guiding Aeneas, whose main purpose was to favour the fortunes of the Aeneadae. In so doing he supplants the Delphic god with a Delian-Actian-Palatine Apollo, despite the far greater historical and literary importance of Delphi. The cult-centre and its title are suppressed, and many of its symbols and legends are trans-ported to Delos and Italy. The result is a very Roman and Augustan Apollo, who finds his final definition in the Palatine temple. Ovid neatly reverses the trend and restores Apollo to Delphi.

Finally, a possible subliminal meaning to Apollo's invita-tion: Apollo tells Ovid to lead his pupils, the readers, 'up the creek' with this teasing pseudo-literary epiphany that leads us nowhere we expect it to.

With the next couplet, however, it immediately becomes clear which manifestation of Apollo has appeared, which temple we are being invited to, and for what purpose (vv. 499–500):

> *est ubi diversum fama celebrata per orbem*
> *littera, cognosci quae sibi quemque iubet.*

. . . where there is the letter celebrated in fame throughout the whole world,
which orders each one to know himself.

We know this is Delphi, and perhaps we are to remember that Delphi is the centre of the world.[54] But is it so clear? Although we quickly realize that *littera* refers to the maxim γνῶθι σαυτόν ('know thyself'), the most basic meaning of *littera* is as a letter of the alphabet, and as such must initially appear to refer to that most indecipherable of inscriptions, the *E* at Delphi. Plutarch's essay of that name (*Mor.* 384d–394c), offering seven possible explanations of the *E*,[55] is a witness to the seeds sown by the god for speculative study and wisdom. That the *E* is *not* what *littera* connotes is a miniature example of the almost continu-ous deception of the reader in this passage. With the entry of the proverbially famous maxim,[56] we settle down. At last we know what is going on.

But the real surprise is yet to come. With the hindsight

[54] Delphi, or rather a round stone in the temple, was called *omphalos*, as marking the middle point of the earth. Cf. Pind. *Pyth.* 4. 74; Bacch. 4. 4; Aesch. *Eum.* 40, 166; Paus. 10. 16. 3.

[55] Or rather, *E*s, since there were three figures by Plutarch's time: a golden *E* supposedly dedicated by Livia, a bronze *E* from the Athenians, and a wooden one, the oldest, believed to be dedicated by the Wise Men who were associated with the maxims. See Plut. *Mor.* 385a–386a.

[56] On which see Otto (1962: 37), who also quotes Cic. *Tusc.* 1. 41; *de fin.* 5. 44; *de leg.* 1. 58; Hor. *Ep.* 1. 14. 44; Prop. 2. 1. 46.

of the god's own explanation, we understand his precept as
applying to the best means of conducting an affair, but that
has not yet been clarified. Even that 'clarification', when it
comes, is undercut by the final couplet of the god's exegesis.
The need to comprehend the extent of one's powers and to
work within its limits is a frequent formulation of Callimachean manifesto. The maxim clarifies with one hand as
it deceives with the other. It shows us that this is the
Delphic *uates* (a prophet), not the Lycian *uates* (a poet), but
still appears to refer to poetry.

Since the reader's appetite for poetic admonition is by
this time well whetted, he may fall victim to the polysemy
of *opus* even in the apparently straightforward precept that
the man who knows himself will love wisely and perform
the whole task according to his powers (vv. 501–2):

> *qui sibi notus erit, solus sapienter amabit*
> *atque opus ad uires exiget omne suas:*

> Whoever knows himself, alone will love wisely
> and will perform his task to his utmost ability.

It would be possible to understand the line both sexually
and poetically.[57] Apollo perhaps does not intend a double
(or treble) meaning, but Ovid usurps the god's words to
wink at the reader between the lines. This type of suggestive
joke on *opus*, as poetry and sex, is found throughout the
Amores. The pupil is learning his lessons and doing all his
homework with all his effort, but the pronouncement reads
subliminally as literary manifesto—a joke on the reader
who is expecting it; and sexually—a joke on the incongruity
of the scene and its subject matter. The precept—for lovers
and poets—is to 'match *materia* to *ingenium*'.

At the magnificent climax of his pronouncement, Apollo's
meaning is ambiguous, in the nature of oracles, despite its
apparent simplicity (v. 506):

---

[57] *Exiget* and *uires* also have double meanings. The agent's *uires* in erotic
terms are his sexual powers, while the term is used in literary contexts of a
writer's poetic powers. Cf. *OLD uis* 18 and e.g. Hor. *Ars* 39 *sumite materiam
uestris, qui scribitis, aequam | uiribus*. For the double meaning of *exiget* (sexual) cf.
peregit in Ov. *Am.* 1. 4. 48 and *Ars* 2. 480, and (poetic) cf. Hor. *Carm.* 3. 30. 1
exegi monumentum; Ov. *Rem.* 811.

> *qui canit arte, canat; qui bibit arte, bibat*

 He who sings well should sing; he who drinks well should drink.

By removing the comma we can read *arte* with *canit* ('he who sings well, let him sing') or with *canat* ('he who sings, let him sing well'). But it is more than 'well'; it is 'with/by art'. In Apollo's hands the precept, an extension of his maxim, is that anyone who can sing well should make use of that talent in interesting his mistress. From Ovid's point of view, however, the point is that anyone who sings should do so artfully. The final, most seductive, most *teneo*-ing reading is the act of working that out. This deception depends on a splitting-up of the reader's various roles, as indeed does much of my reading in this chapter. It is a feature of reading, as I suggested in the first chapter, that we more or less consciously posit a 'reader' working on a different plane from the one on which we consider ourselves to be. Posing as a first-time reader is an essential element in the pleasure of re-reading, allowing us simultaneously to know and 'not to know' that we are being deceived.

4g Apollo as Magister Amoris

Apollo's advice, when it finally comes, turns out to be precepts for the student-lover. What he produces is his own miniature *Ars Amatoria*. So prevalent is the belief in Ovidian facileness that some scholars have been led to believe that the didactic elements in Apollo's speech simply make him into a variant speaker. I suggest, to the contrary, that the speech is like Ovid's own *Ars*, but subtly and significantly unlike. There is an intensification of didactic style, which already hints at burlesque (vv. 497–508):

> *is mihi 'lasciui' dixit 'praeceptor Amoris,*
> *duc age discipulos ad mea templa tuos,*
> *est ubi diuersum fama celebrata per orbem*
> *littera, cognosci quae sibi quemque iubet.*
> *qui sibi notus erit, solus sapienter amabit*
> *atque opus ad uires exiget omne suas:*
> *cui faciem natura dedit, spectetur ab illa;*
> *cui color est, umero saepe patente cubet;*

> *qui sermone placet, taciturna silentia uitet;*
> *qui canit arte, canat; qui bibit arte, bibat.*
> *sed neque declament medio sermone diserti,*
> *nec sua non sanus scripta poeta legat.'*

This god said to me, 'Teacher of wanton love,
come, lead your pupils to my temple,
where there is the letter celebrated in fame throughout the whole
    world,
which orders each one to know himself.
Whoever knows himself, alone will love wisely
and will perform his task to his utmost ability:
whomever nature has endowed with beauty, let him be gazed at
    by his girl;
whoever has a tan, let him often lie with naked shoulder;
he whose speech is pleasing should avoid sullen silence;
he who sings well should sing; he who drinks well should drink.
But let not the eloquent declaim in the midst of conversation,
and let not the mad poet read his writings.'

Apollo opens with a pointedly didactic exhortatory exclamation. The summons or exhortation *age* (colloquial according
to *OLD ago* 24) is a hallmark of didactic diction, as are
imperatives.[58] With hindsight, we realize that the *littera*
which Apollo here proclaims is the god's own didactic
poem, a written precept addressing the whole world.[59]
Apollo, then, is a writer, a writer of advice to all mankind,
with a pedagogic function, and also a literary one—just like
Ovid. Pausanias says of the maxim that it was written for
the good of men—just like the *Ars*. The precept is already a
didactic commandment on how to live, given by a father-
figure, even without the development which specifically
connects it with the *Ars*. As a proverbial piece of wisdom it
wins a place in the tradition of didactic/wisdom literature,
since didactic diction lends itself to proverbial formulations
of this kind.

---

[58] For *age* with another imperative see *OLD ago* 24a. Such constructions are of
course also found in invocation (e.g. Hor. *Carm.* 1. 32. 3 and 3. 4. 1), comedy, and
'speeches of encouragement' even in high-level poetry.

[59] The whole semantic range of *littera* stresses its inherently *written* properties,
from its use as we use ABC, the basic elements of literate education (*OLD littera*
3), through epistles, documents, inscriptions, the written form as opposed to
speech (*OLD littera* 5), the act of writing, to literary works and even erudition,
that is, what is learned from written books (*OLD littera* 9).

In introducing his precept, Apollo maintains his didactic stance. The maxim *orders* (*iubet*), using a basic word in didactic instruction (see Kenney 1958: 204), while *quemque* in v. 500 and the repeated instances of *qui* and *cui* which open the following lines display that universalizing tendency in didactic style with which the whole work opens: *si quis in hoc . . . populo* ('If anyone in this population . . . '). Apollo's precept is universally applicable, to all types and conditions of men—just like Ovid's. The formulation of a precept with *saepe* ('often', v. 504) is didactic. The extension *saepe etiam* (cf. v. 213) occurs six times in Virgil, all in the *Georgics*. Furthermore, in the couplet vv. 505–6, the young lover is told what to do and what to avoid. This is the essence of didactic in the Hesiodic tradition. Finally, Apollo makes a didactic abrupt transition in his closing couplet, employing a didactic *sed* ('but'), just as Ovid himself does, most notably at the beginning of what may be designated the 'second half' of Book 2 (v. 337).[60]

Ovid hails the epiphany with a word, *monere*, whose range of meaning covers the action of a teacher. *Monere*, with its derivatives, is a word of authority, didactic or prophetic. The *Ars* itself is an admonition; Apollo's advice is his *Ars Amatoria*.[61] The word also connotes the teaching which the god or muse gives to the poet.[62] Apollo has favoured both the poet and the students/lovers with his advice. Finally it has a prophetic usage, through which we are reminded that this is the Delphic oracle speaking.[63]

It is a feature of didactic diction—and a favourite of Ovid's—to claim authority for the teacher's precepts, particularly at the opening of a work. This Apollo does when he boasts of the fame of his instructions (v. 499), just as

[60] Cf. also v. 357 and v. 373. The word often facilitates changes of direction in didactic poetry, and elsewhere (e.g. Prop. 2. 10. 1).

[61] Cf. e.g. *Ars* 2. 427–8 *qui modo celabas monitu tua crimina nostro | flecte iter et monitu detege furta meo. Monere* is a *uox propria* for *praecepta* and didacticism, at e.g. Hor. *Ars* 344, the task of the poet being *lectorem delect[are] pariterque mon[ere]*; Sen. *Ben.* 6. 2. 1 *a praeceptis incipere omnes, qui monere aliquem uolunt*; Plin. *Ep.* 4. 24. 7 *uel praeceptis uel exemplis monere.*

[62] As at Virg. *Aen.* 7. 41 *tu uatem, tu, diua, mone*, and the instruction given by the interlocuting gods at *Fast.* 1. 467, 3. 261, 5. 447.

[63] Cf. Tib. 1. 6. 50 *canit euentus quos dea magna monet*; Varro fr. at Serv. Auct. *Aen.* 3. 366 *monstrum, quod monet*; Virg. *Georg.* 1. 353 *quid menstrua luna moneret.*

Ovid boasts of his erotodidactic fame in the epilogue to this book (vv. 733–43). When the call to the temple is clarified by the rest of the speech, it is clear that Apollo is inviting us to go all the way to Delphi for our instruction. In contrast Ovid proclaims (v. 511) *ad propiora uocor*. To extend the thought loosely: 'I am called to things nearer (to home), and you do not need to go to Delphi for amatory wisdom.' Apollo appears on the poet's own ground, but he is hailing from across the world. This is in the nature of the *hekaergos* ('he who works from afar'), who is nearby even when he is far away. Delphic Apollo—the remote god—acts in Greece, but his presence is felt in our poem.

The irony, however, in Apollo's proverbial wisdom is that such proverbs are open to reduction to trite and commonplace moralizing. Apollo's precept γνῶθι σαυτόν ('know thyself') is the greatest wisdom and the greatest platitude. After making his solemn pronouncement, Apollo glosses the precept, now playing the Callimachean part of the god explaining an aspect of his cult. By Plutarch's time, there was such an abundance of exegesis on the maxims that he claims (*Mor.* 408e) that one could not easily find more extensive writings on any other subject.[64] Ovid jokingly has Apollo answer this exegetical tradition (such as was in existence by Ovid's time) by himself giving the true explanation—the maxim is advice for pleasing girls. At last the spell is undone with an anticlimactic crash and Apollo comes to his point: how to love wisely. Instructions on *living* wisely might well be expected from the god of wisdom, particularly in his oracular manifestation. But this is *loving* wisely, an oxymoron, a contradiction in terms which epitomizes the essential paradox (which is not a paradox) of the *Ars*, that love is a skill which can be learned, and done well. Apollo's precept is like the *Ars* in miniature, in the emphasis laid on careful control and aptness, but Apollo states the ideal in so extreme a formulation as to border on absurdity. Likewise, the self-parodying pomposity which Ovid inflicts on Apollo is an exaggerated form of a similar element more subtly present in his own

[64] Cf. *Mor.* 385e: the maxims provided the seed for many philosophical inquiries.

didactic stance. When he takes on Virgil's persona or proclaims himself greater than Hesiod, it is his own pose as well as that of the didactic tradition which is the butt of his parody.

By laying the Delphic inscription under contribution to his precepts, Apollo uses and Ovid burlesques the two traditions of wisdom and love. The injunction *sapienter amare* ('to love wisely') is an anomaly. Love is folly and madness, *furor* and ineptitude.[65] To love wisely then is to be in control: in a sense it is not to love at all. In the context of wisdom, the phrase *solus sapienter* ('alone wisely') is designed to sound like Stoic dogma, recalling Horace's satire on the Stoic *sapiens* ('wise man, philosopher'), who alone is fine, rich, a king, etc.[66] The first *paradoxon* of Cicero's *Paradoxa Stoicorum* is Ὅτι μόνον τὸ καλὸν ἀγαθόν ('only the fine is good', *Parad.* 1. 9). He uses similar phraseology: *quod rectum et honestum et cum uirtute est id solum opinor bonum* ('because I consider that only what is right and honourable and in accordance with virtue is good', 9). To love wisely is to love like a philosopher. It is not to love at all. Apollo does not know what he is talking about. (Or does he?)

Loving wisely, according to Apollo, involves making the best of one's natural resources. The god somewhat undermines his own wisdom in the explanation of it, however, for the injunction γνῶθι σαυτόν in its deepest sense does not normally imply a superficial knowledge of one's face. On the other hand, it is a topos of moral philosophy to use 'looking in a mirror' as a metaphor for introspection. (See J. G. W. Henderson 1976: 63–70; and generally North 1966.) As Maria Wyke shows in her forthcoming essay on female adornment, looking in a mirror is behaviour

---

[65] Cf. Catul. 8. 1 *miser Catulle, desinas ineptire*; Prop. 2. 29. 14; Tib. 1. 4. 24 *iurasset cupide quidquid ineptus amor*; Ov. *Ars* 1. 306. Pichon (1902: 259) says on *sapiens* that 'sapiens dicitur [etiam] qui in amore moderatus manet ac sui compos' and cites Prop. 3. 24. 17, which is in some sense a farewell to love. Fedeli (1985: ad loc.) has useful parallels for coming out of love seen as a return to one's senses. See also *AP* 5. 112 (Philodemus), 12. 117 (Meleager); Virg. *Ecl.* 2. 69; Hor. *Carm.* 3. 26. 1–4; Ov. *Am.* 3. 11; DuQuesnay (1979: 57).

[66] Cf. *Sat.* 1. 3. 124–5 *si diues, qui sapiens est,* | *et sutor bonus et solus formosus et est rex*, 2. 3. 46; *Ep.* 1. 1. 106, 1. 16. 20.

appropriate to a woman, and is only rightly done by a man when it signifies contemplation for spiritual improvement. Here the profound metaphor has been de-metaphored. This reduction of wisdom to triteness, always potentially present, culminates in the brilliantly farcical line at the head of the crescendo of precepts (v. 506):

> *qui canit arte, canat; qui bibit arte, bibat*

he who sings well should sing; he who drinks well should drink.

Although metrically and syntactically the two halves of the line are interchangeable, it is important that artistically they are not. The crescendo must climax on *bibat* ('let him drink') because, from Ovid's and our point of view, it is deliberately and delightfully ridiculous. Artistic singing and drinking are good qualities for a symposiast, but as the climax to the wise pronouncement from the Delphic oracle they overstep the boundary between wisdom and inanity along the precarious line of which the speech has progressed.

Other elements in Apollo's speech can be seen to be both like and unlike Ovid's own practice. The advice to encourage an admiring gaze in potential lovers (v. 504) seems Ovidian, bearing a fairly close affinity to the *magister*'s claim in the first book (*Ars* 1. 99):

> *spectatum ueniunt, ueniunt spectentur ut ipsae.*

They come to look and to be looked at themselves.

But note the differences. Ovid was describing *girls*. The significance of gender difference in the *Ars* should never be underestimated. According to the norms of the Ovidian erotic society, certain patterns of behaviour are strictly gender-linked, and their transgression is usually a sign of subversion in the text's simple message. Apollo's precept seems directly to contradict the more artistic mode of procedure (for men) already developed by Ovid. The very first precept proper in this book was not to trust to *fallaci figurae* ('deceitful figure', v. 143).

> *ut ameris, amabilis esto;*
> *quod tibi non facies solaue forma dabit.*   (vv. 107–8)

> In order to be loved, be lovable;
> which beauty will not give you nor form alone.

Ulysses' approach, of studied natural eloquence, was more effective. Ovid shows the lover how to be actively in control (or at least, so the lover is to understand), but Apollo's advice, passive and unsubtle as it is, at some level could make a fool of him. Moreover, Apollo is out of date. This is crucially important not just for the structure of the poem, but for the interpretation of the Apollo scene. By expounding erotic theories which belong to an earlier part of the instruction and of the affair, he is in fact failing in a central artistic value, that of appropriateness. Displaying one's looks to great advantage might be advantageous in catching a girl, but it will take more subtle seduction to keep her interested in a well-established relationship.

The mention of a tan, and exposed shoulders (v. 504), both have Ovidian authority, but again there is a difference. Ovid himself gave his young lover instructions on his appearance, in the first book (1. 505–22) (and note again that such instruction belongs to an earlier stage in the work), but he strictly rejects any idea of sartorial excess (1. 523–4):

> *cetera lasciuae faciant concede puellae*
> *et si quis male uir quaerit habere uirum.*

> Leave the rest for wanton girls to do,
> and anyone (hardly a man) who wants to have a man.

Now certainly Apollo's *cui color est* ('whoever has a tan') contains the same idea as 1. 513 *fuscentur corpora Campo* ('let bodies be darkened in the field'), but, in keeping with 1. 523–4, it is for *girls* that the baring of shoulders is recommended by Ovid (3. 307–10):[67]

> *pars umeri tamen ima tui, pars summa lacerti*
> *nuda sit, a laeua conspicienda manu:*
> *hoc uos praecipue, niueae, decet; hoc ubi uidi,*
> *oscula ferre umero, qua patet, usque libet.*

> But let the lower part of your shoulder be naked
> and the upper part of your arm, visible from the left hand:

[67] Brandt (1902) on *Ars* 3. 307 compares Hor. *Carm.* 2. 5. 18 *non Chloris albo sic umero nitens*—a woman.

this suits you in particular, snowy-white girls; when I have seen this,
I have wanted to cover the naked shoulder with kisses.

Apollo's suggestion borders on Greek-style effeminacy. The situation envisaged in his instructions is that of a symposium, though not an all-male gathering. The lover is to recline, with his clothing negligently exposing his gymnasium-acquired tan; there is elegant conversation, singing (light lyric poetry?), and drinking.

Next point: the lover is to do what *pleases* the girl (v. 505). The text directly points to the outdatedness of Apollo by having him use the word *placet* ('pleases'). Pleasing, with all the erotic overtones it engenders, was the essence of the first half of this book, and to a lesser extent the first book, but this later stage of the affair, and the book, is less concerned with simply keeping the girl interested and flattered than with manipulating her already-caught feelings—and the lover's. Furthermore, *sermo* ('conversation') was the means of communication appropriate to the beginning of the relationship. The lover is to approach a girl at the Circus and *hic tibi quaeratur socii sermonis origo* ('here you may find a starting point for friendly conversation', 1. 143). Again Apollo's advice is not far from Ovid's own, since this precept, that a good talker should talk, is a diluted version of one aspect of the multiple resonance of the Ulysses story, where learning the art of gentle speech was the favoured artistic alternative to trusting in good looks. Even the advice that a good drinker should drink has an Ovidian ring, and may well echo (1. 595–6):

> *si uox est, canta; si mollia bracchia, salta;*
> *et, quacumque potes dote placere, place.*

If you have a good voice, sing; if you have soft arms, dance;
please by whatever pleasing gifts you have.

Indeed, this jingling line (2. 506) is ultimately Ovidian, but it could not, at this stage in the proceedings at any rate, have been spoken in his persona as *magister amoris*.

In Apollo's last couplet, a verbal reminiscence highlights the misplacement of this scene within the course of the book and the affair. The only other instance of *declamo* in Ovid comes in *Ars* 1. 465:

> *quis, nisi mentis inops, tenerae declamat amicae?*[68]

Who except an idiot would declaim to a tender girlfriend?

Apollo's advice is only *just* out of key, however, and here he does, despite a hint of irony, make a good point. *Declamo* is non-poetic, being found in the poets only at Hor. *Ep.* 1. 2. 2, the two in Ovid, and in Martial and the highly rhetorical Juvenal. It belongs to the world of rhetoric.[69] The *clamo*-element ('shout') may well denote an especially violent style of rhetoric.[70] The contrast is with *sermo*, the everyday speech such as that to which Horace pretends in the *Satires*.[71] Love, or rather art, makes the lover eloquent, but that eloquence must be controlled artistically, and above all be *aptus* ('appropriate'). Eloquence in the context of amatory behaviour is the art of chatting. Love is not in the business of *declamatio* because *declamatio* is long, heavy, and, for all its display, will not further the relationship: there is no communication. A *sermo*, however, gives the girl a chance to chat too, and so a relationship develops. The *Ars* poses as being a *sermo*. After a brief appearance at v. 503, the girl had retired to the background, until it is remembered in this line that there are two sides to a conversation, and to a relationship.

Apollo as Augustan/Callimachean literary adviser remembers the important precept: keep to τὸ πρέπον ('what is appropriate'). The description *diserti* must be ironic here, for true eloquence adapts itself to the context. The ironizing of a word which might apply to the speaker himself (Apollo or Ovid) effects a subversion of the speaker which nevertheless does not entirely undermine his precept. Apollo is at

---

[68] Cf. the *non sanus poeta* in our passage. See Myerowitz (1985: 142) on the *Ars* 1 passage, which she describes as 'stylised naturalness'.

[69] Cf. Seneca's report at *Con.* 1. *praef.* 12 *ait enim Caluus declamare iam se non mediocriter, dicere bene; alterum putat domesticae exercitationis esse, alterum uerae actionis.*

[70] Cic. *Ver.* 4. 149 *ille ... insanus, qui pro isto uehementissime contra me declamasset.*

[71] *Sat.* 1. 4. 42, 47–8 *nisi quod pede certo | differt sermoni, sermo merus*, 1. 10. 23, 2. 4. 9.

the same time both burlesqued and allowed to be a genuine Callimachean adviser. We have seen that two Callimachean Apollos and two Callimachean source texts are involved in this passage. One stems from the *Aetia* and the *reuocatio* to a true Callimachean programme; the other stems from the *Hymn to Apollo* and the complexities of the 'short is good' metaphor. In our scene, both themes are and are not present. The *reuocatio* is ostentatiously paraded, next withdrawn, and then subversively hinted at as a sting in the tail. The 'short is good' metaphor is never paraded, only subliminally present, and put to important although not straightforward use. But it is the point of the whole thing.

We have seen previously that there is a sense in which Apollo *does* perform a *reuocatio*. Despite his apparent undercutting of the entire role of poetry in love, himself as god of poetry, and even the *Ars* itself in his final pronouncement, there is another side to this, and Apollo makes a genuinely Callimachean point. It is specifically the *non sanus* poet who is being banned from speaking, the poet who relies on frenzied divine inspiration, *ingenium*, not on *ars*. Ancient literary criticism provides the terms, when Horace makes the connection between the *ars*/*ingenium* opposition and the *non sanus poeta* (*Ars* 295–7):

> *ingenium misera quia fortunatius arte*
> *credit et excludit sanos Helicone poetas*
> *Democritus*

> Because Democritus deemed intellect to be more fortunate
> than piffling art and excluded sane poets from Helicon . . .

The poem ends with a satire on the artless mad poet, like the Stoic *sapiens* of the *Satires*. Likewise, Apollo addresses Propertius as *demens* ('mad') for trying to be other than Callimachean and to sing of gods and battles (3. 3. 15). We should remember again Ovid's judgements on Callimachus and Ennius discussed in Chapter 3.

With oracular ambiguity, the scene also plays with the 'short is good' metaphor. On the one hand, we might note the redundant reduplication in Apollo's style, when he describes the *littera* as *fama celebrata* ('celebrated in fame'), when he speaks of *taciturna silentia* ('sullen silence'), and when he repeats his maxim as he begins to gloss it. On the other hand, this is Apollo Loxias, of whom it is said that καὶ Λοξίας καλεῖται [Apollo] διὰ τὸ φεύγειν τὴν ἀδολεσχίαν μᾶλλον ἢ τὴν ἀσάφειαν ('Apollo is called "Loxias" because he avoids garrulity rather than obscurity', Plut. *Mor.* 511b). Apollo Loxias gives his whole *ars* here, from start to finish. The less he says the more he 'says' (conveys). Question: how do I keep a mistress? Answer: γνῶθι σαυτόν ('know thyself'). This is the point Ovid is making about length: Ulysses provides an excellent paradigm for the precept about using one's eloquence, but did we *really* need twenty lines of digression to make the point? The answer, of course, is yes: not to drive the precept home, but to produce and allow us to absorb the subtle wealth of complication produced by the story. Apollo makes the point briefly, succinctly, and clearly, but Ovid develops the *ars*. Ovid's *Ars*, stripped of its padding, might look very like Apollo's speech—but it would lack *ars*.

The whole question of artistic 'shortness' against succinctness is at issue here. The maxim γνῶθι σαυτόν ('know thyself') and its companion μηδὲν ἄγαν ('nothing in excess') provide a succinct formulation of that feature of Augustan-Callimachean poetics known as τὸ πρέπον, the need for propriety, as suggested above. Their very succinctness is 'Callimachean'. If Plutarch's judgement on the maxims (quoted above) reflects the ancient *communis opinio*, then they are particularly suited to the examination of Augustan-Callimachean principles which I believe Ovid to be making, for he says καὶ τὰ τοιαῦτα μὲν ἀποφθέγματα τῶν σοφῶν ταὐτὸ τοῖς εἰς στενὸν συνθλιβεῖσι πέπονθε ῥεύμασιν. οὐ γὰρ ἔχει τοῦ νοῦ δίοψιν οὐδὲ διαύγειαν ('now such sayings as these of the Wise Men are in the same case with streams forced into a narrow channel, for they do not keep the transparency or translucence of the sentiment, but if you will investigate what has been written and said about them . . . you will not easily find more extensive writings on any other subject': *Mor.* 408e, trans. W. G. Helmbold). The maxims are ultimately dense: artistic in their succintness, obscure in their need for unpacking, yet (and this is not specifically Callimachean, but rather relates to didactic) they are also educa-

tive in their provocation of exegesis. The question of succinctness is the problem Horace faced and formulated as
breuis esse laboro, | *obscurus fio* ('I strive to be brief and end
up being obscure', *Ars* 25–6). Be brief, or be clear? The
important thing is to be apt. Ovid incorporates this notion
of propriety into his amatory prescriptions, for example in
the precepts of the previous section: the lover is told, stay
away—but not for long; and make her angry—but make up
soon. Art is knowing how much is enough, in both the
erotic and the artistic spheres. The programme of this
passage is that the measure of artistic success and of the
right artistic length is artistic effectiveness. But, in the
nature of oracles, Apollo's response leaves not a clear poetic
admonition, but a puzzle. Poetically, he poses more problems than he solves.

4h Ovid's Answer

> *ad propiora uocor: quisquis sapienter amabit,*
> *uincet et e nostra, quod petit, arte feret.*
> *credita non semper sulci cum fenere reddunt,*
> *nec semper dubias adiuuat aura rates.*
> *quod iuuat, exiguum, plus est, quod laedat amantes:* 515
> *proponant animo multa ferenda suo.*
> *quot lepores in Atho, quot apes pascuntur in Hybla,*
> *caerula quot bacas Palladis arbor habet,*
> *litore quot conchae, tot sunt in amore dolores;*
> *quae patimur, multo spicula felle madent.* 520
> *dicta erit isse foras, quam tu fortasse uidebis:*
> *isse foras et te falsa uidere puta.*
> *clausa tibi fuerit promissa ianua nocte:*
> *perfer et inmunda ponere corpus humo.*
> *forsitan et uultu mendax ancilla superbo* 525
> *dicet 'quid nostras obsidet iste fores?'*
> *postibus et durae supplex blandire puellae*
> *et capiti demptas in fore pone rosas.*
> *cum uolet, accedes; cum te uitabit, abibis:*
> *dedecet ingenuos taedia ferre sui.* 530
> *'effugere hunc non est' quare tibi possit amica*
> *dicere? non omni tempore †sensus obest†.*
> *nec maledicta puta nec uerbera ferre puellae*
> *turpe nec ad teneros oscula ferre pedes.* (vv. 511–34)

I am called to things nearer to hand; whoever loves wisely,
will conquer and will bear off from my art what he seeks.
Furrows do not always return with interest what has been
    entrusted to them,
nor does the breeze always aid the doubtful ship.
There is little which delights lovers, more which hurts:
let them put forward in their minds many things to be borne.
As many as there are hares on Mt. Athos, as bees which feed in
    Hybla,
as green olives borne on Pallas' tree,
as shells on the shore, so many are the pains in love.
The arrows which we suffer are wet with poison.
She will be said to have gone outdoors,
when perhaps you have seen her in.
Think that she has gone outdoors and that you saw falsely.
The door will be closed against you on the promised night:
endure even to place your body on the dirty ground.
Perhaps also a lying servant-girl with arrogant expression will
    say,
'Why is that one besieging our door?'
Humbly coax the doorposts and the hard girl
and place on the door the roses taken from your brow.
When she wants you, approach her; when she avoids you, go
    away.
It is unseemly for freeborn men to make a nuisance of
    themselves.
Why should your girlfriend be able to say 'You can't get away
    from this one'?
†Good sense is not always an obstacle†
Do not think it foul to bear the curses and lashes
of your mistress, or to bring kisses to her tender feet.

The Epiphany of Apollo provokes a response in which
the poet rises to the poetic challenge thrown out by the god.
He begins (vv. 511–12):

> *ad propiora uocor: quisquis sapienter amabit,*
> *uincet et e nostra, quod petit, arte feret.*

I am called to things nearer to hand; whoever loves wisely,
will conquer and will bear off from my art what he seeks.

On this reading, *ad propiora* comes to mean 'nearer to
home', and is an answer to *diuersum . . . per orbem* ('throughout the whole world'). You do not need to go to Greece for

your instruction: you can get it here in Rome. The passive mood of *uocor* ('I am called') suggests poetic inspiration: perhaps, given the connection between inspiration and madness, a little incongruous after Apollo's rejection of the mad poet,[72] and after Ovid's own disclaimers of divine inspiration for his poetry.

Ovid echoes the universalizing didactic formula which Apollo had also used:

> *qui sibi notus erit, solus sapienter amabit*   (v. 501)
> Whoever knows himself, alone will love wisely.

> *quisquis sapienter amabit*
> *uincet*   (vv. 511–12)
> Whoever loves wisely,
> will conquer and will bear off from my art what he seeks.

Ovid's *sententia*-like quotation of Apollo's dictum is problematical. Does he repeat Apollo's instruction, or replace it? In Ovid's adopted role as the 'priest responding to the oracle', the echo appears clearly as an interpretation and expansion of the god's intent. But the following pentameter undermines that apparent simplicity, since it is from Ovid's art that the prize will be won: *nostra . . . arte* is a clear and overt reference to the book itself. The victory celebrations of this couplet combine with Apolline contextuality to remind us of the triumphal opening of the book.

> *Dicite 'io Paean' et 'io' bis dicite 'Paean'.*
> Cry 'io Paean' and twice cry 'io Paean'.

This was an acclamation to Apollo in yet another of his manifestations, but it was into *Ovid's* trap that the plunder had fallen (v. 2):

> *decidit in casses praeda petita meos*
> The desired prey has fallen into my trap.

The lover is to be the victor, and carry off the prize, as he did under the guises of Paris and Pelops (vv. 5–8). The

---

[72] For the passive voice and the general sense of wild poetic inspiration cf. Hor. *Carm.* 3. 25. 1–3 *quo me, Bacche, rapis tui | plenum? quae nemora aut quos agor in specus | uelox mente noua?*

lover's conquest is the poet's also, because it is through his contriving and it fulfils his aim of keeping the lover in the book. This erotic prize echoes the poetic prize which the lover brought to Ovid in the opening triumph (v. 3):

> *laetus amans donat uiridi mea carmina palma.*

The happy lover presents my songs with a triumphal crown.

The contest is for poetic success as well as erotic. Ovid's *Ars* will conquer Apollo's brief erotodidactic essay, by the criterion of effectiveness.

But in contrast with Apollo's positive statements about the way to love wisely, Ovid opens with failure and negativity. This is a victory which looks very like defeat (vv. 513–14):

> *credita non semper sulci cum fenere reddunt,*
> *nec semper dubias adiuuat aura rates.*

Furrows do not always return with interest what has been
  entrusted to them,
nor does the breeze always aid the doubtful ship.

As ever, the ship in question is both erotic and poetic. Both love and poetry may doubt the aid of the winds. Erotically, this is the lover's first taste of the pains of love, which will be presented in their most bitter-sweet romantic form for his masochistic pleasure. Poetically, the line points to the upset in the quasi-narrative thread: Apollo has sent the poem off course, and the ship is sailing in the wrong direction. The insecure unreliability of this couplet—fields not giving return from the seed entrusted (*credita*) to them, and the winds not driving the ship in the expected direction—throw suspicion on to Ovid's pious acclamation of the oracle's reliability, *certa . . . fides* ('sure faith', v. 510). Moreover, *dubias* is a doubtful word, being applicable either to the agent of doubting or the object of doubt.[73] The ship is unsure what to make of the fickle breeze. Any mention of 'trust' by Ovid is susceptible to ironic reading, but especially so when it applies to an oracle, when it is spoken in a pose of pseudo-naïve piety, and when the object of the

---

[73] *OLD dubius* 1 and 2 for the former, 3, 6, and 8 for the latter.

'trust' will be supplanted to the point of contradiction in the ensuing couplets.

Apollo's succinct erotodidaxis instructs the lover on the conduct of his affair, but Ovid's actually seduces him into following it, and the reader into reading it. This he does by a variant of the age-old device, proposed by Ovid himself elsewhere, of inflaming passion by delay.[74] Just as the lover was to rekindle his mistress's declining interest in him by a skilfully judged absence and an artistically dropped hint of someone else, so too Ovid revives the lover's interest in the affair, and therefore the book, by calling him to picture himself in the guise of the great romantic, elegiac, and particularly locked-out lovers. In his 'advice to women', Ovid is explicit about the deception being played on the lover here. He instructs women to make their established lovers perform the traditional song of the locked-out lover (the paraclausithyron) in order to stimulate desire which may by now be flagging (*Ars* 3. 579–82). By telling the lover 'what to do if his mistress keeps him outside', Ovid *is* keeping the lover *out*—and longing. Apollo's style in his specific messages of vv. 503–8 is more overtly didactic, more directly instructive than Ovid's. In contrast, consider the Ovidian *excursus* before the mistress's locked door (vv. 523–32), surrounded as it is by exhortation, platitudinizing, and thoughts and instructions about the general policy of the lover.

This miniature *Ars Amatoria* both repeats and differs from the macro-*Ars*, bearing a relationship to it analogous to that between the *Ars* and the elegiac corpus. The passage parades its dual ancestry in didactic poetry and elegy, and programmatically displays the community of discourse between elegy and epigram on the one hand, and comedy on the other. Throughout this passage, programmatically elegiac as it is, the language, thought, and scenario of both epigram and comedy play a part. Representation of degraded public life, a picture of people making fools of themselves, is a feature shared between elegy and comedy, and here, as often in the first half of this book, the pupil's

[74] See e.g. *Ars* 2. 349–56, 3. 473–4 *mora semper amantes* | *incitat*.

role is fudged between the comic and Comic *adulescens* and the elegiac lover. Elegy shares the erotic discourse of epigram from within—as loving subject; and that of comedy from without—as detached observer. Hellenistic epigram, although indeed an 'ancestor' of elegy and a locus for the consideration of what it means to be Callimachean, is exposed by this passage as limited by comparison with Ovid's greater undertaking, however valuable it might be for the construction of elegiac erotic discourse. The passage exposes elegiac love as a bittersweet love, manipulating and seducing the reader into its erotic web. Just as the addressee is manipulated into picturing himself as a romantic, so too the reader is seduced into a self-image as a 'sophisticated reader', who recognizes and takes pleasure in recognizing the interplays of literary allusion and generic advertisement, as we shall now do.

We have seen before that abrupt transitions are a feature of didactic style, and that Ovid both employs abrupt transitions and also subliminally prepares for them. The very existence of this scene comes into that category. What does all this about being locked out have to do with Apollo on loving wisely, or the erotic history of mankind, or adultery (wherever you wish the text to have diverted from)? The answer is, of course, 'everything and nothing'. Within this passage, a further abrupt transition takes us to the threshold of a house door, at which the lover knocks in vain. But where else could this language of pain, exclusion, and underscored *elegiac* desire lead us but to the closed door of elegy?

Abrupt transitions, then, are a didactic feature employed by the passage. Although, as I said, the passage is not so starkly instructive as Apollo's speech, nevertheless the poet highlights his didactic stance. The didactic formula *quisquis* ('whoever') echoes the opening of the whole work, *Si quis in hoc . . . populo* ('Whoever in this population'). Ovid places his didactic stance in answer and opposition to that of Apollo, who also employed that element of didactic diction (vv. 500 and 501). Ovid also makes some use of the compressed instructions characteristic of didactic writing and reminiscent of Apollo's didactic style (v. 529):

cum uolet, accedes; cum te uitabit, abibis

When she wants you, approach her; when she avoids you, go
away.

As an example of 'didactic style', we might usefully take the
ten couplets vv. 197–216.

> *cede repugnanti: cedendo uictor abibis;*
> *fac modo, quas partes illa iubebit, agas.*
> *arguet: arguito; quidquid probat illa, probato;*
> *quod dicet, dicas; quod negat illa, neges.* 200
> *riserit: adride; si flebit, flere memento:*
> *imponat leges uultibus illa tuis.*
> *seu ludet numerosque manu iactabit eburnos,*
> *tu male iactato, tu male iacta dato;*
> *seu iacies talos, uictam ne poena sequatur,* 205
> *damnosi facito stent tibi saepe canes.*
> *siue latrocinii sub imagine calculus ibit,*
> *fac pereat uitreo miles ab hoste tuus.*
> *ipse tene distenta suis umbracula uirgis,*
> *ipse fac in turba, qua uenit illa, locum.* 210
> *nec dubita tereti scamnum producere lecto,*
> *et tenero soleam deme uel adde pedi.*
> *saepe etiam dominae, quamuis horrebis et ipse,*
> *algenti manus est calficienda sinu.*
> *nec tibi turpe puta (quamuis sit turpe, placebit)* 215
> *ingenua speculum sustinuisse manu.*

Yield to her when she resists: by yielding you will depart as
  victor;
just make sure that you play the part she orders.
If she finds fault with something, you find fault with it;
whatever she approves, approve;
say what she says; deny what she denies.
If she laughs, laugh back; if she weeps, remember to weep:
let her impose laws on your face.
If she is playing at throwing ivory dice,
you throw badly, you give bad throws;
if you are throwing knuckle-bones, lest punishment follow from
  her losing,
make sure your dogs often stand to your loss.
If the pebble goes under the image of a band of robbers,
make your soldier perish by his glassy enemy.
You yourself hold up her sun-shade, spread out on its rods;

you yourself make her a way through the crowd.
Do not hesitate to place a footstool by her smooth bed,
or to take her shoes from her tender feet, or put them on.
Often you must even warm your mistress's hand in your cold
    lap,
even if you are shivering yourself;
and do not think it foul (although it may be foul, it will be
    pleasing)
to hold up her mirror with your freeborn hand.

Here we have a succession of direct, terse instructions,
between the *excursus* on the power of *obsequium* (vv. 179–
96), culminating in the exemplum of Milanion, and the
exemplum of Hercules (vv. 217–22). In ten couplets there
are sixteen imperatives, three jussive subjunctives, and one
gerundive, plus examples of the didactic features *fac* +
subjunctive (see Kenney 1958: 203), *tu* + imperative, *me-
mento* + infintive, *nec dubita* (all in Kenney 1958: 202), *nec
tibi turpe puta*. What is remarkable about the *Ars Amatoria*
stylistically is that so *little* of the poem is like this. It is
there when it is poetically useful, and not when it risks, to
misquote Ovid, *taedia ferens* ('bringing boredom').

Generalization is endemic in pedagogy, particularly in
the tradition of wisdom literature. As the experienced
teacher and love-poet, Ovid associates with his disciples
through the first person plural, *patimur* ('we suffer', v. 520),
when describing the poisoned darts of love. Another generalizing comment rounds off the precept that one should not
taedia ferre ('bring boredom/irritation').

> non omni tempore †sensus obest† (v. 532)

The possible corruption of the text is an additional hin-
drance to the interpretation of this difficult passage. I
favour retention of the well-attested *obest* (RAω), in view
of the abundance of barrier imagery in the passage. For a
defence of the reading see Goold (1965: 40), who translates
'discretion is not always a bad thing'. Also characteristic of
the teacher is the observation of the colour of the olive trees
in v. 518. We might compare Lucr. 5. 1374–5 *olearum |
caerula . . . plaga* ('the green belt of olives'); Manil. 5. 260
caeruleum . . . oleis . . . collem ('a hill green with olives').

The olive tree was sacred to Pallas. The periphrasis combines with the scientific observation on the colour of the trees to enhance the *magister*'s learned aura, while playing incongruously against the light eroticism of the context. Such incongruity is characteristic of the *Ars*.

It is to a very considerable extent by association with and definition against his great predecessors in the genre that Ovid constructs his didactic persona. As I mentioned in the first chapter, Ovid is involved in a particularly complex intertextuality with Virgil's *Georgics*. This showpiece passage opens with a link to its formal predecessor through the use of technical agricultural terminology (v. 513):

> *credita non semper sulci cum fenere reddunt*

> Furrows do not always return with interest what has been
> entrusted to them.

Every operative word has agricultural-technical associations.[75] The specific connection with Virgil is accentuated by *sulci*, a word which links the passage to one where he too uses agricultural sexual imagery,[76] to explain the reason for horse-breeders keeping mares short of food and hard at work, in the period before they want conception to take place (*Georg.* 3. 135–7):

[75] For *credita* cf. Virg. *Georg.* 1. 221–4 *ante . . . debita quam sulcis committas semina quamque | inuitae properes anni spem credere terrae*; Tib. 2. 6. 21–2 *spes alit agricolas, spes sulcis credit aratis | semina quae magno faenore reddat ager*; Ov. *Ars* 1. 401 *nec semper credenda Ceres fallacibus aruis*, 2. 351 *da requiem: requietus ager bene credita reddit*; Manil. 3. 152 *seu Cererem plena uincentem credita messe*; Col. 2. 12. 1; Sen. *Suas.* 3. 1 *creditum sibi terra non retinet*; Plin. *Nat.* 17. 29 *salsaeque terrae multa melius creduntur*. The term *faenus* is technical in crop-growing: cf. Cic. *Cato* 51 *nec umquam terra sine usura reddit quod accepit, sed alios minore, plerumque maiore cum fenore*; Col. 4. 3. 5; Manil. 5. 273 *semina . . . in faenus sulcatis credere terris* (possibly a direct allusion to our passage); Plin. *Nat.* 18. 162. See *TLL* 6. 1. 483. 66. The word has developed a pecuniary metaphorical sense deriving from pre-monetary fertility: Varro in Gel. 16. 12. 7–8 *fenus . . . a fetu et quasi a fetura quadam pecuniae parientis atque increscentis*; Paul. *Fest.* p. 86 *fenus et feneratores . . . a fetu dicta, quod crediti nummi alios pariant, ut apud Graecos eadem res 'tokos' dicitur. Reddunt* also is technical: cf. Ov. *Ars* 2. 351 quoted above; *Pont.* 1. 5. 56 *hanc messem satis est si mea reddit humus*; Manil. 4. 558 *in domibus maturas reddet aristas*; Plin. *Nat.* 18. 67 on how much bread different types of wheat can produce; Mart. 2. 38. 1 *quid mihi reddat ager quaeris*.

[76] Adams (1982: 84) (cf. 24, 28) says on *sulcus* that 'clearly the word had an inoffensive tone'.

hoc faciunt, nimio ne luxu obtunsior usus
sit genitali aruo et sulcos oblimet inertis,
sed rapiat sitiens Venerem interiusque recondat.

They do this, lest by excessive indulgence
the fertile field should become thick and the furrows become
   blocked up and useless,
but rather that the thirsty field should seize the seed and bury it
   deep within.

In Lucretius' lecture on sex, a fertile ground for Ovidian
didactic allusion, he too uses the metaphor, to explain why
movement by women during sex is detrimental to conception (4. 1272–3):

eicit enim sulcum recta regione uiaque
uomeris atque locis auertit seminis ictum.

For she diverts the furrow from the correct region and path
of the plough-share, and turns away the blow from the seed's
   place.

Perhaps the best example of *Georgic* allusion in our passage
is in the catalogue of *dolores* ('pains') in *amor* (vv. 517–19):

quot lepores in Atho, quot apes pascuntur in Hybla,
caerula quot bacas Palladis arbor habet,
litore quot conchae, tot sunt in amore dolores

As many as there are hares on Mt. Athos, as bees which feed on
   Hybla,
as green olives borne on Pallas' tree
as shells on the shore, so many are the pains in love.

The formula may owe its origin to the *arithmētikon* ('arith-
metical poem'),[77] which in Virgil and Ovid becomes a
didactic feature (*Georg.* 2. 103–8)

sed neque quam multae species nec nomina quae sint
est numerus, neque enim numero comprendere refert;
quem qui scire uelit, Libyci uelit aequoris idem
dicere quam multae Zephyro turbentur harenae
aut, ubi nauigiis uiolentior incidit Eurus,
nosse quot Ionii ueniant ad litora fluctus.

[77] See *AP* 14 *passim*; Catul. 5, 7, and 48; and Cairns (1973). The genre is more
clearly alluded to at *Ars* 2. 447–8 *o quater et quotiens numero comprendere non est |*
felicem, de quo laesa puella dolet!, which echoes Virgil's *comprendere* in *Georg.* 2.
104, to be quoted shortly.

But there is no limit to the types and their names,
nor can they be counted;
if someone wanted to know them, he would want to say
how many sands of the Libyan sea are tossed about by the West
    Wind
or, when the East comes, more violent to sailors,
to know how many waves come to the Ionian shore.

The number of plagues which affect animals receives similar treatment (*Georg.* 3. 470–1):

> *non tam creber agens hiemem ruit aequore turbo*
> *quam multae pecudum pestes.*

Not so many are the raging winds which rush over the sea
bringing storms, as are the plagues of cattle.

In the *Ars* (1. 57–9), the number of girls in Rome are compared to

> *Gargara quot segetes, quot habet Methymna racemos,*
>   *aequore quot pisces, fronde teguntur aues,*
> *quot caelum stellas*

As many as Gargara has crops, as Methymna has grape-clusters,
as fish are covered by the sea, birds by leaves,
as the sky has stars . . .

The girls are the raw material for the book as the plagues were for Virgil. In the same way, the variations of hair-style are as many as acorns on a holm-oak, Hyblaean bees, and wild animals in the Alps (*Ars* 3. 149–52); and different dyes are as many as the spring brings forth flowers (*Ars* 3. 185). Such comparisons have a proverbial ring which, together with the ostentatious display of learning, suits them to didactic diction.

But the referents are not simply inert representations of numerousness. The plagues in *Georg.* 3. 470 are like driving storms (harmful and frightening), while the possible girl-friends are like corn, grapes, fish,[78] birds, stars, things which are pleasant, natural, beautiful, and full of fertile promise. The fairly obvious connection between dyes and

[78] Mr P. Callaghan has informed me that fish are commonly found on erotic pots.

flowers comes both from the fact that flowers are of many colours, and that many dyes are actually made from plants. A little strange, then, when the sorrows of love are compared to hares, Hyblaean bees, olives, and shells. The fact that the comparisons are taken from the natural world is of course a general connection with Virgil. If Ovid were simply following didactic practice, however, they would be compared to storms (plagues for cattle, plagues in love). They are not in fact so compared, because this is love elegy, and the referents tell us about love, the sorrows of which are well alloyed with sweetness. We might usefully compare an exile passage full of echoes of the *Ars* (*Tr.* 5. 2. 23–8):

> *litora quot conchas, quot amoena rosaria flores,*
> *quotue soporiferum grana papauer habet,*
> *silua feras quot alit, quot piscibus unda natatur,*
> *quot tenerum pennis aera pulsat auis,*
> *tot premor aduersis: quae si conprendere coner,*
> *Icariae numerum dicere coner aquae.*

As many as the shores have shells, pleasant rose gardens flowers,
or as many as the sleep-bearing poppy has grains,
as many as the wood nourishes wild animals,
as many as the fish which swim in the sea,
as many as the feathers with which a bird beats the thin air,
by so many trials I am oppressed: if I were to try to count them
I would be trying to tell the number of the Icarian sea.

After the build-up of pleasant comparisons, including the escapist poppy-seed drug, *tot premor aduersis* ('by so many trials I am oppressed') comes as a surprise. But Ovid's exile, and all the troubles it brought, were highly fertile— for poetry.[79] Counting his troubles is like counting the drops of the Icarian sea (substituted for Virgil's Ionian sea in *Georg.* 2. 108): if my reading of the Icarus story is accepted, then the poetic interpretation of those drops is hard to resist.

To return to the matter in hand: another classic example of the Ovidian use of the *Georgics* concludes the passage under discussion in this section (vv. 533–4):

[79] Compare also *Tr.* 5. 6. 37–41.

nec maledicta puta nec uerbera ferre puellae
turpe nec ad teneros oscula ferre pedes.

Do not think it foul to bear the curses and lashes
of your mistress, or to bring kisses to her tender feet.

The formula 'do not be ashamed to . . .' accords with
Virgil's didactic diction. Early in the first book, Virgil
encourages the farmer to fertilize his fields: that is, to do
something which, although unpleasant in itself, will further
his cause (*Georg.* 1. 79–81):

arida tantum
ne saturare fimo pingui pudeat sola neue
effetos cinerem immundum iactare per agros.

Only do not be ashamed to saturate dry ground with rich dung
   nor
to toss dirty ashes over worn-out fields.

Ovid amusingly, ironically uses and abuses the Virgilian
formula. Muck-spreading is physically *turpis* ('foul') but
spiritually noble and ennobling. Ovid appropriates and inverts Virgil's moral language to apply it to behaviour at
which moral repugnance might indeed be expected, if this
work belonged to the discourse of Roman moral philosophy,
rather than, as it does, to its anti-discourse. The joke works
because everyone knows that the lover's behaviour is *turpis*.
Or are we privileging moralistic discourse as *the* central
Roman discourse? Turpitude can only be judged relative to
the moral norms of the society assigning it, and in the
society—so to speak—of Ovidian erotics the deciding ethi-
cal factor is effectiveness. The Ovidian lover wallows in his
turpitude, as the master himself did in his subjective elegy
(*Am.* 2. 17. 1–2):

Si quis erit, qui turpe putet seruire puellae,
illo conuincar iudice turpis ego.

If anyone thinks it foul to be a slave to a girl,
by his judgement I shall be convicted of being foul.

To do what pleases the mistress is wisdom, not turpitude,
whether it is the torture of lashes or the not-too-unpleasant
humiliation of kissing her feet. Ovid has usurped the lan-

guage of 'official' Roman morality previously in this passage, when the lover is told that *dedecet ingenuos taedia ferre sui* ('it is unseemly for free-born men to make a nuisance of themselves', v. 530).[80] *TLL* 7. 1. 1545. 56 provides a whole section of 'illustrations of things which might be considered worthy or unworthy of free-born men'. This moralizing stance, highly appropriate to Ovid's status as teacher, may be intended specifically to recall Horace worrying about *taedia ferens* ('being a nuisance') to Maecenas (*Sat.* 1. 3. 63–6):[81]

> *simplicior quis et est qualem me saepe libenter*
> *obtulerim tibi, Maecenas, ut forte legentem*
> *aut tacitum inpellat quouis sermone molestus:*
> *'communi sensu plane caret' inquimus.*

If someone is a bit innocent and such as I have often willingly been to you, Maecenas, when a troublesome person accosts one who is reading, perhaps, or being quiet, with some conversation or other:
'He is clearly lacking in social sense,' we say.

But—amusingly—*taedia ferre* is hardly the least decorous of the lover's activities. Conversely, *oscula ferre (ad) pedes* ('to bring kisses to her feet', v. 534) is not normally a *decus* ('honourable activity')—except according to the moral norms of Ovidian erotic society. When previously the lover was a slave, he was not to think it *turpe* to hold up his mistress's mirror, like her slave-attendant (2. 215–16):

> *nec tibi turpe puta (quamuis sit turpe, placebit)*
> *ingenua speculum sustinuisse manu.*

Do not think it foul (although it may be foul, it will be pleasing)
to hold up her mirror with your free-born hand.

The measure of decorum is the amatory effectiveness of the act—if it works, *decet*.

This passage is and is not more of the same. The lover is to 'go back to basics' and play the role of an *Amores*-type lover (so that he will not become one again), and by allowing

---

[80] Compare *Am.* 3. 11. 9–12 for the ironic contrast between the *ingenuus* and the slave.

[81] The moralizing poetry of Horace is an important and largely unacknowledged source text for Ovidian moralizing.

himself to be treated as a locked-out elegiac failure, he will find a new means to *tenere* his girl; he holds on to her by staying outside. This is victory through simulated defeat, the precept *cedendo uictor abibis* ('by yielding you will depart as victor', v. 197) given a new perspective. The section is striving to look like traditional *Amores*-style love, and Ovid self-consciously employs the traditional topoi of elegy and its antecedents, often topoi that he has already used in the book. In case we fail to notice the elegiac programme of this section, our awareness is jogged at the end by what is probably an allusion to the father of Roman elegy, Gallus. The *teneros . . . pedes* to which the lover will bring kisses echo what are probably echoes of Gallus' elegiac diction.

> *a, tibi ne teneras glacies secet aspera plantas*   (Virg. *Ecl.* 10. 49)
> Ah, may the harsh ice not cut your tender soles.

> *tu pedibus teneris positas fulcire pruinas*
> *. . . potes.*   (Prop. 1. 8. 7–8)
> You could tread with tender feet the frost on the ground.

The passage, then, displays the very excesses of which Ovid is accused, perhaps by Apollo as well as more recent critics, and overturns them by the resulting art. At the same time Ovid is accentuating both the similarities between the *Ars* and elegy, and also the otherness of his Art. It is essential that the scene be one that is already well established to the point of petrifaction, because it is into that clearly defined image that Ovid seduces the lover. Classic elegiac topoi present themselves here. The paraclausithyron, for example, has already been employed once in the book, albeit briefly, at vv. 237–8; the military imagery of *quid nostras obsidet iste fores?* ('Why is that one besieging our door?' v. 516) has also found expression in the poem before (vv. 233–6). It receives its fullest and best known treatment in *Am.* 1. 9, where the specific situation of the besieging lover occurs at vv. 19–20.

Classically elegiac also is the conceit of *seruitium amoris*. The lover is to be less than a slave, since the slave-girl looks arrogantly down on him lying in the dust. A new position, this, for the lover, who had recently been the skilled juggler of many women. But earlier again he had spent nearly 200 lines performing the part of an amatory slave in the main body of the first half of Book 2, which plays around with the metaphor of *seruitium amoris*. At that stage, however, *he* was the clever, controlling slave of comedy, *playing the part* of the elegiac slave of love.[82] Now he is actually to become the elegiac slave, who is painfully aware of the degradation of his free-born dignity. In the first half of this book the lover acted as a slave in order to please his mistress; now slavery metaphorically expresses the enthralment and suffering of his emotional situation. These two sides to the image are not completely distinct, but differentiation between them can help to elucidate the effect of the image.

As was mentioned above, Ovid's advice for suiting one's actions to those of the beloved here closely echoes similar advice given earlier:

> *cum uolet, accedes; cum te uitabit, abibis*   (v. 529)

When she wants you, approach her; when she avoids you, go away.

> *arguet: arguito; quicquid probat illa, probato;*
>   *quod dicet, dicas; quod negat illa, neges.*
> *riserit: adride; si flebit, flere memento:*
>   *imponat leges uultibus illa tuis.*   (vv. 199–202)

If she finds fault with something, you find fault with it;
whatever she approves, approve;
say what she says; deny what she denies.
If she laughs, laugh back; if she weeps, remember to weep:
let her impose laws on your face.

The same and not the same. Then the lover had simply to copy—mirror-like—and agree (or at last act as if he did): now he has genuinely to comply.

When does an echo constitute the same material? The pessimistic introduction to this section creates a close echo of an earlier line in the book.

---

[82] See esp. vv. 197–202, where the lover is told to act the part suggested for him by the mistress. The terminology echoes the programmes of slaves and parasites in comedy. Cf. Pl. *Am.* 960–1; *As.* 210–12; Ter. *Eu.* 248–53; Juv. 3. 100–8. For *seruitium amoris* see Copley (1947) and Lyne (1979).

> *credita non semper sulci cum fenere reddunt*   (v. 513)

Furrows do not always return with interest what has been
entrusted to them.

> *da requiem: requietus ager bene credita reddit*   (v. 351)

Give her a rest: a rested field gives good returns on what has
been entrusted to it.

The verbal parallels *credita* and *reddunt/reddit* reinforce the
thematic allusion. The echo supports the suggestion that
the passage is a deliberate miniature *Ars*, but brings with it
a problem. Our line seems to *answer* the earlier one, and to
renege on the promise. This time the well-sown fields are
not going to yield a good harvest. The lover is not going to
get an easy and immediate return on his investment of
effort, but rather he is going to learn the art of suffering.
The reason for this is that it is the *lover* who now needs to
lie fallow to increase his productivity.

Another point on the self-conscious generic display of
this scene: love's arrows are highly conventional, and Ovid
uses the motif here and earlier in the poem, to different
effect. Ovid had promised the lover that he need not feel
the arrows either of the Centaurs or of Cupid in his erotic
experiences (vv. 191–6):

> *pectora nec missis iubeo praebere sagittis;*
> *artis erunt cautae mollia iussa meae.*   (vv. 195–6)

Nor do I order you to offer your breast to the arrows sent against
you;
the commands of my cautious art will be soft.

At that point in the poem, the young man was enticed into
the relationship by the assurance that it would not hurt.
Now, however, we have something of a volte-face (v. 520):

> *quae patimur, multo spicula felle madent*

The arrows which we suffer are wet with poison.

Now the lover must learn to feel the pleasure of being hurt,
and his and the reader's interest is kept alive.

Repetition and difference are apparent also in the treatment of *taedia*. During the transition from the instructions

for behaviour early in the relationship to those to be applied later, the lover was told *dum capias, taedia nulla fuge* ('while you are catching her, spare no effort', v. 346). The girl was to see and hear him all the time, until he was sure enough of his position to leave her alone, and in enough danger of boring her for separation to produce an improvement. Earlier still he had to be indefatigable in kissing, *nec taedeat oscula ferre* (v. 325). In each of these cases, the identity of the recipient of *taedia* (that is, who was likely to be bored) was deliberately ambiguous, but now that the lover sees himself as a suffering martyr it is clearly *her* state of interest with which the poem is concerned. Or is it? Perhaps a whole night on the doorstep might dampen the lover's newly-inflamed passion?

4i *Tot sunt in amore dolores*

After the lover had embarked on his course at the beginning of this book in an atmosphere of exultant success, and has even now been told that he will carry off the prize, it comes as a surprise that the instruction which he is about to receive is hardly the most pleasant and encouraging: he is to endure all sorts of trials for love's sake. Endurance is the theme of the passage, accentuated by the repeated occurrence of *fero* ('bear') and connected words: *feret* (v. 512), *ferenda* (v. 516), *perfer* (v. 524), *ferre* (v. 530), *ferre* (v. 533), *ferre* (v. 534). Obviously, not in all these occurrences does *ferre* mean 'endure', and indeed that is my point. In this show-piece of Ovidian erotodidaxis, a long-running verbal play serves to underscore the theme of the passage, and is heralded by its double-edged appearance in the transitional couplet: double-edged, that is, because the prize which the lover will bear off is also that which he will endure—a mistress, with all the troubles she brings, and the pleasure/ pain of being locked out. As we have seen elsewhere, the abrupt transition is subliminally prepared, and the double meaning of *fero* acts as a pivot for the change. The play is intensified towards the end, particularly in the final couplet. (vv. 533–4):

nec maledicta puta nec uerbera ferre puellae
turpe nec ad teneros oscula ferre pedes

Do not think it foul to bear the curses and lashes
of your mistress, or to bring kisses to her tender feet.

The lover is to act the part of the lover of the *Amores*, and
so is made to *feel* like a lover; a motif employed earlier is re-
used, that motif is very traditional, and belongs to the very
essence of elegy; the Ovidian play on *ferre* continues, in
that the lover is to bear curses and bring kisses. By these
means the couplet reflects in miniature the essence of the
passage, itself a miniature of the *Ars*.

Holding (*tenere*) is the central aim of this book. As one
point of reference for the Daedalus story shows us, the girl
must be rendered unable to escape once she has been
caught in the trap.[83] Her projected complaint in v. 531,
effugere hunc non est ('this one cannot be escaped'), is, then,
exactly the situation required. But she must be held on to
not against her will, but through it, through the love which
has been inspired in her and the bond which has been
contrived. She should not, therefore, be aware of her imprisonment. If she can make the remark, she has broken the
spell which bound her, and is able to take control. Knowledge is power: the seduction of beloved and lover must be
subtly and insidiously—artistically—contrived.

It is the accentuated elegiac and romantic pose which
manipulates the addressee/lover's self-image into that of the
super-romantic, dying to have his heart broken, and so
helps to keep alive his interest in the relationship and in the
general idea of love. By a mixture of subtle suggestion and
eroticism he is drawn further into the discourse of eros. By
taking on the self-image of a desperate romantic lover, the
addressee might in fact end up in love. Such was the hint
made by Ovid in an aside to the girls in the first book (*Ars*
1. 617–18):

quo magis, o, faciles imitantibus este, puellae:
fiet amor uerus, qui modo falsus erat

---

[83] With *effugere* here cf. *effugio* (v. 21) and *effugiendus* (v. 52) in the Daedalus
episode.

Therefore, girls, be easy on men who pretend to be in love:
  love which just now was false will become true.

The hint is made more explicit in *Rem*. 501–2 (quoted at the
beginning of Chapter 2), which to some extent exposes the
workings of ours. The lover as well as the beloved (and the
reader) has fallen into Ovid's trap.

Reflection on the pains of love seduces both Reader and
reader (vv. 515–20):

> quod iuuat, exiguum, plus est, quod laedat amantes:
>   proponant animo multa ferenda suo.
> quot lepores in Atho, quot apes pascuntur in Hybla,
>   caerula quot bacas Palladis arbor habet,
> litore quot conchae, tot sunt in amore dolores;
>   quae patimur, multo spicula felle madent.

There is little which delights lovers, more which hurts:
let them put forward in their minds many things to be borne.
As many as there are hares on Mt. Athos, as bees which feed in
    Hybla,
as green olives borne on Pallas' tree,
as shells on the shore, so many are the pains in love.
The arrows which we suffer are wet with poison.

Subtle manipulative suggestion under the guise of advice
captures the young man, through his imagination, by picturing him to himself in different guises. A little while ago he
was the skilled lover playing the field and juggling one girl
off against another; now he is the passionate lover wallowing
in his pain. The romantic lover not only faces problems,
but masochistically pictures them to himself, even imagines
them. Such is the force of *proponant*.[84] It is Ovid who is
proposing the things to be suffered by the lover, but in
such a way as to suggest that the lover does it himself, that
it is an inevitable part of being a lover.

Latin Love Elegy is in large part poetry of longing, for
there is far more lamentation than celebration. In particular,
the locked-out and cheated lover is far more *elegiac* than the
sexually fulfilled lover. With these features in mind, the
statement that *quod iuuat, exiguum, plus est, quod laedat
amantes* ('there is little which delights lovers, more which

---

[84] Cf. *OLD propono* 5b 'to picture to oneself, imagine'; Cic. *Catil*. 4. 12 *cum . . .
mihi proposui regnantem Lentulum*; Lucr. 3. 627.

hurts', v. 515) can be read as a comment on the nature of elegy. The phrase *quod iuuat* occurs twice elsewhere in this book, vv. 308 and 682, both overtly referring to sexual pleasure.[85] The word *laedat*, on the other hand, has the specific amatory sense of suffering from a partner's infidelity.[86] The intrinsic link between love and pain is emphasized by the sound-play of *amORE dolOREs*, with *litORE* adding a weak precursor (the syllable being short). 'Saepius,' says Pichon (1902: 132), 'dolere ... dicuntur ii quorum amor est spretus.' ('More often those whose love is spurned are said to *dolere*.') Moreover, *dolor* can imply the pain specifically of desire.[87] According to the precept which precedes the advent of Apollo, the *medicamina* of sex *feri requiem sola doloris habent* ('alone contain peace for wild pain', v. 490). The referent of *dolor* there is in the long-term context the mistress's distress at her lover's infidelity, but, in the short term, the *furias* ('madness') into which sex drives the mares (v. 497). To return to v. 515: the line suggests that 'there is not much sex in elegy, but an awful lot of erotic pain'. Elegiac love can only find full expression, can only be fulfilled, through its pains. Love brings pain whether it is frustrated or successful.

I have suggested above that the attractive referents for the sorrows of love serve both to seduce the lover and to expose the nature of that love. The hare plays a suggestive role in erotic discourse.[88] It is used as a term of endearment at for example Pl. *Cas.* 138 *meu' pullus passer, mea columba, mi lepus* ('my little sparrow, my dove, my hare'). A hare is a love-gift at Ov. *Met.* 13. 832, Calp. *Ecl.* 3. 77, Nemes. *Ecl.* 2. 67, and on many a Greek pot, where the suppliant lover carries the gift of a hare.[89] At *Ars* 3. 662, the woman's lover is seen as a hare in a proverbial use (see Otto 1962:

---

[85] Likewise at 1. 673–4 *uim licet appelles: grata est uis ista puellis;* | *quod iuuat, inuitae saepe dedisse uolunt.* Pichon (1902: 179) says 'nec raro Veneris gaudia hoc uerbum significat', and gives examples.

[86] See Pichon (1902) 182 for examples. He comments 'saepe hoc uerbum dicitur de fallacibus et proditionibus infidorum'.

[87] Cf. Catul. 2. 7 *solaciolum sui doloris*, 50. 17; Prop. 1. 10. 13 *non solum uestros didici reticere dolores* (cf. v. 5), 2. 15. 35; Ov. *Am.* 2. 10. 11–12.

[88] For hares on Athos see Nisbet and Hubbard (1970) on Hor. *Carm.* 1. 37. 18. Athos is a mountain on the peninsula of Acte in Chalcidice.

[89] Boardman (1974: 211), (1975: 215), Dover (1978: 92).

190) of the hunt metaphor: *et lepus hic aliis exagitatus erit* ('and this hare will be chased by others'). The specific contribution of the hare to the metaphorical system of erotic hunting can be seen in Propertius 2. 19, a poem tense with the *amor*/hunt opposition, where Propertius anticipates hunting not lions and boars, but hares and birds, and the hares are graced with the erotic epithet *mollis* ('soft', v. 23).[90] In *Ars* 1, when Ovid begins to instruct the lover on how to catch a girl, we are told that sooner will the Maenalian hound flee the hare than a girl reject a suitor if she is artistically approached (vv. 271–2). Converting the image, the girl is a fleeing hare, and the lover is to feel the excitement of the chase.[91]

If hares suggest 'women running away', then bees may also suggest 'women', as they do at *Ars* 1. 95—a hint at the specific *dolor* which the lover will suffer.[92] Hybla (Sicily) was proverbially famous for its bees. (See Otto 1962: 168.) Hyblaean bees are part of the furniture of pastoral, occurring in the *locus amoenus* description at Virg. *Ecl.* 1. 54. A feature of pastoral beauty, then, provides the comparison with the sorrows of love, and moreover one which contains a byword for sweetness, the bees. The whole line has a pastoral flavour, hares being love-gifts in Calpurnius and Nemesianus as mentioned above,[93] evoking natural beauty in far-away places. Shells, also, belong to erotic discourse. In *Am.* 2. 11. 13, shells on the shore are one of the attractions enumerated to persuade Corinna to stay with the poet. The shore is the place of love, while its antithesis, the high sea

---

[90] The metaphor has been studied by Murgatroyd (1984), who collects examples in an survey of the figure from Ibycus to the 6th cent. AD. As he says, a start was made in this field by Kenney (1970: 386–8), and Davis (1983), who examines in more detail the erotic tensions between love and hunting. Carson (1986: 19–20), examining the discourse of eros as lack, mentions flight and the hunt as contributors: '[p]ursuit and flight are a topos of Greek erotic poetry and iconography from the archaic period onwards.'

[91] Cf. Carson (1986: 19): 'the moment of ideal desire on which vase-painters as well as poets are inclined to focus is not the moment of the *coup de foudre* ... What is pictured is the moment when the beloved turns and runs.'

[92] An obvious corroboration for the association of bees and women is the term *melissai*—bees and priestesses. Cf. esp. Call. *Hymn* 2. 110, to which Hor. *Carm.* 4. 2. 27 clearly alludes.

[93] These poets being later than Ovid, their works are not, of course, offered as allusions by Ovid, although they may be alluding to him.

(the beloved having left), is the place of not-love. Again the comparison is erotically suggestive, since *concha* is some-times used of the female *pudenda*.[94] It receives its erotic suggestion, in part at least, from the story that Venus was born from a shell.[95]

All these erotic commonplaces serve to seduce the Reader into becoming a suffering elegiac lover. More subtle, how-ever, is the seduction of the 'clever reader'. A change in quantity to the middle syllable of *lepores* ('hares') would produce a pun with *lepos*—grace, charm, wit—which can also be used as a term of endearment (*OLD lepos* 1b). There was an ancient popular etymology connecting the two words, arising from (or initiating) the superstition that eating hare increased the consumer's attractions.[96] It is the signifier *lepos*—the pun between hare and charm—which seduces the reader.[97]

The seduction of the Reader climaxes in the double-edged poisoned arrows whose pain the lover must learn to love. The conceit of the Archer Cupid is extremely common. Propertius, in his study of the god's traditional attributes, devotes two couplets to archery (2. 12. 9–12):

> *et merito hamatis manus est armata sagittis,*
> *et pharetra ex umero Cnosia utroque iacet:*
> *ante ferit quoniam tuti quam cernimus hostem,*
> *nec quisquam ex illo uulnere sanus abit.*

Rightly his hand is armed with hooked arrows,
and a Cretan quiver lies across his shoulders,
since he strikes us, while we are safe, before we perceive our
enemy,
nor does anyone escape with his health from that wound.

In *Am.* 1. 1, Cupid's archery provides the erotic motivation of the work, as his usurpation of Apollo's role does the poetic (*Am.* 1. 1. 21–4):

---

[94] Cf. Pl. *Rud.* 704; *TLL* 4. 29. 25. In Propertius shells are symbols of wealth (3. 13. 6, 4. 5. 22).

[95] Cf. Lygd. 3. 34; Stat. *Silv.* 1. 2. 118, 3. 4. 5.

[96] Cf. Plin. *Nat.* 28. 260 *somnos fieri lepore sumpto in cibis Cato arbitrabatur, uulgus et gratiam corpori in octo dies.* It was derived by etymologists from *leuipes.* See *TLL* 7. 1180. 69.

[97] Might the too-clever reader even be seduced into hearing a hint of *leptotēs*?

questus eram, pharetra cum protinus ille soluta
legit in exitium spicula facta meum
lunauitque genu sinuosum fortiter arcum
'quod'que 'canas, uates, accipe' dixit 'opus.'

I had finished my complaint, when straight away, undoing his quiver,
he picked out arrows made for my destruction,
and strongly bent his curving bow on his knee and said,
'here is a work you can sing, bard.'

In the Lament for Tibullus (*Am.* 3. 9), Cupid appears carrying *euersam ... pharetram | et fractos arcus* ('upturned quiver and broken arrows', vv. 7–8). The image is very common in Hellenistic epigram. Among the more famous examples is in *AP* 5. 177 (Meleager), the 'Lost Love' poem, where he has the epithets *pharetrophoros* ('quiver-bearer', v. 4) and *toxota* ('bowman', v. 10). But the poisoning of Love's arrows is unusual. Brandt (1902) compares Theocr. 23. 5 πικρὰ βέλη, which could bear that meaning.[98] The darts (*spicula*) of love reappear towards the end of *Ars*, as the prickles of sexual pleasure (vv. 707–8):

inuenient digiti quod agant in partibus illis,
in quibus occulte spicula tingit Amor.

Your fingers will find what they can do in those parts
in which Love dips his hidden darts.

They are tainted with pharmacological poison, because the pain brings pleasure, and the pleasure brings pain when fulfilment serves to increase desire. The pain of being locked out increases the desire to be granted entry. Love the *pharmakon* is as bitter as poison and as sweet as Hyblaean bees.

Suddenly the lover appears in his most classic elegiac position, before the locked door of his loved one (vv. 521–8):

dicta erit isse foras, quam tu fortasse uidebis:
isse foras et te falsa uidere puta.
clausa tibi fuerit promissa ianua nocte:
perfer et inmunda ponere corpus humo.
forsitan et uultu mendax ancilla superbo

---

[98] Cf. Sappho's epithet for Eros, *glukupikron* (*LP* fr. 130). See Carson's perceptive study (1986) of the bittersweet paradox of love (esp. pp. 3–9).

dicet 'quid nostras obsidet iste fores?'
postibus et durae supplex blandire puellae
et capiti demptas in fore pone rosas.

She will be said to have gone outdoors,
when perhaps you have seen her in.
Think that she has gone outdoors and that you saw falsely.
The door will be closed against you on the promised night:
endure even to place your body on the dirty ground.
Perhaps also a lying servant-girl with arrogant expression will
say,
'Why is that one besieging our door?'
Humbly coax the doorposts and the hard girl
and place on the door the roses taken from your brow.

Ovid controls the lover's mind, while teaching him to
control his own thoughts. The didactic imperative, *puta*
('think'), combines paradoxically with the meaning of the
word. Ovid provides a drug as powerful as that prescribed
for Delia's husband by Tibullus so that he would believe in
her innocence even if he caught the couple in bed (1. 2. 55–
6). Tibullus himself did not have this skill (1. 6. 7–8), lacking
the *Ars*. This is wisdom—to see black as white. Wisdom is
what works.[99] The model for the lover is the wise and
understanding *uir* ('husband/lover') of *Am.* 2. 2, who, Ovid
assures the *custos* ('guard'), would disbelieve him even in
the face of evidence (*Am.* 2. 2. 57–8):

uiderit ipse licet, credet tamen ille neganti
damnabitque oculos et sibi uerba dabit.

Even if he sees it himself, he will believe her if she denies it
and will condemn his eyes and lie to himself.

The self-blinding lover appears again in *Am.* 3. 14. 45–6:

quae bene uisa mihi fuerint, bene uisa negato:
concedent uerbis lumina nostra tuis.

---

[99] A similar point is made by Labate (1984: 171): 'La *sapientia* amorosa non si
rivela soltanto nella capacità di simulare con gli altri, ma anche con sé stessi: non
vedere ciò che si vede, non sentire ciò che si sente.' The lover began the lesson in
control over his thoughts at v. 297, where not only was the girl's appearance to
provide fuel for his flattery, but he was actually to believe what he said. The value
of self-delusion espoused by the *Ars* is studied by Shulman (1981), who shows
how this value parodies Lucretius' call for clear-sightedness in order to avoid the
snares of Venus.

> Deny that I have seen rightly what I have seen rightly:
> my eyes will yield to your words.

In Plautus *Miles*, Sceledrus, the girl's guardian, is made to believe that he did not see her with the *adulescens*. Elegy extends the idea to the lover himself.

The trainee lover is clearly being taught how to perform a paraclausithyron. The paraclausithyron is not exclusive to elegy, but is foregrounded in such a way as to make it programmatically charged for elegy.[100] The most famous elegiac paraclausithyra are of course Tibullus 1. 2, Propertius 1. 16, and *Amores* 1. 6, but phrases like ours here can alone conjure up the scene, often developing the programmatic function.[101] Perhaps the most programmatic is *Am.* 2. 1, an opening poem where the girl's closed door performs a quasi-Apolline redirectory function. While the poet was playing about with the idea of writing epic, the closed door of elegy cuts his pretension down to size. He addresses Jupiter as the thunderer and as the subject matter of epic (*Am.* 2. 1. 20):

> *clausa tuo maius ianua fulmen habet*
> The closed door has a bigger bolt than yours.

The 'closed door', then, says 'elegiac love'. Insidiously, the instruction to perform the actions of the elegiac lover seduces the unwary pupil into love. Elegiac love is about the act of gaining entry, far more than the consummated inside.

---

[100] Copley (1942 and 1947) provides a helpful general introduction to the subject. Cairns (1975) provides a useful analysis, mostly concerned with Propertius 2. 17. His interest in genre leads to over-dogmatic differentiation between what is and is not a *komos*. 'Tibullus wrote two *komoi* (1. 2 and 1. 5) and Ovid one in elegy (1. 6) and one in the *Metamorphoses* (14. 698–758)' (Cairns 1975: 8). See also Yardley (1978), Fedeli (1980) on Prop. 1. 16, Ogle (1911) Hendrickson (1925), Haight (1950).

[101] Compare esp. Tib. 2. 6. 11–12 *magna loquor, sed magnifice mihi magna locuto | excutiunt clausae fortia uerba fores*; and also Tib. 1. 2. 6 *clauditur et dura ianua firma sera*, 2. 4. 22 *ne iaceam clausam flebilis ante domum* (where again the programmatic aspect is highlighted); Prop. 2. 5. 22 *nec mea praeclusas fregerit ira fores*, 2. 23. 12 *a pereant, si quos ianua clausa iuuat* (may they die of love, perhaps, since there is a certain perverse pleasure for the locked-out lover/poet), 3. 3. 49 *ut per te clausas sciat excantare puellas*; Ov. *Am.* 2. 19. 38 *incipe iam prima claudere nocte forem*, 3. 8. 7 *laudato ianua clausa est*, 3. 11. 12 *excubui clausam seruus ut ante domum?*; *Rem.* 506 *ueneris, et fuerit ianua clausa: feres*, where the lover is expressly told not to perform a *komos*.

The coacervation of words for 'door' (the repeated *foras* of vv. 521–2, then *ianua* (v. 523), *fores* (v. 526), *postibus* (v. 527), and *fore* (v. 528)) stresses the *barriers* involved in the entry-seeking paraclausithyron. It is a frequent, though not an essential, topos of the genre that the lover is unjustly excluded since he had been promised entry that night, the withdrawal of the promise being calculated to inflame his frustrated desire. It is particularly common in epigram.[102]

The ultimate romantic touch comes in the instruction *perfer* ('endure'), in an echo of Catullus' famous phrase, *perfer, obdura* ('endure, harden yourself', 8. 11). The echo was even clearer, though the context slightly different, earlier in our book (vv. 177–8):

> *si nec blanda satis nec erit tibi comis amanti,*
> *perfer et obdura: postmodo mitis erit.*

If she will not be compliant enough nor companionable to you as lover,
endure and harden yourself: soon she will be kindly.

So again we have romanticism, again repetition. Again the lover acts the role of the *Amores*, for there the echo of Catullus also appeared, in a poem where the lover was trying to give up love (*Am.* 3. 11. 7):

> *perfer et obdura: dolor hic tibi proderit olim.*

Endure and harden yourself: this pain will benefit you sooner or later.

In the *Remedia Amoris*, *perfer* is twice used of the determination and self-control necessary for the cure of love (vv. 218, 642). In the *Ars*, the tradition is taken up—and overturned, since the 'endurance' involved is just the opposite of Catullus' idea and Ovid's own more straightforward allusions.[103] Where Catullus tried to make himself resistant to love, Ovid tells his pupil to persevere in his attempts to further the relationship.

[102] Cf. *AP* 5. 150 (Asclepiades), 152 (Meleager), 265 (Cometas Chartularius), 279 (Paulus Silentarius), 12. 201 (Strato), to mention just a few examples. It occurs in Latin e.g. at Hor. *Sat.* 1. 5. 82; Tib. 1. 8. 63–4, 2. 6. 49; Prop. 2. 17. 1, 4. 5. 33; Ov. *Ars* 3. 461; *Rem.* 400, 505–6. See Cairns (1975) 9.

[103] Pease (1935) on Virg. *Aen.* 4. 420 has a useful note on *perferre* in amatory contexts.

The traditionality continues with the erotic-elegiac topos of the lover physically lying on the threshold. Again it is very common in epigram.[104] An important, because programmatic, example of this topos occurs in Tibullus' opening poem, as essentially the first indication that his work is love elegy (Tib. 1. 1. 55–6):

> *me retinent uinctum formosae uincla puellae,*
> *et sedeo duras ianitor ante fores*

> The bonds of a beautiful girl hold me bound,
> and I sit as a janitor before her hard door.

There, as here, the lover is an elegiac slave. A close verbal parallel for our line is to be found in one of Ovid's own paraclausithyra (*Am.* 3. 11. 9–10):

> *ergo ego sustinui, foribus tam saepe repulsus,*
> *ingenuum dura ponere corpus humo?*

> Have I, then, so often repulsed from the door, endured to place my free-born body on the hard ground?

Ovid the elegist adopts the pose of the lover hardening himself to love; as teacher he suggests this role to his pupil, so that he fuels his love by dwelling on it.

It frequently happens that the unyielding girl and her door are compared, almost identified.[105] Here the motif is accentuated by the position of the two words both beginning with *p* at the two ends of the line, with the suppliant lover in the middle, with two *p*s in the middle of that. The balance of opposites between *durae* ('hard') and *blandire* ('flatter, coax'), forming an inner surround for the lover, completes the structure. The appeal to the door allows the lover to avoid accepting his total exclusion by the girl, but in so doing it distances the girl, thus emphasizing the

---

[104] Cf. (for example) *AP* 5. 23 (Callimachus) Οὕτως ὑπνώσαις, Κωνώπιον, ὡς ἐμὲ ποιεῖς | κοιμᾶσθαι ψυχροῖς τοῖσδε παρὰ προθύροις; [Theocr]. 23 (the lover hanging himself before his beloved's door is a dramatic extension of the topos); Tib. 1. 2. 3–4, 2. 4. 22 *ne iaceam clausam flebilis ante domum*; Prop. 1. 16. 23–4 *me mediae noctes, me sidera plena iacentem, | frigidaque Eoo me dolet aura gelu.*

[105] For the motif compare Tib. 1. 2, esp. 7–14, an anti-hymn to the *ianua*; Ov. *Am.* 1. 6, where a *ianitor* takes the place of the *ianua*; Hor. *Carm.* 1. 25, 3. 10; Prop. 1. 16. For *supplex* as a word of erotic pleading cf. Pease (1935) on Virg. *Aen.* 4. 424; Tib. 1. 2. 14, 2. 6. 33; Prop. 1. 9. 3, 1. 16. 14, 2. 14. 11, 2. 20. 33, 4. 5. 37; Ov. *Am.* 1. 7. 61, 2. 5. 49; *Ars* 1. 713.

barrier to be penetrated above the notional target inside.
The epithet *durae*, frequently applied to the unwilling
girl,[106] subliminally (although not grammatically) transfers
itself on to the *postibus*, the doorposts which are both
literally and metaphorically, both actually and morally,
duris.

The crowning glory of the *komos* is the reveller's garland
left as a token on his mistress's doorpost. The topos is
common in epigram.[107] The lover's body was a dedicatory
offering to his beloved (*ponere*, v. 524), just like the withering
garland (*pone*, v. 528). The coaxing flattery which the lover
is to pour forth on to the deaf ears of girl and door is the
song of the elegiac paraclausithyron. If he is learning to be
an elegiac lover, he is also learning to be an elegiac poet—
he is learning poetry for access. In the self-conscious and
self-centred psychology of elegy, it is the lover himself on
whom the *blanditiae* ('blandishments') are most effective,
feeding his love through concentration and frustration. As
the lover coaxes the doorpost, he himself is coaxed by the
poem, and the *Ars* itself is the ultimate *blanditia*.

Yardley (1987: 182), in his study of comic influences on
Roman elegy, says that *blandiri* is Plautine, and is very rare
in elegy, occurring only in *Am*. 1. 8. 103, 2. 11. 54, *Her*. 20.
195, and our passage. What the elegiac lover does is certainly *blandiri*, however. The outspoken signifier of the
lover's behaviour, taken from the more forthright diction of
comedy, exposes the workings of elegy, about which elegy
itself is more discreet. The slave go-between is also a comic
character, who also appears in Hellenistic epigram, and it is
a convention in comedy, adopted by Ovid, that slaves are
deceitful (see Duckworth 1971: particularly 151–75), so
that all those bribes and kindly services which the lover
gave (vv. 251–60) have been conveniently forgotten. The *iste*
with which the *ancilla* dismisses the lover is, according to
Tränkle (1960: 162) and Axelson (1945: 71) an 'unpoetic

---

[106] Cf. e.g. Tib. 1. 8. 50, 2. 6. 28; Hor. *Carm*. 3. 7. 32; Prop. 1. 1. 10, 1. 7. 6;
Ov. *Am*. 1. 9. 19.

[107] Cf. *AP* 5. 145 (Asclepiades) Αὐτοῦ μοι στέφανοι παρὰ δικλίσι ταῖσδε κρεμα-
στοὶ | μίμνετε, 191. 5–6 (Meleager) ἐπὶ προθύροισι μαράνας | δάκρυσιν ἐκδήσω τοὺς
ἱκέτας στεφάνους. In Latin cf. Tib. 1. 2. 13–14 *te meminisse decet quae plurima uoce
peregi* | *supplice cum posti florida serta darem*. See Murgatroyd (1980) for parallels.

word', belonging to *uox uulgaris*, and as such it is appropriate to the context.[108] Appropriately, the slave-girl's diction is comic. Military imagery such as we have in *obsidet* is even more common in comedy than in elegy;[109] and *foras* ('outdoors') is a colloquial word, common in comedy.[110]

In the sense that we have met this figure before, our *ancilla* is decidedly *mendax*, since we have reason to believe that she knows the lover very well, not only from his services at vv. 251–60, but also from the suggestion of 1. 375–98. There Ovid considers the advantages and disadvantages of seducing the slave-girl as well as the mistress. His conclusion is that the mistress should come first, but that the most important point to remember is that if the lover makes advances to the slave, he must carry it through, as the speaker himself showed in *Am.* 2. 7 and 8.

The final three couplets of this section are about power (vv. 529–34):

> *cum uolet, accedes; cum te uitabit, abibis:*
> *dedecet ingenuos taedia ferre sui.*
> *'effugere hunc non est' quare tibi possit amica*
> *dicere? non omni tempore †sensus obest†.*
> *nec maledicta puta nec uerbera ferre puellae*
> *turpe nec ad teneros oscula ferre pedes.*

When she wants you, approach her; when she avoids you, go away.
It is unseemly for free-born men to make a nuisance of themselves.
Why should your girlfriend be able to say 'You can't get away from this one'?
†Good sense is not always an obstacle†
Do not think it foul to bear the curses and lashes
of your mistress, or to bring kisses to her tender feet.

---

[108] Tränkle's note refers to Prop. 1. 8. 3 *et tibi iam tanti, quicumque est, iste uidetur*. There, as here, the speaker disparages the person referred to, and tries to pretend he neither knows nor cares who he is.

[109] Cf. e.g. Pl. *Bac.* 948, in an extended military metaphor, *nunc facio opsidium Ilio, Mil.* 219–29 (no surprising place for military imagery).

[110] Cf. *TLL* 6. 1. 1034. 74, 'uoces praecipue sermonis uulgaris. legitur inde a Plauto, raro apud poetas melioris latinitatis', Axelson (1945) 96, who shows that it is fairly common (33 occurrences) in Lucretius.

In the first couplet, it is the mistress who calls the tune; in the second, she (potentially) despises the lover; and in the third, he is a helpless elegiac slave enthralled to his mistress and willing to undergo the most servile punishments for her sake.[111] The girl is now signified by her most elegiac sobriquet, *puella*. All three scenes are ways of keeping the lover involved and moulding his self-image. They are also paradoxical ways of 'holding' a mistress. You can win by losing; you can hold on by letting go; you can be in control by being a slave.

Variation, as here in these different scenes from erotic life offered, is a device by which girls, lovers, readers are held. But perhaps it is the modern critic who is most in danger of seduction here, for the passage seems to offer clues to that 'great unsolved question' of Roman elegy about the social status of the mistress. I shall argue that it is in a sense a non-question, but since it is one which has been frequently debated it remains important within the discourse of the criticism of elegy, and therefore is very much a question.[112] The discussion, which often seeks to construct a precise social situation into which the beloved can be slotted, is concerned with her social status, and therefore necessarily with her marital status. It is an interest which stems from the biographical imperative, and at times may reflect a desire to protect the morality (or at least emotional acceptability) of the man, who tends to be identified to a greater or lesser extent with the poet himself, and whose social status appears to be assumed to be unproblematical. The possibilites for social status are many, since social status is so nebulous and shifting a concept: those most commonly introduced into the discussion are (*a*) 'common' prostitute (usually rejected); (*b*) someone else's wife (popu-

---

[111] See Murgatroyd (1980) on Tib. 1. 5. 5, 1. 9. 21 for the motif of servile punishments. Prostration is not honourable supplication but degraded self-abasement. Cf. Tib. 1. 9. 30 *nunc pudet ad teneros procubuisse pedes* (with Murgatroyd's note). Kissing the hand which oppresses one is a 'cliché of degradation' (J. G. W. Henderson 1976: 253–4 on Phaed. 5. 1) and an act of submission. Kissing the foot takes this act to extremes.

[112] On this point see my forthcoming article on 'Ovid and the Politics of Reading'. For the debate see e.g. Sullivan (1961), Sabot (1976: 459–64), Wyke (1987).

lar with some, but more often rejected); (*c*) a single or widowed woman of 'respectable' (i.e. middle- or upper-class) status (not often suggested); (*d*) something in between—a courtesan (usually the favourite, but in my opinion a dangerously deceptive piece of rhetoric). It is hardly surprising that no consensus has been reached on this matter, since it is not the right question. That is not to say that social distinctions are irrelevant, however, for we are invited to imagine many scenarios in which questions of social status are foregrounded,[113] but we are not given a set of consistent clues from which a simple, absolute answer will pop out.

In the case of the first two couplets here (vv. 529–32), we are in the world of comedy, as indeed is much of this passage, while still playing with elegy (they are not, of course, two separate worlds). In this scene, where the mistress comes unusually vividly to life, she takes on something of the role of a prostitute. If the girl can say '*effugere hunc non est*' ('You can't get away from this one'), then she is showing her meretricious elements. The scornful *hunc* matches the slave's *iste*. In this comic scene, the signifier for the mistress is telling: *amica* is not a simply neutral feminine of *amicus*, nor an equivalent to our 'girl-friend'. Of all the terms used for beloveds in Latin love poetry it seems to be the least respectful, although it is particularly difficult to determine the shades of its meaning. The four occurrences in Catullus all apply to a prostitute or make that derogatory suggestion. Catullus 110, an epigram concerned with the broken promise of sex, addresses Aufellina using the language of prostitution, while ostentatiously emphasizing her high social status. Tibullus does not have the word, while Propertius and Ovid show a marked preference against it. The statistics for their usage of *amica*, *domina*, and *puella* (not necessarily applying to their mistress) are as follows: Propertius—9:32:122, Ovid—30 (28 in the amatory poetry):129 (96):260 (221). Ovid does not use *amica* in the *Metamorphoses*, and only twice in the *Fasti*. In many, although by no means all, of the instances of *amica*, the

---

[113] *Am.* 1. 4 is an obvious example.

context suggests a relatively low tone.[114] The word is 'non-poetic', its cruder associations occurring in situations suitable for comic treatment. One would have to argue the case for almost every occurrence of the word in Propertius. What, for example, should one make of the paradoxical 2. 30. 23 [*nec*] *una contentum pudeat me uiuere amica* ('I would not be ashamed to live content with one girlfriend')? At 2. 6. 41–2 there is clearly an opposition between *amica* and respectable wife:

> *nos uxor numquam, numquam seducet amica:*
> *semper amica mihi, semper et uxor eris.*

> No wife will ever seduce me from you, nor any girlfriend:
> you will always be wife and girlfriend to me.

Wife and whore perhaps? This is one of the few occasions where the word is used in a poem actually addressing the beloved.[115]

How should we imagine the elegiac mistress? More to the point, should we imagine the elegiac mistress at all, in the sense of trying to give her a unified reality? Her status is not consistent, for she is made to play out a variety of social and erotic roles in different situations. Although the language of ordinary social discourse is involved in the way a lover envisages himself and his beloved, nevertheless poetry does not map on to 'real life' so simply. But then, one might say, neither does life, for as is becoming increasingly recognized, our social roles are constructs in a way similar to the constructions of fiction. The implication in elegy of particular social categories in particular situations may indeed have contributed to the construction of those categories.

4*j* Afterword: Where do we Go from Here?

My criteria for the selection of passages for this study are subjective and constitute an imposition on the text. It is an imposition, however, which may facilitate the exposition of reading for which I am aiming: for, first, all of us in

---

[114] Note e.g. Ov. *Am.* 1. 6. 45, addressed to the slave janitor, *forsitan et tecum tua nunc requiescit amica.*

[115] Now didn't I say that the modern critic is in danger of seduction here?

our reading practices subdivide texts and, perhaps semi-consciously, find 'paragraphs', so to speak, to make the whole more manageable, and those divisions are subjective, although not usually chaotic; and, more importantly, I would suggest that the excising for hermeneutic purposes of the Daedalus episode should be no more (and no less) comfortable than that of Apollo, or that of the disquisition on magic. I take further justification for choosing this section, the epiphany of Apollo and its sequel, from the disruption to the thread of the book which the passage has caused. That 'disruption' is of course itself the result of an act of interpretation, not an absolute within the text, but it has been the argument of this book that *all* encounters with texts are acts of interpretation, and that texts do not have internal absolutes. Since this confusion to the quasi-narrative line has made an important contribution to my reading, it has seemed appropriate to link the Apollo scene and its sequel to the surrounding passages (but how wide is a 'wider context'?). On leaving Ovid's miniature *Ars Amatoria*, we receive advice on how to cope with a rival, for which the manipulation of the lover's self-image into 'suffering lover' was essential, and on into the politically charged story of the adultery of Mars and Venus.[116] That is, we are going to have some more manipulation, more generic play, and most importantly, some more 'repetition', of the commonplaces of elegy and of the stories of myth. But after the entry of Apollo, we have learned how to read art. The Apollo scene and its sequel together constitute a paradigm for a reading strategy, for they parade the intertextuality which is the necessary component of the intelligibility of any work: that is, of the act of reading itself. Varied repetition, paraded intertextuality, literary playfulness: these are elements of Ovid's Callimacheanism, with which this chapter, and to a greater or lesser extent the whole book, has been concerned. Ovid's song contest with Apollo shows us that the shortness in the judgement that 'short is good' must depend on criteria other than simple number of verses.

---

[116] On which see my forthcoming article on 'Ovid and the Politics of Reading'.

A final point: this passage with which Ovid replies to Apollo illustrates the hard work necessary to be a truly artistic lover, in preparation for Ovid's eroticized version of the proverb that success involves a struggle (v. 537):[117]

> *ardua molimur, sed nulla, nisi ardua, uirtus.*
>
> Hard is the path we strive along, yet there is no virtue which is not hard.

Ovid's answer to his critics, characterized by Apollo, is that there is more to the sophisticated management of an advanced erotic relationship than simple display of prowess in singing or drinking. There is more to writing love poetry than the simple arrangement of erotic topoi. Lover, beloved, and reader must all be subtly and subliminally manipulated into playing the roles defined for them by the *artifex amoris*—and that can only be done by *ars*.

> *per ardua ad astra*
>
> It's not easy being a lover.

[117] See Otto (1962: 36), Hor. *Carm.* 3. 2.

5

Thus We See? Re-reading 'Reading the *Ars Amatoria*'

So how *do* you keep a reader? Answer: you repeat the seduction—differently. Keeping a girl involves finding new ways of catching, seducing, 'wooing' her, over and over again, the same old story: *aliter idem*, the same differently. But when is repetition 'the same'? The phrase 'I love you' is always and never a quotation, always and never the same.[1] It is always a repetition and as such is general, but also always particular. In interaction (intercourse?) with the text of Ovid, the acts of reading and loving are collapsed into an identification, according to which the story Ovid tells of the maintenance of a relationship is as poetic as it is erotic. It is a story of metapoetry. We make sense of relationships against the background of other relationships, both our own and those we encounter at second hand: likewise, we make sense of reading, as of any act of communication, by means of reference to other readings. Ovid's display of repetition as the root of erotic success could perhaps be taken as paragidmatic for communication itself, for it is the iterability of any piece of language that makes it intelligible.[2]

I have been concerned throughout this book with the nature of reading as re-reading: the reader's re-reading of any given text; the reader's reading of other readings of a text; 'the text's reading' of other texts and readings (but what is the difference between a text and a reading? when are they 'the same'?); and all of those *re*peated. Where has this reading brought us? Back to the beginning, to a

---

[1] In thoughts of this nature I am generally indebted to Barthes (1979).
[2] This is of course a 'Derridean' point.

re-reading of *Reading Ovid's Ars Amatoria*.[3] Will this retrospect, which seeks to draw together something of what the book has been about, be a repetition? Will it be the same or different? I seek to make it a paradigmatic iteration, a 'difference in sameness', but will it turn out to have changed the original reading? Perhaps re-reading always does.

In any act of reading, there will always be many levels at work. Indeed, this is one way of visualizing the simultaneous difference and sameness involved in iteration: every time we read something, we play the role of a reader for whom this is new, while at the same time playing other reading roles which are not. It is in both the gap and the communication between these levels of reading that intelligibility can occur. The simultaneous separation and identification between levels of reading has been crucial to my thesis, in the argument that the foregrounded Reader of didactic is both a fictional construct of the text, whose education we are to witness from a vantage-point of distant superiority, and also a focus for our own act of reading: he is us.[4] When he is caught, so are we.

And what about the author? I have written much about the status of Reader and reader in the *Ars*, and about the need for both identification and separation between the two. The author also plays out many roles: poet—elegiac, didactic, Callimachean; teacher—kindly and a little pedantic, in the didactic tradition; manipulator—both erotic and poetic; lover—both passing on his wisdom as acquired as the lover in straight elegy, and directly as lover of his pupil. As both readers and pupils, we will also identify with the author/teacher. We will identify, but we will also confront. Of the many possible metaphors for the relationship of reader and author, that of confrontation and the struggle for interpretative authority has been particularly often employed in the field of reader-response criticism. I wonder whether the story I am telling of that relationship in the

---

[3] That, approximately, was the title of the dissertation out of which this book grew. Now, at some years' remove, I am re-reading my reading. This is a preface.

[4] See my forthcoming article for discussion of the 'need' to play out the role of the pupil in didactic.

Ars Amatoria could be seen as a metaphor for the struggle between text and reader for authority as the locus of interpretation. (Do texts make meaning, the discussion goes, or do readers?) Ovid contends as teacher, seducer, manipulator, Author for supremacy over the reader/pupil, in such a way that perhaps the text wins, for the poet controls the reader. Or does he? It depends on how we read the reader. In so far as we see the reader (ourselves) as the passive recipient of advice, instruction, and poetry, the text wins. But if we see the reader as the constructor of the reading in which the poet is controller, the reader wins, for the reader has constructed the meaning. Readers make meaning according to various strategies (of which estimations as to the author's intention might be one), as prescribed by the text but wholly controlling it. To that extent, it would not be right to see meaning as arising in the negotiation between text and reader, attractive as that hypothesis might be: rather, one would need to see the generation of meaning as stemming from the creative power of the reader, using among other things the material of the text. Ovid only controls us through *our* act of reading, so perhaps we control him.

When in this story of desire I collapse the poet and the reader, I am reminded that a common criticism of Ovid has been excessive desire for himself. On this telling, Ovid becomes (his own) Narcissus. So, what is the value of Ovidian poetry?[5] The notion of repetition has been a way into this debate, for the frequent complaint has been that Ovid simply repeats the themes of earlier writers, and of himself, but less well. I cannot prove such critics wrong, for reading is a subjective business, although not an isolated one; but rather I have sought to offer a reading of Ovid in which repetition is given positive value. Moreover, this reading of positively charged repetition is a sign for the functioning of literature more generally, in that a discernible relationship with a tradition provides one important strategy for comprehension.

---

[5] Is Ovid facile? as the examination question asks. The answer, of course, is 'yes, and no'.

The big (or is it little?) question which has been at issue throughout much of this book is the nature of Ovid's Callimacheanism. Is Ovid Callimachean? We should note first the extent to which we have internalized the Roman poets' values, in that the implication of my question makes 'Callimachean' equal to 'good'. Callimachus himself is not, of course, universally admired by modern critics, but the dominant trend in Roman literary studies has been to rate at least the -ism favourably. Indeed, the 'excess' with which Ovid is so often charged could be seen as an objection in Callimachean terms. (It is bad for Ovid to be excessive because it is anti-Callimachean, the argument might go.) Perhaps, however, it is useful for us to have internalized the value, for it is in terms of a positive value rather than a rigid set of poetic principles that Callimachean language functions in Roman poetry. All Latin poets, at least from Catullus on, claim to be Callimachean, although the terms of their claim may vary according to their particular pro-grammatic purpose at the time. Even Virgil writing the *Aeneid*, in some sense as anti-Callimachean an act as you could ask for, can be described as Callimachean. What is so great about his endeavour is that it involves braving the high seas of epic while still maintaining Callimachean princi-ples, when 'Callimachean' equals 'good artistic'. That's one way the language can be manipulated: another is to view the 'great endeavour' as something which transcends the activities of ordinary mortals and so transcends Callimache-anism without losing poetic success, and indeed without destroying the positive value of Callimacheanism. And there would be other ways of playing it as well.

To return to the question: is Ovid Callimachean? My answer would be yes, but in a complex manner, always remembering the possibility that it is a circular question. Ovid is playing around with the idea of being and also of *not* being Callimachean, which (being playful, that is) is a Callimachean thing to do. But isn't he excessive? Isn't excess the opposite of Callimacheanism? Yes (to both), and on the other hand no. A simple way of approaching this problem is the claim, which I would indeed want to make, that many instances of so-called Ovidian excess are in fact highly functional. I have taken the story of Daedalus and Icarus as paradigmatic of this functionality of excess for two reasons: (1) it constitutes an extreme case of excess, in its magnificent disproportion (on a simple level) with the point supposedly illustrated by it; and (2) its function is itself, in my reading, to do with the nature of Callimacheanism. It is a story which both in medium and in message confronts the issue of excess. I have linked the story of Daedalus and Icarus with the epiphany of Apollo for similar reasons. Apollo, as god of Callimachean poetry, comes and tells Ovid he is doing it wrong: Ovid tells him he isn't.

When we come to consider the nature of Ovid's Callimacheanism, however, things become a little more problematical. It should always be borne in mind that Ovid, in common with other Roman poets, uses the language of Callimachean poetics not as one coherent system but as it suits him at any one time. We cannot simply solve the puzzle and read off a set of principles for writing poetry. One can perhaps take refuge in paradox and say that the *Ars Amatoria* teaches you how to be excessive and still be Callimachean; but surely one of the distinguishing factors of Callimachean poetry would be precisely littleness? So is it a 'little' poem? In my analysis of both Daedalus and Apollo, I have suggested that a sort of stylized programmatic 'littleness' is paraded while at the same time the possibility of 'writing big' is affirmed. Big can be beautiful: perhaps we should call it a littleness posing as being big while at the same time proclaiming its littleness. 'Little' is a metaphor for art, and art is good: that still seems a valid point to me. Yet, also, there is a sense in which when Ovid claims that his poem is 'little' (in the Callimachean sense) he is saying more than simply that it is good: he is saying that it is greater than elegy but less than epic, quite literally in its length and more nebulously in its style, and couching that in Callimachean terms—clever, learned, playful, ironic. The metaphor 'flight is daring' signifies that poetry is daring; that Callimachean poetry is daring, and that's a paradox which may undermine—but not destroy—the poetry's claim to be Callimachean; that you can be

Callimachean in any genre, but it is more daring to be so the 'higher' you go.[6]

Repetition—*referre aliter idem* ('to relate the same thing in different ways')—has been a sign under which I have examined the nature of Ovid's Callimacheanism, for it confronts the issue of originality which is always at stake in Callimachean poetics and in the common criticisms of Ovid. I have said that repetition is a means of seduction; and poetry itself is a form of seduction, as Icarus found when he flew to the heights. On whom, besides Icarus, does this seduction work? Reader-response criticism is not the only discursive field with an interest in power-relations: so, notoriously, has ancient love poetry. It has been a frequent sub-text in this book that the balance of power in Ovidian erotic society involves complex interactions, and that the question of who is seducing whom is always at issue. I have examined those relationships under the metaphor of magic, arguing that the *Ars* itself is a spell (a *carmen*) with great seductive power. Sex is magic; love is itself a seductive spell; poetry is magic, a spell by which both reader and poet are seduced. Just as texts are magically seductive, so is interpretation, so is theory. It is the act of reading that draws us into the poem. Reading about desire provokes the desire to read.

[6] I would not, incidentally, use this as an argument for a simple and absolute claim that poetry gets less or more Callimachean as you go up and down a scale of genres, but that the poets sometimes pose as making an equation between low genres and Callimacheanism.

REFERENCES

For a note on the abbreviations used please refer to the list on pp. xiii–xiv.

ADAMS, J. N. (1982), *Latin Sexual Vocabulary*, London.

AHERN, C. F. JUN. (1989), 'Daedalus and Icarus in the *Ars Amatoria*', *H.S.Ph.* 92: 273–96.

——(1990), 'Ovid as *Vates* in the Proem to the *Ars Amatoria*', *C.Ph.* 85: 44–8.

AHL, F. M. (1985), *Metaformations: Soundplay and Wordplay in Ovid and Other Classical Poets*, New York.

ALBRECHT, M. VON (1977), ' "Epische" und "elegische" Erzähl-ung. Ovids zwei Daedalus-Fassungen: Dichtung in psycholo-gischer und universaler Dimension', in *Römische Poesie: Text und Interpretation*, Heidelberg: 63–79.

——(1982), 'Ovide et ses lecteurs', *REL* 59: 207–15.

ALLEN, W. S. (1965), *Vox Latina*, Cambridge.

AMANDRY, P. (1950), *La Mantique apollinienne à Delphes*, Paris.

ANDERSON, W. S. (1969*a*), *The Art of the Aeneid*, Englewood Cliffs, NJ.

——(1969*b*), Review of Bernbeck (1967), *A.J.Ph.* 90: 352–5.

Arethusa, 19/2 (1986), *Audience-Oriented Criticism and the Classics.*

ARMSTRONG, D. (1964), 'Second Thoughts on Fraenkel's Horace', *Arion*, 3: 116–28.

ASHTON, J. W. (1941), 'The Fall of Icarus', *Ph.Q.* 20: 345–51.

AXELSON, B. (1945), *Unpoetische Wörte*, Lund.

BAILEY, C. (1947), *Titi Lucreti Cari De Rerum Natura Libri Sex*, vol. ii, Oxford.

BARSBY, J. A. (1978), *Ovid*, Greece and Rome New Surveys in the Classics, Oxford.

BARTHES, R. (1979), *A Lover's Discourse: Fragments*, trans. R. Nice, London.

BASSI, K. (1989), 'The Poetics of Exclusion in Callimachus' *Hymn to Apollo*', *T.A.Ph.A.* 119: 219–31.

BASTO, R. (1982), 'Horace's Propempticon to Vergil: A Re-exami-nation', *Vergilius*, 28: 30–43.

BECATTI, G. (1953–4), 'La leggenda di Dedalo', *MDAI(R)* 40–1: 22–36.

BECKER, O. (1937), *Das Bild des Weges*, Hermes Einzelschriften, 4, Wiesbaden.

BERGREN, A. L. T. (1981), 'Helen's "Good Drug": Odyssey IV 1–305', in S. Kresic (ed.), *Contemporary Literary Hermeneutics*, Ottawa: 201–14.

BERNBECK, E. (1967), *Beobachtungen zur Darstellungsart in Ovids Metamorphosen*, Zetemata, 43, Munich.

BINNICKER, C. M. (1967), 'Didactic Qualities in Ovid's Ars Amatoria', Ph.D. diss., University of N. Carolina at Chapel Hill.

BLODGETT, E. D. (1973), 'The Well Wrought Void: Reflections on the *Ars Amatoria*', *CJ* 68: 322–33.

BOARDMAN, J. (1974), *Athenian Black Figure Vases*, London.

——(1975), *Athenian Red Figure Vases*, London.

BÖMER, F. (1969–86), *P. Ovidius Naso: Metamorphosen*, Heidelberg.

BONNER, S. F. (1977), *Education in Ancient Rome*, London.

BOWRA, C. M. (1964), *Pindar*, Oxford.

BOYLE, A. J. (1972), 'The Meaning of the *Aeneid*. Critical Inquiry II: *Homo Immemor*. Book 6 and its Thematic Ramifications', *Ramus*, 1: 113–51.

BRAMBLE, J. (1974), '*Qui non dictus Hylas puer?*: Propertius 1.20', in A. J. Woodman and D. West (eds.), *Quality and Pleasure in Latin Poetry*, Cambridge: 81–93.

BRANDT, P. (1902), *Ovid: De Arte Amatoria Libri Tres*, Leipzig.

BRINK, C. O. (1971), *Horace on Poetry: The Ars Poetica*, Cambridge.

BRUNNER, T. F. (1966), 'The Function of Simile in Ovid's *Metamorphoses*', *CJ* 61: 354–63.

——(1971), 'Δεινόν vs. ἐλεεινόν: Heinze Revisited', *A.J.Ph.* 92: 275–84.

BUNDY, E. L. (1972), 'The Quarrel between Kallimachos and Apollonios', *CSCA* 5: 39–94.

BURMAN, P. (1727), *Ovid: Opera Omnia*, Amsterdam.

CAIRNS, F. J. (1969), 'Catullus I', *Mnemosyne*, 22: 153–8.

——(1972), *Generic Composition in Greek and Roman Poetry*, Edinburgh.

——(1973), 'Catullus' *Basia* Poems (5, 7, 48)', *Mnemosyne*, 26: 15–22.

——(1975), *Further Adventures of a Locked-out Lover: Propertius 2.17*, Liverpool.

——(1984a), 'Propertius and the Battle of Actium', in A. J.

Woodman and D. West (eds.), *Poetry and Politics in the Age of Augustus*, Cambridge: 129–68.

——(1984*b*), 'Theocritus' First *Idyll*: The Literary Programme', *WS* 18: 89–113.

CANTER, H. V. (1933), 'The Mythological Paradigm in Greek and Latin Poetry', *A.J.Ph.* 54: 201–24.

CARRUBBA, R. W. (1982), 'The White Swan and Daedalian Icarus', *Eranos*, 80: 145–9.

CARSON, A. (1986), *Eros the Bittersweet*, Princeton, NJ.

CARTLEDGE, P. (1981), 'The Politics of Spartan Pederasty', *P.C.Ph.S.* 27: 17–36.

CHAMBERS, R. (1984), *Story and Situation: Narrative Seduction and the Power of Fiction*, Minneapolis.

CLASSEN, C. J. (1968), 'Poetry and Rhetoric in Lucretius', *T.A.Ph.A.* 99: 77–118.

CLAUSEN, W. (1976), '*Cynthius*', *A.J.Ph.* 97: 245–7.

——(1977), '*Cynthius*: Addendum', *A.J.Ph.* 98: 362.

CLAY, D. (1983), *Lucretius and Epicurus*, Ithaca, NY, and London.

COLETTI, M. L. (1981), 'Rassegna bibliografico-critica degli studi sulle opere amatorie di Ovidio dal 1958 al 1978', *ANRW* 2.31.4: 2385–435.

COPLEY, F. O. (1942), 'On the Origins of Certain Features of the Paraclausithyron', *T.A.Ph.A.* 73: 96–107.

——(1947), '*Seruitium amoris* in the Roman Elegists', *T.A.Ph.A.* 78: 285–300.

——(1956), *Exclusus amator: A Study in Latin Love Poetry*, Madison, Wis. (= Ann Arbor, Mich., 1978).

CRABBE, A. M. (1977), '*Ignoscenda quidem* . . . Catullus 64 and the Fourth Georgic', *CQ* 27: 342–51.

——(1981), 'Structure and Content in Ovid's *Metamorphoses*', *ANRW* 2.31.4: 2275–327.

CULLER, J. (1975), *Structuralist Poetics*, Ithaca, NY.

——(1981), *The Pursuit of Signs*, London.

——(1983), *On Deconstruction: Theory and Criticism after Structuralism*, London.

——(1988), *Framing the Sign: Criticism and its Institutions*, Oxford.

CUNNINGHAM, M. P. (1958), 'Ovid's Poetics', *CJ* 53: 253–9.

DAVIS, G. (1983), *The Death of Procris: 'Amor' and the Hunt in Ovid's Metamorphoses*, Rome.

DAVISSON, M. T. (1984), 'Parents and Children in Ovid's Poems from Exile', *CW* 78: 111–14.

DEFRADAS, J. (1954), *Les Thèmes de la propagande Delphique*, Paris.

DELCOURT, M. (1957), *Héphaïstos ou la légende du magicien*, Paris.

DERRIDA, J. (1981), *Dissemination*, trans. B. Johnson, London.

DILKE, O. A. W. (1982), 'La Tradition didactique chez Ovide', in R. Chevallier (ed.), *Colloque présence d'Ovide*, Paris: 9–15.

DODDS, E. R. (1951), *The Greeks and the Irrational*, Sather Classical Lectures 25, Berkeley, Calif., and Los Angeles.

DONNET, D. (1983), 'Intersections de schèmes sonores dans les Hymnes II et V de Callimaque', *LEC* 51: 219–31.

DOVER, K. J. (1971), *Theocritus: Select Poems*, London.

——(1978), *Greek Homosexuality*, London.

DuBOIS, P. (1982), *History, Rhetorical Description, and the Epic: From Homer to Spenser*, Cambridge and Totowa, NJ.

DUCKWORTH, G. E. (1971), *The Nature of Roman Comedy*, Princeton, NJ.

DUE, O. S. (1974), *Changing Forms: Studies in the Metamorphoses of Ovid*, Copenhagen.

DuQUESNAY, I. M. LeM. (1976), 'Virgil's Fourth *Eclogue*', *PLLS* 1: 25–99.

——(1979), 'From Polyphemus to Corydon: Virgil *Eclogue* 2 and the *Idylls* of Theocritus', in A. J. Woodman and D. West (eds.) *Creative Imitation and Latin Literature*, Cambridge: 35–69.

DURLING, R. M. (1958), 'Ovid as *praeceptor amoris*', *CJ* 53: 157–67.

EFFE, B. (1977), *Dichtung und Lehre: Untersuchungen zur Typologie des antiken Lehrgedichts*. Zetemata, 69, Munich.

EISENHUT, W. (1975), '*Deducere carmen*: Ein Beitrag zum Problem der literarischen Beziehungen zwischen Horaz und Properz', in W. Eisenhut (ed.), *Properz*, Darmstadt: 247–63.

ELDER, J. P. (1961), '*Non iniussa cano*: Virgil's Sixth *Eclogue*', *H.S.Ph.* 65: 109–25.

FARRINGTON, B. (1965), 'Form and Purpose in the *de Rerum Natura*', in D. R. Dudley (ed.) *Lucretius*, London: 19–34.

FAUTH, W. (1980), '*Venena Amoris*: die Motive des Liebeszaubers und der erotischen Verzauberung in der augusteischen Dichtung', *Maia*, 32: 265–82.

FEDELI, P. (1980), *Sesto Properzio: il primo libro delle Elegie*, Florence.

——(1985), *Sesto Properzio: il libro terzo delle Elegie*, Bari.

FEENEY, D. C. (1986), '"Stat magni nominis umbra": Lucan on the Greatness of Pompeius Magnus', *CQ* 36: 239–44.

FETTERLY, J. (1978), *The Resisting Reader: A Feminist Approach to American Literature*, Bloomington, Ind.

FISH, S. (1980), *Is There a Text in This Class? The Authority of Interpretative Communities*, Cambridge, Mass.

—— (1989), *Doing What Comes Naturally: Change, Rhetoric, and the Practice of Theory in Literary and Legal Studies*, Oxford.

FITZGERALD, W. (1984), 'Aeneas, Daedalus, and the Labyrinth', *Arethusa*, 17: 51–65.

FONTENROSE, J. (1959), *Python: a Study of the Delphic Myth and its Origins*, Berkeley, Calif.

FOWLER, D. P. (1991), 'Narrate and Describe: the Problem of Ekphrasis', *JRS* 81: 25–35.

FRAENKEL, E. (1957), *Horace*, Oxford.

FRÄNKEL, H. (1945), *Ovid: a Poet between Two Worlds*, Sather Classical Lectures 18, Berkeley, Calif., and Los Angeles (reprinted 1969).

FRÉCAUT, J.-M. (1972), *L'esprit et l'humour chez Ovide*, Grenoble.

FREUND, E. (1987), *The Return of the Reader: Reader-Response Criticism*, London and New York.

FRONTISI-DUCROUX, F. (1975), *Dédale: mythologie de l'artisan en Grèce ancienne*, Paris.

FYLER, J. M. (1971), '*Omnia uincit amor*: Incongruity and the Limitations of Structure in Ovid's Elegiac Poetry', *CJ* 66: 196–203.

GALINSKY, G. K. (1975), *Ovid's Metamorphoses: an Introduction to the Basic Aspects*, Oxford.

GAMEL, M. K. (1985), (ed.) *Contemporary Interpretations of Ovid*, In Memoriam Alison Goddard Elliot, *Helios*, 12.

GARIÉPY, R. J. JUN. (1970), 'Recent Scholarship on Ovid (1958–1968)', *CW* 64: 37–56.

GELZER, T. (1975), *Musaeus: Hero and Leander*, Loeb Classical Library, London.

GENETTE, G. (1972), *Figures III collection poétique* (Paris), trans. J. E. Lewis (1980), *Narrative Discourse*, Oxford: 65–282.

GOLDHILL, S. (1983), 'Narrative Sequence in Bacchylides 5', *Eranos*, 81: 65–81.

—— (1986), 'Framing and Polyphony: Readings in Hellenistic Poetry', *P.C.Ph.S.* 32: 25–52.

GOOLD, G. P. (1965), 'Amatoria Critica', *H.S.Ph.* 69: 1–107.

GOW, A. S. F. (1952), *Theocritus: Edited with a Translation and Commentary*, vol. ii, Cambridge.

GRIFFITH, M. (1983), 'Personality in Hesiod', *Cl.Ant.* 2: 37–65.

GRIFFITHS, F. T. (1979), *Theocritus at Court*, Mnemosyne suppl. 55, Leiden.

GRIGGS, M. J. (1971), *Ars Amatoria: Selections*, London.

HAIGHT, E. H. (1950), *Symbolism of the House Door in Classical Poetry*, New York.

HALPERIN, D. M., WINKLER, J. J., and ZEITLIN, F. I. (1989), *Before Sexuality: the Construction of Erotic Experience in the Ancient Greek World*, Princeton, NJ.

HARDIE, P. R. (1986), *Virgil's Aeneid: Cosmos and Imperium*, Oxford.

HEATH, M. (1985), 'Hesiod's Didactic Poetry', *CQ* 35: 245–63.

HEINZE, R. (1919), *Ovids Elegische Erzählung*, Leipzig (= Stuttgart, 1960: 308–403).

HELDMANN, V. K. (1981), '*Ovidius amoris artifex, Ovidius praeceptor Amoris* (zu *Ars am.* 1, 1–24)', *MH* 38: 162–6.

HENDERSON, A. A. R. (1983), *Manifestus deus: il motivo della teofania nella poesia d'amore di Ovidio*, Ovidiana, 6, Sulmona.

HENDERSON, J. G. W. (1976), 'Anecdote and Satire in Phaedrus: Commentary and Discussion', D.Phil. diss., Oxford.

HENDRICKSON, G. L. (1925), 'Verbal Imagery, Magic, or Erotic Comus', *C.Ph.* 20: 289–308.

HEYER, H. (1933), *Hymnische Stilelemente in der frühgriechischen Dichtung*, Wurzburg.

HINDS, S. E. (1985), 'Booking the Return Trip: Ovid and *Tristia* 1', *P.C.Ph.S.* 31: 13–32.

—— (1987), *The Metamorphosis of Persephone*, Cambridge.

—— (1992), '*Arma* in Ovid's *Fasti*', *Arethusa*, 25: 81–153.

HOLLIS, A. S. (1970), *Ovid: Metamorphoses Book 8*, Oxford.

—— (1973), 'The *Ars Amatoria* and *Remedia Amoris*', in J. W. Binns (ed.), *Ovid*, London: 84–115.

—— (1977), *Ovid: Ars Amatoria Book I*, Oxford.

HOLZBERG, N. (1981), 'Ovids erotische Lehrgedichte und die römische Liebeselegie', *WS* 15: 185–204.

HOPKINSON, N. (1984), *Callimachus: Hymn to Demeter*, Cambridge.

—— (1988), *A Hellenistic Anthology*, Cambridge.

HUNT, J. M. (1979), Review of Willis (1972), *C.Ph.* 74: 340–50.

HUTCHINSON, G. O. (1988), *Hellenistic Poetry*, Oxford.

INNES, D. C. (1979), 'Gigantomachy and Natural Philosophy', *CQ* 29: 165–71.

ISER, W. (1978), *The Act of Reading: A Theory of Aesthetic Response*, Baltimore.

JACKSON-KNIGHT, W. F. (1929), 'Virgil and the Maze', *CR* 43: 212–13.

JACOBUS, M. (1986), *Reading Woman: Essays in Feminist Criticism*, Columbia and London.

JAUSS, H. R. (1982), *Towards an Aesthetic of Reception*, trans. T. Bahti, Brighton.

JOHNSON, W. R. (1966), 'The Boastful Bird: Notes on Horatian Modesty', *CJ* 61: 272–5.

KENNEDY, D. F. (1980), 'A Commentary on Culex 1–156, with an Introductory Section Indicating the Poem's Likely Dependence on Cornelius Gallus', Ph.D. diss., Cambridge.

——(1983), 'Shades of Meaning: Virgil *Eclogue* 10. 75–7', *LCM* 8.8: 124.

——(1993), *The Arts of Love: Five Studies in the Discourse of Roman Love Elegy*, Cambridge.

KENNEY, E. J. (1958), '*Nequitiae Poeta*', in N. I. Herescu (ed.), *Ovidiana: recherches sur Ovide*, Paris: 201–9.

——(1959), 'Notes on Ovid 2', *CQ* 9: 240–60.

——(1970), 'Doctus Lucretius', *Mnemosyne*, 23: 366–92.

——(1972), Review of Bömer (1969), *CR* 22: 38–42.

——(1976), '*Ovidius Prooemians*', *P.C.Ph.S.* 22: 46–53.

KER, A. (1958), 'Notes on Some Passages in the Amatory Poems', in N. I. Herescu (ed.), *Ovidiana: recherches sur Ovide*, Paris: 224–8.

KETTEMANN, U. (1979), *Interpretationen zu Satz und Vers in Ovids erotischem Lehrgedicht*, Frankfurt.

KIDD, D. A. (1971), 'The Metamorphosis of Horace', *AUMLA* 35: 5–16.

KINSEY, T. E. (1986), 'Pictures on Temple Doors: Virgil *Aeneid* 6. 9–14', *LCM* 11.8: 137.

KIRK, G. J., and RAVEN, J. E. (1957), *The Pre-Socratic Philosophers*, Cambridge.

KIRKWOOD, G. M. (1981), 'Pindar's Ravens: *Olymp.* 2. 87', *CQ* 31: 240–3.

KLEVE, K. (1983), 'NASO MAGISTER ERAT—sed quis Nasonis magister?', *SO* 58: 89–109.

KLING, H. (1970), 'Zur Komposition des 2. Buches der "Ars Amatoria"', in E. Zinn (ed.), *Ovids Ars Amatoria und Remedia Amoris: Untersuchungen zum Aufbau*, Stuttgart: 35–43.

KNAAK, G. (1902), 'Zur Sage von Daidalos und Ikaros', *Hermes*, 37: 267–71.

KNAUER, G. N. (1964), 'Vergil's *Aeneid* and Homer', *GRBS* 5: 61–84.

KNOX, P. E. (1986), *Ovid's Metamorphoses and the Tradition of Elegy*, P.C.Ph.S. Suppl. 11, Cambridge.

KOSTER, S. (1983), *Tessera: Sechs Beiträge zur Poesie und poetischen Theorie der Antike*, Erlangen.

KRIS, E., and KURZ, O. (1979), *Legend, Myth, and Magic in the Image of the Artist: A Historical Experiment*, New Haven, Conn., and London.

KROKOWSKI, J. (1963), '*Ars Amatoria*—poème didactique', *Eos*, 53: 143–56.

KROLL, W. (1924), *Studien zum Verständnis der römischen Literatur*, Stuttgart.

KROMER, G. (1979), 'The Didactic Tradition in Virgil's *Georgics*', in A. J. Boyle (ed.), *Virgil's Ascraean Song: Ramus Essays on the Georgics*, Victoria: 7–21.

KÜHNER, R., and STEGMANN, C. (1966), *Ausführliche Grammatik der Lateinischen Sprache*, Hanover.

KÜPPERS, E. (1981), 'Ovids *Ars Amatoria* und *Remedia Amoris* als Lehrdichtungen', *ANRW* 2.31.4: 2507–551.

LABATE, M. (1984), *L'arte di farsi amare: modelli culturali e progetto didascalico nell'elegia ovidiana*, Pisa.

LATEINER, D. (1984), 'Mythic and Non-mythic Artists in Ovid's *Metamorphoses*', *Ramus*, 13: 1–30.

LEACH, E. W. (1964), 'Georgic Imagery in the *Ars Amatoria*', *T.A.Ph.A.* 95: 142–54.

——(1974), 'Ekphrasis and the Theme of Artistic Failure in Ovid's *Metamorphoses*', *Ramus*, 3: 102–42.

LEFKOWITZ, M. R. (1969), 'Bacchylides Ode 5', *H.S.Ph.* 73: 45–96.

——(1981), *Lives of the Greek Poets*, London.

LENZ, F. W. (1939), 'Ovid: Bericht über das Schrifttum der Jahre 1928–1937', *Bursians Jahresbericht* 264: 1–168.

——(1961), 'Das Proömium von Ovids *Ars Amatoria*', *Maia*, 13: 131–42.

LEUMANN, M., HOFMANN, J. B., and SZANTYR, A. (1965–79), *Lateinische Grammatik*, Munich.

LÉVI-STRAUSS, C. (1958), *Anthropologie Structurale*, Paris.

LEWIS, J. M. (1985), 'Eros and the Polis in Theognis Book II', in T. J. Figueira and G. Nagy (eds.), *Theognis of Megara: Poetry and the Polis*, Baltimore: 197–222.

LIPKING, L. (1981), *The Life of the Poet: Beginning and Ending Poetic Careers*, Chicago.

LITTLE, D. (1970), 'Richard Heinze: *Ovids elegische Erzählung*', in E. Zinn (ed.), *Ovids Ars Amatoria und Remedia Amoris*, Stuttgart: 64–105.

LLOYD, G. E. R. (1979), *Magic, Reason, and Experience*, Cambridge.

—— (1983), *Science, Folklore, and Ideology*, Cambridge.

LLOYD-JONES, H., and PARSONS, P. (1983), *Supplementum Hellenisticum*, Berlin and New York.

LOCKYER, C. W. (1967), 'Horace's Propemptikon and Virgil's Voyage', *CW* 61: 42–5.

LUCK, G. (1985), *Arcana Mundi*, Baltimore.

LYNE, R. O. A. M. (1979), '*Seruitium Amoris*' *CQ* 29: 117–30.

—— (1984), 'Ovid's *Metamorphoses*, Callimachus, and l'art pour l'art', *MD* 12: 9–34.

McLAUGHLIN, J. D. (1975), 'The Relevancy of the Mythological Episodes to Ovid's Ars Amatoria', Ph.D. diss., Ann Arbor, Mich.

MARCHESI, C. (1918), 'Il secondo e il terzo libro dell' *Ars Amatoria*', *RFIC* 46: 41–77.

MARTINDALE, C. A. (1993), *Redeeming the Text: Latin Poetry and the Hermeneutics of Reception*, Cambridge.

MASTERS, J. (1992), *Poetry and Civil War in Lucan's Bellum Civile* (Cambridge).

MILES, G. B. (1980), *Virgil's Georgics: a New Interpretation*, Berkeley, Calif., and Los Angeles.

MILLER, J. F. (1983), 'Callimachus and the *Ars Amatoria*', *C.Ph.* 78: 26–34.

—— (1986), 'Disclaiming Divine Inspiration: a Programmatic Pattern', *WS* 20: 151–64.

MOST, G. (1987), 'The 'Virgilian' *Culex*', in M. Whitby, P. Hardie, and M. Whitby (eds.), *Homo Viator: Classical Essays for John Bramble*, Bristol: 199–209.

MURGATROYD, P. (1980), *Tibullus I*, Pietermaritzburg.

—— (1982), *Ovid with love: Selections from Ars Amatoria I and II*, Chicago.

—— (1984), 'Amatory Hunting, Fishing, and Fowling', *Latomus*, 43: 362–8.

MURGIA, C. E. (1986), 'The Date of Ovid's *Ars Amatoria*', *A.J.Ph.* 107: 74–94.

MYEROWITZ, M. (1985), *Ovid's Games of Love*, Detroit.

NAGLE, B. R. (1988), 'A Trio of Love-triangles in Ovid's *Metamorphoses*', *Arethusa*, 21: 75–98.

NEWMAN, J. K. (1967), *The Concept of Vates in Augustan Poetry*, Coll. Latomus 89, Brussels.

NISBET, R. G. M. (1978), 'Virgil's Fourth *Eclogue*: Easterners and Westerners', *BICS* 25: 59–78.

—— and HUBBARD, M. (1970), *A Commentary on Horace Odes I*, Oxford.

—— (1978), *A Commentary on Horace Odes II*, Oxford.

NORDEN, E. (1913), *Agnostos Theos: Untersuchungen zur Formengeschichte religiöser Rede*, Leipzig and Berlin.

——(1916), *P Vergilius Maro: Aeneis Buch VI*, Berlin.

NORTH H. (1966), *Sophrosyne: Self-Knowledge and Self-Restraint in Greek Literature*, Ithaca, NY.

OGLE, M. B. (1910), 'Laurel in Ancient Religion and Folk-lore', *A.J.Ph.* 31: 287–311.

——(1911), 'The House Door in Greek and Roman Religion and Folk-lore', *A.J.Ph.* 32: 251–71.

OSBOURNE, C. (1987), 'Empedocles Recycled', *CQ* 37: 24–50.

OTIS, B. (1966), *Ovid as an Epic Poet*, Cambridge.

OTTO, A. (1962), *Die Sprichwörter und sprichwörtlichen Redensarten der Römer*, Hildesheim.

OWEN, S. G. (1924), *Ovid: Tristium Liber Secundus*, Oxford.

PARKE, H. W., and WORMELL, D. E. W. (1956), *The Delphic Oracle*, Oxford.

PARSONS, P. J. (1977), 'Callimachus: *Victoria Berenices*', *ZPE* 25: 1–50.

PASCAL, C. B. (1980), 'Another Look at the Swan Ode', *Latomus*, 39: 98–108.

PASCHALIS, M. (1986), 'Virgil and the Delphic Oracle', *Philologus*, 130: 44–68.

PEARSON, C. S. (1969), 'Aspects of Imagery in the Works of Ovid', Ph.D. diss., Baltimore.

PEASE, A. S. (1935), *Vergil: Aeneidos Liber Quartus*, Darmstadt.

PENWILL, J. L. (1978), 'Men in Love: Aspects of Plato's Symposium', *Ramus*, 7: 143–75.

PFEIFFER, R. (1922), *Kallimachosstudien*, Munich.

——(1949), *Callimachus*, vol. 1, Oxford.

——(1952), 'The Image of Delian Apollo and Apolline Ethics', *JWI*: 20–32.

——(1953), *Callimachus*, vol. 2, Oxford.

PICHON, R. (1902), *Index Verborum Amatoriorum*, Paris (= Hildesheim, 1966).

PLATNAUER, M. (1951), *Latin Elegiac Verse*, Cambridge.

PÖHLMANN, E. (1973), 'Charakteristike des römischen Lehrgedichts', *ANRW* 1.3: 813–901.

PORTER, D. H. (1975), 'The Recurrent Motifs of Horace, *Carmina* IV', *H.S.Ph.* 79: 189–228.

——(1987), *Horace's Poetic Journey: A Reading of Odes 1–3*, Princeton, NJ.

PÖSCHL, V. (1962), *The Art of Virgil: Image and Symbol in the Aeneid*, Ann Arbor, Mich.

PRESCOTT, H. W. (1927), *The Development of Virgil's Art*, Chicago.

PRIDIK, K.-H. (1970), 'Bibliographie zu den Carmina amatoria (1936–1968)', in E. Zinn (ed.), *Ovids Ars amatoria und Remedia amoris: Untersuchungen zum Aufbau*, Stuttgart: 110–16.

PRINZ, K. (1914), 'Untersuchungen zu Ovids *Remedia Amoris*', *WS* 36: 36–83.

PUCCI, P. (1979), 'The Song of the Sirens', *Arethusa*, 12: 121–32.

PUTNAM, M. C. J. (1979), *Virgil's Poem of the Earth: Studies in the Georgics*, Princeton, NJ.

——(1987), 'Daedalus, Virgil, and the End of Art', *A.J.Ph.* 108: 173–98.

QUINN, K. (1980), *Horace: the Odes*, London.

REITZENSTEIN, E. (1931), 'Zur Stiltheorie des Kallimachos', in *Festschrift Richard Reitzenstein*, Leipzig and Berlin: 23–69.

RENZ, H. (1935), *Mythologische Beispiele in Ovids erotischer Elegie*, Ph.D. diss., Tubingen.

RIFFATERRE, M. (1990), 'Compulsory Reader Response: the Intertextual Drive', in M. Worton and J. Still (eds.), *Intertextuality: Theories and Practices*, Manchester: 56–78.

ROMANO, A. C. (1972), 'Ovid's *Ars Amatoria* or the Art of Outmanœuvering the Partner', *Latomus*, 31: 814–19.

ROSE, H. J. (1928), *A Handbook of Greek Mythology*, London.

ROSS, D. O. (1975), *Backgrounds to Augustan Poetry: Gallus, Elegy and Rome*, Cambridge.

RUCK, C. A. P. (1972), 'Marginalia Pindarica, 4–6', *Hermes*, 100: 143–69.

RUDD, N. (1976), *Lines of Enquiry: Studies in Latin Poetry*, Cambridge.

——(1988), 'Daedalus and Icarus (i): from Rome to the End of the Middle Ages', in C. Martindale (ed.), *Ovid Renewed*, Cambridge: 21–35.

RUSTEN, J. S. (1982), 'Ovid, Empedocles, and the Minotaur', *A.J.Ph.* 103: 332–3.

RUTLEDGE, H. C. (1967), 'Vergil's Daedalus', *CJ* 62: 309–11.

SABBADINI, R. (1909), 'Per la cronologia delle poesie amorose d'Ovidio', *RFIC* 37: 166–9.

SABOT, A.-F. (1976), *Ovide: poète de l'amour dans ses œuvres de jeunesse*, Ophrys.

ST DENIS, E. DE (1935), *Le Rôle de la mer dans la poésie latine*, Paris.

SCIVOLETTO, N. (1976), *Musa iocosa: studio sulla poesia giovanile di Ovidio*, Rome.

SCOTT, K. (1930), 'Emperor Worship in Ovid', *T.A.Ph.A.* 61: 43–69.

SEGAL, C. P. (1965), '*Aeternum per saecula nomen*: the Golden Bough and the Tragedy of History', *Arion*, 4: 617–57.

—— (1989), *Orpheus: the Myth of the Poet*, Baltimore.

SHAPIRO, H. A. (1981), 'Courtship Scenes in Attic Vase-painting', *AJA* 85: 133–43.

SHARROCK, A. R. (1987), '*Ars Amatoria* 2.123–42: Another Homeric Scene in Ovid', *Mnemosyne*, 40: 406–12.

—— (1990), '*Alternae Voces*—Again', *CQ* 40: 570–1.

—— (1991), 'The Love of Creation' *Ramus* 20: 169–82.

—— (forthcoming), 'Ovid and the Politics of Reading', *MD*.

SHULMAN, J. (1981), '*Te quoque falle tamen*: Ovid's Anti-Lucretian Didactics', *CJ* 76: 242–53.

SILK, E. T. (1956), 'A Fresh Approach to Horace 2.20', *A.J.Ph.* 77: 255–63.

SMITH, K. F. (1913), *The Elegies of Albius Tibullus: the Corpus Tibullianum*, New York.

SMITH, M. F. (1975), *Lucretius: De Rerum Natura*, Loeb Classical Library, London.

SOLODOW, J. B. (1977), 'Ovid's *Ars Amatoria*: The Lover as Cultural Ideal', *WS* 11: 106–27.

STEWART, D. J. (1967), 'The Poet as Bird in Aristophanes and Horace', *CJ* 62: 357–61.

STEWART, Z. (1959), 'The Song of Silenus', *H.S.Ph.* 64: 179–205.

STONEMAN, R. (1976), 'The Theban Eagle', *CQ* 26: 188–92.

SULLIVAN, J. P. (1961), 'Two Problems in Roman Love Elegy', *T.A.Ph.A.* 92: 522–36.

SYME, SIR R. (1978), *History in Ovid*, Oxford.

SYNDIKUS, H. P. (1972), *Die Lyrik des Horaz*, Darmstadt.

TATUM, J. (1973), 'Non usitata nec tenui ferar', *A.J.Ph.* 94: 4–25.

THOMAS, R. F. (1983), 'Callimachus, the *Victoria Berenices*, and Roman Poetry', *CQ* 33: 92–113.

—— (1986), Review of Sullivan (1980), *Phoenix*, 40: 112–14.

THOMPSON, G. H. (1958), *Selections from the Ars Amatoria and Remedia Amoris of Ovid*, Hampden and Sidney.

THURY, E. M. (1987), 'Lucretius' Poem as a *Simulacrum* of the *Rerum Natura*', *A.J.Ph.* 108: 270–94.

TOLKIEHN, J. (1903), 'Ovids Liebeskunst', *Neue Jahrbücher* 12: 326–39.

TOMPKINS, J. P. (1980) (ed.), *Reader Response Criticism: From Formalism to Post-Structuralism*, Baltimore.

TOWNEND, G. B. (1978), 'The Fading of Memmius', *CQ* 28: 267–83.

TRÄNKLE, H. (1960), *Die Sprachkunst des Properz und die Tradition der Lateinischen Dichtersprache*', Hermes Einzelschriften, 15, Weisbaden.

TRYPANIS, C. A. (1958), *Callimachus: Aetia, Iambi, Hecale, and other Fragments*, Loeb Classical Library, London.

TUPET, A. M. (1976), *La Magie dans la poésie latine*, Paris.

VAHLEN, I. (1903), *Ennianae Poesis Reliquiae*, Leipzig.

VERDUCCI, F. (1980), 'The Contest of Rational Libertinism and Imaginative License in Ovid's *Ars Amatoria*', *Pacific Coast Philology*, 15.2: 29–39.

VIAN, F. (1952), 'La Guerre des géants devant les penseurs de l'antiquité', *REG* 65: 1–39.

WALSH, G. B. (1984), *The Varieties of Enchantment*, Chapel Hill, NC, and London.

WARDEN, J. (1982), (ed.) *Orpheus: The Metamorphosis of a Myth*, Toronto.

WATSON, P. (1983), 'Mythological *exempla* in Ovid's *Ars Amatoria*', *C.Ph.* 78: 117–26.

—— (1984), 'Love as Civiliser: *Ars Amatoria* 2.467–92', *Latomus*, 43: 389–95.

WEBER, M. (1983), *Die mythologische Erzählung in Ovids Liebeskunst*, Frankfurt.

WEINREICH, O. (1968), *Religionsgeschichtliche Studien*, Darmstadt.

WEST, M. L. (1966), *Hesiod: Theogony*, Oxford.

—— (1969), 'Near Eastern Material in Hellenistic and Roman Literature', *H.S.Ph.* 73: 113–34.

—— (1972), *Iambi et Elegi Graeci 2*, Oxford.

—— (1978), *Hesiod: Works and Days*, Oxford.

WILKINS, E. G. (1932), 'A Classification of the Similes of Ovid', *CW* 25: 73–86.

WILKINSON, L. P. (1950), 'The Intention of Virgil's *Georgics*', *G&R*: 19–28.

—— (1955), *Ovid Recalled*, Cambridge.

—— (1956), 'Greek Influence on the Poetry of Ovid', *L'influence grecque sur la poésie latine de Catulle à Ovide*, Geneva.

—— (1969), *The Georgics of Virgil*, Cambridge.

WILLIAMS, F. (1978), *Callimachus: Hymn to Apollo*, Oxford.

WILLIAMS, G. (1968), *Tradition and Originality in Roman Poetry*, Oxford.

—— (1969), *The Third Book of Horace's Odes*, Oxford.

WILLIS, J. (1972), *Latin Textual Criticism*, Urbana, Ill.

WIMMEL, W. (1960), *Kallimachos in Rom: Die Nachfolge seines apologetischen Dichtens in der Augusteerzeit*, Hermes Einzel-schriften, 16.

WINKLER, J. J. (1990), *The Constraints of Desire: the Anthropology of Sex and Gender in Ancient Greece*, New York and London.

WISE, V. M. (1977), 'Flight Myths in Ovid's *Metamorphoses*', *Ramus*, 6: 44–59.

WOODMAN, T., and WEST, D. (1979), *Creative Imitation and Latin Literature* (Cambridge).

WORTON, M., and STILL, J. (eds.) (1990), *Intertextuality: Theories and Practices*, Manchester.

WRIGHT, E. F. (1984), '*Profanum sunt genus*: the Poets of the *Ars Amatoria*', *Ph.Q.* 63: 1–15.

WRIGHT, J. R. G. (1983), 'Virgil's Pastoral Programme: Theocritus, Callimachus, and *Eclogue* 1', *P.C.Ph.S.* 29: 107–58.

WYKE, M. (1987), 'Written Women: Propertius' *scripta puella*', *JRS* 77: 47–61.

—— (forthcoming), 'Woman in the Mirror: the Rhetoric of Adornment in the Roman World', in L. Archer, S. Fischler, and M. Wyke (eds.), *Women in Ancient Societies: an Illusion of the Night*.

YARDLEY, J. C. (1978), 'The Elegiac Paraclausithyron', *Eranos*, 76: 19–34.

—— (1987), 'Propertius 4.5, Ovid *Amores* 1.6, and Roman Comedy', *P.C.Ph.S.* 33: 179–89.

ZETZEL, J. E. G. (1982), 'Poetics of Patronage', in B. K. Gold (ed.), *Literary and Artistic Patronage in Ancient Rome*, Austin, Tex.: 87–102.

ZINGERLE, A. (1869–71), *Ovidius und sein Verhältniß zu den Vorgängern und gleichzeitigen römischen Dichtern*, Innsbruck.

INDEX LOCORUM

Not all passages cited in the text appear in this list. Where, for example, a citation occurs in a list of usages of a particular word, it has not been included in the index.

Aeschylus *Ag.* 52: 142
  Choeph. 559: 226 n. 36
AP 5. 12 (Rufinus) 40
  5. 28 (Rufinus) 40, 43
  5. 79 (Plato) 40
  5. 177 (Meleager) 279
  12. 29 (Alcaeus) 40
  12. 32 (Thymocles) 40
Apollodorus *Epit.* 1. 12: 134, 190
  lib. 3. 15. 8: 190
Apollonius Rhodius 1. 1207–72: 37
  3. 744–6: 150
Aratus 37–8: 150
  91–3: 151
  97: 152
  323–5: 151
  581–9: 152
  728–31: 150
Ausonius *Epistle* 23: 127

Bacchylides 5. 16: 97
  5. 24–30: 101

Callimachus *Aet.* fr. 1: 199–201
  fr. 1. 20: 116
  fr. 1. 21–4: 206–7
  fr. 1. 25–8: 98
  fr. 1. 32: 98, 125
  fr. 23. 3: 92
  fr. 43. 48–9: 92
  frr. 68–70: 29, 211
  fr. 114: 210, 224
  Hymn 1. 64: 192
  2: 202–4, 214–29
  4. 2–3: 188–9
Catullus 8. 11: 282
  22: 201
  36: 201
  50: 38–9
  64: 105, 157
  110: 287

Cicero *ND* 2. 121: 139
  Orat. 91: 102
  131: 185–6
  Parad. 1. 9: 249
  Part. 56: 185

Diodorus 4. 77. 5–7: 190–1
  4. 77. 9: 134

Ennius fr. 125V: 97

Homer *Il.* 2. 145: 92
  2. 672–5: 35
  2. 731–2: 233
  4. 200–1: 233
  4. 461: 160
  6. 474: 182
  18. 590–2: 92–3
  22. 338: 185
  23. 306–48: 147
  Od. 5. 272–4: 152–3
  7. 245: 82
  8. 281: 83
  9. 32: 83
  10. 213: 52–3
  11. 125: 142
  19. 173: 158
  21. 252: 158
Horace *Ars* 9–10: 141
  25–6: 256
  38–9: 238
  230: 102
  295–7: 254
  Epod. 3. 12: 74
  5: 69
  15. 22: 36
  Carm. 1. 1. 35–6: 115
  1. 3: 112–17, 139, 162, 167
  1. 25: 40
  2. 10. 5: 134
  2. 12. 7: 116

Horace *Carm.* (*cont.*):
 2. 20: 117–22, 139
 2. 20. 12: 125
 3. 4. 42: 116
 3. 20: 29, 36
 3. 30: 118
 4. 2: 122–6
 4. 2. 10: 141
 4. 2. 11: 146
 4. 2. 27: 176
 4. 10. 3–5: 42
 4. 13. 2: 40
 4. 15. 1–4: 208–9
 Sat. 1. 3. 63–6: 269
Hyginus *Astr.* 2. 1–2: 151

Isidore 3. 71. 8–10: 154

Longinus, (Pseudo-) *On the Sublime*
 33–6: 102, 164
Lucretius 1. 136–7: 140
 3. 1–30: 154
 3. 59–84: 13
 3. 968: 17
 4. 1272–3: 265
 5. 110–12: 227
 5. 878–80: 129
 5. 1218–21: 15 n. 20
 5. 1374–5: 263
 6. 86 and 380: 15–16

Manilius 1. 501–5: 153–4
 5. 260: 263
Musaeus *Hero and Leander* 203–20:
 153

Nonnus *D.* 38. 334–7: 153 n. 114

Ovid *Am.* 1. 1: 212, 224, 278–9
 1. 1. 17 and 27: 102
 1. 8: 84–6
 1. 8. 49: 40
 1. 15. 13–19: 164–5
 2. 1: 281
 2. 1. 11–12: 116–17
 2. 1. 17–28: 64, 117
 2. 2: 280
 2. 10. 9–10: 99 n. 19
 2. 11. 13: 277–8
 2. 17. 1–2: 268
 2. 17. 22: 131
 3. 7: 76
 3. 9: 279

 3. 11. 7: 282
 3. 11. 9–10: 283
 3. 14. 45–6: 280–1
Ars 1. 1: 6–7
 1. 3–4: 99
 1. 7–10: 240
 1. 17: 239
 1. 25–6: 227
 1. 29: 226, 227
 1. 35–40: 18–20
 1. 45–6: 156
 1. 57–9: 266
 1. 99: 250
 1. 143: 252
 1. 271–2: 277
 1. 341–2: 77–8
 1. 375–98: 285
 1. 382: 149
 1. 465: 253
 1. 505–24: 251
 1. 595–6: 252
 1. 617–18: 274–5
 1. 645–6: 22
 2. 1–3: 227, 258–9
 2. 2: 21–2, 156
 2. 3–4: 35–6
 2. 5–10: 99–100
 2. 9–10: 155
 2. 11–12: 22–4
 2. 14: 146
 2. 17: 49
 2. 19–20: 192
 2. 21–98: 87–195
 2. 21: 100, 111, 139, 189–90
 2. 22: 140
 2. 23–4: 129–31, 190
 2. 25–30: 184–8
 2. 27–8: 169–70
 2. 29–30: 179
 2. 31–2: 186–7
 2. 33–42: 134–9, 178–9, 187
 2. 35: 191
 2. 36: 101
 2. 37: 97–8, 187
 2. 42: 111, 122, 139–40
 2. 43: 136, 147, 191
 2. 45–8: 111, 141–2, 177
 2. 49–50: 163, 178, 182
 2. 51–64: 148–55
 2. 52: 126
 2. 54: 141
 2. 58: 166
 2. 59–62: 132–3

2. 61: 102
2. 63: 165
2. 65: 147
2. 66: 139, 181
2. 69–70: 182
2. 71–2: 128–9, 180
2. 74: 160
2. 75–84: 155–9, 165
2. 75–6: 167
2. 77–8: 180–1, 194
2. 81: 176
2. 82: 189
2. 85–90: 159–60
2. 91: 67, 160–1
2. 92: 100, 160–1
2. 94: 195
2. 96: 100
2. 97–8: 170–1, 192
2. 98: 25
2. 99–144: 24–86
2. 99–122: 24–5
2. 99–108: 50–86
2. 99–107: 66
2. 99: 64–5, 72
2. 100: 38, 72
2. 102–7: 68–72
2. 105–6: 75–8
2. 107–22: 26–50
2. 107–8: 33–7, 78
2. 109–10: 34–9
2. 111: 26, 43
2. 112: 32, 34, 38
2. 113–18: 39–47
2. 119–22: 47–50
2. 123–44: 78–83
2. 128: 2
2. 136: 72
2. 139: 231
2. 143: 250
2. 164: 63 n. 65, 152 n. 112
2. 177–8: 282
2. 191–6: 272
2. 197–216: 262–3, 270
2. 199–202: 271
2. 215–16: 269
2. 233–6: 270
2. 237–8: 270
2. 251–60: 285
2. 287–94 (with 261–84 and 145–336): 17
2. 319–36: 55–6
2. 325: 273
2. 337–8: 99 n. 19, 247

2. 346: 273
2. 351: 272
2. 355–72: 199–200
2. 357–92: 48–9
2. 415–24: 54
2. 459–60: 230
2. 467–80: 231–2, 234, 236
2. 487: 78
2. 489–92: 230, 233, 276
2. 493–534: 197–290
2. 493–6: 216–28
2. 497–508: 245–56
2. 499–500: 237, 242–3
2. 501–2: 244, 258
2. 506: 244–5
2. 507–8: 237
2. 509: 217, 226
2. 510: 225, 259
2. 511–34: 256–88
2. 511–12: 232, 257–8
2. 511: 226, 248
2. 513–14: 259, 264, 272
2. 515–20: 275–9
2. 517–19: 265
2. 520: 263, 272
2. 521–8: 279–85
2. 529–34: 285–7
2. 529: 261–2, 271
2. 530: 269
2. 531: 274
2. 532: 263
2. 533–4: 267–8, 269, 273–4
2. 535–42: 228–9
2. 535: 233, 236
2. 537: 290
2. 549: 232–3
2. 683–4: 27
2. 707–8: 279
2. 725–6: 26
2. 733–43: 248
2. 733: 20
3. 43–56: 210–11
3. 59–82: 44–6
3. 99–100: 166
3. 149–52: 266
3. 185: 266
3. 307–10: 251–2
3. 329–45: 20
3. 579–82: 260
3. 662: 276–7
3. 789–94: 227–8
3. 797–8: 228
Fast. 3. 830: 241

Ovid *Fast.* (*cont.*):
  4. 385: 231
  6. 83: 232
 Her. 14. 89–92: 131–2
  15. 253–4: 181
 Met. 1. 1–4: 174–5
  1. 452–73: 212
  1. 637–41: 131–2
  2. 496–507: 151
  3. 339–510: 28–9
  8. 183–235: 171–88
  8. 191–2: 145
  15. 75–479: 171–2
 Pont. 1. 1. 35: 102
  2. 7. 47–8: 49
  3. 3. 46–8: 241
 Rem. 249–90: 56
  249–50: 65
  371–82: 174
  501–2: 22, 275
  555–76: 211
  648: 63
  811: 100
 Tr. 1. 1: 161, 166, 168–70
  1. 1. 67: 239–40
  1. 1. 112: 7
  1. 2. 13–14: 161
  2. 329–30: 141
  2. 424: 164
  2. 555–6: 173
  2. 559: 102
  3. 1. 60: 225
  3. 4. 21–2: 167, 170
  3. 14. 33: 147
  4. 1. 35–6: 165
  5. 1: 136
  5. 2. 23–8: 267
  5. 7. 31–2: 172

Pausanias 9. 11. 4: 191
Peruigilium Veneris 32: 43
Phaedrus *A.* 6. 3: 218
  6. 4: 221
  8. 4: 222
Philostratus *Epist.* 57: 36
Pindar fr. 169 Bowra: 143
 Isthm. 4. 1: 101
 Nem. 5. 20–1: 97
 Ol. 1. 29: 94
  1. 105: 94
  2. 86–8: 97, 124
 Pyth. 3: 233
Plato *Rep.* 377D–403C: 192

 Symp. 189d: 55
  197e: 61–2
  201d: 84
Plutarch *Mor.* 141b–c: 61 n. 58
  384d–394c: 243
  408e: 248, 255
  511b: 255
Propertius 1. 1: 57–8
  1. 1. 7: 77
  1. 1. 22–3: 76–7
  1. 2. 6: 34
  1. 8. 7–8: 270
  1. 11. 11: 144
  1. 20: 38
  2. 1: 58–60
  2. 1. 39–40: 116
  2. 6. 41–2: 288
  2. 10. 11: 103
  2. 12. 9–12: 278
  2. 19: 277
  2. 28. 57: 40–1
  2. 30. 23: 288
  2. 31: 219–21
  3. 3. 13–16: 208–9, 220
  3. 3. 15–24: 237–8, 254
  3. 3. 23–4: 166
  3. 9. 47–8: 116
  4. 1. 71–4: 238
  4. 5: 86
  4. 6: 219–21

Quintilian *Inst.* 10. 1. 98: 88 and n. 3

Sappho 1. 2: 66
Seneca (elder) *Contr.* 2. 2. 12: 88 n. 3, 129
Seneca (younger) *Ep.* 9. 6: 71–2
Silius Italicus 12. 89–103: 175
  12. 95: 140
  12. 97–8: 145
Sophocles *Trach.* 584 and 1142: 54–5
 Phil. 1333: 233
Strabo 14. 1. 19: 134

Theocritus 2. 51: 77
  11: 62
  13. 5–7: 37
  29. 26: 40
[Theocritus] 23. 29–33: 41–2
  27. 8: 40
Theognis 237: 97
  1305–7: 40
  1386: 66

Tibullus 1. 1. 55–6: 283
   1. 2. 41–58: 60, 280
   1. 4. 3–4: 33
   1. 5: 60, 75–6
   1. 6. 7–8: 280
   1. 6. 77–84: 40
   1. 8: 23–6, 76
   1. 8. 41: 40
   1. 9. 13: 40
   2. 5: 220–1, 223
   2. 6. 23: 156

Virgil *Aen.* 1. 106–7: 159–60
   1. 456–93: 106
   1. 661: 50
   1. 688: 66–7
   2. 589–91: 219
   2. 729: 187
   3. 90–9: 238
   3. 90: 217, 219
   3. 92: 221–2
   3. 101: 226
   3. 188: 226
   4. 515–16: 73
   6. 14–33: 104–11, 183
   6. 19: 142
   6. 45–7: 217–18

   6. 49: 219
   6. 100: 238
   7. 282: 119
   8. 729–31: 163
   12. 440: 182
   12. 935–6: 185
Ecl. 1. 44–5: 213
   4. 1–2: 103
   6. 3–5: 207–10
   6. 43–4: 38
   6. 63–73: 208
   6. 70–1: 61
   10. 49: 38, 270
   10. 70–1: 143
Georg. 1. 40: 140
   1. 79–81: 268
   2. 103–8: 265–6
   2. 108: 267
   2. 175–6: 140–1
   3. 6: 38 n. 21, 157
   3. 8–9: 97
   3. 17–19: 98
   3. 26–7: 106
   3. 135–7: 264–5
   3. 470–1: 266–7
   4. 334–70: 189
   4. 562: 115

GENERAL INDEX

Acanthis 86
Achilles 36
Acontius 29, 211
Actaeon 171
adfecto 137 n. 80
Aemilius Macer 65
Aeneadae 238, 242
Aeneas 104–10, 182, 187, 226
  in relation to Apollo 242
agriculture:
  as metaphor 264–7, 272
  as myth 14
Alcman 97
Amor/amor 240–1; *see also* Cupid;
  love
Apollo Ch. 4 *passim*
  and hair 224
  and lyre 220–4
  and wisdom 211, 224, 238, 246, 248–
    50
  as *euorkos* 225–6
  as *hekaergos* 225, 248
  as teacher of love 245–56
  authority rejected 226–7, 259–60
  conflation of various 208, 210–11,
    225, 254
  epiphany in *Aen.* 3 and 6: 215–23
  his speech 204
  in *Met.* 212
  programmatic epiphany 206–10, 212,
    216, 231, 235–6, 281
  statues of 219–20
  temple of in *Aen.* 6: 106–7
apotropaic formula 71
Arcas 151
Aristaeus 176
Aristotle 35
arithmetikon 265–7
ars indicating *Ars Amatoria* 96
ars magica 65
art:
  as directing the lover's activities 245,
    252–3
  as means of judgement 200–1, 256
  failure of 109, 170

opposed to nature/*ingenium* 95, 133,
    135, 163–4, 254
artistry/artists 88, 94–6
astronomy 148–54
Astypalaea 157–8
audax 110–11, 140–1, 167–8
Augustus 136–8, 168–9
  and Palatine temple 225

beloved 27–9
benefaction (of poet) 140
biographical imperative 11, 13, 17,
    286–7
bird, poet as 118–19; *see also* Daedalus
books, no. of in *Ars* 2: 18–20, 117–18
Bootes 151–3
boredom (of reader) 4, 235, 263

Callimacheanism Chs. 3 and 4 *passim*,
  esp. 198–204, 253–6, 294–5
  in *recusatio* 138
  'opposed' to Ennius 164–5; to epic
    114–17, 126, 133, 207; to
    Pindaricism 121–6, 162
  using sea image 141, 161–2
  see also length; size
Callisto 150
Calymne 157–8
Calypso, *see* Ulysses
carmen 63–4
Cassiodorus 218
Catalogue of Islands 157, 176, 188–9
Circe 56, 61 n. 60, 67 n. 72, 74–5
Clarius 157–9, 225
comedy 260, 284–5, 287
cosmology 233–5
couplet, *see* elegiac couplet
Cupid 212, 224, 240–1
  as archer 278–9
Cydippe 29
Cynthius 211

Daedalus 24, 25, Ch. 3 *passim*, 242
  and caution/fear 155, 160, 162, 165–
    7, 187; see also *audax*

and invention 138–40, 191–2
as archetypal artist 92
as bird 95–6, 128–30, 139
as signifier/signified of art 90, 94,
    107–8, 126–8, 141–5, 184, 194
as teacher 146–55
connected with metamorphosis 119,
    128
in exile 168–71
in Horace 112–26
in *Met.* 95, 145, 173–83; regarding
    exile 171–3
in Virgil 103–13
daidalos 93–4, 96
death:
    erotic 58–60
    magical 70, 77
    of Icarus, *see* Icarus
deception 66–7, 82–3, 94, 236–44, 260
deification 115, 137
delay 23–6, 48–9, 150, 260
Delos 157–8
    temple of Apollo at 210–11
Delphi 210–11, 223, 242–3, 248
    E at 243
desire, see *dolor*; love
detinere 56, 194
didactic formulae/vocabulary 7, 80,
    149, 193, 231, 261–3
    in Apollo's speech 246–8
didactic tradition 4, 7, 11–12, 51, 249
    exempla in 89–90
Dido 53 n. 50, 66, 73
digression 90, 103, 192–5, 206, 229,
    233
Diotima 84
Dipsas 84–6
disponere 142–3
doctrina 188, 236
dolor 276–7
domina 26, 287–8
Donatus 1, 112

effugium 184
ekphrasis 105–10
elegiac couplet 128–33, 142, 176–9
elegiac mistress, social status of 286–8
elegy:
    and epic 133–4
    Gigantomachy opposed to 117
    magical love in 57–61
    tradition of 3–4, 260, 270, 283
    see also stylistic level

elevation, metaphor of 102–3, 132–4,
    156–7, 160
eloquence 81–2; *see also* rhetoric
embossing/engraving 94, 106–7
Empedocles 31, 130
encomium 58, 113–14, 116, 123
Ennius 164; *see also* Callimacheanism;
    Icarus
epic:
    hexameter standing for 102
    impersonality of 108
    Lucan on size of 202
    positive value of 2
    simile in 181–2
    temple doors as metaphor for 106
    see also genre; Gigantomachy;
        Icarus; stylistic level
epicness of *Met.* 174–5
Epicurus/Epicureanism 12, 15, 51–2
epigram 260
epinicia 113, 123
epyllion 104–6
erōmenos 28–44
erotics of text 21, 24, 26–7, 50–3 (*and
    see* magic), 75, 204–5, 296
    as seduction of reader *esp.* 66, 261,
        278
    in desirability of unstable signifiers
        57
    see also delay; narrative
excess 3, 87–9, 193, 199, 255, 270,
    295
exempla 3, 36, 74
    as didactic strategy 87
    as paradigm for reading 87
    instability of 80–1
    relationship with main text *esp.* 94,
        109, 175
    transition from 78–81, 89–90, 231
exile:
    Daedalus' 185
    Ovid's 141, 147, 161, 168–73

fallax figura 82–3, 250–1
fame 97, 120–2, 168–70; *see also* Icarus
feminist criticism 6
ferre 273–4, 282
fishing and hunting imagery 156, 277 n.
    90; *see also* hare
flight 95–6, 96–8, 118–20, 124–5, 133
    path of Icarus 158–9
flower imagery 41–2, 46
forma/formosus 33, 43

Gallus 38, 62, 208, 210, 215, 270
Gellius, Aulus 52, 69
gender 6, 8–9, 28, 66, 250
genre:
  consistency of 174, 188
  development through 1–2, 296 n. 6
  difference in narrative 179–81
  mix-up of 128–32
  see also didactic; elegy; epic; stylistic
  level
Gigantomachy 114–17, 134–5, 137,
  168
γνῶθι σαυτόν 210, 233, 237–8, 243–4,
  248–9, 255
goddess, courting mortal 28, 82
Golden Age 234–5
Greek/Roman relationship 16, 32, 49–
  50
  mixing of Greek/Latin sounds 68

hair (as sign of ageing) 42–7
hare 276–8
Hecato of Rhodes 71
Helen 61
Helice 150
Hellenistic device 105–6, 189–90
Hephaestus 83, 92–3
Hercules 36, 37–9, 54–5, 113, 263
hippomanes 52, 72–3
hybrids 90, 128–33
hybris 101, 114–18, 120–3, 127, 137–8,
  186
  and Icarus 163
Hylas 34, 36–9, 43, 74
hymnic style 214–29
  clarity 219–20
  gold 222–3
  movement 222
  noise 221
  soundplay 216–17
  suddenness 217–18

Icarian Sea 87, 92, 120, 170–1, 267
Icarus 24, 67, Ch. 3 *passim*
  and elevation 156–9
  and fame 120–2, 162
  and incaution 159
  as epic failure 155–68
  connected with Aeneas 159–60,
  163
  death overcome by fame 120–2, 126,
  162–3
  in exile poetry 169

in Horace 112–26
  in Virgil 108–9
impotence 60, 75–6
infidelity 205, 230, 276
intention, authorial viii, 5, 292–3
interpretation, *see* reader
intertextuality 4, 87–8, 104, 110, 206,
  213–14
  with *Georgics* 264–8

journey imagery 67, 98–102, 112, 161,
  166
Juno (temple of in *Aen.* 1) 106
Jupiter 101, 134, 136–8

komos 39, 284; *see also*
  paraclausithyron

labyrinth 110, 190
laurel 221, 223
Leander 153
length:
  as Callimachean value 146, 198–204,
  254–6, 294–6
  of Daedalus story 89
  of time as problematized 48–9, 199–
  200, 205
  see also size
leuis:
  as programmatic term 106, 143
  of mistress 48
life of the poet, *see* poetic career
longing, poetry of 48, 59–60, 260, 275–
  6
love 22, 26, 259–88
  apparent failure in 259, 270, 273
  as desire 232
  as universal force 7, 55
  bittersweetness of 56, 259, 266–7,
  272–86
  induced in Reader 205, 259–82

Machaon 224, 233
madness 57, 77–8, 232, 249, 254, 258
Maecenas 6, 9, 13–14
magic 50–86
  art as 92
  in bewitching power of words 81,
  165
  language of 68–78
  plants 70 n. 80
  poetry as 61–4
mala 147

manifestus 218
Marathus 29–30, 76
mares 78, 231–2; *see also* hippomanes
Marsians 69–70
materia 135–6
maxim, *see* γνῶθι σαυτόν; proverb
Medea 28, 56, 70, 74
medicine 52–6, 58, 233
Memmius 6, 12–13, 15, 17, 33
meta 20
military imagery 142, 149, 177, 270, 285
Minos 89–90, 92, 100, 169, 187, 193
  as judge 184, 191
Minotaur 129–30, 184, 190
monere 147–8, 247
monogamy 48, 205 n. 12
movement (as metaphor) 100, 159; *see also* journey imagery

Narcissus 28–9
  as metaphor for Ovid 293
narrative 188–92, 229–36, 288–90; *see also* genre
nenia 69, 71
Nicander 38, 54, 65
Nireus 29, 34–6, 74
nocere 75–7
novelty, *see* originality
nurse 84–6; *see also* witch

Odysseus 152–3; *see also* Ulysses
opus (sex and poetry) 20, 143, 147–8, 244
oracle 218, 223, 226, 238, 244, 247, 259–60
originality 4, 97–8, 111, 139–40, 146, 213–14, 296
Orion 150–4

Palatine 225, 242–3
pallor 58, 70 n. 83, 77
paraclausithyron 64, 260–1, 270, 279–84
pedagogy 9, 47, 145–6, 241–3, 263–4
  ingenuae artes 49
  poet as teacher *esp.* 79
pederasty Ch. 2 *passim* and esp. 27, 30–2, 49, 84
Perdix 184, 190–1
Persephone 173–4
Perses 6, 11, 17
persuasion to love 39–40, 44, 46–7

Phaedra 59, 84
Phaethon 95
pharmakeus 84
pharmakon 52–78, 232, 279
Phasias 68 n. 74
Philetas 145
Philostephanus 92
philtron 52, 54, 68–9, 75–8
phthonos 114, 123, 199, 202–3, 215
'pity and fear' 131, 173–4, 182–3, 185–6; *see also* stylistic level
Plautus 281, 284
Pliny (elder) 54, 189
poetic career 1–2, 171
politics 10 n. 9, 14, 126, 207–8
Polyphemus 62
Priapus 33, 210–11
proem 90, 134, 136–7, 247
Prometheus 113–14
propemptikon 112–14
proverb 41, 71, 72 n. 88, 80, 82, 166

rape 77
reader *esp.* Chs. 1 and 2
  as addressee 6–17
  distinction between reader and Reader 44, 63, 74, 86
  doubling of readers 8, 18–19
  identification between reader and Reader 7–9, 10–17, 21, 62, 204–5
  involvement in the text 7, 204, 236–45, 289; *see also* erotics of text
  power to create meaning 5, 168, 292–3
  superiority of *esp.* 16, 21, 82
reader-response criticism 5–6, 9 n. 8, 291–2
reading performance 10
reception ix, 2, 87–8; *see also* reader-response criticism
recusatio 116, 137–8, 207
redirection (poetic programme) 231–5, 243
renuntiatio amoris 62–3
repetition 2–4, 8, 199, 204–6, 291–6
  as *uariatio* 206, 286
  between Apollo and Ovid 250–3, 258
  between *Ars* 2. 509–34 and rest of *Ars*: 260–5, 269–73, 282
  in Apollo's style 254–5
  in Daedalus story 88, 176
  in incantation 69
re-reading Ch. 1 *passim*, 74, 85, 245, 291–6

reuocatio 206–14, 241–2, 254; *see also* Apollo; redirection
rhetoric 47–8, 85–6, 91, 253
    Daedalus as orator 183–8
rhetoric of disclaimer, *see* tact, literary
ring composition 79, 202, 216
ritualism, *see* hymnic style
rosa 43

seduction, *see* erotics of text; reader
shells 189, 277–8
shipwreck 160–1
size as Callimachean value 125, 138; *see also* length
slaves (erotic) 17, 26, 58, 236, 270–1, 286
    as go-between 284–5
Socrates 31, 62
soluere 145–6
spell 52–3, 56, 64, 69, 74–5, 83
    importance of words in 71–2, 78
stylistic level 127–8, 133–4, 173–83; *see also* elevation
Styx, *see* death, of Icarus

tact, literary 7, 13, 118–21, 168, 195
Tantalus 60
Telchines 199–200, 206–7
tenere 23–4, 26, 194, 228–9
    and magic 78
    and Medea and Circe 74
    and *sustinere* 160
    in play with *tenuis* 144
    lover holding the beloved 270, 274, 286
Theognis 31

threat, erotic 39, 44
transition 80 n. 98, 261; *see also* exempla
trap, for girl/reader 21–2, 82, 274–5
turpis 268–9

Ulysses 50, 78–83, 199–200, 251–2

uariatio, *see* repetition
Varro 83
uates 118, 220, 226, 239, 244
uenia 136–7
Venus:
    born from a shell 278
    in Lucretius 16
Virgo (constellation) 152

wax 144–6
weaving 143
wings:
    as metaphor for couplet 177
    as oars 111, 142
    as ships 99, 191
    creation of 142–4
    in Horace 122, 126
    of Cupid 192
wisdom, Ovidian, didactic claims to 15, 31–2, 49, 229, 280
wisdom literature 31–2, 147, 246
witch 55, 57, 60–2, 74, 76–7; *see also* Acanthis; Circe; Diotima; Dipsas; Medea; nurse

Xenophanes 116

youth, transience of 39–42, 46–7